2009 Supplement to

AMERICAN CRIMINAL PROCEDURE

CASES AND COMMENTARY

Eighth Edition

By

Stephen A. Saltzburg

Wallace and Beverley Woodbury University Professor
George Washington University Law School

Daniel J. Capra

Philip D. Reed Professor of Law
Fordham University School of Law

AMERICAN CASEBOOK SERIES®

WEST®

A Thomson Reuters business

Mat #40850090

© 1996 WEST PUBLISHING CO.
© West, a Thomson business, 1997–2001, 2003–2008
© 2009 Thomson Reuters
    610 Opperman Drive
    St. Paul, MN 55123
    1–800–313–9378
Printed in the United States of America

ISBN: 978–0–314–20633–6

Table of Contents

*

Table of Cases

The principal cases are in bold type. Cases cited or discussed in the text are in roman type. References are to pages. Cases cited in principal cases and within other quoted materials are not included.

2009 Supplement to

AMERICAN CRIMINAL PROCEDURE

CASES AND COMMENTARY
Eighth Edition

*

Chapter One

BASIC PRINCIPLES

III. TWO SPECIAL ASPECTS OF CONSTITUTIONAL LAW: THE INCORPORATION DOCTRINE AND RETROACTIVE APPLICATION OF CONSTITUTIONAL DECISIONS

B. RETROACTIVITY

3. *Current Supreme Court Approach to Retroactivity*

Page 29. Add the following after the runover paragraph:

Overruling Creates a New Rule; and New "Watershed" Rules Are Extremely Unlikely: Whorton v. Bockting

What follows is the latest Supreme Court application of *Teague.*

WHORTON v. BOCKTING

Supreme Court of the United States, 2007.
549 U.S. 406.

Justice Alito **delivered the opinion of the Court.**

This case presents the question whether, under the rules set out in Teague v. Lane, 489 U.S. 288 (1989), our decision in Crawford v. Washington, 541 U.S. 36 (2004), is retroactive to cases already final on direct review. We hold that it is not.

I

A

Respondent Marvin Bockting lived in Las Vegas, Nevada, with his wife, Laura Bockting, their 3–year-old daughter Honesty, and Laura's 6–year-old daughter from a previous relationship, Autumn. One night, while respondent was at work, Autumn awoke from a dream crying, but she refused to tell her mother what was wrong, explaining: " 'Daddy said you would make

1

him leave and that he would beat my butt if I told you.' "After her mother reassured her, Autumn said that respondent had frequently forced her to engage in numerous and varied sexual acts with him.

The next day, Laura Bockting confronted respondent and asked him to leave the house. He did so but denied any wrongdoing. Two days later, Laura called a rape crisis hotline and brought Autumn to the hospital for an examination. At the hospital, Detective Charles Zinovitch from the Las Vegas Metropolitan Police Department Sexual Assault Unit attempted to interview Autumn but found her too distressed to discuss the assaults. Detective Zinovitch then ordered a rape examination, which revealed strong physical evidence of sexual assaults.

Two days later, Detective Zinovitch interviewed Autumn in the presence of her mother, and at that time, Autumn provided a detailed description of acts of sexual assault carried out by respondent; Autumn also demonstrated those acts using anatomically correct dolls. Respondent was then arrested, and a state grand jury indicted him on four counts of sexual assault on a minor under 14 years of age.

* * *

At trial, the court held a hearing outside the presence of the jury to determine whether Autumn could testify. After it became apparent that Autumn was too distressed to be sworn in, the State moved under Nev. Rev. Stat. § 51.385 (2003) to allow Laura Bockting and Detective Zinovitch to recount Autumn's statements regarding the sexual assaults. Under the Nevada statute,

out-of-court statements made by a child under 10 years of age describing acts of sexual assault or physical abuse of the child may be admitted if the court finds that the child is unavailable or unable to testify and that "the time, content and circumstances of the statement provide sufficient circumstantial guarantees of trustworthiness." Over defense counsel's objection that admission of this testimony would violate the Confrontation Clause, the trial court found sufficient evidence of reliability to satisfy § 51.385.

As a result of this ruling, Laura Bockting and Detective Zinovitch were permitted at trial to recount Autumn's out-of-court statements about the assaults. * * *

The jury found respondent guilty of three counts of sexual assault on a minor under the age of 14, and the trial court imposed two consecutive life sentences and another concurrent life sentence.

B

Respondent took an appeal to the Nevada Supreme Court, which handed down its final decision in 1993, more than a decade before *Crawford*. In analyzing respondent's contention that the admission of Autumn's out-of-court statements had violated his Confrontation Clause rights, the Nevada Supreme Court looked to Ohio v. Roberts, 448 U.S. 56 (1980), which was then the governing precedent of this Court. *Roberts* had held that the Confrontation Clause permitted the admission of a hearsay statement made by a declarant who was unavailable to testify if the statement bore sufficient indicia of reliability, either because the statement fell within a firmly rooted hearsay exception or because there were "particularized guarantees of trustworthiness" relating to the statement in question. Applying *Roberts*, the Nevada Supreme Court held that the admission of Autumn's statements was constitutional because the circumstances surrounding the making of the statements provided particularized guarantees of trustworthiness. The Court cited the "natural spontaneity" of Autumn's initial statements to her mother, her reiteration of the same account to Detective Zinovitch several days later, her use of anatomically correct dolls to demonstrate the assaults, and her detailed descriptions of sexual acts with which a 6–year-old would generally not be familiar.

C

Respondent then filed a petition for a writ of habeas corpus with the United States District Court for the District of Nevada, arguing that the Nevada Supreme Court's decision violated his Confrontation Clause rights. The District Court denied the petition, holding that respondent was not entitled to relief under the habeas statute, 28 U.S.C. § 2254(d), because the Nevada Supreme Court's decision was not "contrary to" and did not "involve an unreasonable application of, clearly established Federal law, as determined by the Supreme Court of the United States."

While this appeal was pending, we issued our opinion in *Crawford*, in which we overruled *Roberts* and held that "testimonial statements of witnesses absent from trial" are admissible "only where the declarant is unavailable, and only where the defendant has had a prior opportunity to cross-examine [the witness]." We noted that the outcome in *Roberts*—as well as the outcome in all similar cases decided by this Court—was consistent with the rule announced in *Crawford*, but we concluded that the interpretation of the Confrontation Clause set out in *Roberts* was unsound in several respects. * * * First, we observed that *Roberts* potentially excluded too much testimony because it imposed Confrontation Clause restrictions on nontestimonial hearsay not governed by that Clause. At the same time, we noted, the *Roberts* test was too "malleable" in permitting the admission of *ex parte* testimonial statements. * * *

D

On appeal from the denial of his petition for writ of habeas corpus, respondent contended that if the rule in *Crawford* had been applied to his case, Autumn's out-of-court statements could not have been admitted into evidence and the jury would not have convicted him. Respondent further argued that *Crawford* should have been applied to his case because the *Crawford* rule was either (1) an old rule in existence at the time of his conviction or (2) a "watershed" rule that implicated "the fundamental fairness and accuracy of the criminal proceeding."

A divided panel of the Ninth Circuit reversed the District Court, holding that *Crawford* applies retroactively to cases on collateral review. * * *

The panel's decision that *Crawford* is retroactive to cases on collateral review conflicts with the decision of every other Court of Appeals and State Supreme Court that has addressed this issue. We granted certiorari to resolve this conflict.

II

A

In *Teague* and subsequent cases, we have laid out the framework to be used in determining whether a rule announced in one of our opinions should be applied retroactively to judgments in criminal cases that are already final on direct review. Under the *Teague* framework, an old rule applies both on direct and collateral review, but a new rule is generally applicable only to cases that are still on direct review. See Griffith v. Kentucky, 479 U.S. 314 (1987). A new rule applies retroactively in a collateral proceeding only if (1) the rule is substantive or (2) the rule is a "watershed rule of criminal procedure implicating the fundamental fairness and accuracy of the criminal proceeding."

B

In this case, it is undisputed that respondent's conviction became final on direct appeal well before *Crawford* was decided. We therefore turn to the question whether *Crawford* applied an old rule or announced a new one. A new rule is defined as "a rule that . . . was not dictated by precedent existing at the time the defendant's conviction became final."

Applying this definition, it is clear that *Crawford* announced a new rule. The *Crawford* rule was not "dictated" by prior precedent. Quite the opposite is true: The *Crawford* rule is flatly inconsistent with the prior governing precedent,

Roberts, which *Crawford* overruled. The explicit overruling of an earlier holding no doubt creates a new rule.

* * *

Because the *Crawford* rule was not dictated by the governing precedent existing at the time when respondent's conviction became final, the *Crawford* rule is a new rule.

III

A

Because *Crawford* announced a "new rule" and because it is clear and undisputed that the rule is procedural and not substantive, that rule cannot be applied in this collateral attack on respondent's conviction unless it is a "watershed rule of criminal procedure implicating the fundamental fairness and accuracy of the criminal proceeding." This exception is "extremely narrow." We have observed that it is unlikely that any such rules have yet to emerge. And in the years since *Teague*, we have rejected every claim that a new rule satisfied the requirements for watershed status. * * *

In order to qualify as watershed, a new rule must meet two requirements. First, the rule must be necessary to prevent an impermissibly large risk of an inaccurate conviction. Second, the rule must alter our understanding of the bedrock procedural elements essential to the fairness of a proceeding. We consider each of these requirements in turn.

B

The *Crawford* rule does not satisfy the first requirement relating to an impermissibly large risk of an inaccurate conviction. To be sure, the *Crawford* rule reflects the Framers' preferred mechanism (cross-examination) for ensuring that inaccurate out-of-court testimonial statements are not used to convict an accused. But in order for a new rule to meet the accuracy requirement at issue here, it is not enough to say that the rule is aimed at improving the accuracy of trial, or that the rule is directed toward the enhancement of reliability and accuracy in some sense. Instead, the question is whether the new rule remedied "an impermissibly large risk" of an inaccurate conviction.

Guidance in answering this question is provided by Gideon v. Wainwright, 372 U.S. 335 (1963), to which we have repeatedly referred in discussing the meaning of the *Teague* exception at issue here. In *Gideon*, the only case that we have identified as qualifying under this exception, the Court held that counsel must be appointed for any indigent defendant charged with a felony. When a defendant who wishes to be represented by counsel is denied representation, *Gideon* held, the risk of an unreliable verdict is intolerably high. The new rule announced in *Gideon* eliminated this risk.

The *Crawford* rule is in no way comparable to the *Gideon* rule. The *Crawford* rule is much more limited in scope, and the relationship of that rule to the accuracy of the fact-finding process is far less direct and profound. *Crawford* overruled *Roberts* because *Roberts* was inconsistent with the original understanding of the meaning of the Confrontation Clause, not because the Court

reached the conclusion that the overall effect of the *Crawford* rule would be to improve the accuracy of fact finding in criminal trials. * * * Accordingly, it is not surprising that the overall effect of *Crawford* with regard to the accuracy of fact-finding in criminal cases is not easy to assess.

With respect to *testimonial* out-of-court statements, *Crawford* is more restrictive than was *Roberts*, and this may improve the accuracy of fact-finding in some criminal cases. Specifically, under *Roberts*, there may have been cases in which courts erroneously determined that testimonial statements were reliable. But whatever improvement in reliability *Crawford* produced in this respect must be considered together with *Crawford*'s elimination of Confrontation Clause protection against the admission of unreliable out-of-court nontestimonial statements. Under *Roberts*, an out-of-court nontestimonial statement not subject to prior cross-examination could not be admitted without a judicial determination regarding reliability. Under *Crawford*, on the other hand, the Confrontation Clause has no application to such statements and therefore permits their admission even if they lack indicia of reliability.

It is thus unclear whether *Crawford*, on the whole, decreased or increased the number of unreliable out-of-court statements that may be admitted in criminal trials. But the question here is not whether *Crawford* resulted in some net improvement in the accuracy of fact finding in criminal cases. Rather, the question is whether testimony admissible under *Roberts* is so much more unreliable than that admissible under *Crawford* that the *Crawford* rule is one without which the likelihood of an accurate conviction is *seriously* diminished. *Crawford* did not effect a change of this magnitude.

C

The *Crawford* rule also did not "alter our understanding of the *bedrock procedural elements* essential to the fairness of a proceeding." Contrary to the suggestion of the Court of Appeals (relying on the conclusion that "the right of cross-examination as an adjunct to the constitutional right of confrontation" is a "bedrock procedural rule"), this requirement cannot be met simply by showing that a new procedural rule is *based on* a "bedrock" right. We have frequently held that the *Teague* bar to retroactivity applies to new rules that are based on "bedrock" constitutional rights. Similarly, that a new procedural rule is "fundamental" in some abstract sense is not enough.

Instead, in order to meet this requirement, a new rule must itself constitute a previously unrecognized bedrock procedural element that is essential to the fairness of a proceeding. In applying this requirement, we again have looked to the example of *Gideon*, and we have not hesitated to hold that less sweeping and fundamental rules do not qualify.

In this case, it is apparent that the rule announced in *Crawford*, while certainly important, is not in the same category with *Gideon*. *Gideon* effected a profound and "sweeping" change. The *Crawford* rule simply lacks the "primacy" and "centrality" of the *Gideon* rule, and does not qualify as a rule that altered our understanding of the bedrock procedural elements essential to the fairness of a proceeding.

IV

In sum, we hold that *Crawford* announced a "new rule" of criminal procedure and that this rule does not fall within the *Teague* exception for watershed rules. We therefore reverse the judgment of the Court of Appeals and remand the case for further proceedings consistent with this opinion.

———

Page 30. Add the following after the section on the relationship between *Teague* and AEDPA, which begins on page 29:

Can States Apply a New Supreme Court Rule Retroactively Even if the Supreme Court Does Not? Danforth v. Minnesota.

The Court held in *Teague* that federal habeas petitioners generally will not be able to take advantage of any new rule that the Supreme Court promulgates. The following case addresses a pretty narrow point: whether a state court may apply a new Supreme Court rule retroactively in state postconviction proceedings, even though the Supreme Court has found the rule to be inapplicable to federal habeas proceedings. But underlying this narrow point are two fundamental questions, vigorously disputed by the majority and dissent: 1) what is the meaning of "retroactivity"?; and 2) does allowing the state to apply a new rule retroactively, when the Supreme Court would not, undermine the Supreme Court's authority to "say what the law is"?

DANFORTH v. MINNESOTA

Supreme Court of the United States, 2008.
128 S.Ct. 1029.

JUSTICE STEVENS delivered the opinion of the Court.

New constitutional rules announced by this Court that place certain kinds of primary individual conduct beyond the power of the States to proscribe, as well as "watershed" rules of criminal procedure, must be applied in all future trials, all cases pending on direct review, and all federal habeas corpus proceedings. All other new rules of criminal procedure must be applied in future trials and in cases pending on direct review, but may not provide the basis for a federal collateral attack on a state-court conviction. This is the substance of the "*Teague* rule" described by Justice O'Connor in * * * Teague v. Lane, 489 U.S. 288 (1989). The question in this case is whether *Teague* constrains the authority of state courts to give broader effect to new rules of criminal procedure than is required by that opinion. We have never suggested that it does, and now hold that it does not.

I

In 1996 a Minnesota jury found petitioner Stephen Danforth guilty of first-degree criminal sexual conduct with a minor. The 6–year-old victim did not testify at trial, but the jury saw and heard a videotaped interview of the child. On appeal from his conviction, Dan-

forth argued that the tape's admission violated the Sixth Amendment's guarantee that "[i]n all criminal prosecutions, the accused shall enjoy the right ... to be confronted with the witnesses against him." Applying the rule of admissibility set forth in Ohio v. Roberts, 448 U.S. 56 (1980), the Minnesota Court of Appeals concluded that the tape "was sufficiently reliable to be admitted into evidence," and affirmed the conviction. The conviction became final in 1998 when the Minnesota Supreme Court denied review and petitioner's time for filing a writ of certiorari elapsed. After petitioner's conviction had become final, we announced a "new rule" for evaluating the reliability of testimonial statements in criminal cases. In Crawford v. Washington, 541 U.S. 36, 68–69 (2004), we held that where testimonial statements are at issue, "the only indicium of reliability sufficient to satisfy constitutional demands is the one the Constitution actually prescribes: confrontation."

Shortly thereafter, petitioner filed a state postconviction petition, in which he argued that he was entitled to a new trial because the admission of the taped interview violated the rule announced in *Crawford*. Applying the standards set forth in *Teague,* the Minnesota trial court and the

Minnesota Court of Appeals concluded that *Crawford* did not apply to petitioner's case. The State Supreme Court granted review to consider two arguments: (1) that the lower courts erred in holding that *Crawford* did not apply retroactively under *Teague;* and (2) that the state court was "free to apply a broader retroactivity standard than that of *Teague*," and should apply the *Crawford* rule to petitioner's case even if federal law did not require it to do so. The court rejected both arguments.

* * * The Minnesota Court acknowledged that other state courts had held that *Teague* does not apply to state postconviction proceedings, but concluded that "we are not free to fashion our own standard of retroactivity for *Crawford*."

Our recent decision in Whorton v. Bockting, 127 S. Ct. 1173 (2007), makes clear that the Minnesota court correctly concluded that federal law does not *require* state courts to apply the holding in *Crawford* to cases that were final when that case was decided. Nevertheless, we granted certiorari, to consider whether *Teague* or any other federal rule of law *prohibits* them from doing so.

II

* * *

III

Our decision today must * * * be understood against the backdrop of our somewhat confused and confus-

ing "retroactivity" cases decided in the years between 1965 and 1987. Indeed, we note at the outset that the very word "retroactivity" is misleading because it speaks in temporal terms. "Retroactivity" suggests that when we declare that a new constitutional rule of criminal procedure is "nonretroactive," we are implying that the right at issue was not in existence prior to the date the "new rule" was announced. But this is incorrect. As we have already explained, the source of a "new rule" is the Constitution itself, not any judicial power to create new rules of law. Accordingly, the underlying right necessarily pre-exists our articulation of the new rule. What we are actually determining when we assess the "retroactivity" of a new rule is not the temporal scope of a newly announced right, but whether a violation of the right that occurred prior to the announcement of the new rule will entitle a criminal defendant to the relief sought.[5]

[Justice Stevens discusses the Court's retroactivity jurisprudence, which culminated in *Griffith* (applying new rules retroactively to all cases on direct review) and *Teague* (holding that new rules generally cannot be invoked by federal habeas petitioners). These cases are discussed in the Text.]

IV

* * * A close reading of the *Teague* opinion makes clear that the rule it established was tailored to the unique context of federal habeas

---

5. It may, therefore, make more sense to speak in terms of the "redressability" of violations of new rules, rather than the "retroactivity" of such rules. Unfortunately, it would likely create, rather than allevi-

ate, confusion to change our terminology at this point. Accordingly, we will continue to utilize the existing vocabulary, despite its shortcomings.

and therefore had no bearing on whether States could provide broader relief in their own postconviction proceedings than required by that opinion. Because the case before us now does not involve either of the "*Teague* exceptions," it is Justice O'Connor's discussion of the general rule of nonretroactivity that merits the following three comments.

First, not a word in Justice O'Connor's discussion—or in either of the opinions of Justice Harlan that provided the blueprint for her entire analysis—asserts or even intimates that her definition of the class eligible for relief under a new rule should inhibit the authority of any state agency or state court to extend the benefit of a new rule to a broader class than she defined.

Second, Justice O'Connor's opinion clearly indicates that *Teague's* general rule of nonretroactivity was an exercise of this Court's power to interpret the federal habeas statute. Chapter 153 of Title 28 of the U.S. Code gives federal courts the authority to grant "writs of habeas corpus," but leaves unresolved many important questions about the scope of available relief. This Court has interpreted that congressional silence—along with the statute's command to dispose of habeas petitions "as law and justice require," 28 U.S.C. § 2243—as an authorization to adjust the scope of the writ in accordance with equitable and prudential considerations. *Teague* is plainly grounded in this authority, as the opinion expressly situated the rule it announced in this line of cases adjusting the scope of

federal habeas relief in accordance with equitable and prudential considerations. Since *Teague* is based on statutory authority that extends only to federal courts applying a federal statute, it cannot be read as imposing a binding obligation on state courts.

Third, the text and reasoning of Justice O'Connor's opinion also illustrate that the rule was meant to apply only to federal courts considering habeas corpus petitions challenging state-court criminal convictions. Justice O'Connor made numerous references to the "Great writ" and the "writ," and expressly stated that "[t]he relevant frame of reference" for determining the appropriate retroactivity rule is defined by "the purposes for which the writ of habeas corpus is made available." Moreover, she justified the general rule of nonretroactivity in part by reference to comity and respect for the finality of state convictions. Federalism and comity considerations are unique to *federal* habeas review of state convictions. If anything, considerations of comity militate in favor of allowing state courts to grant habeas relief to a broader class of individuals than is required by *Teague*. And while finality is, of course, implicated in the context of state as well as federal habeas, finality of state convictions is a *state* interest, not a federal one. It is a matter that States should be free to evaluate, and weigh the importance of, when prisoners held in state custody are seeking a remedy for a violation of federal rights by their lower courts.

The dissent correctly points out that *Teague* was also grounded in concerns over uniformity and the inequity inherent in the [pre-*Teague/Griffith*] approach. * * * This interest in uniformity, however, does not outweigh the general principle that States are independent sovereigns with plenary authority to make and enforce their own laws as long as they do not infringe on federal constitutional guarantees. The fundamental interest in federalism that allows individual States to define crimes, punishments, rules of evidence, and rules of criminal and civil procedure in a variety of different ways—so long as they do not violate the Federal Constitution—is not otherwise limited by any general, undefined federal interest in uniformity. Nonuniformity is, in fact, an unavoidable reality in a federalist system of government. Any State could surely have adopted the rule of evidence defined in *Crawford* under state law even if that case had never been decided. It should be equally free to give its citizens the benefit of our rule in any fashion that does not offend federal law.

It is thus abundantly clear that the *Teague* rule of nonretroactivity was fashioned to achieve the goals of federal habeas while minimizing federal intrusion into state criminal proceedings. It was intended to limit the authority of federal courts to overturn state convictions—not to limit a state court's authority to grant relief for violations of new rules of constitutional law when reviewing its own State's convictions.

* * *

In sum, the *Teague* decision limits the kinds of constitutional violations that will entitle an individual to relief on federal habeas, but does not in any way limit the authority of a state court, when reviewing its own state criminal convictions, to provide a remedy for a violation that is deemed "nonretroactive" under *Teague*.

V

* * *

VI

Finally, while the State acknowledges that it may grant its citizens broader protection than the Federal Constitution requires by enacting appropriate legislation or by judicial interpretation of its own Constitution, it argues that it may not do so by judicial misconstruction of federal law. * * * But the States that give broader retroactive effect to this Court's new rules of criminal procedure do not do so by misconstruing the federal *Teague* standard. Rather, they have developed *state* law to govern retroactivity in state post-conviction proceedings. The issue in this case is whether there is a federal rule, either implicitly announced in *Teague*, or in some other source of federal law, that prohibits them from doing so.

The absence of any precedent for the claim that *Teague* limits state collateral review courts' authority to provide remedies for federal constitutional violations is a sufficient reason for concluding that there is no such rule of federal law. That conclusion is confirmed by several additional considerations. First, if there is such a federal rule of law, presumably the Supremacy Clause in Article V of the Federal Constitution would require all state entities—not just state judges—to comply with it. We have held that States can waive a *Teague* defense, during the course of litigation, by expressly choosing not to rely on it, see Collins v. Youngblood, 497 U.S. 37, 41 (1990), or by failing to raise it in a timely manner, see Schiro v. Farley, 510 U.S. 222, 228–229 (1994). It would indeed be anomalous to hold that state legislatures and executives are not bound by *Teague*, but that state courts are.

Second, the State has not identified, and we cannot discern, the source of our authority to promulgate such a novel rule of federal law. While we have ample authority to control the administration of justice in the federal courts—particularly in their enforcement of federal legislation—we have no comparable supervisory authority over the work of state judges. And while there are federal interests that occasionally justify this Court's development of common-law rules of federal law, our normal role is to interpret law created by others and not to prescribe what it shall be. Just as constitutional doubt may tip the scales in favor of one construction of a statute rather than another, so does uncertainty about the source of authority to impose a federal limit on the power of state judges to remedy wrongful state convictions outweigh any possible policy arguments favoring the rule that respondent espouses.

Finally, the dissent contends that the "end result [of this opinion] is startling" because "two criminal defendants, each of whom committed the same crime, at the same time, whose convictions became final on the same day, and each of whom raised an identical claim at the same time under the Federal Constitution" could obtain different results.

This assertion ignores the fact that the two hypothetical criminal defendants did not actually commit the "same crime." They violated different state laws, were tried in and by different state sovereigns, and may—for many reasons—be subject to different penalties. As previously noted, such nonuniformity is a necessary consequence of a federalist system of government.

VII

It is important to keep in mind that our jurisprudence concerning the "retroactivity" of "new rules" of constitutional law is primarily concerned, not with the question whether a constitutional violation occurred, but with the availability or nonavailability of remedies. The former is a pure question of federal law, our resolution of which should be applied uniformly throughout the Nation, while the latter is a mixed question of state and federal law.

A decision by this Court that a new rule does not apply retroactively under *Teague* does not imply that there was no right and thus no violation of that right at the time of trial—only that no remedy will be provided in federal habeas courts. It is fully consistent with a government of laws to recognize that the finality of a judgment may bar relief. It would be quite wrong to assume, however, that the question whether constitutional violations occurred in trials conducted before a certain date depends on how much time was required to complete the appellate process.

Accordingly, the judgment of the Supreme Court of Minnesota is reversed, and the case is remanded for further proceedings not inconsistent with this opinion. * * * [T]he Minnesota Court is free to reinstate its judgment disposing of the petition for state postconviction relief.

————

CHIEF JUSTICE ROBERTS, **with whom** JUSTICE KENNEDY **joins, dissenting.**

Some of our new rulings on the meaning of the United States Constitution apply retroactively—to cases already concluded—and some do not. This Court has held that the question whether a particular ruling is retroactive is itself a question of federal law. It is basic that when it comes to any such question of federal law, it is "the province and duty" of this Court "to say what the law is." Marbury v. Madison, 5 U.S. 137, 1 Cranch 137, 177 (1803). State courts are the final arbiters of their own state law; this Court is the final arbiter of federal law. State courts are therefore bound by our rulings on whether our cases construing federal law are retroactive.

The majority contravenes these bedrock propositions. The end result is startling: Of two criminal defendants, each of whom committed the same crime, at the same time, whose convictions became final on the same day, and each of whom raised an identical claim at the same time under the Federal Constitution, one may be executed while the other is set free—the first despite being correct on his claim, and the second because of it. That result is contrary to the Supremacy Clause and the Framers' decision to vest in "one supreme Court" the responsibility and authority to ensure the uniformity of federal law. Because the Constitution requires us to be more jealous of that re-

sponsibility and authority, I respectfully dissent.

I

* * *

A

* * *

B

* * *

* * * *Teague* did not purport to distinguish between federal and state collateral review. * * * [O]ur unqualified holding—that "[u]nless they fall within an exception to the general rule, new constitutional rules of criminal procedure will not be applicable to those cases which have become final before the new rules are announced"—is enough to decide this case.

Moreover, the reasons the *Teague* Court provided for adopting Justice Harlan's view apply to state as well as federal collateral review. The majority is quite right that *Teague* invoked the interest in comity between the state and federal sovereigns. But contrary to the impression conveyed by the majority, there was more to *Teague* than that. *Teague* also relied on the interest in finality: "Application of constitutional rules not in existence at the time a conviction became final seriously undermines the principle of finality which is essential to the operation of our criminal justice system. Without finality, the criminal law is deprived of much of its deterrent effect." The Court responds by flatly stating that "finality of state convictions is a *state* interest, not a federal one." But while it is certainly true that finality of state convictions is a state interest, that does mean it is not also a federal one. After all, our decision in *Griffith* made finality the touchstone for retroactivity of new federal rules, and bound States to that judgment. [It stated that] new rules are "to be applied retroactively to all cases, *state or federal*, pending on direct review or not yet final" (emphasis added).

It is quite a radical proposition to assert that this Court has nothing to say about an interest "essential to the operation of our criminal justice system," without which "the criminal law is deprived of much of its deterrent effect," when the question is whether this interest is being undermined by the very rules of *federal* constitutional procedure that we are charged with expounding. A State alone may "evaluate, and weigh the importance of" finality interests, when it decides which substantive rules of criminal procedure *state law* affords; it is quite a leap to hold, as the Court does, that they alone can do so in the name of the Federal Constitution.

Teague was also based on the inequity of the [previous] approach to retroactivity. After noting that the disparate treatment of similarly situated defendants led us in *Griffith* to adopt Justice Harlan's view for cases on direct appeal, the Court then explained that the [previous] standard "also led to unfortunate disparity in the treatment of similarly situated defendants on collateral review." 489 U.S., at 305. See also *id.*, at 316 (the Court's new approach

to retroactivity "avoids the inequity resulting from the uneven application of new rules to similarly situated defendants").

This interest in reducing the inequity of haphazard retroactivity standards and disuniformity in the application of federal law is quite plainly a predominantly federal interest. Indeed, it was one of the main reasons we cited in *Griffith* for imposing a uniform rule of retroactivity upon *state* courts for cases on direct appeal. And, more to the point, it is the very interest that animates the Supremacy Clause and our role as the "one supreme Court" charged with enforcing it.

* * * States are free to announce their own state-law rules of criminal procedure, and to apply them retroactively in whatever manner they like. That is fully consistent with the principle that "a single sovereign's law should be applied equally to all." But the Court's opinion invites just the sort of disuniformity in federal law that the Supremacy Clause was meant to prevent. The same determination of a federal constitutional violation at the same stage in the criminal process can result in freedom in one State and loss of liberty or life in a neighboring State. The Court's opinion allows "a single sovereign's law"—the Federal Constitution, as interpreted by this Court—to be applied differently in every one of the several States.

Finally * * * we have always emphasized that determining whether a new federal right is retroactive turns on the nature of the substantive federal rule at issue. That is how we determine retroactivity—by carefully examining the underlying federal right. When this Court decides that a particular right shall not be applied retroactively, but a state court finds that it should, it is at least in part because of a different assessment by the state court of the nature of the underlying federal right—something on which the Constitution gives this Court the final say. The nature and scope of the new rules we announce directly determines whether they will be applied retroactively on collateral review. Today's opinion stands for the unfounded proposition that while we alone have the final say in expounding the former, we have no control over the latter.

II

The Court's holding is not only based on a misreading of our retroactivity cases, but also on a misunderstanding of the nature of retroactivity generally. The majority's decision is grounded on the erroneous view that retroactivity is a remedial question. But * * * when we ask whether and to what extent a rule will be retroactively applied, we are asking what law—new or old—will apply. As we have expressly noted, "[t]he *Teague* doctrine ... does not involve a special 'remedial' limitation on the principle of 'retroactivity' as much as it reflects a limitation inherent in the principle itself." Reynoldsville Casket Co. v. Hyde, 514 U.S. 749, 758 (1995).

* * *

The majority explains that when we announce a new rule of law, we are not "*creating* the law," but rather "*declaring* what the law already is." But this has nothing to do with the question before us. The point may lead to the conclusion that

nonretroactivity of our decisions is improper—the position the Court has adopted in both criminal and civil cases on direct review—but everyone agrees that full retroactivity is not required on collateral review. It necessarily follows that we must choose whether "new" or "old" law applies to a particular category of cases. Suppose, for example, that a defendant, whose conviction became final before we announced our decision in Crawford v. Washington, 541 U.S. 36 (2004), argues (correctly) on collateral review that he was convicted in violation of both *Crawford* and Ohio v. Roberts, 448 U.S. 56 (1980), the case that *Crawford* overruled. Under our decision in Whorton v. Bockting 549 U.S. 406 (2007), the "new" rule announced in *Crawford* would not apply retroactively to the defendant. But I take it to be uncontroversial that the defendant would nevertheless get the benefit of the "old" rule of *Roberts*, even under the view that the rule not only is but always has been an incorrect reading of the Constitution. Thus, the question whether a particular federal rule will apply retroactively is, in a very real way, a choice between new and old law. The issue in this case is who should decide.

The proposition that the question of retroactivity—that is, the choice between new or old law in a particular case—is distinct from the question of remedies has several important implications for this case. To begin with, whatever intuitive appeal may lie in the majority's statement that "the remedy a state court chooses to provide its citizens for violations of the Federal Constitution is primarily a question of state law," the statement misses the mark. The relevant inquiry is not about remedy; it is about choice of law—new or old. There is no reason to believe, either legally or intuitively, that States should have any authority over this question when it comes to which *federal* constitutional rules of criminal procedure to apply.

Indeed, when the question is what federal rule of decision from this Court should apply to a particular case, no Court but this one—which has the ultimate authority "to say what the law is," *Marbury*, 5 U.S. 137, 1 Cranch, at 177—should have final say over the answer. This is enough to rebut the proposition that there is no "source of [our] authority" to bind state courts to follow our retroactivity decisions. Retroactivity is a question of federal law, and our final authority to construe it cannot, at this point in the Nation's history, be reasonably doubted.

Principles of federalism protect the prerogative of States to extend greater rights under their own laws than are available under federal law. The question here, however, is the availability of protection under the Federal Constitution—specifically, the Confrontation Clause of the Sixth Amendment. It is no intrusion on the prerogatives of the States to recognize that it is for this Court to decide such a question of federal law, and that our decision is binding on the States under the Supremacy Clause.

Consider the flip side of the question before us today: If a State interprets its own constitution to provide protection beyond that available under the Federal Constitution, and has ruled that this interpretation is not retroactive, no one would suppose that a federal court could hold otherwise, and grant relief under state law that a state court would refuse to grant. The result should be the same when a state court is asked to give retroactive effect to a right under the Federal Constitution that this Court has held is not retroactive.

The distinction between retroactivity and available remedies highlights the fact that the majority's assertion "that *Teague's* general rule of nonretroactivity was an exercise of this Court's power to interpret the federal habeas statute"— even if correct—is neither here nor there. [4]While Congress has substantial control over federal courts' ability to grant relief for violations of the Federal Constitution, the Constitution gives us the responsibility to decide what its provisions mean. And with that responsibility necessarily comes the authority to determine the scope of those provisions—when they apply and when they do not.

* * *

Lurking behind today's decision is of course the question of just how free state courts are to define the retroactivity of our decisions interpreting the Federal Constitution. I do not see any basis in the majority's logic for concluding that States are free to hold our decisions retroactive when we have held they are not, but not free to hold that they are not when we have held they are. Under the majority's reasoning, in either case the availability of relief in state court is a question for those courts to evaluate independently. * * *

Nor is there anything in today's decision suggesting that States could not adopt more nuanced approaches to retroactivity. For example, suppose we hold that the Sixth Amendment right to be represented by particular counsel of choice, recently announced in United States v. Gonzalez–Lopez, 548 U.S. 140 (2006) [see Chapter Ten; holding that a violation of the right is never harmless], is a new rule that does not apply retroactively. Under the majority's rationale, a state court could decide that it nonetheless will apply *Gonzalez-Lopez* retroactively, but only if the defendant could prove prejudice, or some other criterion we had rejected as irrelevant in defining the substantive right. Under the majority's logic, that would not be a misapplication of our decision in *Gonzalez-Lopez*— which specifically rejected any required showing of prejudice—but

simply a state decision on the scope of available remedies in state court. The possible permutations—from State to State, and federal right to federal right—are endless.

————

Perhaps all this will be dismissed as fine parsing of somewhat arcane precedents, over which reasonable judges may disagree. Fair enough; but I would hope that enough has been said at least to refute the majority's assertion that its conclusion is dictated by our prior cases. This dissent is compelled not simply by disagreement over how to read those cases, but by the fundamental issues at stake—our role under the Constitution as the final arbiter of federal law, both as to its meaning and its reach, and the accompanying duty to ensure the uniformity of that federal law.

Chapter Two

SEARCHES AND SEIZURES OF PERSONS AND THINGS

V. TO APPLY OR NOT APPLY THE WARRANT CLAUSE

A. ARRESTS IN PUBLIC AND IN THE HOME

3. *The Constitutional Rule: Arrests in Public*

Page 172. Add at the bottom of the page:

Application of Tennessee v. Garner to a High– Speed Vehicle Chase: Scott v. Harris

SCOTT v. HARRIS

Supreme Court of the United States, 2007.
550 U.S. 372.

JUSTICE SCALIA **delivered the opinion of the Court.**

We consider whether a law enforcement official can, consistent with the Fourth Amendment, attempt to stop a fleeing motorist from continuing his public-endangering flight by ramming the motorist's car from behind. Put another way: Can an officer take actions that place a fleeing motorist at risk of serious injury or death in order to stop the motorist's flight from endangering the lives of innocent bystanders?

I

In March 2001, a Georgia county deputy clocked respondent's vehicle traveling at 73 miles per hour on a road with a 55–mile-per-hour speed limit. The deputy activated his blue flashing lights indicating that respondent should pull over. Instead, respondent sped away, initiating a chase down what is in most portions a two-lane road, at speeds exceeding 85 miles per hour. The deputy radioed his dispatch to report that he was pursuing a fleeing vehicle, and broadcast its license plate number. Petitioner, Deputy Timothy Scott, heard the radio com-

17

munication and joined the pursuit along with other officers. In the midst of the chase, respondent pulled into the parking lot of a shopping center and was nearly boxed in by the various police vehicles. Respondent evaded the trap by making a sharp turn, colliding with Scott's police car, exiting the parking lot, and speeding off once again down a two-lane highway.

Following respondent's shopping center maneuvering, which resulted in slight damage to Scott's police car, Scott took over as the lead pursuit vehicle. Six minutes and nearly 10 miles after the chase had begun, Scott decided to attempt to terminate the episode by employing a "Precision Intervention Technique ('PIT') maneuver, which causes the fleeing vehicle to spin to a stop." Having radioed his supervisor for permission, Scott was told to " 'go ahead and take him out.' "Instead, Scott applied his push bumper to the rear of respondent's vehicle. As a result, respondent lost control of his vehicle, which left the roadway, ran down an embankment, overturned, and crashed. Respondent was badly injured and was rendered a quadriplegic.

Respondent filed suit against Deputy Scott and others under 42 U.S.C. § 1983, alleging, inter alia, a violation of his federal constitutional rights, viz. use of excessive force resulting in an unreasonable seizure under the Fourth Amendment. In response, Scott filed a motion for summary judgment based on an assertion of qualified immunity. The District Court denied the motion, finding that "there are material issues of fact on which the issue of qualified immunity turns which present sufficient disagreement to

require submission to a jury." On interlocutory appeal, the United States Court of Appeals for the Eleventh Circuit affirmed the District Court's decision to allow respondent's Fourth Amendment claim against Scott to proceed to trial. Taking respondent's view of the facts as given, the Court of Appeals concluded that Scott's actions could constitute "deadly force" under Tennessee v. Garner, 471 U.S. 1 (1985), and that the use of such force in this context "would violate [respondent's] constitutional right to be free from excessive force during a seizure. Accordingly, a reasonable jury could find that Scott violated [respondent's] Fourth Amendment rights." The Court of Appeals further concluded that "the law as it existed [at the time of the incident], was sufficiently clear to give reasonable law enforcement officers 'fair notice' that ramming a vehicle under these circumstances was unlawful." The Court of Appeals thus concluded that Scott was not entitled to qualified immunity. We granted certiorari and now reverse.

II

In resolving questions of qualified immunity, courts are required to resolve a "threshold question: Taken in the light most favorable to the party asserting the injury, do the facts alleged show the officer's conduct violated a constitutional right? This must be the initial inquiry." Saucier v. Katz, 533 U.S. 194, 201 (2001). If, and only if, the court finds a violation of a constitutional right, "the next, sequential step is to ask whether the right was clearly established . . . in light of the specific context of the case." * * * We therefore turn to the threshold inquiry: whether Deputy Scott's actions violated the Fourth Amendment.

III

A

The first step in assessing the constitutionality of Scott's actions is to determine the relevant facts. As this case was decided on summary judgment, there have not yet been factual findings by a judge or jury, and respondent's version of events (unsurprisingly) differs substantially from Scott's version. When things are in such a posture, courts are required to view the facts and draw reasonable inferences "in the light most favorable to the party opposing the [summary judgment] motion." In qualified immunity cases, this usually means adopting (as the Court of Appeals did here) the plaintiff's version of the facts.

There is, however, an added wrinkle in this case: existence in the record of a videotape capturing the events in question. There are no allegations or indications that this videotape was doctored or altered in any way, nor any contention that what it depicts differs from what actually happened. The videotape quite clearly contradicts the version of the story told by respondent and adopted by the Court of Appeals. For example, the Court of Appeals adopted respondent's assertions that, during the chase, "there was little, if any, actual threat to pedestrians or other motorists, as the roads were mostly empty and [respondent] remained in control of his vehicle." Indeed, reading the lower court's opinion, one gets the impression that respondent, rather than fleeing from police, was attempting to pass his driving test. * * *

The videotape tells quite a different story. There we see respondent's vehicle racing down narrow, two-lane roads in the dead of night at speeds that are shockingly fast. We see it swerve around more than a dozen other cars, cross the double-yellow line, and force cars traveling in both directions to their respective shoulders to avoid being hit. We see it run multiple red lights and travel for considerable periods of time in the occasional center left-turn-only lane, chased by numerous police cars forced to engage in the same hazardous maneuvers just to keep up. Far from being the cautious and controlled driver the lower court depicts, what we see on the video more closely resembles a Hollywood-style car chase of the most frightening sort, placing police officers and innocent bystanders alike at great risk of serious injury.

* * * Respondent's version of events is so utterly discredited by the record that no reasonable jury could have believed him. The Court of Appeals should not have relied on such visible fiction; it should have viewed the facts in the light depicted by the videotape.

B

Judging the matter on that basis, we think it is quite clear that Deputy Scott did not violate the Fourth Amendment. Scott does not contest that his decision to terminate the car chase by ramming his bumper into respondent's vehicle constituted a "seizure." * * * The question we need to answer is whether Scott's actions were objectively reasonable.

Respondent urges us to analyze this case as we analyzed *Garner*. We must first decide, he says, whether the actions Scott took constituted "deadly force." (He defines "deadly force" as "any use of force which creates a substantial likelihood of causing death or serious bodily injury.") If so, respondent claims that *Garner* prescribes certain preconditions that must be met before Scott's actions can survive Fourth Amendment scrutiny: (1) The suspect must have posed an immediate threat of serious physical harm to the officer or others; (2) deadly force must have been necessary to prevent escape; and (3) where feasible, the officer must have given the suspect some warning. Since these *Garner* preconditions for using deadly force were not met in this case, Scott's actions were *per se* unreasonable.

Respondent's argument falters at its first step; *Garner* did not establish a magical on/off switch that triggers rigid preconditions whenever an officer's actions constitute "deadly force." *Garner* was simply an application of the Fourth Amendment's "reasonableness" test to the use of a particular type of force in a particular situation. *Garner* held that it was unreasonable to kill a "young, slight, and unarmed" burglary suspect by shooting him "in the back of the head" while he was running away on foot, and when the officer "could not reasonably have believed that [the suspect] ... posed any threat," and "never attempted to justify his actions on any basis other than the need to prevent an escape." Whatever *Garner* said about the factors that *might have* justified shooting the suspect in that case, such "pre-

conditions" have scant applicability to this case, which has vastly different facts. * * * Nor is the threat posed by the flight on foot of an unarmed suspect even remotely comparable to the extreme danger to human life posed by respondent in this case. Although respondent's attempt to craft an easy-to-apply legal test in the Fourth Amendment context is admirable, in the end we must still slosh our way through the factbound morass of "reasonableness." Whether or not Scott's actions constituted application of "deadly force," all that matters is whether Scott's actions were reasonable.

2

In determining the reasonableness of the manner in which a seizure is effected, "we must balance the nature and quality of the intrusion on the individual's Fourth Amendment interests against the importance of the governmental interests alleged to justify the intrusion." United States v. Place, 462 U.S. 696, 703 (1983). Scott defends his actions by pointing to the paramount governmental interest in ensuring public safety, and respondent nowhere suggests this was not the purpose motivating Scott's behavior. Thus, in judging whether Scott's actions were reasonable, we must consider the risk of bodily harm that Scott's actions posed to respondent in light of the threat to the public that Scott was trying to eliminate. Although there is no obvious way to quantify the risks on either side, it is clear from the videotape that respondent posed an actual and imminent threat to the lives of any pedestrians who might have been present, to other civilian motorists, and to the officers involved in the chase. It is equally clear that Scott's actions posed a high likelihood of serious injury or death to respondent—though not the near *certainty* of death posed by, say, shooting a fleeing felon in the back of the head, or pulling alongside a fleeing motorist's car and shooting the motorist. So how does a court go about weighing the perhaps lesser probability of injuring or killing numerous bystanders against the perhaps larger probability of injuring or killing a single person? We think it appropriate in this process to take into account not only the number of lives at risk, but also their relative culpability. It was respondent, after all, who intentionally placed himself and the public in danger by unlawfully engaging in the reckless, high-speed flight that ultimately produced the choice between two evils that Scott confronted. Multiple police cars, with blue lights flashing and sirens blaring, had been chasing respondent for nearly 10 miles, but he ignored their warning to stop. By contrast, those who might have been harmed had Scott not taken the action he did were entirely innocent. We have little difficulty in concluding it was reasonable for Scott to take the action that he did.[1]

But wait, says respondent: Couldn't the innocent public equally have been protected, and the tragic accident entirely avoided, if the police had simply ceased their pursuit? We think the police need not have taken that chance and hoped for the best. Whereas Scott's action—ramming respondent off the road—was *certain* to eliminate the risk that respondent posed to the public, ceasing pursuit was not. First of all, there would have been no way to convey convincingly to respondent that the chase was off, and that he was free to go. Had respondent looked in his rear-view mirror and seen the police cars deactivate their flashing lights and turn around, he would have had no idea whether they were truly letting him get away, or simply devising a new strategy for capture. Perhaps the police knew a shortcut he didn't know, and would reappear down the road to intercept him; or perhaps they were setting up a roadblock in his path. Given such uncertainty, respondent might have been just as likely to respond by continuing to drive recklessly as by slowing down and wiping his brow.

Second, we are loath to lay down a rule requiring the police to allow fleeing suspects to get away whenever they drive *so recklessly* that they put other people's lives in danger. It is obvious the perverse incentives such a rule would create: Every fleeing motorist would know that escape is within his grasp, if only he accelerates to 90 miles per hour, crosses the double-yellow line

---

1. The Court of Appeals cites Brower v. County of Inyo, 489 U.S. 593, 595 (1989), for its refusal to "countenance the argument that by continuing to flee, a suspect absolves a pursuing police officer of any possible liability for all ensuing actions during the chase," The only question in *Brower* was whether a police roadblock constituted a *seizure* under the Fourth Amendment. In deciding that question, the relative culpability of the parties is, of course, irrelevant; a seizure occurs whenever the police are "responsible for the termination of [a person's] movement," regardless of the reason for the termination. Culpability *is* relevant, however, to the *reasonableness* of the seizure—to whether preventing possible harm to the innocent justifies exposing to possible harm the person threatening them.

a few times, and runs a few red lights. The Constitution assuredly does not impose this invitation to impunity-earned-by-recklessness. Instead, we lay down a more sensible rule: A police officer's attempt to terminate a dangerous high-speed car chase that threatens the lives of innocent bystanders does not violate the Fourth Amendment, even when it places the fleeing motorist at risk of serious injury or death.

* * *

The car chase that respondent initiated in this case posed a substantial and immediate risk of serious physical injury to others; no reasonable jury could conclude otherwise. Scott's attempt to terminate the chase by forcing respondent off the road was reasonable, and Scott is entitled to summary judgment. The Court of Appeals' decision to the contrary is reversed.

It is so ordered.

JUSTICE GINSBURG, concurring.

* * * I do not read today's decision as articulating a mechanical, *per se* rule. The inquiry described by the Court is situation-specific. Among relevant considerations: Were the lives and well-being of others (motorists, pedestrians, police officers) at risk? Was there a safer way, given the time, place, and circumstances, to stop the fleeing vehicle? "Admirable" as "[an] attempt to craft an easy-to-apply legal test in the Fourth Amendment context [may be]," the Court explains, "in the end we must still slosh our way through the factbound morass of 'reasonableness.'"

* * *

[The concurring opinion of JUSTICE BREYER is omitted.]

JUSTICE STEVENS, dissenting.

Today, the Court asks whether an officer may "take actions that place a fleeing motorist at risk of serious injury or death in order to stop the motorist's flight from endangering the lives of innocent bystanders." Depending on the circumstances, the answer may be an obvious "yes," an obvious "no," or sufficiently doubtful that the question of the reasonableness of the officer's actions should be decided by a jury, after a review of the degree of danger and the alternatives available to the officer. A high speed chase in a desert in Nevada is, after all, quite different from one that travels through the heart of Las Vegas.

Relying on a *de novo* review of a videotape of a portion of a nighttime chase on a lightly traveled road in Georgia where no pedestrians or other "bystanders" were present, buttressed by uninformed speculation about the possible consequences of discontinuing the chase, eight of the jurors on this Court reach a verdict that differs from the views of the judges on both the District Court and the Court of Appeals who are surely more familiar with the hazards of driving on Georgia roads than we are. The Court's justification for this unprecedented departure from our well-settled standard of review of factual determinations made by a district court and affirmed by a court of appeals is based on its mistaken view that the Court of Appeals' description of the facts was "blatantly contradicted by the record" and that respondent's version of the events was "so utterly discredited by the record that no reasonable jury could have believed him."

Rather than supporting the conclusion that what we see on the video "resembles a Hollywood-style car chase of the most frightening sort,"[1] the tape actually confirms, rather than contradicts, the lower courts' appraisal of the factual questions at issue. More important, it surely does not provide a principled basis for depriving the respondent of his right to have a jury evaluate the question whether the police officers' decision to use deadly force to bring the chase to an end was reasonable.

* * *

My colleagues on the jury saw respondent "swerve around more than a dozen other cars," and "force cars traveling in both directions to their respective shoulders," but they apparently discounted the possibility that those cars were already out of the pursuit's path as a result of hearing the sirens. Even if that were not so, passing a slower vehicle on a two-lane road always involves some degree of swerving and is not especially dangerous if there are no cars coming from the opposite direction. At no point during the chase did respondent pull into the opposite lane other than to pass a car in front of him; he did the latter no more than five times and, on most of those occasions, used his turn signal. On none of these occasions was there a car traveling in the opposite direction. In fact, at one point, when respondent found him-

self behind a car in his own lane and there were cars traveling in the other direction, he slowed and waited for the cars traveling in the other direction to pass before overtaking the car in front of him while using his turn signal to do so. This is hardly the stuff of Hollywood. To the contrary, the video does not reveal any incidents that could even be remotely characterized as "close calls."

* * *

I recognize, of course, that even though respondent's original speeding violation on a four-lane highway was rather ordinary, his refusal to stop and subsequent flight was a serious offense that merited severe punishment. It was not, however, a capital offense, or even an offense that justified the use of deadly force rather than an abandonment of the chase. The Court's concern about the "imminent threat to the lives of any pedestrians who might have been present," while surely valid in an appropriate case, should be discounted in a case involving a nighttime chase in an area where no pedestrians were present.

What would have happened if the police had decided to abandon the chase? We now know that they could have apprehended respondent later because they had his license plate number. Even if that were not true, and even if he would have escaped any punishment at all, the use of deadly force in this case was no more appropriate than the

---

1. I can only conclude that my colleagues were unduly frightened by two or three images on the tape that looked like bursts of lightning or explosions, but were in fact merely the headlights of vehicles zooming by in the opposite lane. Had they learned to drive when most high-speed driv-

ing took place on two-lane roads rather than on superhighways—when split-second judgments about the risk of passing a slowpoke in the face of oncoming traffic were routine—they might well have reacted to the videotape more dispassionately.

use of a deadly weapon against a fleeing felon in Tennessee v. Garner. * * *

Although *Garner* may not, as the Court suggests, "establish a magical on/off switch that triggers rigid preconditions" for the use of deadly force, it did set a threshold under which the use of deadly force would be considered constitutionally unreasonable: * * *

Whether a person's actions have risen to a level warranting deadly force is a question of fact best reserved for a jury. Here, the Court has usurped the jury's factfinding function and, in doing so, implicitly

labeled the four other judges to review the case unreasonable. * * *

* * * In my view, the risks inherent in justifying unwarranted police conduct on the basis of unfounded assumptions are unacceptable, particularly when less drastic measures—in this case, the use of stop sticks[2] or a simple warning issued from a loudspeaker—could have avoided such a tragic result. In my judgment, jurors in Georgia should be allowed to evaluate the reasonableness of the decision to ram respondent's speeding vehicle in a manner that created an obvious risk of death and has in fact made him a quadriplegic at the age of 19.

B. STOP AND FRISK

1. *Stop and Frisk Established*

Page 205. Add after the entry on Maryland v. Wilson

Protective Search of a Passenger in a Car Stopped for a Traffic Violation: Arizona v. Johnson

In Maryland v. Wilson [Text page 204] the Court held that during a lawful stop of a car, an officer has an automatic right to order a passenger out of a car. *Wilson* was based on the need for officer safety during a vehicle stop. It authorized a seizure of the passenger (moving him from one place to another) but did not involve a search. In Arizona v. Johnson, 129 S.Ct. 781 (2009), the Court considered the legality of a protective search of a passenger during a traffic stop. Justice Ginsburg, writing for the Court, recounted the facts:

> On April 19, 2002, Officer Maria Trevizo and Detectives Machado and Gittings, all members of Arizona's gang task force, were on patrol in Tucson near a neighborhood associated with the Crips gang. At approximately 9 p.m., the officers pulled over an automobile after a license plate check revealed that the vehicle's registration had been suspended for an insurance-related violation. Under Arizona law, the violation for which the vehicle was stopped constituted a civil infraction warranting a citation. At the time of the stop,

---

2. "Stop sticks" are a device which can be placed across the roadway and used to flatten a vehicle's tires slowly to safely terminate a pursuit.

the vehicle had three occupants-the driver, a front-seat passenger, and a passenger in the back seat, Lemon Montrea Johnson, the respondent here. In making the stop the officers had no reason to suspect anyone in the vehicle of criminal activity.

The three officers left their patrol car and approached the stopped vehicle. Machado instructed all of the occupants to keep their hands visible. He asked whether there were any weapons in the vehicle; all responded no. Machado then directed the driver to get out of the car. Gittings dealt with the front-seat passenger, who stayed in the vehicle throughout the stop. While Machado was getting the driver's license and information about the vehicle's registration and insurance, Trevizo attended to Johnson.

Trevizo noticed that, as the police approached, Johnson looked back and kept his eyes on the officers. When she drew near, she observed that Johnson was wearing clothing, including a blue bandana, that she considered consistent with Crips membership. She also noticed a scanner in Johnson's jacket pocket, which "struck [her] as highly unusual and cause [for] concern," because "most people" would not carry around a scanner that way "unless they're going to be involved in some kind of criminal activity or [are] going to try to evade the police by listening to the scanner." In response to Trevizo's questions, Johnson provided his name and date of birth but said he had no identification with him. He volunteered that he was from Eloy, Arizona, a place Trevizo knew was home to a Crips gang. Johnson further told Trevizo that he had served time in prison for burglary and had been out for about a year.

Trevizo wanted to question Johnson away from the front-seat passenger to gain "intelligence about the gang [Johnson] might be in." For that reason, she asked him to get out of the car. Johnson complied. Based on Trevizo's observations and Johnson's answers to her questions while he was still seated in the car, Trevizo suspected that "he might have a weapon on him." When he exited the vehicle, she therefore "patted him down for officer safety." During the patdown, Trevizo felt the butt of a gun near Johnson's waist. At that point Johnson began to struggle, and Trevizo placed him in handcuffs.

Johnson was charged in state court with, inter alia, possession of a weapon by a prohibited possessor. He moved to suppress the evidence as the fruit of an unlawful search. The trial court denied the motion, concluding that the stop was lawful and that Trevizo had cause to suspect Johnson was armed and dangerous.

The Arizona appellate court found that the search was improper because it was unrelated to the traffic stop. But the Court unanimously rejected that reasoning and found that a search of a passenger is permissible under the *Terry* doctrine, so long as the officer has a reasonable belief that the passenger is armed and dangerous. Justice Ginsburg made the following points:

1. "Johnson was lawfully detained incident to the legitimate stop of the vehicle in which he was a passenger."

2. "A lawful roadside stop begins when a vehicle is pulled over for investigation of a traffic violation. The temporary seizure of driver and passengers ordinarily continues, and remains reasonable, for the duration of the stop. Normally, the stop ends when the police have no further need to control the scene, and inform the driver and passengers they are free to leave. An officer's inquiries into matters unrelated to the justification for the traffic stop, this Court has made plain, do not convert the encounter into something other than a lawful seizure, so long as those inquiries do not measurably extend the duration of the stop."

3. "[A] traffic stop of a car communicates to a reasonable passenger that he or she is not free to terminate the encounter with the police and move about at will. Nothing occurred in this case that would have conveyed to Johnson that, prior to the frisk, the traffic stop had ended or that he was otherwise free to depart without police permission."

4. "Officer Trevizo surely was not constitutionally required to give Johnson an opportunity to depart the scene after he exited the vehicle without first ensuring that, in so doing, she was not permitting a dangerous person to get behind her."

Justice Ginsburg concluded that "officers who conduct routine traffic stops may perform a patdown of a driver and any passengers upon reasonable suspicion that they may be armed and dangerous."

The lower court had assumed, without deciding, that the officer in fact had reasonable suspicion that Johnson was armed and dangerous. The Court reminded the case for a finding on this question.

Page 209. Add at the end of the section:

Summers and Mena Applied: Los Angeles County v. Rettele

In Los Angeles County v. Rettele, 550 U.S. 609 (2007) (per curiam), the Court summarily reversed the court of appeals and held that county deputies did not conduct a search in an unreasonable manner. The deputies had a search warrant for two houses where they thought they could find four suspects in a fraud and identity-theft ring. The four suspects were known to be African–Americans, and one had a registered 9–millimeter Glock handgun. Unbeknownst to the deputies, one of the houses was sold two months before the warrants were obtained. When officers entered that house they found a Caucasian man and women in bed. The deputies ordered the couple, who were unclothed, to get out of the bed and raise their hands. The couple was held at gunpoint for a minute or two before the male was permitted to retrieve a robe for the female, and then the male was permitted to dress. The two "suspects" left the bedroom within three or four minutes to sit on a couch in the living room, and the deputies realized that they had made a mistake and apologized. They executed the search warrant for the second house where they found three suspects who were arrested and convicted. The couple brought an action for the violation of their Fourth Amendment rights. They did not challenge the officers' probable cause to enter the premises on the basis of the warrant they had obtained, but claimed that the search and seizure were unreasonable under the circumstances given the fact that they clearly did not match the description of the suspects the officers were seeking.

The Court found the police actions objectively reasonable. It first rejected the proposition that the officers should have left the premises as soon as they saw that the couple were Caucasian:

> Because respondents were of a different race than the suspects the deputies were seeking, the Court of Appeals held that "after taking one look at [respondents], the deputies should have realized that [respondents] were not the subjects of the search warrant and did not pose a threat to the deputies' safety." We need not pause long in rejecting this unsound proposition. When the deputies ordered respondents from their bed, they had no way of knowing whether the African–American suspects were elsewhere in the house. The presence of some Caucasians in the residence did not eliminate the possibility that the suspects lived there as well. As the deputies stated in their affidavits, it is not uncommon in our society for people of different races to live together. Just as people of different races live and work together, so too might they engage in joint criminal activity. The deputies, who were searching a house where they believed a suspect might be armed, possessed authority to secure the premises before deciding whether to continue with the search.

The Court held that the reasonableness of the officers' actions in detaining the couple was controlled by its prior opinions in *Summers* and *Mena*. It elaborated as follows:

> In Michigan v. Summers, 452 U.S. 692 (1981), this Court held that officers executing a search warrant for contraband may "detain the occupants of the premises while a proper search is conducted." In weighing whether the search in *Summers* was reasonable the Court first found that "detention represents only an incremental intrusion on personal liberty when the search of a home has been authorized by a valid warrant." Against that interest, it balanced "preventing flight in the event that incriminating evidence is found"; "minimizing the risk of harm to the officers"; and facilitating "the orderly completion of the search." See Muehler v. Mena, 544 U.S. 93 (2005).
>
> In executing a search warrant officers may take reasonable action to secure the premises and to ensure their own safety and the efficacy of the search. Id., at 98–100. The test of reasonableness under the Fourth Amendment is an objective one. Unreasonable

actions include the use of excessive force or restraints that cause unnecessary pain or are imposed for a prolonged and unnecessary period of time. *Mena,* supra, at 100.

The Court found the officers' actions in ordering the couple out of the bed, and detaining them for a short period of time, to be reasonable under the circumstances:

> The orders by the police to the occupants, in the context of this lawful search, were permissible, and perhaps necessary, to protect the safety of the deputies. Blankets and bedding can conceal a weapon, and one of the suspects was known to own a firearm, factors which underscore this point. The Constitution does not require an officer to ignore the possibility that an armed suspect may sleep with a weapon within reach. The reports are replete with accounts of suspects sleeping close to weapons. See United States v. Enslin, 327 F.3d 788, 791 (CA9 2003) ("When [the suspect] put his hands in the air and began to sit up, his movement shifted the covers and the marshals could see a gun in the bed next to him"); see also United States v. Jones, 336 F.3d 245, 248 (CA3 2003) (suspect kept a 9–millimeter Luger under his pillow while he slept); United States v. Hightower, 96 F.3d 211 (CA7 1996) (suspect kept a loaded five-shot handgun under his pillow). The deputies needed a moment to secure the room and ensure that other persons were not close by or did not present a danger. Deputies were not required to turn their backs to allow Rettele and Sadler to retrieve clothing or to cover themselves with the sheets. Rather, "the risk of harm to both the police and the occupants is minimized if the officers routinely exercise unquestioned command of the situation." *Summers,* 452 U.S., at 702–703.

The Court noted that there were limits to the permissible length or intrusiveness of the detention, but concluded that those limits were not approached in this case.

> This is not to say, of course, that the deputies were free to force Rettele and Sadler to remain motionless and standing for any longer than necessary. We have recognized that special circumstances, or possibly a prolonged detention might render a search unreasonable. There is no accusation that the detention here was prolonged. The deputies left the home less than 15 minutes after arriving. The detention was shorter and less restrictive than the 2-to 3–hour handcuff detention upheld in *Mena.* And there is no allegation that the deputies prevented Sadler and Rettele from dressing longer than necessary to protect their safety. Sadler was unclothed for no more than two minutes, and Rettele for only slightly more time than that. Sadler testified that once the police were satisfied that no immediate threat was presented, "they wanted us to get dressed and they were pressing us really fast to hurry up and get some clothes on."

The Court summed up as follows:

The Fourth Amendment allows warrants to issue on probable cause, a standard well short of absolute certainty. Valid warrants will issue to search the innocent, and people like Rettele and Sadler unfortunately bear the cost. Officers executing search warrants on occasion enter a house when residents are engaged in private activity; and the resulting frustration, embarrassment, and humiliation may be real, as was true here. When officers execute a valid warrant and act in a reasonable manner to protect themselves from harm, however, the Fourth Amendment is not violated.

Justice Souter did not join the per curiam opinion, stating that he would have denied the petition for certiorari. Justice Stevens, joined by Justice Ginsburg, wrote an opinion concurring in the judgment; he did not disagree with the majority's conclusion that the officers acted reasonably.

2. When Does a Seizure Occur? The Line Between "Stop" and "Encounter"

Page 225. After the Note on *Brower v. County of Inyo*, add the following:

Is a Passenger in a Car "Seized" When an Officer Stops the Car? Brendlin v. California

In the following case, the Court considered prior precedents such as *Mendenhall*, *Bostick* and *Brower* in determining whether a passenger had a right to complain about the illegal stop of the car in which he was riding.

BRENDLIN v. CALIFORNIA

Supreme Court of the United States, 2007.
551 U.S. 249.

JUSTICE SOUTER delivered the opinion of the Court.

When a police officer makes a traffic stop, the driver of the car is seized within the meaning of the Fourth Amendment. The question in this case is whether the same is true of a passenger. We hold that a passenger is seized as well and so may challenge the constitutionality of the stop.

I

Early in the morning of November 27, 2001, Deputy Sheriff Robert Brokenbrough and his partner saw a parked Buick with expired registration tags. In his ensuing conversation with the police dispatcher, Brokenbrough learned that an application for renewal of registration was being processed. The officers saw the car again on the road, and this time Brokenbrough noticed its display of a temporary operating permit with the number "11," indicating it was legal to drive the car through November. The officers decided to pull the Buick over to verify that the permit matched the vehicle, even though, as Brokenbrough admitted later, there was nothing unusual about the permit or the way it was affixed. Brokenbrough asked the driver, Karen Simeroth, for her license and saw a passenger in the front seat, petitioner Bruce Brendlin, whom he recognized as "one of the Brendlin brothers." He recalled that either Scott or Bruce Brendlin had dropped out of parole supervision and asked Brendlin to identify himself. Brokenbrough returned to his cruiser, called for backup, and verified that Brendlin was a parole violator with an outstanding no-bail warrant for his arrest. While he was in the patrol car, Brokenbrough saw Brendlin briefly open and then close the passenger door of the Buick. Once reinforcements arrived, Brokenbrough went to the passenger side of the Buick, ordered him out of the car at gunpoint, and declared him under arrest. When the police searched Brendlin incident to arrest, they found an orange syringe cap on his person. A patdown search of Simeroth revealed syringes and a plastic bag of a green leafy substance, and she was also formally arrested. Officers then searched the car and found tubing, a scale, and other things used to produce methamphetamine.

Brendlin was charged with possession and manufacture of methamphetamine, and he moved to suppress the evidence obtained in the searches of his person and the car as fruits of an unconstitutional seizure, arguing that the officers lacked probable cause or reasonable suspicion to make the traffic stop. He did not assert that his Fourth Amendment rights were violated by the search of Simeroth's vehicle, cf. Rakas v. Illinois, 439 U.S. 128 (1978), but claimed only that the traffic stop was an unlawful sei-

zure of his person. The trial court denied the suppression motion after finding that the stop was lawful and Brendlin was not seized until Brokenbrough ordered him out of the car and formally arrested him. Brendlin pleaded guilty, subject to appeal on the suppression issue, and was sentenced to four years in prison.

The California Court of Appeal reversed the denial of the suppression motion, holding that Brendlin was seized by the traffic stop, which they held unlawful. By a narrow majority, the Supreme Court of California reversed. The State Supreme Court noted California's concession that the officers had no reasonable basis to suspect unlawful operation of the car, but still held suppression unwarranted because a passenger "is not seized as a constitutional matter in the absence of additional circumstances that would indicate to a reasonable person that he or she was the subject of the peace officer's investigation or show of authority." The court reasoned that Brendlin was not seized by the traffic stop because Simeroth was its exclusive target, that a passenger cannot submit to an officer's show of authority while the driver controls the car, and that once a car has been pulled off the road, a passenger "would feel free to depart or otherwise to conduct his or her affairs as though the police were not present." In dissent, Justice Corrigan said that a traffic stop entails the seizure of a passenger even when the driver is the sole target of police investigation because a passenger is detained for the purpose of ensuring an officer's safety and would not feel free to leave the car without the officer's permission.

We granted certiorari to decide whether a traffic stop subjects a passenger, as well as the driver, to Fourth Amendment seizure. We now vacate.

II

A

A person is seized by the police and thus entitled to challenge the government's action under the Fourth Amendment when the officer, "by means of physical force or show of authority," terminates or restrains his freedom of movement, Florida v. Bostick, 501 U.S. 429, 434 (1991), "*through means intentionally applied*," Brower v. County of Inyo, 489 U.S. 593, 597 (1989) (emphasis in original). Thus, an "unintended person . . . [may be] the object of the detention," so long as the detention is "willful" and not merely the consequence of "an unknowing act." *Id.*, at 596; cf. County of Sacramento v. Lewis, 523 U.S. 833, 844 (1998) (no seizure where a police officer accidentally struck and killed a motorcycle passenger during a high-speed pursuit). A police officer may make a seizure by a show of authority and without the use of physical force, but there is no seizure without actual submission; otherwise, there is at most an attempted seizure, so far as the Fourth Amendment is concerned. See California v. Hodari D., 499 U.S. 621, 626, n. 2 (1991).

When the actions of the police do not show an unambiguous intent to restrain or when an individual's submission to a show of governmental authority takes the form of passive acquiescence, there needs to be some test for telling when a seizure occurs in response to authority, and when it does not. The test was devised by Justice Stewart in United States v. Mendenhall, 446 U.S. 544 (1980), who wrote that a seizure occurs if "in view of all of the circumstances surrounding the incident, a reasonable person would have believed that he was not free to leave." Later on, the Court adopted Justice Stewart's touchstone, *see, e.g., Hodari D., supra*, at 627; INS v. Delgado, 466 U.S. 210, 215 (1984), but added that when a person "has no desire to leave" for reasons unrelated to the police presence, the "coercive effect of the encounter" can be measured better by asking whether "a reasonable person would feel free to decline the officers' requests or otherwise terminate the encounter," *Bostick, supra*, at 435–436.

The law is settled that in Fourth Amendment terms a traffic stop entails a seizure of the driver "even though the purpose of the stop is limited and the resulting detention quite brief." Delaware v. Prouse, 440 U.S. 648, 653 (1979). And although we have not, until today, squarely answered the question whether a passenger is also seized, we have said over and over in dicta that during a traffic stop an officer seizes everyone in the vehicle, not just the driver. * * *

B

The State concedes that the police had no adequate justification to pull the car over, but argues that the passenger was not seized and thus cannot claim that the evidence was tainted by an unconstitutional stop. We resolve this question by asking whether a reasonable person in Brendlin's position when the car stopped would have believed himself free to "terminate the encounter" between the police and himself. We think that in these circumstances any reasonable passenger would have understood the police officers to be exercising control to the point that no one in the car was free to depart without police permission.

A traffic stop necessarily curtails the travel a passenger has chosen just as much as it halts the driver, diverting both from the stream of traffic to the side of the road, and the police activity that normally amounts to intrusion on privacy and personal security does not normally (and did not here) distinguish between passenger and driver. An officer who orders one particular car to pull over acts with an implicit claim of right based on fault of some sort, and a sensible person would not expect a police officer to allow people to come and go freely from the physical focal point of an investigation into faulty behavior or wrongdoing. If the likely wrongdoing is not the driving, the passenger will reasonably feel subject to suspicion owing to close association; but even when the wrongdoing is only bad driving, the passenger will expect to be subject to some scrutiny, and his attempt to leave the scene would be so obviously likely to prompt an objection from the officer that no passenger would feel free to leave in the first place.

It is also reasonable for passengers to expect that a police officer at the scene of a crime, arrest, or investigation will not let people move around in ways that could jeopardize his safety. In Maryland v. Wilson, 519 U.S. 408 (1997), we held that during a lawful traffic stop an officer may order a passenger out of the car as a precautionary measure, without reasonable suspicion that the passenger poses a safety risk. * * * In fashioning this rule, we invoked our earlier statement that " '[t]he risk of harm to both the police and the occupants is minimized if the officers routinely exercise unquestioned command of the situation.' "What we have said in these opinions probably reflects a societal expectation of " 'unquestioned [police] command' "at odds with any notion that a passenger would feel free to leave, or to terminate the personal encounter any other way, without advance permission.

Our conclusion comports with the views of all nine Federal Courts of Appeals, and nearly every state court, to have ruled on the question. * * * And the treatise writers share this prevailing judicial view that a passenger may bring a Fourth Amendment challenge to the legality of a traffic stop. * * *

C

The contrary conclusion drawn by the Supreme Court of California, that seizure came only with formal arrest, reflects three premises as to which we respectfully disagree. First, the State Supreme Court reasoned that Brendlin was not seized by the stop because Deputy Sheriff Brokenbrough only intended to investigate Simeroth and did not direct a show of authority toward Brendlin. The court saw Brokenbrough's "flashing lights [as] directed at the driver," and pointed to the lack of record evidence that Brokenbrough "was even aware [Brendlin] was in the car prior to the vehicle stop." But that view of the facts ignores the objective *Men-*

denhall test of what a reasonable passenger would understand. To the extent that there is anything ambiguous in the show of force (was it fairly seen as directed only at the driver or at the car and its occupants?), the test resolves the ambiguity, and here it leads to the intuitive conclusion that all the occupants were subject to like control by the successful display of authority. The State Supreme Court's approach, on the contrary, shifts the issue from the intent of the police as objectively manifested to the motive of the police for taking the intentional action to stop the car, and we have repeatedly rejected attempts to introduce this kind of subjectivity into Fourth Amendment analysis. * * *

California defends the State Supreme Court's ruling on this point by citing our cases holding that seizure requires a purposeful, deliberate act of detention. But * * * [t]he intent that counts under the Fourth Amendment is the intent that has been conveyed to the person confronted, and the criterion of willful restriction on freedom of movement is no invitation to look to subjective intent when determining who is seized. Our most recent cases are in accord on this point. In *Lewis*, 523 U.S. 833, we considered whether a seizure occurred when an officer accidentally ran over a passenger who had fallen off a motorcycle during a high-speed chase, and in holding that no seizure took place, we stressed that the officer stopped Lewis's movement by accidentally crashing into him, not "through means intentionally applied." We did not even consider, let alone emphasize, the possibility that the officer had meant to detain the driver only and not the passenger. Nor is *Brower* to the contrary, where it was dispositive that "Brower was meant to be stopped by the physical obstacle of the roadblock—and that he was so stopped." California reads this language to suggest that for a specific occupant of the car to be seized he must be the motivating target of an officer's show of authority, as if the thrust of our observation were that Brower, and not someone else, was "meant to be stopped." But our point was not that Brower alone was the target but that officers detained him "through means intentionally applied"; if the car had had another occupant, it would have made sense to hold that he too had been seized when the car collided with the roadblock. Neither case, then, is at odds with our holding that the issue is whether a reasonable passenger would have perceived that the show of authority was at least partly directed at him, and that he was thus not free to ignore the police presence and go about his business.

Second, the Supreme Court of California assumed that Brendlin, "as the passenger, had no ability to submit to the deputy's show of authority" because only the driver was in control of the moving vehicle. But what may amount to submission depends on what a person was doing before the show of authority: a fleeing man is not seized until he is physically overpowered, but one sitting in a chair may submit to authority by not getting up to run away. Here, Brendlin had no effective way to signal submission while the car was still moving on the roadway, but once it came to a stop he could, and apparently did, submit by staying inside.

Third, the State Supreme Court shied away from the rule we apply today for fear that it "would encompass even those motorists following the vehicle subject to the traffic stop who, by virtue of the original detention, are forced to slow down and perhaps even come to a halt in order to accommodate that vehicle's submission to police authority." But an occupant of a car who knows that he is stuck in traffic because another car has been pulled over (like the motorist who can't even make out why the road is suddenly clogged) would not perceive a show of authority as directed at him or his car. Such incidental restrictions on freedom of movement would not tend to affect an individual's "sense of security and privacy in traveling in an automobile." Nor would the consequential blockage call for a precautionary rule to avoid the kind of "arbitrary and oppressive interference by [law] enforcement officials with the privacy and personal security of individuals" that the Fourth Amendment was intended to limit.[3]

Indeed, the consequence to worry about would not flow from our conclusion, but from the rule that almost all courts have rejected. Holding that the passenger in a private car is not (without more) seized in a traffic stop would invite police officers to stop cars with passengers regardless of probable cause or reasonable suspicion of anything illegal. The fact that evidence uncovered as a result of an arbitrary traffic stop would still be admissible against any passengers would be a powerful incentive to run the kind of "roving patrols" that would still violate the driver's Fourth Amendment right. * * *

* * *

Brendlin was seized from the moment Simeroth's car came to a halt on the side of the road, and it was error to deny his suppression motion on the ground that seizure occurred only at the formal arrest. It will be for the state courts to consider in the first instance whether suppression turns on any other issue. The judgment of the Supreme Court of California is vacated, and the case is remanded for further proceedings not inconsistent with this opinion.

It is so ordered.

C. SEARCH INCIDENT TO ARREST: THE ARREST POWER RULE

4. *The Arrest Power Rule Applied to Automobiles*

Page 324. Add at the end of the section:

Limitations on Arrest Power After the Arrest of a Recent Occupant: Arizona v. Gant

In the following case, the Court rejected the *Belton* rule, insofar as it allowed the automatic search of the passenger compartment of a car

---

3. California claims that, under today's rule, "all taxi cab and bus passengers would be 'seized' under the Fourth Amendment when the cab or bus driver is pulled over by the police for running a red light." But the relationship between driver and passenger is not the same in a common carrier as it is in a private vehicle, and the expectations of police officers and passengers differ accordingly. In those cases, as here, the crucial question would be whether a reasonable person in the passenger's position would feel free to take steps to terminate the encounter.

after a recent occupant of the car was arrested. But it substitutes Justice Scalia's evidence-based view of the arrest power, articulated in his separate opinion in *Thornton*.

ARIZONA v. GANT　2009

Supreme Court of the United States, 2009.
129 S.Ct. 1710.

JUSTICE STEVENS delivered the opinion of the Court.

After Rodney Gant was arrested for driving with a suspended license, handcuffed, and locked in the back of a patrol car, police officers searched his car and discovered cocaine in the pocket of a jacket on the backseat. Because Gant could not have accessed his car to retrieve weapons or evidence at the time of the search, the Arizona Supreme Court held that the search-incident-to-arrest exception to the Fourth Amendment's warrant requirement, as defined in Chimel v. California, 395 U.S. 752 (1969), and applied to vehicle searches in New York v. Belton, 453 U.S. 454 (1981), did not justify the search in this case. We agree with that conclusion.

Under *Chimel*, police may search incident to arrest only the space within an arrestee's " 'immediate control,' "meaning "the area from within which he might gain possession of a weapon or destructible evidence." The safety and evidentiary justifications underlying *Chimel's* reaching-distance rule determine *Belton's* scope. Accordingly, we hold that *Belton* does not authorize a vehicle search incident to a recent occupant's arrest after the arrestee has been secured and cannot access the interior of the vehicle. Consistent with the holding in Thornton v. United States, 541 U.S. 615 (2004), and following the suggestion in Justice SCALIA's opinion concurring in the judgment in that case, we also conclude that circumstances unique to the automobile context justify a search incident to arrest when it is reasonable to believe that evidence of the offense of arrest might be found in the vehicle.

I

On August 25, 1999, acting on an anonymous tip that the residence at 2524 North Walnut Avenue was being used to sell drugs, Tucson police officers Griffith and Reed knocked on the front door and asked to speak to the owner. Gant answered the door and, after identifying himself, stated that he expected the owner to return later. The officers left the residence and conducted a records check, which revealed that Gant's driver's license had been suspended and there was an outstanding warrant for his arrest for driving with a suspended license.

When the officers returned to the house that evening, they found a man near the back of the house and a woman in a car parked in front of it. After a third officer arrived, they arrested the man for providing a false name and the woman for possessing drug paraphernalia. Both ar-

restees were handcuffed and secured in separate patrol cars when
Gant arrived. The officers recognized his car as it entered the driveway, and Officer Griffith confirmed
that Gant was the driver by shining
a flashlight into the car as it drove
by him. Gant parked at the end of
the driveway, got out of his car, and
shut the door. Griffith, who was
about 30 feet away, called to Gant,
and they approached each other,
meeting 10–to–12 feet from Gant's
car. Griffith immediately arrested
Gant and handcuffed him.

Because the other arrestees were
secured in the only patrol cars at
the scene, Griffith called for backup. When two more officers arrived,
they locked Gant in the backseat of
their vehicle. After Gant had been
handcuffed and placed in the back
of a patrol car, two officers searched
his car: One of them found a gun,
and the other discovered a bag of
cocaine in the pocket of a jacket on
the backseat.

Gant was charged with two offenses—possession of a narcotic
drug for sale and possession of
drug paraphernalia (i.e., the plastic
bag in which the cocaine was
found). He moved to suppress the
evidence seized from his car on the
ground that * * * *Belton* did not
authorize the search of his vehicle
because he posed no threat to the
officers after he was handcuffed in
the patrol car and because he was
arrested for a traffic offense for
which no evidence could be found
in his vehicle. When asked at the
suppression hearing why the search
was conducted, Officer Griffith responded: "Because the law says we
can do it." [The Trial Court refused
to suppress the evidence and Gant
was convicted.]

After protracted state-court proceedings, the Arizona Supreme
Court concluded that the search of
Gant's car was unreasonable within
the meaning of the Fourth Amendment. The court's opinion discussed at length our decision in
Belton, which held that police may
search the passenger compartment
of a vehicle and any containers
therein as a contemporaneous incident of an arrest of the vehicle's
recent occupant. The court distinguished *Belton* as a case concerning
the permissible scope of a vehicle
search incident to arrest and concluded that it did not answer "the
threshold question whether the police may conduct a search incident
to arrest at all once the scene is
secure." Relying on our earlier decision in *Chimel*, the court observed
that the search-incident-to-arrest exception to the warrant requirement
is justified by interests in officer
safety and evidence preservation.
When "the justifications underlying
Chimel no longer exist because the
scene is secure and the arrestee is
handcuffed, secured in the back of a
patrol car, and under the supervision of an officer," the court concluded, a "warrantless search of the
arrestee's car cannot be justified as
necessary to protect the officers at
the scene or prevent the destruc-
tion of evidence." Accordingly, the
court held that the search of Gant's
car was unreasonable.

The dissenting justices would
have upheld the search of Gant's
car based on their view that "the
validity of a *Belton* search . . . clearly does not depend on the presence
of the *Chimel* rationales in a particular case." Although they disagreed
with the majority's view of *Belton*,

the dissenting justices acknowledged that "[t]he bright-line rule embraced in *Belton* has long been criticized and probably merits reconsideration." They thus "add[ed their] voice[s] to the others that have urged the Supreme Court to revisit *Belton*."

The chorus that has called for us to revisit *Belton* includes courts, scholars, and Members of this Court who have questioned that decision's clarity and its fidelity to Fourth Amendment principles. We therefore granted the State's petition for certiorari.

II

* * * Among the exceptions to the warrant requirement is a search incident to a lawful arrest. See Weeks v. United States, 232 U.S. 383, 392 (1914). The exception derives from interests in officer safety and evidence preservation that are typically implicated in arrest situations. See United States v. Robinson, 414 U.S. 218, 230–234 (1973); *Chimel*, 395 U.S., at 763.

In *Chimel*, we held that a search incident to arrest may only include "the arrestee's person and the area 'within his immediate control'— construing that phrase to mean the area from within which he might gain possession of a weapon or destructible evidence." That limitation, which continues to define the boundaries of the exception, ensures that the scope of a search incident to arrest is commensurate with its purposes of protecting arresting officers and safeguarding any evidence of the offense of arrest that an arrestee might conceal or destroy. If there is no possibility that an arrestee could reach into the area that law enforcement officers seek to search, both justifications for the search-incident-to-arrest exception are absent and the rule does not apply.

In *Belton*, we considered *Chimel*'s application to the automobile context. [The Court discusses the facts and arguments of the parties in *Belton*.] There was no suggestion by the parties or amici that *Chimel* authorizes a vehicle search incident to arrest when there is no realistic possibility that an arrestee could access his vehicle.

After considering these arguments, we held that when an officer lawfully arrests "the occupant of an automobile, he may, as a contemporaneous incident of that arrest, search the passenger compartment of the automobile" and any containers therein. That holding was based in large part on our assumption "that articles inside the relatively narrow compass of the passenger compartment of an automobile are in fact generally, even if not inevitably, within 'the area into which an arrestee might reach.' "

The Arizona Supreme Court read our decision in *Belton* as merely delineating "the proper scope of a search of the interior of an automobile" incident to an arrest. That is, when the passenger compartment is within an arrestee's reaching distance, *Belton* supplies the generalization that the entire compartment and any containers therein may be reached. On that view of *Belton*, the state court concluded that the search of Gant's car was unreasonable because Gant clearly could not have accessed his car at the time of the search. It also found that no other exception to the warrant requirement applied in this case.

Gant now urges us to adopt the reading of *Belton* followed by the Arizona Supreme Court.

III

Despite the textual and evidentiary support for the Arizona Supreme Court's reading of *Belton*, our opinion has been widely understood to allow a vehicle search incident to the arrest of a recent occupant even if there is no possibility the arrestee could gain access to the vehicle at the time of the search. This reading may be attributable to Justice Brennan's dissent in *Belton*, in which he characterized the Court's holding as resting on the "fiction ... that the interior of a car is always within the immediate control of an arrestee who has recently been in the car." Under the majority's approach, he argued, "the result would presumably be the same even if [the officer] had handcuffed *Belton* and his companions in the patrol car" before conducting the search.

Since we decided *Belton*, Courts of Appeals have given different answers to the question whether a vehicle must be within an arrestee's reach to justify a vehicle search incident to arrest, but Justice Brennan's reading of the Court's opinion has predominated. As Justice O'Connor observed, "lower court decisions seem now to treat the ability to search a vehicle incident to the arrest of a recent occupant as a police entitlement rather than as an exception justified by the twin rationales of *Chimel*." *Thornton*, 541 U.S., at

624 (opinion concurring in part). Justice SCALIA has similarly noted that, although it is improbable that an arrestee could gain access to weapons stored in his vehicle after he has been handcuffed and secured in the backseat of a patrol car, cases allowing a search in "this precise factual scenario ... are legion." Id., at 628 (opinion concurring in judgment) (collecting cases). * * *

Under this broad reading of *Belton*, a vehicle search would be authorized incident to every arrest of a recent occupant notwithstanding that in most cases the vehicle's passenger compartment will not be within the arrestee's reach at the time of the search. To read *Belton* as authorizing a vehicle search incident to every recent occupant's arrest would thus untether the rule from the justifications underlying the *Chimel* exception—a result clearly incompatible with our statement in *Belton* that it "in no way alters the fundamental principles established in the *Chimel* case regarding the basic scope of searches incident to lawful custodial arrests." Accordingly, we reject this reading of *Belton* and hold that the *Chimel* rationale authorizes police to search a vehicle incident to a recent occupant's arrest only when the arrestee is unsecured and within reaching distance of the passenger compartment at the time of the search.[4]

Although it does not follow from *Chimel*, we also conclude that cir-

---

4. Because officers have many means of ensuring the safe arrest of vehicle occupants, it will be the rare case in which an officer is unable to fully effectuate an arrest so that a real possibility of access to the arrestee's vehicle remains. Cf. 3 W. LaFave, Search and Seizure § 7.1(c), p. 525 (4th

ed.2004) (hereinafter LaFave) (noting that the availability of protective measures "ensur[es] the nonexistence of circumstances in which the arrestee's 'control' of the car is in doubt"). But in such a case a search incident to arrest is reasonable under the Fourth Amendment.

cumstances unique to the vehicle context justify a search incident to a lawful arrest when it is "reasonable to believe evidence relevant to the crime of arrest might be found in the vehicle." *Thornton*, 541 U.S., at 632 (SCALIA, J., concurring in judgment). In many cases, as when a recent occupant is arrested for a traffic violation, there will be no reasonable basis to believe the vehicle contains relevant evidence. But in others, including *Belton* and *Thornton*, the offense of arrest will supply a basis for searching the passenger compartment of an arrestee's vehicle and any containers therein.

Neither the possibility of access nor the likelihood of discovering offense-related evidence authorized the search in this case. Unlike in *Belton*, which involved a single officer confronted with four unsecured arrestees, the five officers in this case outnumbered the three arrestees, all of whom had been handcuffed and secured in separate patrol cars before the officers searched Gant's car. Under those circumstances, Gant clearly was not within reaching distance of his car at the time of the search. An evidentiary basis for the search was also lacking in this case. Whereas *Belton* and Thornton were arrested for drug offenses, Gant was arrested for driving with a suspended license-an offense for which police could not expect to find evidence in the passenger compartment of Gant's car. Because police could not reasonably have believed either that Gant could have accessed his car at the time of the search or that evidence of the offense for which he was arrested might have been found

therein, the search in this case was unreasonable.

IV

The State does not seriously disagree with the Arizona Supreme Court's conclusion that Gant could not have accessed his vehicle at the time of the search, but it nevertheless asks us to uphold the search of his vehicle under the broad reading of *Belton* discussed above. The State argues that *Belton* searches are reasonable regardless of the possibility of access in a given case because that expansive rule correctly balances law enforcement interests, including the interest in a bright-line rule, with an arrestee's limited privacy interest in his vehicle.

For several reasons, we reject the State's argument. First, the State seriously undervalues the privacy interests at stake. Although we have recognized that a motorist's privacy interest in his vehicle is less substantial than in his home, the former interest is nevertheless important and deserving of constitutional protection. It is particularly significant that *Belton* searches authorize police officers to search not just the passenger compartment but every purse, briefcase, or other container within that space. A rule that gives police the power to conduct such a search whenever an individual is caught committing a traffic offense, when there is no basis for believing evidence of the offense might be found in the vehicle, creates a serious and recurring threat to the privacy of countless individuals. Indeed, the character of that threat implicates the central concern underlying the Fourth Amendment— the concern about giving police officers unbridled discretion to rummage at will among a person's private effects.

At the same time as it undervalues these privacy concerns, the State exaggerates the clarity that its reading of *Belton* provides. Courts that have read *Belton* expansively are at odds regarding how close in time to the arrest and how proximate to the arrestee's vehicle an officer's first contact with the arrestee must be to bring the encounter within *Belton* 's purview and whether a search is reasonable when it commences or continues after the arrestee has been removed from the scene. The rule has thus generated a great deal of uncertainty, particularly for a rule touted as providing a "bright line."

Contrary to the State's suggestion, a broad reading of *Belton* is also unnecessary to protect law enforcement safety and evidentiary interests. Under our view, *Belton* and *Thornton* permit an officer to conduct a vehicle search when an arrestee is within reaching distance of the vehicle or it is reasonable to believe the vehicle contains evidence of the offense of arrest. Other established exceptions to the warrant requirement authorize a vehicle search under additional circumstances when safety or evidentiary concerns demand. For instance, Michigan v. Long, 463 U.S. 1032 (1983), permits an officer to search a vehicle's passenger compartment when he has reasonable suspicion that an individual, whether or not the arrestee, is "dangerous" and might access the vehicle to "gain immediate control of weapons." If there is probable cause to believe a vehicle contains evidence of criminal activity, United States v. Ross,

456 U.S. 798 (1982), authorizes a search of any area of the vehicle in which the evidence might be found. Unlike the searches permitted by Justice SCALIA's opinion concurring in the judgment in *Thornton*, which we conclude today are reasonable for purposes of the Fourth Amendment, *Ross* allows searches for evidence relevant to offenses other than the offense of arrest, and the scope of the search authorized is broader. Finally, there may be still other circumstances in which safety or evidentiary interests would justify a search. Cf. Maryland v. Buie, 494 U.S. 325, 334 (1990) (holding that, incident to arrest, an officer may conduct a limited protective sweep of those areas of a house in which he reasonably suspects a dangerous person may be hiding).

These exceptions together ensure that officers may search a vehicle when genuine safety or evidentiary concerns encountered during the arrest of a vehicle's recent occupant justify a search. Construing *Belton* broadly to allow vehicle searches incident to any arrest would serve no purpose except to provide a police entitlement, and it is anathema to the Fourth Amendment to permit a warrantless search on that basis. For these reasons, we are unpersuaded by the State's arguments that a broad reading of *Belton* would meaningfully further law enforcement interests and justify a substantial intrusion on individuals' privacy. [Justice Stevens, in a footnote, observes that eight states had rejected *Belton* under their own constitutions.]

V

Our dissenting colleagues argue that the doctrine of stare decisis requires adherence to a broad reading of *Belton* even though the justifications for searching a vehicle incident to arrest are in most cases absent. The doctrine of stare decisis is of course "essential to the respect accorded to the judgments of the Court and to the stability of the law," but it does not compel us to follow a past decision when its rationale no longer withstands "careful analysis."

We have never relied on stare decisis to justify the continuance of an unconstitutional police practice. And we would be particularly loath to uphold an unconstitutional result in a case that is so easily distinguished from the decisions that arguably compel it. The safety and evidentiary interests that supported the search in *Belton* simply are not present in this case. Indeed, it is hard to imagine two cases that are factually more distinct, as *Belton* involved one officer confronted by four unsecured arrestees suspected of committing a drug offense and this case involves several officers confronted with a securely detained arrestee apprehended for driving with a suspended license. This case is also distinguishable from *Thornton*, in which the petitioner was arrested for a drug offense. It is thus unsurprising that Members of this Court who concurred in the judgments in *Belton* and Thornton also concur in the decision in this case.

We do not agree with the contention in Justice ALITO's dissent (hereinafter dissent) that consideration of police reliance interests requires a different result. Although it appears that the State's reading of *Belton* has been widely taught in police academies and that law en-

forcement officers have relied on the rule in conducting vehicle searches during the past 28 years, many of these searches were not justified by the reasons underlying the *Chimel* exception. Countless individuals guilty of nothing more serious than a traffic violation have had their constitutional right to the security of their private effects violated as a result. The fact that the law enforcement community may view the State's version of the *Belton* rule as an entitlement does not establish the sort of reliance interest that could outweigh the countervailing interest that all individuals share in having their constitutional rights fully protected. If it is clear that a practice is unlawful, individuals' interest in its discontinuance clearly outweighs any law enforcement "entitlement" to its persistence. * * *

The experience of the 28 years since we decided *Belton* has shown that the generalization underpinning the broad reading of that decision is unfounded. We now know that articles inside the passenger compartment are rarely "within 'the area into which an arrestee might reach,' "and blind adherence to *Belton*'s faulty assumption would authorize myriad unconstitutional searches. The doctrine of stare decisis does not require us to approve routine constitutional violations.

VI

Police may search a vehicle incident to a recent occupant's arrest only if the arrestee is within reaching distance of the passenger compartment at the time of the search or it is reasonable to believe the vehicle contains evidence of the offense of arrest. When these justifications are absent, a search of an arrestee's vehicle will be unreasonable unless police obtain a warrant or show that another exception to the warrant requirement applies. The Arizona Supreme Court correctly held that this case involved an unreasonable search. Accordingly, the judgment of the State Supreme Court is affirmed.

It is so ordered.

JUSTICE SCALIA, concurring.

To determine what is an "unreasonable" search within the meaning of the Fourth Amendment, we look first to the historical practices the Framers sought to preserve; if those provide inadequate guidance, we apply traditional standards of reasonableness. Since the historical scope of officers' authority to search vehicles incident to arrest is uncertain, see Thornton v. United States, 541 U.S. 615, 629–631 (2004) (SCALIA, J., concurring in judgment), traditional standards of reasonableness govern. It is abundantly clear that those standards do not justify what I take to be the rule set forth in New York v. Belton, and *Thornton*: that arresting officers may always search an arrestee's vehicle in order to protect themselves from hidden weapons. When an arrest is made in connection with a roadside stop, police virtually always have a less intrusive and more effective means of ensuring their safety-and a means that is virtually always employed: ordering the arrestee away from the vehicle, patting him down in the open, handcuffing him, and placing him in the squad car.

Law enforcement officers face a risk of being shot whenever they pull a car over. But that risk is at its height at the time of the initial confrontation; and it is not at all reduced by allowing a search of the stopped vehicle after the driver has been arrested and placed in the squad car. I observed in *Thornton* that the government had failed to provide a single instance in which a formerly restrained arrestee escaped to retrieve a weapon from his own vehicle; Arizona and its amici have not remedied that significant deficiency in the present case.

It must be borne in mind that we are speaking here only of a rule automatically permitting a search when the driver or an occupant is arrested. Where no arrest is made, we have held that officers may search the car if they reasonably believe "the suspect is dangerous and . . . may gain immediate control of weapons." Michigan v. Long, 463 U.S. 1032, 1049 (1983). In the no-arrest case, the possibility of access to weapons in the vehicle always exists, since the driver or passenger will be allowed to return to the vehicle when the interrogation is completed. The rule of Michigan v. Long is not at issue here.

Justice STEVENS acknowledges that an officer-safety rationale cannot justify all vehicle searches incident to arrest, but asserts that that is not the rule *Belton* and Thornton adopted. (As described above, I read those cases differently). Justice STEVENS would therefore retain the application of Chimel v. California in the car-search context but would apply in the future what he believes our cases held in the past: that officers making a roadside stop may search the vehicle so long as the "arrestee is within reaching distance of the passenger compartment at the time of the search." I believe that this standard fails to provide the needed guidance to arresting officers and also leaves much room for manipulation, inviting officers to leave the scene unsecured (at least where dangerous suspects are not involved) in order to conduct a vehicle search. In my view we should simply abandon the *Belton-Thornton* charade of officer safety and overrule those cases. I would hold that a vehicle search incident to arrest is ipso facto "reasonable" only when the object of the search is evidence of the crime for which the arrest was made, or of another crime that the officer has probable cause to believe occurred. Because respondent was arrested for driving without a license (a crime for which no evidence could be expected to be found in the vehicle), I would hold in the present case that the search was unlawful.

Justice ALITO insists that the Court must demand a good reason for abandoning prior precedent. That is true enough, but it seems to me ample reason that the precedent was badly reasoned and produces erroneous (in this case unconstitutional) results. We should recognize *Belton's* fanciful reliance upon officer safety for what it was: "a return to the broader sort of [evidence-gathering] search incident to arrest that we allowed before *Chimel*." *Thornton, supra,* at 631 (SCALIA, J., concurring in judgment; citations omitted).

* * *

No other Justice, however, shares my view that application of *Chimel* in this context should be entirely abandoned. It seems to me unacceptable for the Court to come forth with a 4–to–1–to–4 opinion that leaves the governing rule uncertain. I am therefore confronted with the choice of either leaving the current understanding of *Belton* and *Thornton* in effect, or acceding to what seems to me the artificial narrowing of those cases adopted by Justice STEVENS. The latter, as I have said, does not provide the degree of certainty I think desirable in this field; but the former opens the field to what I think are plainly unconstitutional searches—which is the greater evil. I therefore join the opinion of the Court.

———

JUSTICE BREYER, dissenting.

I agree with Justice ALITO that New York v. Belton is best read as setting forth a bright-line rule that permits a warrantless search of the passenger compartment of an automobile incident to the lawful arrest of an occupant-regardless of the danger the arrested individual in fact poses. I also agree with Justice STEVENS, however, that the rule can produce results divorced from its underlying Fourth Amendment rationale. For that reason I would look for a better rule—were the question before us one of first impression.

The matter, however, is not one of first impression, and that fact makes a substantial difference. The *Belton* rule has been followed not only by this Court in Thornton v. United States, but also by numerous other courts. Principles of stare decisis must apply, and those who wish this Court to change a well-established legal precedent—where, as here, there has been considerable reliance on the legal rule in question—bear a heavy burden. I have not found that burden met. Nor do I believe that the other considerations ordinarily relevant when determining whether to overrule a case are satisfied. I consequently join Justice ALITO's dissenting opinion with the exception of Part II–E.

JUSTICE ALITO, with whom THE CHIEF JUSTICE and JUSTICE KENNEDY join, and with whom JUSTICE BREYER joins except as to Part II–E, dissenting.

Twenty-eight years ago, in New York v. Belton, this Court held that "when a policeman has made a lawful custodial arrest of the occupant of an automobile, he may, as a contemporaneous incident of that arrest, search the passenger compartment of that automobile." Five years ago, in Thornton v. United States—a case involving a situation not materially distinguishable from the situation here—the Court not only reaffirmed but extended the holding of Belton, making it applicable to recent occupants. Today's decision effectively overrules those important decisions, even though respondent Gant has not asked us to do so.

To take the place of the overruled precedents, the Court adopts a new two-part rule under which a police officer who arrests a vehicle occupant or recent occupant may search the passenger compartment if (1) the arrestee is within reaching distance of the vehicle at the time of the search or (2) the officer has reason to believe that the vehicle contains evidence of the offense of arrest. The first part of this new rule may endanger arresting officers and is truly endorsed by only four Justices; Justice SCALIA joins solely for the purpose of avoiding a "4–to–1–to 4 opinion." The second part of the new rule is taken from Justice SCALIA's separate opinion in *Thornton* without any independent expla-

nation of its origin or justification and is virtually certain to confuse law enforcement officers and judges for some time to come. The Court's decision will cause the suppression of evidence gathered in many searches carried out in good-faith reliance on well-settled case law, and although the Court purports to base its analysis on the landmark decision in *Chimel*, the Court's reasoning undermines *Chimel*. I would follow *Belton*, and I therefore respectfully dissent.

I

Although the Court refuses to acknowledge that it is overruling *Belton* and Thornton, there can be no doubt that it does so.

* * *

The precise holding in *Belton* could not be clearer. The Court stated unequivocally: "[W]e hold that when a policeman has made a lawful custodial arrest of the occupant of an automobile, he may, as a contemporaneous incident of that arrest, search the passenger compartment of that automobile."

Despite this explicit statement, the opinion of the Court in the present case curiously suggests that *Belton* may reasonably be read as adopting a holding that is narrower than the one explicitly set out in the *Belton* opinion, namely, that an officer arresting a vehicle occupant may search the passenger compartment "when the passenger compartment is within an arrestee's reaching distance." According to the Court, the broader reading of *Belton* that has gained wide acceptance "may be attributable to Justice Brennan's dissent."

Contrary to the Court's suggestion, however, Justice Brennan's *Belton* dissent did not mischaracterize the Court's holding in that case or cause that holding to be misinterpreted. As noted, the *Belton* Court explicitly stated precisely what it held. In *Thornton*, the Court recognized the scope of *Belton's* holding. So did Justice SCALIA's separate opinion. ("In [*Belton*] we set forth a bright-line rule for arrests of automobile occupants, holding that ... a search of the whole [passenger] compartment is justified in every case"). So does Justice SCALIA's opinion in the present case. This "bright-line rule" has now been interred.

II

Because the Court has substantially overruled *Belton* and *Thornton*, the Court must explain why its departure from the usual rule of stare decisis is justified. I recognize that stare decisis is not an "inexorable command," and applies less rigidly in constitutional cases. But the Court has said that a constitutional precedent should be followed unless there is a "special justification" for its abandonment. Dickerson v. United States, 530 U.S. 428, 443 (2000). Relevant factors identified in prior cases include whether the precedent has engendered reliance, whether there has been an important change in circumstances in the outside world, whether the precedent has proved to be unworkable, whether the precedent has been undermined by later decisions, and whether the decision was badly reasoned. These factors weigh in favor of retaining the rule established in *Belton*.

A

Reliance. While reliance is most important in "cases involving property and contract rights," the Court has recognized that reliance by law enforcement officers is also entitled to weight. In *Dickerson*, the Court held that principles of stare decisis "weigh[ed]" heavily against overruling Miranda v. Arizona, because the *Miranda* rule had become "embedded in routine police practice."

If there was reliance in *Dickerson*, there certainly is substantial reliance here. The *Belton* rule has been taught to police officers for more than a quarter century. Many searches—almost certainly including more than a few that figure in cases now on appeal—were conducted in scrupulous reliance on that precedent. It is likely that, on the very day when this opinion is announced, numerous vehicle searches will be conducted in good faith by police officers who were taught the *Belton* rule.

The opinion of the Court recognizes that "*Belton* has been widely taught in police academies and that law enforcement officers have relied on the rule in conducting vehicle searches during the past 28 years." But for the Court, this seemingly counts for nothing. The Court states that "[w]e have never relied on stare decisis to justify the continuance of an unconstitutional police practice," but of course the Court routinely relies on decisions sustaining the constitutionality of police practices without doing what the Court has done here—sua sponte considering whether those decisions should be overruled. And the Court cites no authority for the proposition that stare decisis may be disregarded or provides only lesser protection when the precedent that is challenged is one that sustained the constitutionality of a law enforcement practice.

* * *

B

Changed circumstances. Abandonment of the *Belton* rule cannot be justified on the ground that the dangers surrounding the arrest of a vehicle occupant are different today than they were 28 years ago. The Court claims that "[w]e now know that articles inside the passenger compartment are rarely within the area into which an arrestee might reach," but surely it was well known in 1981 that a person who is taken from a vehicle, handcuffed, and placed in the back of a patrol car is unlikely to make it back into his own car to retrieve a weapon or destroy evidence.

C

Workability. The *Belton* rule has not proved to be unworkable. On the contrary, the rule was adopted for the express purpose of providing a test that would be relatively easy for police officers and judges to apply. The Court correctly notes that even the *Belton* rule is not perfectly clear in all situations. Specifically, it is sometimes debatable whether a search is or is not contemporaneous with an arrest, but that problem is small in comparison with the problems that the Court's new two-part rule will produce.

The first part of the Court's new rule—which permits the search of a vehicle's passenger compartment if it is within an arrestee's reach at the time of the search—reintroduces the same sort of case-by-case, fact-specific decisionmaking that the *Belton* rule was adopted to avoid. As the situation in *Belton* illustrated, there are cases in which it is unclear whether an arrestee could retrieve a weapon or evidence in the passenger compartment of a car.

Even more serious problems will also result from the second part of the Court's new rule, which requires officers making roadside arrests to determine whether there is reason to believe that the vehicle contains evidence of the crime of arrest. What this rule permits in a variety of situations is entirely unclear.

D

Consistency with later cases. The *Belton* bright-line rule has not been undermined by subsequent cases. On the contrary, that rule was reaffirmed and extended just five years ago in *Thornton*.

E

Bad reasoning. The Court is harshly critical of *Belton*'s reasoning, but the problem that the Court perceives cannot be remedied simply by overruling *Belton*. *Belton* represented only a modest—and quite defensible—extension of *Chimel*, as I understand that decision.

Prior to *Chimel*, the Court's precedents permitted an arresting officer to search the area within an arrestee's "possession" and "control" for the purpose of gathering evidence. Based on this "abstract doctrine," the Court had sustained searches that extended far beyond an arrestee's grabbing area. See United States v. Rabinowitz, 339 U.S. 56 (1950) (search of entire office); Harris v. United States, 331 U.S. 145 (1947) (search of entire apartment).

The *Chimel* Court, in an opinion written by Justice Stewart, overruled these cases. Concluding that there are only two justifications for a warrantless search incident to arrest—officer safety and the preservation of evidence—the Court stated that such a search must be confined to "the arrestee's person" and "the area from within which he might gain possession of a weapon or destructible evidence."

Unfortunately, *Chimel* did not say whether "the area from within which [an arrestee] might gain possession of a weapon or destructible evidence" is to be measured at the time of the arrest or at the time of the search, but unless the *Chimel* rule was meant to be a specialty rule, applicable to only a few unusual cases, the Court must have intended for this area to be measured at the time of arrest.

This is so because the Court can hardly have failed to appreciate the following two facts. First, in the great majority of cases, an officer making an arrest is able to handcuff the arrestee and remove him to a secure place before conducting a search incident to the arrest. Second, because it is safer for an arresting officer to secure an arrestee before searching, it is likely that this is what arresting officers do in the great majority of cases. * * * Thus, if the area within an arrestee's reach were assessed, not at the time of arrest, but at the time of the search, the *Chimel* rule would rarely come into play.

Moreover, if the applicability of the *Chimel* rule turned on whether an arresting officer chooses to secure an arrestee prior to conducting a search, rather than searching first and securing the arrestee later, the rule would "create a perverse incentive for an arresting officer to prolong the period during which the arrestee is kept in an area where he could pose a danger to the officer." United States v. Abdul–Saboor, 85 F.3d 664, 669 (C.A.D.C. 1996). If this is the law, the D.C. Circuit observed, "the law would truly be, as Mr. Bumble said, 'a ass.'" See also United States v. Tejada, 524 F.3d 809, 812 (C.A.7 2008) ("[I]f the police could lawfully have searched the defendant's grabbing radius at the moment of arrest, he has no legitimate complaint if, the better to protect themselves from him, they first put him outside that radius").

I do not think that this is what the *Chimel* Court intended. Handcuffs were in use in 1969. The ability of arresting officers to secure arrestees before conducting a search—and their incentive to do so—are facts that can hardly have escaped the Court's attention. I therefore believe that the *Chimel* Court intended that its new rule apply in cases in which the arrestee is handcuffed before the search is conducted.

The *Belton* Court, in my view, proceeded on the basis of this interpretation of *Chimel*. Again speaking through Justice Stewart, the *Belton* Court reasoned that articles in the passenger compartment of a car are "generally, even if not inevitably" within an arrestee's reach. This is undoubtedly true at the time of the arrest of a person who is seated in a car but plainly not true when the person has been removed from the car and placed in handcuffs. Accordingly, the *Belton* Court must have proceeded on the assumption that the *Chimel* rule was to be applied at the time of arrest. And that is why the *Belton* Court was able to say that its decision "in no way alter[ed] the fundamental principles established in the *Chimel* case regarding the basic scope of searches incident to lawful custodial arrests." Viewing *Chimel* as having focused on the time of arrest, *Belton*'s only new step was to eliminate the need to decide on a case-by-case basis whether a particular person seated in a car actually could have reached the part of the passenger compartment where a weapon or evidence was hidden. For this reason, if we are going to reexamine *Belton*, we should also reexamine the reasoning in *Chimel* on which *Belton* rests.

F

The Court, however, does not reexamine *Chimel* and thus leaves the law relating to searches incident to arrest in a confused and unstable state. The first part of the Court's new two-part rule—which permits an arresting officer to search the area within an arrestee's reach at the time of the search—applies, at least for now, only to vehicle occupants and recent occupants, but there is no logical reason why the same rule should not apply to all arrestees.

The second part of the Court's new rule, which the Court takes uncritically from Justice SCALIA's separate opinion in *Thornton*, raises doctrinal and practical problems that the Court makes no effort to address. Why, for example, is the standard for this type of evidence-gathering search "reason to believe" rather than probable cause? And why is this type of search restricted to evidence of the offense of arrest? It is true that an arrestee's vehicle is probably more likely to contain evidence of the crime of arrest than of some other crime, but if reason-to-believe is the governing standard for an evidence-gathering search incident to arrest, it is not easy to see why an officer should not be able to search when the officer has reason to believe that the vehicle in question possesses evidence of a crime other than the crime of arrest.

Nor is it easy to see why an evidence-gathering search incident to arrest should be restricted to the passenger compartment. The *Belton* rule was limited in this way because the passenger compartment was considered to be the area that vehicle occupants can generally reach, but since the second part of the new rule is not based on officer safety or the preservation of evidence, the ground for this limitation is obscure.

III

Respondent in this case has not asked us to overrule *Belton*, much less *Chimel*. Respondent's argument rests entirely on an interpretation of *Belton* that is plainly incorrect, an interpretation that disregards *Belton*'s explicit delineation of its holding. I would therefore leave any reexamination of our prior precedents for another day, if such a reexamination is to be undertaken at all. In this case, I would simply apply *Belton* and reverse the judgment below.

Page 326. Add the following new section after the *Question on Knowles*:

6. *The Arrest Power Rule Where the Arrest Violates State Law*

In the following case, the Court applies *Atwater, Robinson* and *Knowles* to a search incident to an arrest made in violation of state law, but permissible under the Federal Constitution.

VIRGINIA v. MOORE
2008

Supreme Court of the United States, 2008.
128 S.Ct. 1598.

JUSTICE SCALIA delivered the opinion of the Court.

We consider whether a police officer violates the Fourth Amendment by making an arrest based on probable cause but prohibited by state law.

I

On February 20, 2003, two City of Portsmouth police officers stopped a car driven by David Lee Moore. They had heard over the police radio that a person known as "Chubs" was driving with a suspended license, and one of the officers knew Moore by that nickname. The officers determined that Moore's license was in fact suspended, and arrested him for the misdemeanor of driving on a suspended license, which is punishable under Virginia law by a year in jail and a $2,500 fine. The officers subsequently searched Moore and found that he was carrying 16 grams of crack cocaine and $516 in cash.

Under state law, the officers should have issued Moore a summons instead of arresting him. Driving on a suspended license, like some other misdemeanors, is not an arrestable offense except as to those who "fail or refuse to discontinue" the violation, and those whom the officer reasonably believes to be likely to disregard a summons, or likely to harm themselves or others. Va. Code Ann. § 19.2–74. The intermediate appellate court found none of these circumstances applicable, and Virginia did not appeal that determination. * * *

Moore was charged with possessing cocaine with the intent to distribute it in violation of Virginia law. He filed a pretrial motion to suppress the evidence from the arrest search. Virginia law does not, as a general matter, require suppression of evidence obtained in violation of state law. Moore argued, however, that suppression was required by the Fourth Amendment. The trial court denied the motion, and after a bench trial found Moore guilty of the drug charge and sentenced him to a 5–year prison term, with one year and six months of the sentence suspended. The conviction was reversed by a panel of Virginia's intermediate court on Fourth Amendment grounds, reinstated by the intermediate court sitting en banc, and finally reversed again by the Virginia Supreme Court. The Court reasoned that since the arresting officers should have issued Moore a citation under state law, and the Fourth Amendment does not permit search incident to citation, the arrest search violated the Fourth Amendment. We granted certiorari.

II

The Fourth Amendment protects "against unreasonable searches and seizures" of (among other things) the person. In determining whether a search or seizure is unreasonable, we begin with history. We look to the statutes and common law of the founding era to determine the norms that the Fourth Amendment was meant to preserve.

We are aware of no historical indication that those who ratified the Fourth Amendment understood it as a redundant guarantee of whatever limits on search and seizure legislatures might have enacted. The immediate object of the Fourth Amendment was to prohibit the general warrants and writs of assistance that English judges had employed against the colonists. That suggests, if anything, that founding-era citizens were skeptical of using the rules for search and seizure set by government actors as the index of reasonableness.

Joseph Story, among others, saw the Fourth Amendment as "little more than the affirmance of a great constitutional doctrine of the common law," 3 Commentaries on the Constitution of the United States § 1895, p. 748 (1833) * * *. No early case or commentary, to our knowledge, suggested the Amendment was intended to incorporate subsequently enacted statutes. None of the early Fourth Amendment cases that scholars have identified sought to base a constitutional claim on a violation of a state or federal statute concerning arrest.

See Davies, Recovering the Original Fourth Amendment, 98 Mich. L. Rev. 547, 613–614 (1999); see also T. Taylor, Two Studies in Constitutional Interpretation 44–45 (1969).

* * * [A]s Moore adduces neither case law nor commentaries to support his view that the Fourth Amendment was intended to incorporate statutes, this is "not a case in which the claimant can point to a clear answer that existed in 1791 and has been generally adhered to by the traditions of our society ever since." Atwater v. Lago Vista, 532 U.S. 318, 345 (2001).

III

A

When history has not provided a conclusive answer, we have analyzed a search or seizure in light of traditional standards of reasonableness by assessing, on the one hand, the degree to which it intrudes upon an individual's privacy and, on the other, the degree to which it is needed for the promotion of legitimate governmental interests. That methodology provides no support for Moore's Fourth Amendment claim. In a long line of cases, we have said that when an officer has probable cause to believe a person committed even a minor crime in his presence, the balancing of private and public interests is not in doubt. The arrest is constitutionally reasonable.

Our decisions counsel against changing this calculus when a State chooses to protect privacy beyond the level that the Fourth Amendment requires. We have treated additional protections exclusively as matters of state law. In Cooper v. California, 386 U.S. 58 (1967), we reversed a state court that had held the search of a seized vehicle to be in violation of the Fourth Amendment because state law did not explicitly authorize the search. We concluded that whether state law authorized the search was irrelevant. States, we said, remained free "to impose higher standards on searches and seizures than required by the Federal Constitution," but regardless of state rules, police could search a lawfully seized vehicle as a matter of federal constitutional law.

In California v. Greenwood, 486 U.S. 35 (1988), we held that search of an individual's garbage forbidden by California's Constitution was not forbidden by the Fourth Amendment. "[W]hether or not a search is reasonable within the meaning of the Fourth Amendment," we said, has never "depend[ed] on the law of the particular State in which the search occurs." while "[i]ndividual States may surely construe their own constitutions as imposing more stringent constraints on police conduct than does the Federal Constitution," state law did not alter the content of the Fourth Amendment.

We have applied the same principle in the seizure context. Whren v. United States, 517 U.S. 806 (1996), held that police officers had acted reasonably in stopping a car, even though their action violated regulations limiting the authority of plainclothes officers in unmarked vehicles. We thought it obvious that the Fourth Amendment's meaning did not change with local law enforcement practices—even practices set by rule. While those practices "vary from place to place and from time to time," Fourth Amendment protections are not "so variable" and cannot "be made to turn upon such trivialities."

B

We are convinced that the approach of our prior cases is correct, because an arrest based on probable cause serves interests that have long been seen as sufficient to justify the seizure. Arrest ensures that a suspect appears to answer charges and does not continue a crime, and it safeguards evidence and enables officers to conduct an in-custody investigation.

Moore argues that a State has no interest in arrest when it has a policy against arresting for certain crimes. That is not so, because arrest will still ensure a suspect's appearance at trial, prevent him from continuing his offense, and enable officers to investigate the incident more thoroughly. State arrest restrictions are more accurately characterized as showing that the State values its interests in forgoing arrests more highly than its interests in making them, or as showing that the State places a higher premium on privacy than the Fourth Amendment requires. A State is free to prefer one search-and-seizure policy among the range of constitutionally permissible options, but its choice of a more restrictive option does not render the less restrictive ones unreasonable, and hence unconstitutional.

If we concluded otherwise, we would often frustrate rather than further state policy. Virginia chooses to protect individual privacy and dignity more than the Fourth Amendment requires, but it also chooses not to attach to violations of its arrest rules the potent remedies that federal courts have applied to Fourth Amendment violations. Virginia does not, for example, ordinarily exclude from criminal trials evidence obtained in violation of its statutes. Moore would allow Virginia to accord enhanced protection against arrest only on pain of accompanying that protection with federal remedies for Fourth Amendment violations, which often include the exclusionary rule. States unwilling to lose control over the remedy would have to abandon restrictions on arrest altogether. This is an odd consequence of a provision designed to protect against searches and seizures.

Even if we thought that state law changed the nature of the Commonwealth's interests for purposes of the Fourth Amendment, we would adhere to the probable-cause standard. In determining what is reasonable under the Fourth Amendment, we have given great weight to the "essential interest in readily administrable rules." *Atwater,* 532 U.S., at 347. In *Atwater*, we acknowledged that nuanced judgments about the need for warrantless arrest were desirable, but we nonetheless declined to limit to felonies and disturbances of the peace the Fourth Amendment rule allowing arrest based on probable cause to believe a law has been broken in the presence of the arresting officer. The rule extends even to minor misdemeanors, we concluded, because of the need for a bright-line constitutional standard. If the constitutionality of arrest for minor offenses turned in part on inquiries as to risk of flight and danger of repetition, officers might be deterred from making legitimate arrests. * * *

Incorporating state-law arrest limitations into the Constitution would produce a constitutional regime no less vague and unpredictable than the one we rejected in *Atwater*. The constitutional standard would be only as easy to apply as the underlying state law, and state law can be complicated indeed. The Virginia statute in this case, for example, calls on law enforcement officers to weigh just the sort of case-specific factors that *Atwater* said would deter legitimate arrests if made part of the constitutional inquiry. It would authorize arrest if a misdemeanor suspect fails or refuses to discontinue the unlawful act, or if the officer believes the suspect to be likely to disregard a summons. Va. Code Ann. § 19.2–74.A.1. *Atwater* specifically noted the "extremely poor judgment" displayed in arresting a local resident who would "almost certainly" have discontinued the offense and who had "no place to hide and no incentive to flee." It nonetheless declined to make those considerations part of the constitutional calculus. *Atwater* differs from this case in only one significant respect: It considered (and rejected) federal constitutional remedies for *all* minor-misdemeanor arrests; Moore seeks them in only that *subset* of minor-misdemeanor arrests in which there is the least to be gained—that is, where the State has already acted to constrain officers' discretion and prevent abuse. Here we confront fewer horribles than in *Atwater*, and less of a need for redress.

Finally, linking Fourth Amendment protections to state law would cause them to "vary from place to place and from time to time," *Whren,* 517 U.S., at 815. Even at the same place and time, the Fourth Amendment's protections might vary if federal officers were not subject to the same statutory constraints as state officers. In Elkins v. United States, 364 U.S. 206 (1960), we noted the practical difficulties posed by the "silver-platter doctrine," which had imposed more stringent limitations on federal officers than on state police acting independent of them. It would be strange to construe a constitutional provision that did not apply to the States at all when it was adopted to now restrict state officers more than federal officers, solely because the States have passed search-and-seizure laws that are the prerogative of independent sovereigns.

We conclude that warrantless arrests for crimes committed in the presence of an arresting officer are reasonable under the Constitution, and that while States are free to regulate such arrests however they desire, state restrictions do not alter the Fourth Amendment's protections.

IV

Moore argues that even if the Constitution allowed his arrest, it did not allow the arresting officers to search him. We have recognized, however, that officers may perform searches incident to constitutionally permissible arrests in order to ensure their safety and safeguard evidence. United States v. Robinson, 414 U.S. 218 (1973). We have described this rule as covering any "lawful arrest," with constitutional law as the reference point. That is to say, we have equated a lawful arrest with an arrest based on prob-

able cause: "A custodial arrest of a suspect based on probable cause is a reasonable intrusion under the Fourth Amendment; *that intrusion being lawful*, a search incident to the arrest requires no additional justification." *Id.* (emphasis added). * * *

The interests justifying search are present whenever an officer makes an arrest. A search enables officers to safeguard evidence, and, most critically, to ensure their safety during "the extended exposure which follows the taking of a suspect into custody and transporting him to the police station." *Robinson, supra,* at 234–235. Officers issuing citations do not face the same danger, and we therefore held in Knowles v. Iowa, 525 U.S. 113 (1998), that they do not have the same authority to search. We cannot agree with the Virginia Supreme Court that *Knowles* controls here. The state officers *arrested* Moore, and therefore faced the risks that are "an adequate basis for treating all custodial arrests alike for purposes of search justification." *Robinson, supra,* at 235.

The Virginia Supreme Court may have concluded that *Knowles* required the exclusion of evidence seized from Moore because, under state law, the officers who arrested Moore should have issued him a citation instead. This argument might have force if the Constitution forbade Moore's arrest, because we have sometimes excluded evidence obtained through unconstitutional methods in order to deter constitutional violations. See Wong Sun v. United States, 371 U.S. 471, 484–485 (1963). But the arrest rules that the officers violated were those of state law alone, and as we have just concluded, it is not the province of the Fourth Amendment to enforce state law. That Amendment does not require the exclusion of evidence obtained from a constitutionally permissible arrest.

————

We reaffirm against a novel challenge what we have signaled for more than half a century. When officers have probable cause to believe that a person has committed a crime in their presence, the Fourth Amendment permits them to make an arrest, and to search the suspect in order to safeguard evidence and ensure their own safety. The judgment of the Supreme Court of Virginia is reversed, and the case is remanded for further proceedings not inconsistent with this opinion.

[Justice Ginsburg's opinion concurring in the judgment is omitted.]

H. ADMINISTRATIVE SEARCHES AND OTHER SEARCHES BASED ON "SPECIAL NEEDS"

3. Searches and Seizures of Individuals Pursuant to "Special Needs"

a. Searches and Seizures on the Basis of Reasonable Suspicion Rather Than Probable Cause

Page 397. Add at the end of the note on more intrusive searches

Reasonableness of Strip Searches of Students: Safford v. Unified School District #1 v. Redding

SAFFORD UNIFIED SCHOOL DISTRICT #1 v. REDDING

Supreme Court of the United States, 2009.
129 S.Ct. 2633.

Justice Souter **delivered the opinion of the Court.**

The issue here is whether a 13–year-old student's Fourth Amendment right was violated when she was subjected to a search of her bra and underpants by school officials acting on reasonable suspicion that she had brought forbidden prescription and over-the-counter drugs to school. Because there were no reasons to suspect the drugs presented a danger or were concealed in her underwear, we hold that the search did violate the Constitution, but because there is reason to question the clarity with which the right was established, the official who ordered the unconstitutional search is entitled to qualified immunity from liability.

I

The events immediately prior to the search in question began in 13–year-old Savana Redding's math class at Safford Middle School one October day in 2003. The assistant principal of the school, Kerry Wilson, came into the room and asked

Savana to go to his office. There, he showed her a day planner, unzipped and open flat on his desk, in which there were several knives, lighters, a permanent marker, and a cigarette. Wilson asked Savana whether the planner was hers; she said it was, but that a few days before she had lent it to her friend, Marissa Glines. Savana stated that none of the items in the planner belonged to her.

Wilson then showed Savana four white prescription-strength ibuprofen 400–mg pills, and one over-the-counter blue naproxen 200–mg pill, all used for pain and inflammation but banned under school rules without advance permission. He asked Savana if she knew anything about the pills. Savana answered that she did not. Wilson then told Savana that he had received a report that she was giving these pills to fellow students; Savana denied it and agreed to let Wilson search her belongings. Helen Romero, an administrative assistant, came into the office, and together with Wilson they searched Savana's backpack, finding nothing.

At that point, Wilson instructed Romero to take Savana to the school nurse's office to search her clothes for pills. Romero and the nurse, Peggy Schwallier, asked Savana to remove her jacket, socks, and shoes, leaving her in stretch pants and a T-shirt (both without pockets), which she was then asked to remove. Finally, Savana was told to pull her bra out and to the side and shake it, and to pull out the elastic on her underpants, thus exposing her breasts and pelvic area to some degree. No pills were found.

Savana's mother filed suit against Safford Unified School District #1, Wilson, Romero, and Schwallier for conducting a strip search in violation of Savana's Fourth Amendment rights. The individuals (hereinafter petitioners) moved for summary judgment, raising a defense of qualified immunity. The District Court for the District of Arizona granted the motion on the ground that there was no Fourth Amendment violation, and a panel of the Ninth Circuit affirmed.

A closely divided Circuit sitting en banc, however, reversed. Following the two-step protocol for evaluating claims of qualified immunity, the Ninth Circuit held that the strip search was unjustified under the Fourth Amendment test for searches of children by school officials set out in New Jersey v. T. L. O., 469 U. S. 325 (1985). The Circuit then applied the test for qualified immunity, and found that Savana's right was clearly established at the time of the search: "these notions of personal privacy are 'clearly established' in that they inhere in all of us, particularly middle school teenagers, and are inherent in the privacy component of the Fourth Amendment's proscription against unreasonable searches. "The upshot was reversal of summary judgment as to Wilson, while affirming the judgments in favor of Schwallier, the school nurse, and Romero, the administrative assistant, since they had not acted as independent decisionmakers.

We granted certiorari, and now affirm in part, reverse in part, and remand.

II

The Fourth Amendment "right of the people to be secure in their persons ... against unreasonable searches and seizures" generally requires a law enforcement officer to have probable cause for conducting a search. "Probable cause exists where the facts and circumstances within an officer's knowledge and of which he had reasonably trustworthy information are sufficient in themselves to warrant a man of reasonable caution in the belief that an offense has been or is being committed," Brinegar v. United States, 338 U. S. 160, 175–176 (1949), and that evidence bearing on that offense will be found in the place to be searched.

In *T. L. O.*, we recognized that the school setting "requires some modification of the level of suspicion of illicit activity needed to justify a search," and held that for searches by school officials "a careful balancing of governmental and private interests suggests that the public interest is best served by a Fourth Amendment standard of reasonableness that stops short of probable cause." We have thus applied a standard of reasonable suspicion to determine the legality of a school administrator's search of a student, and have held that a school search "will be permissible in its scope when the measures adopted are reasonably related to the objectives of the search and not excessively intrusive in light of the age and sex of the student and the nature of the infraction."

A number of our cases on probable cause have an implicit bearing on the reliable knowledge element of reasonable suspicion, as we have attempted to flesh out the knowl-

edge component by looking to the degree to which known facts imply prohibited conduct, see, e.g., Adams v. Williams, 407 U. S. 143, 148 (1972), the specificity of the information received, see, e.g., Spinelli v. United States, 393 U. S. 410, 416–417 (1969), and the reliability of its source, see, e.g., Aguilar v. Texas, 378 U. S. 108, 114 (1964). At the end of the day, however, we have realized that these factors cannot rigidly control, Illinois v. Gates, 462 U. S. 213, 230 (1983), and we have come back to saying that the standards are "fluid concepts that take their substantive content from the particular contexts" in which they are being assessed. Ornelas v. United States, 517 U. S. 690, 696 (1996).

Perhaps the best that can be said generally about the required knowledge component of probable cause for a law enforcement officer's evidence search is that it raise a "fair probability," Gates, 462 U. S., at 238, or a "substantial chance," id., at 244, n. 13, of discovering evidence of criminal activity. The lesser standard for school searches could as readily be described as a moderate chance of finding evidence of wrongdoing.

III

A

In this case, the school's policies strictly prohibit the nonmedical use, possession, or sale of any drug on school grounds, including "[a]ny prescription or over-the-counter drug, except those for which permission to use in school has been granted pursuant to Board policy."[5]

---

5. When the object of a school search is the enforcement of a school rule, a valid search assumes, of course, the rule's legitimacy. But the legitimacy of the rule usually

A week before Savana was searched, another student, Jordan Romero (no relation of the school's administrative assistant), told the principal and Assistant Principal Wilson that "certain students were bringing drugs and weapons on campus," and that he had been sick after taking some pills that "he got from a classmate." On the morning of October 8, the same boy handed Wilson a white pill that he said Marissa Glines had given him. He told Wilson that students were planning to take the pills at lunch.

Wilson learned from Peggy Schwallier, the school nurse, that the pill was Ibuprofen 400 mg, available only by prescription. Wilson then called Marissa out of class. Outside the classroom, Marissa's teacher handed Wilson the day planner, found within Marissa's reach, containing various contraband items. Wilson escorted Marissa back to his office.

In the presence of Helen Romero, Wilson requested Marissa to turn out her pockets and open her wallet. Marissa produced a blue pill, several white ones, and a razor blade. Wilson asked where the blue pill came from, and Marissa answered, "I guess it slipped in when she gave me the IBU 400s." When Wilson asked whom she meant, Marissa replied, "Savana Redding." Wilson then enquired about the day planner and its contents; Marissa

denied knowing anything about them. Wilson did not ask Marissa any followup questions to determine whether there was any likelihood that Savana presently had pills: neither asking when Marissa received the pills from Savana nor where Savana might be hiding them.

Schwallier did not immediately recognize the blue pill, but information provided through a poison control hotline indicated that the pill was a 200–mg dose of an anti-inflammatory drug, generically called naproxen, available over the counter. At Wilson's direction, Marissa was then subjected to a search of her bra and underpants by Romero and Schwallier, as Savana was later on. The search revealed no additional pills.

It was at this juncture that Wilson called Savana into his office and showed her the day planner. Their conversation established that Savana and Marissa were on friendly terms: while she denied knowledge of the contraband, Savana admitted that the day planner was hers and that she had lent it to Marissa. Wilson had other reports of their friendship from staff members, who had identified Savana and Marissa as part of an unusually rowdy group at the school's opening dance in August, during which alcohol and cigarettes were found in the girls'

---

goes without saying as it does here. The Court said plainly in New Jersey v. T. L. O., 469 U. S. 325, 342, n. 9 (1985), that standards of conduct for schools are for school administrators to determine without second-guessing by courts lacking the experience to appreciate what may be needed. Except in patently arbitrary instances, Fourth Amendment analysis takes the rule as a given, as it obviously should do in this case. There is no need here either to explain

the imperative of keeping drugs out of schools, or to explain the reasons for the school's rule banning all drugs, no matter how benign, without advance permission. Teachers are not pharmacologists trained to identify pills and powders, and an effective drug ban has to be enforceable fast. The plenary ban makes sense, and there is no basis to claim that the search was unreasonable owing to some defect or shortcoming of the rule it was aimed at enforcing.

bathroom. Wilson had reason to connect the girls with this contraband, for Wilson knew that Jordan Romero had told the principal that before the dance, he had been at a party at Savana's house where alcohol was served. Marissa's statement that the pills came from Savana was thus sufficiently plausible to warrant suspicion that Savana was involved in pill distribution.

This suspicion of Wilson's was enough to justify a search of Savana's backpack and outer clothing.[3] If a student is reasonably suspected of giving out contraband pills, she is reasonably suspected of carrying them on her person and in the carryall that has become an item of student uniform in most places today. If Wilson's reasonable suspicion of pill distribution were not understood to support searches of outer clothes and backpack, it would not justify any search worth making. And the look into Savana's bag, in her presence and in the relative privacy of Wilson's office, was not excessively intrusive, any more than Romero's subsequent search of her outer clothing.

B

Here it is that the parties part company, with Savana's claim that extending the search at Wilson's behest to the point of making her pull out her underwear was constitutionally unreasonable. The exact label for this final step in the intrusion is not important, though strip search is a fair way to speak of it. Romero and Schwallier directed Savana to remove her clothes down to

her underwear, and then "pull out" her bra and the elastic band on her underpants. Although Romero and Schwallier stated that they did not see anything when Savana followed their instructions, we would not define strip search and its Fourth Amendment consequences in a way that would guarantee litigation about who was looking and how much was seen. The very fact of Savana's pulling her underwear away from her body in the presence of the two officials who were able to see her necessarily exposed her breasts and pelvic area to some degree, and both subjective and reasonable societal expectations of personal privacy support the treatment of such a search as categorically distinct, requiring distinct elements of justification on the part of school authorities for going beyond a search of outer clothing and belongings.

Savana's subjective expectation of privacy against such a search is inherent in her account of it as embarrassing, frightening, and humiliating. The reasonableness of her expectation (required by the Fourth Amendment standard) is indicated by the consistent experiences of other young people similarly searched, whose adolescent vulnerability intensifies the patent intrusiveness of the exposure. See Hyman & Perone, The Other Side of School Violence: Educator Policies and Practices that may Contribute to Student Misbehavior, 36 J. School Psychology 7, 13 (1998) (strip search can "result in serious

---

3. There is no question here that justification for the school officials' search was required in accordance with the *T. L. O.* standard of reasonable suspicion, for it is common ground that Savana had a reason-able expectation of privacy covering the personal things she chose to carry in her backpack, and that Wilson's decision to look through it was a "search" within the meaning of the Fourth Amendment.

emotional damage"). The common reaction of these adolescents simply registers the obviously different meaning of a search exposing the body from the experience of nakedness or near undress in other school circumstances. Changing for gym is getting ready for play; exposing for a search is responding to an accusation reserved for suspected wrongdoers and fairly understood as so degrading that a number of communities have decided that strip searches in schools are never reasonable and have banned them no matter what the facts may be.

The indignity of the search does not, of course, outlaw it, but it does implicate the rule of reasonableness as stated in *T. L. O.*, that "the search as actually conducted [be] reasonably related in scope to the circumstances which justified the interference in the first place." The scope will be permissible, that is, when it is "not excessively intrusive in light of the age and sex of the student and the nature of the infraction."

Here, the content of the suspicion failed to match the degree of intrusion. Wilson knew beforehand that the pills were prescription-strength ibuprofen and over-the-counter naproxen, common pain relievers equivalent to two Advil, or one Aleve. He must have been aware of the nature and limited threat of the specific drugs he was searching for, and while just about anything can be taken in quantities that will do real harm, Wilson had no reason to suspect that large amounts of the drugs were being passed around, or that individual students were receiving great numbers of pills.

Nor could Wilson have suspected that Savana was hiding common painkillers in her underwear. Petitioners suggest, as a truth universally acknowledged, that "students ... hid[e] contraband in or under their clothing," and cite a smattering of cases of students with contraband in their underwear. But when the categorically extreme intrusiveness of a search down to the body of an adolescent requires some justification in suspected facts, general background possibilities fall short; a reasonable search that extensive calls for suspicion that it will pay off. But nondangerous school contraband does not raise the specter of stashes in intimate places, and there is no evidence in the record of any general practice among Safford Middle School students of hiding that sort of thing in underwear; neither Jordan nor Marissa suggested to Wilson that Savana was doing that, and the preceding search of Marissa that Wilson ordered yielded nothing. Wilson never even determined when Marissa had received the pills from Savana; if it had been a few days before, that would weigh heavily against any reasonable conclusion that Savana presently had the pills on her person, much less in her underwear.

In sum, what was missing from the suspected facts that pointed to Savana was any indication of danger to the students from the power of the drugs or their quantity, and any reason to suppose that Savana was carrying pills in her underwear. We think that the combination of these deficiencies was fatal to finding the search reasonable.

In so holding, we mean to cast no ill reflection on the assistant principal, for the record raises no doubt that his motive throughout was to eliminate drugs from his school and protect students from what Jordan Romero had gone through. Parents are known to overreact to protect their children from danger, and a school official with responsibility for safety may tend to do the same. The difference is that the Fourth Amendment places limits on the official, even with the high degree of deference that courts must pay to the educator's professional judgment.

We do mean, though, to make it clear that the T. L. O. concern to limit a school search to reasonable scope requires the support of reasonable suspicion of danger or of resort to underwear for hiding evidence of wrongdoing before a search can reasonably make the quantum leap from outer clothes and backpacks to exposure of intimate parts. The meaning of such a search, and the degradation its subject may reasonably feel, place a search that intrusive in a category of its own demanding its own specific suspicions.

IV

A school official searching a student is entitled to qualified immunity where clearly established law does not show that the search violated the Fourth Amendment. To be established clearly, however, there is no need that "the very action in question [have] previously been held unlawful." Wilson v. Layne, 526 U. S. 603, 615 (1999). The unconstitutionality of outrageous conduct obviously will be unconstitutional, this being the reason, as Judge Posner has said, that "[t]he easiest cases don't even arise." K. H. v. Morgan, 914 F. 2d 846, 851 (CA7 1990). But even as to action

less than an outrage, "officials can still be on notice that their conduct violates established law . . . in novel factual circumstances." Hope v. Pelzer, 536 U. S. 730, 741 (2002).

T. L. O. directed school officials to limit the intrusiveness of a search, "in light of the age and sex of the student and the nature of the infraction," and as we have just said at some length, the intrusiveness of the strip search here cannot be seen as justifiably related to the circumstances. But we realize that the lower courts have reached divergent conclusions regarding how the T. L. O. standard applies to such searches.

A number of judges have read T. L. O. as the en banc minority of the Ninth Circuit did here. The Sixth Circuit upheld a strip search of a high school student for a drug, without any suspicion that drugs were hidden next to her body. Williams v. Ellington, 936 F. 2d 881, 882–883, 887 (1991). And other courts considering qualified immunity for strip searches have read T. L. O. as "a series of abstractions, on the one hand, and a declaration of seeming deference to the judgments of school officials, on the other," Jenkins v. Talladega City Bd. of Ed., 115 F. 3d 821, 828 (CA11 1997) (en banc), which made it impossible "to establish clearly the contours of a Fourth Amendment right . . . [in] the wide variety of possible school settings different from those involved in T. L. O." itself. Ibid. See also Thomas v. Roberts, 323 F. 3d 950 (CA11 2003) (granting qualified immunity to a teacher and police officer who conducted a group strip search of a fifth grade class when looking for a missing $26).

We think these differences of opinion from our own are substantial enough to require immunity for the school officials in this case. We would not suggest that entitlement to qualified immunity is the guaranteed product of disuniform views of the law in the other federal, or state, courts, and the fact that a single judge, or even a group of judges, disagrees about the contours of a right does not automatically render the law unclear if we have been clear. That said, however, the cases viewing school strip searches differently from the way we see them are numerous enough, with well-reasoned majority and dissenting opinions, to counsel doubt that we were sufficiently clear in the prior statement of law. We conclude that qualified immunity is warranted.

V

The strip search of Savana Redding was unreasonable and a violation of the Fourth Amendment, but petitioners Wilson, Romero, and Schwallier are nevertheless protected from liability through qualified immunity. Our conclusions here do not resolve, however, the question of the liability of petitioner Safford Unified School District #1 under Monell v. New York City Dept. of Social Servs., 436 U. S. 658, 694 (1978), a claim the Ninth Circuit did not address. The judgment of the Ninth Circuit is therefore affirmed in part and reversed in part, and this case is remanded for consideration of the *Monell* claim [Editors' Note: Liability under *Monell* would depend on whether the District had a custom or policy that caused the illegal search—it is not

enough under *Monell* to show that a state official acted illegally].

It is so ordered.

———

JUSTICE STEVENS, with whom JUSTICE GINSBURG joins, concurring in part and dissenting in part.

* * * This is, in essence, a case in which clearly established law meets clearly outrageous conduct. I have long believed that it does not require a constitutional scholar to conclude that a nude search of a 13–year-old child is an invasion of constitutional rights of some magnitude. The strip search of Savana Redding in this case was both more intrusive and less justified than the search of the student's purse in *T. L. O.* Therefore, while I join Parts I–III of the Court's opinion, I disagree with its decision to extend qualified immunity to the school official who authorized this unconstitutional search.

The Court reaches a contrary conclusion about qualified immunity based on the fact that various Courts of Appeals have adopted seemingly divergent views about *T. L. O.'s* application to strip searches. But the clarity of a well-established right should not depend on whether jurists have misread our precedents. And while our cases have previously noted the "divergence of views" among courts in deciding whether to extend qualified immunity, we have relied on that consideration only to spare officials from having "to predict the future course of constitutional law." In this case, by contrast, we chart no new constitutional path. We merely decide whether the decision to strip search Savana Redding, on these facts, was prohibited under *T. L. O.* Our conclusion leaves the boundaries of the law undisturbed.

The Court of Appeals properly rejected the school official's qualified immunity defense, and I would affirm that court's judgment in its entirety.

———

JUSTICE GINSBURG, concurring in part and dissenting in part.

I agree with the Court that Assistant Principal Wilson's subjection of 13–year-old Savana Redding to a humiliating stripdown search violated the Fourth Amendment. But I also agree with Justice Stevens, that our opinion in New Jersey v. T. L. O. "clearly established" the law governing this case.

* * *

In contrast to *T. L. O.*, where a teacher discovered a student smoking in the lavatory, and where the search was confined to the student's purse, the search of Redding involved her body and rested on the bare accusation of another student whose reliability the Assistant Principal had no reason to trust. The Court's opinion in *T. L. O.* plainly stated the controlling Fourth Amendment law: A search ordered by a school official, even if "justified at its inception," crosses the constitutional boundary if it becomes "excessively intrusive in light of the age and sex of the student and the nature of the infraction."

Here, "the nature of the [supposed] infraction," the slim basis for suspecting Savana Redding, and her "age and sex," establish beyond doubt that Assistant Principal Wilson's order cannot be reconciled with this Court's opinion in *T. L. O.* Wilson's treatment of Redding was abusive and it was not reasonable

for him to believe that the law permitted it. I join Justice Stevens in dissenting from the Court's acceptance of Wilson's qualified immunity plea, and would affirm the Court of Appeals' judgment in all respects.

———

JUSTICE THOMAS, concurring in the judgment in part and dissenting in part.

I agree with the Court that the judgment against the school officials with respect to qualified immunity should be reversed. Unlike the majority, however, I would hold that the search of Savana Redding did not violate the Fourth Amendment. The majority imposes a vague and amorphous standard on school administrators. It also grants judges sweeping authority to second-guess the measures that these officials take to maintain discipline in their schools and ensure the health and safety of the students in their charge. This deep intrusion into the administration of public schools exemplifies why the Court should return to the common-law doctrine of in loco parentis under which the judiciary was reluctant to interfere in the routine business of school administration, allowing schools and teachers to set and enforce rules and to maintain order. But even under the prevailing Fourth Amendment test established by New Jersey v. T. L. O., all petitioners, including the school district, are entitled to judgment as a matter of law in their favor.

I

* * *

A

* * * As the majority rightly concedes, this search was justified at its inception because there were reasonable grounds to suspect that Redding possessed medication that violated school rules. A finding of reasonable suspicion "does not deal with hard certainties, but with probabilities." United States v. Cortez, 449 U. S. 411, 418 (1981). To satisfy this standard, more than a mere "hunch" of wrongdoing is required, but "considerably" less suspicion is needed than would be required to "satisf[y] a preponderance of the evidence standard." United States v. Arvizu, 534 U. S. 266, 274 (2002).

Furthermore, in evaluating whether there is a reasonable "particularized and objective" basis for conducting a search based on suspected wrongdoing, government officials must consider the totality of the circumstances. School officials have a specialized understanding of the school environment, the habits of the students, and the concerns of the community, which enables them to formulate certain common-sense conclusions about human behavior. And like police officers, school officials are entitled to make an assessment of the situation in light of this specialized training and familiarity with the customs of the school.

Here, petitioners had reasonable grounds to suspect that Redding was in possession of prescription and nonprescription drugs in violation of the school's prohibition of the non-medical use, possession, or sale of a drug on school property or at school events. * * *

B

The remaining question is whether the search was reasonable in scope. * * * The majority concludes that the school officials' search of Redding's underwear was not "reasonably related in scope to the circumstances which justified the interference in the first place", notwithstanding the officials' reasonable suspicion that Redding "was involved in pill distribution." According to the majority, to be reasonable, this school search required a showing of "danger to the students from the power of the drugs or their quantity" or a "reason to suppose that [Redding] was carrying pills in her underwear." Each of these additional requirements is an unjustifiable departure from bedrock Fourth Amendment law in the school setting, where this Court has heretofore read the Fourth Amendment to grant considerable leeway to school officials. Because the school officials searched in a location where the pills could have been hidden, the search was reasonable in scope under T. L. O.

1

[I]n the majority's view, although the school officials had reasonable suspicion to believe that Redding had the pills on her person, they needed some greater level of particularized suspicion to conduct this "strip search." There is no support for this contortion of the Fourth Amendment.

The Court has generally held that the reasonableness of a search's scope depends only on whether it is limited to the area that is capable of concealing the object of the search. See, e.g., Wyoming v. Houghton, 526 U. S. 295, 307 (1999) (Police officers "may inspect passengers' belongings found in the car that are capable of concealing the object of the search"); Florida v. Jimeno, 500 U. S. 248, 251 (1991)

("The scope of a search is generally defined by its expressed object"); United States v. Ross, 456 U. S. 798, 820 (1982) ("A lawful search . . . generally extends to the entire area in which the object of the search may be found").

In keeping with this longstanding rule, the "nature of the infraction" referenced in *T. L. O.* delineates the proper scope of a search of students in a way that is identical to that permitted for searches outside the school—i.e., the search must be limited to the areas where the object of that infraction could be concealed. A search of a student therefore is permissible in scope under *T. L. O.* so long as it is objectively reasonable to believe that the area searched could conceal the contraband. The dissenting opinion below correctly captured this Fourth Amendment standard, noting that "if a student brought a baseball bat on campus in violation of school policy, a search of that student's shirt pocket would be patently unjustified."

* * * The reasonable suspicion that Redding possessed the pills for distribution purposes did not dissipate simply because the search of her backpack turned up nothing. It was eminently reasonable to conclude that the backpack was empty because Redding was secreting the pills in a place she thought no one would look.

Redding would not have been the first person to conceal pills in her undergarments. See Hicks, Man Gets 17–Year Drug Sentence, [Corbin, KY] Times–Tribune, Oct. 7, 2008, p. 1 (Drug courier "told officials she had the [Oxycontin] pills concealed in her crotch"); Conley, Whitehaven: Traffic Stop Yields Hy-drocodone Pills, [Memphis] Commercial Appeal, Aug. 3, 2007, p. B3 ("An additional 40 hydrocodone pills were found in her pants"); Caywood, Police Vehicle Chase Leads to Drug Arrests, [Worcester] Telegram & Gazette, June 7, 2008, p. A7 (25–year-old "allegedly had a cigar tube stuffed with pills tucked into the waistband of his pants"); Hubartt, 23–Year-Old Charged With Dealing Ecstasy, The [Fort Wayne] Journal Gazette, Aug. 8, 2007, p. C2 ("[W]hile he was being put into a squad car, his pants fell down and a plastic bag containing pink and orange pills fell on the ground"); Sebastian Residents Arrested in Drug Sting, Vero Beach Press Journal, Sept. 16, 2006, p. B2 (Arrestee "told them he had more pills 'down my pants' "). Nor will she be the last after today's decision, which announces the safest place to secrete contraband in school.

2

The majority compounds its error by reading the "nature of the infraction" aspect of the *T. L. O.* test as a license to limit searches based on a judge's assessment of a particular school policy. According to the majority, the scope of the search was impermissible because the school official "must have been aware of the nature and limited threat of the specific drugs he was searching for" and because he "had no reason to suspect that large amounts of the drugs were being passed around, or that individual students were receiving great numbers of pills." Thus, in order to locate a rationale for finding a Fourth Amendment violation in this case, the majority retreats from its observation that the school's firm no-drug policy "makes sense, and there is no basis to claim that the search was unreasonable owing to some defect or shortcoming of the rule it was aimed at enforcing."

Even accepting the majority's assurances that it is not attacking the rule's reasonableness, it certainly is attacking the rule's importance. This approach directly conflicts with *T. L. O.* in which the Court was "unwilling to adopt a standard under which the legality of a search is dependent upon a judge's evaluation of the relative importance of school rules." Indeed, the Court in *T. L. O.* expressly rejected the proposition that the majority seemingly endorses—that "some rules regarding student conduct are by nature too 'trivial' to justify a search based upon reasonable suspicion."

The majority's decision in this regard also departs from another basic principle of the Fourth Amendment: that law enforcement officials can enforce with the same vigor all rules and regulations irrespective of the perceived importance of any of those rules. In a long line of cases, we have said that when an officer has probable cause to believe a person committed even a minor crime in his presence, the balancing of private and public interests is not in doubt. The arrest is constitutionally reasonable. The Fourth Amendment rule for searches is the same: Police officers are entitled to search regardless of the perceived triviality of the underlying law. As we have explained, requiring police to make "sensitive, case-by-case determinations of government need," *Atwater v. Lago Vista*, 532 U. S. 318, 347 (2001), for a particular prohibition before conducting a search would

"place police in an almost impossible spot."

The majority has placed school officials in this "impossible spot" by questioning whether possession of Ibuprofen and Naproxen causes a severe enough threat to warrant investigation. Had the suspected infraction involved a street drug, the majority implies that it would have approved the scope of the search. In effect, then, the majority has replaced a school rule that draws no distinction among drugs with a new one that does. As a result, a full search of a student's person for prohibited drugs will be permitted only if the Court agrees that the drug in question was sufficiently dangerous. Such a test is unworkable and unsound. School officials cannot be expected to halt searches based on the possibility that a court might later find that the particular infraction at issue is not severe enough to warrant an intrusive investigation.

* * *

Judges are not qualified to second-guess the best manner for maintaining quiet and order in the school environment. Such institutional judgments * * * involve a host of policy choices that must be made by locally elected representatives, rather than by federal judges interpreting the basic charter of Government for the entire country. It is a mistake for judges to assume the responsibility for deciding which school rules are important enough to allow for invasive searches and which rules are not.

3

Even if this Court were authorized to second-guess the importance of school rules, the Court's assessment of the importance of this district's policy is flawed. It is a crime to possess or use prescription-strength Ibuprofen without a prescription. By prohibiting unauthorized prescription drugs on school grounds—and conducting a search to ensure students abide by that prohibition—the school rule here was consistent with a routine provision of the state criminal code. * * *

Moreover, school districts have valid reasons for punishing the unauthorized possession of prescription drugs on school property as severely as the possession of street drugs; "[t]eenage abuse of over-the-counter and prescription drugs poses an increasingly alarming national crisis." Get Teens Off Drugs, The Education Digest 75 (Dec. 2006). As one study noted, "more young people ages 12–17 abuse prescription drugs than any illicit drug except marijuana-more than cocaine, heroin, and methamphetamine combined." Executive Office of the President, Office of National Drug Control Policy (ONDCP), Prescription for Danger 1 (Jan. 2008). * * * .

School administrators can reasonably conclude that this high rate of drug abuse is being fueled, at least in part, by the increasing presence of prescription drugs on school campuses. The risks posed by the abuse of these drugs are every bit as serious as the dangers of using a typical street drug.

Teenagers are nevertheless apt to "believe the myth that these drugs provide a medically safe high." ONDCP, Teens and Prescription Drugs: An Analysis of Recent Trends on the Emerging Drug Threat 3 (Feb. 2007) (hereinafter Teens and

Prescription Drugs). But since 1999, there has been a dramatic increase in the number of poisonings and even deaths associated with the abuse of prescription drugs. * * * Furthermore, even if a child is not immediately harmed by the abuse of prescription drugs, research suggests that prescription drugs have become "gateway drugs to other substances of abuse." Id., at 4; Healy, Skipping the Street, Los Angeles Times, Sept. 15, 2008, p. F1 ("Boomers made marijuana their 'gateway' . . . but a younger generation finds prescription drugs an easier score").

Admittedly, the Ibuprofen and Naproxen at issue in this case are not the prescription painkillers at the forefront of the prescription-drug-abuse problem. But they are not without their own dangers. As nonsteroidal anti-inflammatory drugs (NSAIDs), they pose a risk of death from overdose. The Pill Book 821, 827 (H. Silverman, ed., 13th ed. 2008) (observing that Ibuprofen and Naproxen are NSAIDs and "[p]eople have died from NSAID overdoses"). Moreover, the side-effects caused by the use of NSAIDs can be magnified if they are taken in combination with other drugs. See, e.g., Reactions Weekly, p. 18 (Issue no. 1235, Jan. 17, 2009) ("A 17–year-old girl developed allergic interstitial nephritis and renal failure while receiving escitalopram and ibuprofen").

If a student with a previously unknown intolerance to Ibuprofen or Naproxen were to take either drug and become ill, the public outrage would likely be directed toward the school for failing to take steps to prevent the unmonitored use of the drug. In light of the risks involved, a school's decision to establish and enforce a school prohibition on the possession of any unauthorized drug is thus a reasonable judgment.

In determining whether the search's scope was reasonable under the Fourth Amendment, it is therefore irrelevant whether officials suspected Redding of possessing prescription-strength Ibuprofen, nonprescription-strength Naproxen, or some harder street drug. Safford prohibited its possession on school property. Reasonable suspicion that Redding was in possession of drugs in violation of these policies, therefore, justified a search extending to any area where small pills could be concealed. The search did not violate the Fourth Amendment.

II

By declaring the search unreasonable in this case, the majority has surrendered control of the American public school system to public school students by invalidating school policies that treat all drugs equally and by second-guessing swift disciplinary decisions made by school officials. The Court's interference in these matters of great concern to teachers, parents, and students illustrates why the most constitutionally sound approach to the question of applying the Fourth Amendment in local public schools would in fact be the complete restoration of the common-law doctrine of in loco parentis.

* * *

If the common-law view that parents delegate to teachers their authority to discipline and maintain order were to be applied in this case, the search of Redding would

stand. There can be no doubt that a parent would have had the authority to conduct the search at issue in this case. * * *

As acknowledged by this Court, this principle is based on the "societal understanding of superior and inferior" with respect to the "parent and child" relationship. Georgia v. Randolph, 547 U. S. 103, 114 (2006). In light of this relationship, the Court has indicated that a parent can authorize a third-party search of a child by consenting to such a search, even if the child denies his consent. Certainly, a search by the parent himself is no different, regardless of whether or not a child would prefer to be left alone.

Restoring the common-law doctrine of in loco parentis would not, however, leave public schools entirely free to impose any rule they choose. If parents do not like the rules imposed by those schools, they can seek redress in school boards or legislatures; they can send their children to private schools or home school them; or they can simply move. Indeed, parents and local government officials have proved themselves quite capable of challenging overly harsh school rules or the enforcement of sensible rules in insensible ways.

For example, one community questioned a school policy that resulted in "an 11–year-old [being] arrested, handcuffed, and taken to jail for bringing a plastic butter knife to school." Downey, Zero Tolerance Doesn't Always Add Up, The Atlanta Journal–Constitution, Apr. 6, 2009, p. A11. In another, "[a]t least one school board member was outraged" when 14 elementary-school students were suspended for "imitating drug activity" after they combined Kool–Aid and sugar in plastic bags. Grant, Pupils Trading Sweet Mix Get Sour Shot of Discipline, Pittsburgh Post–Gazette, May 18, 2006, p. B1. Individuals within yet another school district protested a " 'zero-tolerance' policy toward weapons" that had become "so rigid that it force[d] schools to expel any student who belongs to a military organization, a drum-and-bugle corps or any other legitimate extracurricular group and is simply transporting what amounts to harmless props." Richardson, School Gun Case Sparks Cries For "Common Sense," Washington Times, Feb. 13, 2009, p. A1.

These local efforts to change controversial school policies through democratic processes have proven successful in many cases. See, e.g., Postal, Schools' Zero Tolerance Could Lose Some Punch, Orlando Sentinel, Apr. 24, 2009, p. B3 ("State lawmakers want schools to dial back strict zero-tolerance policies so students do not end up in juvenile detention for some 'goofy thing' "); Richardson, Tolerance Waning for Zero-tolerance Rules, Washington Times, Apr. 21, 2009, p. A3 ("[A] few states have moved to relax their laws. Utah now allows students to bring asthma inhalers to school without violating the zero-tolerance policy on drugs"); see also Nussbaum, Becoming Fed Up With Zero Tolerance, New York Times, Sept. 3, 2000, Section 14, p. 1 (discussing a report that found that "widespread use of zero-tolerance discipline policies was creating as many problems as it was solving and that there were many cases around the country in which students were harshly disciplined for

infractions where there was no harm intended or done").

In the end, the task of implementing and amending public school policies is beyond this Court's function. Parents, teachers, school administrators, local politicians, and state officials are all better suited than judges to determine the appropriate limits on searches conducted by school officials. Preservation of order, discipline, and safety in public schools is simply not the domain of the Constitution. And, common sense is not a judicial monopoly or a Constitutional imperative.

III

The nationwide drug epidemic makes the war against drugs a pressing concern in every school. And yet the Court has limited the authority of school officials to conduct searches for the drugs that the officials believe pose a serious safety risk to their students. By doing so, the majority has confirmed that a return to the doctrine of in loco parentis is required to keep the judiciary from essentially seizing control of public schools. * * * By deciding that it is better equipped to decide what behavior should be permitted in schools, the Court has undercut student safety and undermined the authority of school administrators and local officials. Even more troubling, it has done so in a case in which the underlying response by school administrators was reasonable and justified. I cannot join this regrettable decision. I, therefore, respectfully dissent from the Court's determination that this search violated the Fourth Amendment.

VII. REMEDIES FOR FOURTH AMENDMENT VIOLATIONS

D. THE EXCLUSIONARY RULE IN DETAIL: PROCEDURES, SCOPE AND PROBLEMS

12. *The Good Faith Exception and Warrantless Searches*

Page 592. Add after the section on Arizona v. Evans.

Good-Faith Exception Applied Where Error Was the Result of Negligence Attenuated From the Arrest or Search: Herring v. United States

HERRING v. UNITED STATES

Supreme Court of the United States, 2009.
129 S.Ct. 695.

CHIEF JUSTICE ROBERTS delivered the opinion of the Court.

The Fourth Amendment forbids "unreasonable searches and seizures," and this usually requires the police to have probable cause or a warrant before making an arrest. What if an officer reasonably believes there is an outstanding arrest warrant, but that belief turns out to be wrong because of a negligent bookkeeping error by another police employee? The parties here agree that the ensuing arrest is still a violation of the Fourth Amendment, but dispute whether contraband found during a search incident to that arrest must be excluded in a later prosecution.

Our cases establish that such suppression is not an automatic consequence of a Fourth Amendment violation. Instead, the question turns on the culpability of the police and the potential of exclusion to deter wrongful police conduct. Here the error was the result of isolated negligence attenuated from the arrest. We hold that in these circumstances the jury should not be barred from considering all the evidence.

I

On July 7, 2004, Investigator Mark Anderson learned that Bennie Dean Herring had driven to the Coffee County Sheriff's Department to retrieve something from his impounded truck. Herring was no stranger to law enforcement, and Anderson asked the county's warrant clerk, Sandy Pope, to check for any outstanding warrants for Herring's arrest. When she found none, Anderson asked Pope to check with Sharon Morgan, her counterpart in neighboring Dale County. After checking Dale County's computer database, Morgan replied that there was an active arrest warrant for Herring's failure to appear on a felony charge. Pope relayed the information to Anderson and asked Morgan to fax over a copy of the warrant as confirmation. Anderson and a deputy followed Herring as he left the impound lot, pulled him over, and arrested him. A search incident to the arrest revealed methamphetamine in Herring's pocket, and a pistol (which as a felon he could not possess) in his vehicle.

There had, however, been a mistake about the warrant. The Dale

County sheriff's computer records are supposed to correspond to actual arrest warrants, which the office also maintains. But when Morgan went to the files to retrieve the actual warrant to fax to Pope, Morgan was unable to find it. She called a court clerk and learned that the warrant had been recalled five months earlier. Normally when a warrant is recalled the court clerk's office or a judge's chambers calls Morgan, who enters the information in the sheriff's computer database and disposes of the physical copy. For whatever reason, the information about the recall of the warrant for Herring did not appear in the database. Morgan immediately called Pope to alert her to the mix-up, and Pope contacted Anderson over a secure radio. This all unfolded in 10 to 15 minutes, but Herring had already been arrested and found with the gun and drugs, just a few hundred yards from the sheriff's office.

Herring was indicted in the District Court for the Middle District of Alabama for illegally possessing the gun and drugs. He moved to suppress the evidence on the ground that his initial arrest had been illegal because the warrant had been rescinded. The Magistrate Judge recommended denying the motion because the arresting officers had acted in a good-faith belief that the warrant was still outstanding. Thus, even if there were a Fourth Amendment violation, there was "no reason to believe that application of the exclusionary rule here would deter the occurrence of any future mistakes." The District Court adopted the Magistrate Judge's recommendation, and the Court of Ap-

peals for the Eleventh Circuit affirmed.

The Eleventh Circuit found that the arresting officers in Coffee County "were entirely innocent of any wrongdoing or carelessness." The court assumed that whoever failed to update the Dale County sheriff's records was also a law enforcement official, but noted that "the conduct in question [wa]s a negligent failure to act, not a deliberate or tactical choice to act." Because the error was merely negligent and attenuated from the arrest, the Eleventh Circuit concluded that the benefit of suppressing the evidence "would be marginal or nonexistent," and the evidence was therefore admissible under the good-faith rule of United States v. Leon, 468 U.S. 897 (1984).

Other courts have required exclusion of evidence obtained through similar police errors,, so we granted Herring's petition for certiorari to resolve the conflict. We now affirm the Eleventh Circuit's judgment.

II

When a probable-cause determination was based on reasonable but mistaken assumptions, the person subjected to a search or seizure has not necessarily been the victim of a constitutional violation. The very phrase "probable cause" confirms that the Fourth Amendment does not demand all possible precision. And whether the error can be traced to a mistake by a state actor or some other source may bear on the analysis. For purposes of deciding this case, however, we accept the parties' assumption that there was a Fourth Amendment violation. The issue is whether the exclusionary rule should be applied.

A

The Fourth Amendment protects "[t]he right of the people to be secure in their persons, houses, papers, and effects, against unreasonable searches and seizures," but "contains no provision expressly precluding the use of evidence obtained in violation of its commands," Arizona v. Evans, 514 U.S. 1, 10 (1995). Nonetheless, our decisions establish an exclusionary rule that, when applicable, forbids the use of improperly obtained evidence at trial. See, e.g., Weeks v. United States, 232 U.S. 383, 398 (1914). We have stated that this judicially created rule is "designed to safeguard Fourth Amendment rights generally through its deterrent effect." United States v. Calandra, 414 U.S. 338, 348 (1974).

In analyzing the applicability of the rule, *Leon* admonished that we must consider the actions of all the police officers involved. ("It is necessary to consider the objective reasonableness, not only of the officers who eventually executed a warrant, but also of the officers who originally obtained it or who provided information material to the probable-cause determination"). The Coffee County officers did nothing improper. Indeed, the error was noticed so quickly because Coffee County requested a faxed confirmation of the warrant.

The Eleventh Circuit concluded, however, that somebody in Dale County should have updated the computer database to reflect the recall of the arrest warrant. The court also concluded that this error was negligent, but did not find it to be reckless or deliberate. That fact is crucial to our holding that this error is not enough by itself to require the extreme sanction of exclusion.

B

1. The fact that a Fourth Amendment violation occurred-i.e., that a search or arrest was unreasonable-does not necessarily mean that the exclusionary rule applies. Indeed, exclusion "has always been our last resort, not our first impulse," Hudson v. Michigan, 547 U.S. 586, 591 (2006), and our precedents establish important principles that constrain application of the exclusionary rule.

First, the exclusionary rule is not an individual right and applies only where it results in appreciable deterrence. We have repeatedly rejected the argument that exclusion is a necessary consequence of a Fourth Amendment violation. *Leon, supra,* at 905–906; Pennsylvania Bd. of Probation and Parole v. Scott, 524 U.S. 357, 363 (1998). Instead we have focused on the efficacy of the rule in deterring Fourth Amendment violations in the future.[2]

In addition, the benefits of deterrence must outweigh the costs. "We have never suggested that the exclusionary rule must apply in every circumstance in which it might provide marginal deterrence." *Scott, supra,* at 368. "[T]o the extent that application of the exclusionary rule could provide some incremental deterrent, that possible benefit must

---

2. Justice GINSBURG's dissent champions what she describes as "a more majestic conception of the exclusionary rule" which would exclude evidence even where deterrence does not justify doing so. Majestic or not, our cases reject this conception, see, e.g., United States v. Leon, 468 U.S. 897, 921, n. 22 (1984), and perhaps for this reason, her dissent relies almost exclusively on previous dissents to support its analysis.

be weighed against [its] substantial social costs." Illinois v. Krull, 480 U.S. 340, 352–353 (1987). The principal cost of applying the rule is, of course, letting guilty and possibly dangerous defendants go free-something that "offends basic concepts of the criminal justice system." Leon, supra, at 908. "[T]he rule's costly toll upon truth-seeking and law enforcement objectives presents a high obstacle for those urging [its] application." *Scott, supra*, at 364–365.

These principles are reflected in the holding of *Leon*: When police act under a warrant that is invalid for lack of probable cause, the exclusionary rule does not apply if the police acted "in objectively reasonable reliance" on the subsequently invalidated search warrant. We (perhaps confusingly) called this objectively reasonable reliance "good faith." In a companion case, Massachusetts v. Sheppard, 468 U.S. 981 (1984), we held that the exclusionary rule did not apply when a warrant was invalid because a judge forgot to make "clerical corrections" to it.

Shortly thereafter we extended these holdings to warrantless administrative searches performed in good-faith reliance on a statute later declared unconstitutional. *Krull*, supra, at 349–350. Finally, in *Evans*, we applied this good-faith rule to police who reasonably relied on mistaken information in a court's database that an arrest warrant was outstanding. We held that a mistake made by a judicial employee could not give rise to exclusion for three reasons: The exclusionary rule was crafted to curb police rather than judicial misconduct; court employees were unlikely to try to subvert the Fourth Amendment; and "most important, there [was] no basis for believing that application of the exclusionary rule in [those] circumstances" would have any significant effect in deterring the errors. *Evans* left unresolved "whether the evidence should be suppressed if police personnel were responsible for the error," an issue not argued by the State in that case, but one that we now confront.

2.   The extent to which the exclusionary rule is justified by these deterrence principles varies with the culpability of the law enforcement conduct. As we said in *Leon*, "an assessment of the flagrancy of the police misconduct constitutes an important step in the calculus" of applying the exclusionary rule. * * *

Anticipating the good-faith exception to the exclusionary rule, Judge Friendly wrote that "[t]he beneficent aim of the exclusionary rule to deter police misconduct can be sufficiently accomplished by a practice ... outlawing evidence obtained by flagrant or deliberate violation of rights." The Bill of Rights as a Code of Criminal Procedure, 53 Calif. L.Rev. 929, 953 (1965); see also Brown v. Illinois, 422 U.S. 590, 610–611 (1975) (Powell, J., concurring in part) ("[T]he deterrent value of the exclusionary rule is most likely to be effective" when "official conduct was flagrantly abusive of Fourth Amendment rights").

Indeed, the abuses that gave rise to the exclusionary rule featured intentional conduct that was patently unconstitutional. In *Weeks*, 232 U.S. 383, a foundational exclusionary rule case, the officers had broken into the defendant's home (using a key shown to them by a neighbor), confiscated incriminating papers, then returned again with a U.S. Marshal to confiscate even more. Not only did they have no search warrant, which the Court held was required, but they could not have gotten one had they tried. They were so lacking in sworn and particularized information that "not even an order of court would have justified such procedure." Silverthorne Lumber Co. v. United States, 251 U.S. 385 (1920), on which petitioner repeatedly relies, was similar; federal officials "without a shadow of authority" went to the defendants' office and "made a clean sweep" of every paper they could find. Even the Government seemed to acknowledge that the "seizure was an outrage."

Equally flagrant conduct was at issue in Mapp v. Ohio, 367 U.S. 643 (1961), which * * * extended the exclusionary rule to the States. Officers forced open a door to Ms. Mapp's house, kept her lawyer from entering, brandished what the court concluded was a false warrant, then forced her into handcuffs and canvassed the house for obscenity. An error that arises from nonrecurring and attenuated negligence is thus far removed from the core concerns that led us to adopt the rule in the first place. And in fact since *Leon*, we have never applied the rule to exclude evidence obtained in violation of the Fourth Amendment, where the police conduct was no more intentional or culpable than this.

3. To trigger the exclusionary rule, police conduct must be sufficiently deliberate that exclusion can meaningfully deter it, and sufficiently culpable that such deterrence is worth the price paid by the justice system. As laid out in our cases, the exclusionary rule serves to deter deliberate, reckless, or grossly negligent conduct, or in some circumstances recurring or systemic negligence. The error in this case does not rise to that level.[4]

Our decision in Franks v. Delaware, 438 U.S. 154 (1978), provides an analogy. In *Franks*, we held that police negligence in obtaining a warrant did not even rise to the level of a Fourth Amendment violation, let alone meet the more stringent test for triggering the exclusionary rule. We held that the Constitution allowed defendants, in some circumstances, "to challenge the truthfulness of factual statements made in an affidavit supporting the warrant," even after the warrant had issued. If those false statements were necessary to the Magistrate Judge's probable-cause determination, the warrant would be "voided." But we did not find all false statements relevant: "There must be allegations of deliberate falsehood or of reckless disregard for the truth," and "[a]llegations of negligence or innocent mistake are insufficient."

Both this case and *Franks* concern false information provided by police. Under *Franks*, negligent police miscommunications in the course of acquiring a warrant do

---

4. We do not quarrel with Justice GINSBURG's claim that "liability for negligence ... creates an incentive to act with greater care," and we do not suggest that the exclusion of this evidence could have no deterrent effect. But our cases require any deterrence to be weighed against the substantial social costs exacted by the exclusionary rule, and here exclusion is not worth the cost.

not provide a basis to rescind a warrant and render a search or arrest invalid. Here, the miscommunications occurred in a different context—after the warrant had been issued and recalled—but that fact should not require excluding the evidence obtained.

The pertinent analysis of deterrence and culpability is objective, not an inquiry into the subjective awareness of arresting officers. We have already held that "our good-faith inquiry is confined to the objectively ascertainable question whether a reasonably well trained officer would have known that the search was illegal" in light of "all of the circumstances." *Leon*, 468 U.S., at 922, n. 23. These circumstances frequently include a particular officer's knowledge and experience, but that does not make the test any more subjective than the one for probable cause, which looks to an officer's knowledge and experience, but not his subjective intent, Whren v. United States, 517 U.S. 806, 812–813 (1996).

We do not suggest that all record-keeping errors by the police are immune from the exclusionary rule. In this case, however, the conduct at issue was not so objectively culpable as to require exclusion. In *Leon* we held that "the marginal or nonexistent benefits produced by suppressing evidence obtained in objectively reasonable reliance on a subsequently invalidated search warrant cannot justify the substantial costs of exclusion." The same is true when evidence is obtained in objectively reasonable reliance on a subsequently recalled warrant.

If the police have been shown to be reckless in maintaining a warrant system, or to have knowingly made false entries to lay the groundwork for future false arrests, exclusion would certainly be justified under our cases should such misconduct cause a Fourth Amendment violation. We said as much in *Leon*, explaining that an officer could not "obtain a warrant on the basis of a 'bare bones' affidavit and then rely on colleagues who are ignorant of the circumstances under which the warrant was obtained to conduct the search." Petitioner's fears that our decision will cause police departments to deliberately keep their officers ignorant, are thus unfounded.

The dissent also adverts to the possible unreliability of a number of databases not relevant to this case. In a case where systemic errors were demonstrated, it might be reckless for officers to rely on an unreliable warrant system. See *Evans*, 514 U.S., at 17 (O'Connor, J., concurring) ("Surely it would not be reasonable for the police to rely . . . on a recordkeeping system . . . that routinely leads to false arrests"); *Hudson*, 547 U.S., at 604 (KENNEDY, J., concurring) ("If a widespread pattern of violations were shown . . . there would be reason for grave concern." But there is no evidence that errors in Dale County's system are routine or widespread. Officer Anderson testified that he had never had reason to question information about a Dale County warrant, and both Sandy Pope and Sharon Morgan testified that they could remember no similar miscommunication ever happening on their watch. * * *

Petitioner's claim that police negligence automatically triggers suppression cannot be squared with the principles underlying the exclusionary rule, as they have been explained in our cases. In light of our repeated holdings that the deterrent effect of suppression must be substantial and outweigh any harm to the justice system, we conclude that when police mistakes are the result of negligence such as that described here, rather than systemic error or reckless disregard of constitutional requirements, any marginal deterrence does not pay its way. In such a case, the criminal should not "go free because the constable has blundered." People v. Defore, 242 N.Y. 13, 21, 150 N.E. 585, 587 (1926) (opinion of the Court by Cardozo, J.).

The judgment of the Court of Appeals for the Eleventh Circuit is affirmed.

It is so ordered.

JUSTICE GINSBURG, **with whom JUSTICE STEVENS, JUSTICE SOUTER, and JUSTICE BREYER join, dissenting.**

Petitioner Bennie Dean Herring was arrested, and subjected to a search incident to his arrest, although no warrant was outstanding against him, and the police lacked probable cause to believe he was engaged in criminal activity. The arrest and ensuing search therefore violated Herring's Fourth Amendment right "to be secure . . . against unreasonable searches and seizures." The Court of Appeals so determined, and the Government does not contend otherwise. The exclusionary rule provides redress for Fourth Amendment violations by placing the government in the position it would have been in had there been no unconstitutional arrest and search. The rule thus strongly encourages police compliance with the Fourth Amendment in the future. The Court, however, holds the rule inapplicable because careless recordkeeping by the police—not flagrant or deliberate misconduct—accounts for Herring's arrest.

I would not so constrict the domain of the exclusionary rule and would hold the rule dispositive of this case: "[I]f courts are to have any power to discourage [police] error of [the kind here at issue], it must be through the application of the exclusionary rule." Arizona v. Evans, 514 U.S. 1, 22–23 (1995) (STEVENS, J., dissenting). The unlawful search in this case was contested in court because the police found methamphetamine in Herring's pocket and a pistol in his truck. But the "most serious impact" of the Court's holding will be on innocent persons wrongfully arrested based on erroneous information carelessly maintained in a computer data base.

I

* * *

II

A

The Court states that the exclusionary rule is not a defendant's right, ante, at 700; rather, it is simply a remedy applicable only when suppression would result in appreciable deterrence that outweighs the cost to the justice system. * * *

B

Others have described "a more majestic conception" of the Fourth Amendment and its adjunct, the exclusionary rule. *Evans*, 514 U.S., at 18 (STEVENS, J., dissenting). Protective of the fundamental "right of the people to be secure in their persons, houses, papers, and effects," the Amendment "is a constraint on the power of the sovereign, not merely on some of its agents." Ibid.; see Stewart, The Road to Mapp v. Ohio and Beyond: The Origins, Development and Future of the Exclusionary Rule in Search-and-Seizure Cases, 83 Colum. L.Rev. 1365 (1983). I share that vision of the Amendment.

The exclusionary rule is a remedy necessary to ensure that the Fourth Amendment's prohibitions are observed in fact. The rule's service as an essential auxiliary to the Amendment earlier inclined the Court to hold the two inseparable.

Beyond doubt, a main objective of the rule "is to deter—to compel respect for the constitutional guaranty in the only effectively available way—by removing the incentive to disregard it." Elkins v. United States, 364 U.S. 206, 217 (1960). But the rule also serves other important purposes: It "enables the judiciary to avoid the taint of partnership in official lawlessness, and it assures the people—all potential victims of unlawful government conduct that the government would not profit from its lawless behavior, thus minimizing the risk of seriously undermining popular trust in government." United States v. Ca-

landra, 414 U.S. 338, 357 (1974) (Brennan, J., dissenting).

The exclusionary rule, it bears emphasis, is often the only remedy effective to redress a Fourth Amendment violation. See Mapp v. Ohio, 367 U.S. 643, 652 (1961) (noting "the obvious futility of relegating the Fourth Amendment to the protection of other remedies"); Amsterdam, Perspectives on the Fourth Amendment, 58 Minn. L.Rev. 349, 360 (1974) (describing the exclusionary rule as "the primary instrument for enforcing the [F]ourth [A]mendment"). Civil liability will not lie for "the vast majority of [F]ourth [A]mendment violations—the frequent infringements motivated by commendable zeal, not condemnable malice." Stewart, 83 Colum. L.Rev., at 1389. Criminal prosecutions or administrative sanctions against the offending officers and injunctive relief against widespread violations are an even farther cry.

III

The Court maintains that Herring's case is one in which the exclusionary rule could have scant deterrent effect and therefore would not "pay its way." I disagree.

A

The exclusionary rule, the Court suggests, is capable of only marginal deterrence when the misconduct at issue is merely careless, not intentional or reckless. The suggestion runs counter to a foundational premise of tort law—that liability for negligence, i.e., lack of due care, creates an incentive to act with greater care. * * *

That the mistake here involved the failure to make a computer entry hardly means that application of the exclusionary rule would have minimal value. "Just as the risk of respondeat superior liability encourages employers to supervise ... their employees' conduct [more carefully], so the risk of exclusion of evidence encourages policymakers and systems managers to monitor the performance of the systems they install and the personnel employed to operate those systems." *Evans,* 514 U.S., at 29, n. 5 (GINSBURG, J., dissenting).

Consider the potential impact of a decision applying the exclusionary rule in this case. As earlier observed, the record indicates that there is no electronic connection between the warrant database of the Dale County Sheriff's Department and that of the County Circuit Clerk's office, which is located in the basement of the same building. When a warrant is recalled, one of the many different people that have access to the warrants, must find the hard copy of the warrant in the two or three different places where the department houses warrants, return it to the Clerk's office, and manually update the Department's database. The record reflects no routine practice of checking the database for accuracy, and the failure to remove the entry for Herring's warrant was not discovered until Investigator Anderson sought to pursue Herring five months later. Is it not altogether obvious that the Department could take further precautions to ensure the integrity of its database? The Sheriff's Department "is in a position to remedy the situation and might well do so if the exclusionary rule is there to remove the incentive to do otherwise." 1 W.

LaFave, Search and Seizure § 1.8(e), p. 313 (4th ed.2004).

B

Is the potential deterrence here worth the costs it imposes? In light of the paramount importance of accurate recordkeeping in law enforcement, I would answer yes, and next explain why, as I see it, Herring's motion presents a particularly strong case for suppression.

Electronic databases form the nervous system of contemporary criminal justice operations. In recent years, their breadth and influence have dramatically expanded. Police today can access databases that include not only the updated National Crime Information Center (NCIC), but also terrorist watchlists, the Federal Government's employee eligibility system, and various commercial databases. Moreover, States are actively expanding information sharing between jurisdictions. As a result, law enforcement has an increasing supply of information within its easy electronic reach.

The risk of error stemming from these databases is not slim. Herring's amici warn that law enforcement databases are insufficiently monitored and often out of date. Government reports describe, for example, flaws in NCIC databases, terrorist watchlist databases, and databases associated with the Federal Government's employment eligibility verification system.

Inaccuracies in expansive, interconnected collections of electronic information raise grave concerns for individual liberty. "The offense to the dignity of the citizen who is arrested, handcuffed, and searched on a public street simply because some bureaucrat has failed to maintain an accurate computer data base" is evocative of the use of general warrants that so outraged the authors of our Bill of Rights. *Evans*, 514 U.S., at 23, 115 S.Ct. 1185 (STEVENS, J., dissenting).

C

The Court assures that "exclusion would certainly be justified" if "the police have been shown to be reckless in maintaining a warrant system, or to have knowingly made false entries to lay the groundwork for future false arrests." This concession provides little comfort.

First, by restricting suppression to bookkeeping errors that are deliberate or reckless, the majority leaves Herring, and others like him, with no remedy for violations of their constitutional rights. There can be no serious assertion that relief is available under 42 U.S.C. § 1983. The arresting officer would be sheltered by qualified immunity, see Harlow v. Fitzgerald, 457 U.S. 800 (1982), and the police department itself is not liable for the negligent acts of its employees, see Monell v. New York City Dept. of Social Servs., 436 U.S. 658 (1978). Moreover, identifying the department employee who committed the error may be impossible.

Second, I doubt that police forces already possess sufficient incentives to maintain up-to-date records. The Government argues that police have no desire to send officers out on arrests unnecessarily, because arrests consume resources and place officers in danger. The facts of this case do not fit that description of police motivation. Here the officer wanted to arrest Herring and consulted the Department's records to legitimate his predisposition.[6]

Third, even when deliberate or reckless conduct is afoot, the Court's assurance will often be an empty promise: How is an impecunious defendant to make the required showing? If the answer is that a defendant is entitled to discovery (and if necessary, an audit of police databases), then the Court has imposed a considerable administrative burden on courts and law enforcement.[7]

IV

Negligent recordkeeping errors by law enforcement threaten individual liberty, are susceptible to deterrence by the exclusionary rule, and cannot be remedied effectively through other means. Such errors present no occasion to further erode the exclusionary rule. The rule "is needed to make the Fourth Amendment something real; a guarantee that does not carry with it the exclusion of evidence obtained by its violation is a chimera." *Calandra*, 414 U.S., at 361 (Brennan, J., dissenting). In keeping with the rule's core concerns, suppression should have attended the unconstitutional search in this case.

* * *

---

6. It has been asserted that police departments have become sufficiently "professional" that they do not need external deterrence to avoid Fourth Amendment violations. Hudson v. Michigan, 547 U.S. 586, 598–599 (2006). But professionalism is a sign of the exclusionary rule's efficacy—not of its superfluity.

7. It is not clear how the Court squares its focus on deliberate conduct with its recognition that application of the exclusionary rule does not require inquiry into the mental state of the police.

JUSTICE BREYER, **with whom** JUSTICE SOUTER **joins, dissenting.**

I agree with Justice GINSBURG and join her dissent. I write separately to note one additional supporting factor that I believe important. In Arizona v. Evans, we held that recordkeeping errors made by a court clerk do not trigger the exclusionary rule, so long as the police reasonably relied upon the court clerk's recordkeeping. The rationale for our decision was premised on a distinction between judicial errors and police errors, and we gave several reasons for recognizing that distinction.

First, we noted that "the exclusionary rule was historically designed as a means of deterring police misconduct, not mistakes by court employees." Second, we found "no evidence that court employees are inclined to ignore or subvert the Fourth Amendment or that lawlessness among these actors requires application of the extreme sanction of exclusion." Third, we recognized that there was "no basis for believing that application of the exclusionary rule . . . [would] have a significant effect on court employees responsible for informing the police that a warrant has been quashed. Because court clerks are not adjuncts to the law enforcement team engaged in the often competi-

tive enterprise of ferreting out crime, they have no stake in the outcome of particular criminal prosecutions." Taken together, these reasons explain why police recordkeeping errors should be treated differently than judicial ones.

Other cases applying the "good faith" exception to the exclusionary rule have similarly recognized the distinction between police errors and errors made by others, such as judicial officers or legislatures. See United States v. Leon (police reasonably relied on magistrate's issuance of warrant); Illinois v. Krull, (police reasonably relied on statute's constitutionality).

Distinguishing between police recordkeeping errors and judicial ones not only is consistent with our precedent, but also is far easier for courts to administer than THE CHIEF JUSTICE's case-by-case, multifactored inquiry into the degree of police culpability. I therefore would apply the exclusionary rule when police personnel are responsible for a recordkeeping error that results in a Fourth Amendment violation.

The need for a clear line, and the recognition of such a line in our precedent, are further reasons in support of the outcome that Justice GINSBURG's dissent would reach.

Chapter Three

SELF–INCRIMINATION AND CONFESSIONS

III. FIFTH AMENDMENT LIMITATIONS ON CONFESSIONS

Page 783. Add the following new section at the end of the materials on *Miranda*

F. NON–CONSTITUTIONAL PROTECTION SUPPLEMENTING *MIRANDA*: THE RIGHT TO PROMPT PRESENTMENT TO A MAGISTRATE

Before *Miranda*, the Supreme Court—exercising its supervisory power over federal courts—sought to protect suspects in custody by requiring their prompt presentment before a magistrate. The idea was that the magistrate would inform the suspect of their rights to silence and counsel. If police did not comply with the prompt presentment requirement, statements made after the time in which the suspect should have been brought before a magistrate were held inadmissible. The "prompt presentment" requirement—and exclusion of confessions made in violation of it—became known as the *McNabb-Mallory* rule. That rule was, and still is, embodied in Fed. R. Crim.P. 5.

Congress passed 18 U.S.C. § 3501 shortly after *Miranda* was decided. That statute was designed to legislatively overrule *Miranda* (an attempt found unsuccessful in Dickerson v. United States, page 708 of the Text)—and it was also designed to limit the *McNabb-Mallory* rule. The following case discusses the scope of the *McNabb-Mallory* rule; its relationship to *Miranda*; and the effect of section 3501 on the rule.

CORLEY v. UNITED STATES

Supreme Court of the United States, 2009.
129 S.Ct. 1558.

JUSTICE SOUTER **delivered the opinion of the Court.**

The question here is whether Congress intended 18 U.S.C. § 3501 to discard, or merely to narrow, the rule in McNabb v. United States, 318 U.S. 332 (1943), and Mallory v. United States, 354 U.S. 449 (1957), under which an arrested person's confession is inadmissible if given after an unreasonable delay in bringing him before a judge. We hold that Congress meant to limit, not eliminate, *McNabb-Mallory*.

I

A

The common law obliged an arresting officer to bring his prisoner before a magistrate as soon as he reasonably could. See County of Riverside v. McLaughlin, 500 U.S. 44, 61–62 (1991) (SCALIA, J., dissenting). This "presentment" requirement tended to prevent secret detention and served to inform a suspect of the charges against him, and it was the law in nearly every American State and the National Government.

McNabb v. United States raised the question of how to enforce a number of federal statutes codifying the presentment rule. There, federal agents flouted the requirement by interrogating several murder suspects for days before bringing them before a magistrate, and then only after they had given the confessions that convicted them.

On the defendants' motions to exclude the confessions from evidence, we saw no need to reach any constitutional issue. Instead we invoked the supervisory power to establish and maintain "civilized standards of procedure and evidence" in federal courts, which we exercised for the sake of making good on the traditional obligation embodied in the federal presentment legislation. We saw both the statutes and the traditional rule as aimed not only at checking the likelihood of resort to the third degree but meant generally to "avoid all the evil implications of secret interrogation of persons accused of crime." We acknowledged that "Congress ha[d] not explicitly forbidden the use of evidence ... procured" in derogation of the presentment obligation, but we realized that "permit[ting] such evidence to be made the basis of a conviction in the federal courts would stultify the policy which Congress ha[d] enacted into law," and in the exercise of supervisory authority we held confessions inadmissible when obtained during unreasonable presentment delay.

Shortly after *McNabb*, the combined action of the Judicial Conference of the United States and Congress produced Federal Rule of Criminal Procedure 5(a), which pulled the several statutory presentment provisions together in one place. * * * The rule [provides]: "A person making an arrest within the United States must take the defendant without unnecessary delay before a magistrate judge.... "

* * *

We applied Rule 5(a) * * * in Mallory v. United States, holding a confession given seven hours after arrest inadmissible for "unnecessary delay" in presenting the suspect to a magistrate, where the police questioned the suspect for hours "within the vicinity of numerous committing magistrates." * * * Thus, the rule known simply as *McNabb-Mallory* "generally render[s] inadmissible confessions made during periods of detention that violat[e] the prompt presentment requirement of Rule 5(a)." United States v. Alvarez–Sanchez, 511 U.S. 350, 354 (1994).

There the law remained until 1968, when Congress enacted 18 U.S.C. § 3501 in response to Miranda v. Arizona, 384 U.S. 436 (1966), and to the application of *McNabb-Mallory* in some federal courts. Subsections (a) and (b) of § 3501 were meant to eliminate *Miranda*. See Dickerson v. United States, 530 U.S. 428, 435–437 (2000). Subsection (a) provides that "[i]n any criminal prosecution brought by the United States . . . , a confession . . . shall be admissible in evidence if it is voluntarily given," while subsection (b) lists several considerations for courts to address in assessing voluntariness. Subsection (c), which focused on *McNabb-Mallory*, provides that in any federal prosecution, "a confession made . . . by . . . a defendant therein, while such person was under arrest . . . , shall not be inadmissible solely because of delay in bringing such person before a magistrate judge . . . if such confession is found by the trial judge to have been made voluntarily . . . and if such confession was made . . . within six hours [of arrest]"; the six-

hour time limit is extended when further delay is "reasonable considering the means of transportation and the distance to be traveled to the nearest available [magistrate]."

The issue in this case is whether Congress intended § 3501(a) to sweep *McNabb-Mallory's* exclusionary rule aside entirely, or merely meant § 3501(c) to provide immunization to voluntary confessions given within six hours of a suspect's arrest.

B

Petitioner Johnnie Corley was suspected of robbing a bank in Norristown, Pennsylvania. After federal agents learned that Corley was subject to arrest on an unrelated local matter, some federal and state officers went together to execute the state warrant on September 17, 2003, and found him just as he was pulling out of a driveway in his car. Corley nearly ran over one officer, then jumped out of the car, pushed the officer down, and ran. The agents gave chase and caught and arrested him for assaulting a federal officer. The arrest occurred about 8 a.m.

FBI agents first kept Corley at a local police station while they questioned residents near the place he was captured. Around 11:45 a.m. they took him to a Philadelphia hospital to treat a minor cut on his hand that he got during the chase. At 3:30 p.m. the agents took him from the hospital to the Philadelphia FBI office and told him that he was a suspect in the Norristown bank robbery. Though the office was in the same building as the chambers of the nearest magistrate judges, the agents did not bring Corley before a magistrate, but questioned him instead, in hopes of getting a confession.

The agents' repeated arguments sold Corley on the benefits of cooperating with the Government, and he signed a form waiving his *Miranda* rights. At 5:27 p.m., some 9.5 hours after his arrest, Corley began an oral confession that he robbed the bank, and spoke on in this vein until about 6:30, when agents asked him to put it all in writing. Corley said he was tired and wanted a break, so the agents decided to hold him overnight and take the written statement the next morning. At 10:30 a.m. on September 18 they began the interrogation again, which ended when Corley signed a written confession. He was finally presented to a magistrate at 1:30 p.m. that day, 29.5 hours after his arrest.

Corley was charged with armed bank robbery, conspiracy to commit armed bank robbery, and using a firearm in furtherance of a crime of violence. When he moved to suppress his oral and written confessions under Rule 5(a) and *McNabb-Mallory*, the District Court denied the motion, with the explanation that the time Corley was receiving medical treatment should be excluded from the delay, and that the oral confession was thus given within the six-hour window of § 3501(c). The District Court also held Corley's written confession admissible, reasoning that "a break from interrogation requested by an arrestee who has already begun his confession does not constitute unreasonable delay under Rule 5(a)." [Corley was convicted.]

A divided panel of the Court of Appeals for the Third Circuit affirmed the conviction, though its rationale for rejecting Corley's Rule 5(a) argument was different from the District Court's. The panel majority considered itself bound by Circuit precedent to the effect that § 3501 entirely abrogated the *McNabb-Mallory* rule and replaced it with a pure voluntariness test. As the majority saw it, if a district court found a confession voluntary after considering the points listed in § 3501(b), it would be admissible, regardless of whether delay in presentment was unnecessary or unreasonable. Judge Sloviter * * * dissented with an opinion that "§ 3501 does not displace Rule 5(a)" or abrogate *McNabb-Mallory* for presentment delays beyond six hours.

We granted certiorari to resolve a division in the Circuit Courts on the reach of § 3501. We now vacate and remand.

II

The Government's argument focuses on § 3501(a), which provides that any confession "shall be admissible in evidence" in federal court "if it is voluntarily given." To the Government, subsection (a) means that once a district court looks to the considerations in § 3501(b) and finds a confession voluntary, in it comes; (a) entirely eliminates *McNabb-Mallory* with its bar to admitting even a voluntary confession if given during an unreasonable delay in presentment.

Corley argues that § 3501(a) was meant to overrule *Miranda* and nothing more, with no effect on *McNabb-Mallory*, which § 3501 touches only in subsection (c). By providing that a confession "shall not be inadmissible solely because of delay" in presentment if "made voluntarily and . . . within six hours [of arrest]," subsection (c) leaves *McNabb-Mallory* inapplicable to confessions given within the six hours, but when a confession comes even later, the exclusionary rule applies and courts have to see whether the delay was unnecessary or unreasonable.

Corley has the better argument.

A

The fundamental problem with the Government's reading of § 3501 is that it renders § 3501(c) nonsensical and superfluous. Subsection (c) provides that a confession "shall not be inadmissible solely because of delay" in presentment if the confession is "made voluntarily and . . . within six hours [of arrest]." If (a) really meant that any voluntary confession was admissible, as the Government contends, then (c) would add nothing; if a confession was "made voluntarily" it would be admissible, period, and never "inadmissible solely because of delay," no matter whether the delay went beyond six hours. There is no way out of this * * * .

The Government's reading is thus at odds with one of the most basic interpretive canons, that a statute should be construed so that effect is given to all its provisions, so that no part will be inoperative or superfluous, void or insignificant. The Government attempts to mitigate its problem by rewriting (c) into a clarifying, if not strictly necessary, provision: although Congress wrote that a confession "shall not be inadmissible solely because of delay" if the confession is "made voluntarily and . . . within six hours [of arrest]," the Government tells us that

Congress actually meant that a confession "shall not be [involuntary] solely because of delay" if the confession is "[otherwise voluntary] and . . . [made] within six hours [of arrest]." Thus rewritten, (c) would coexist peacefully (albeit inelegantly) with (a), with (c) simply specifying a bright-line rule applying (a) to cases of delay: it would tell courts that delay alone does not make a confession involuntary unless the delay exceeds six hours.

To this proposal, the short answer is that Congress did not write the statute that way .. The Government may say that we can sensibly read "inadmissible" as "involuntary" because the words are "virtually synonymous . . . in this statutory context," but this is simply not so. To begin with, Congress used both terms in (c) itself, and we would not presume to ascribe this difference to a simple mistake in draftsmanship. And there is, in fact, every reason to believe that Congress used the distinct terms very deliberately. Subsection (c) specifies two criteria that must be satisfied to prevent a confession from being "inadmissible solely because of delay": the confession must be "[1] made voluntarily and . . . [2] within six hours [of arrest]." Because voluntariness is thus only one of several criteria for admissibility under (c), "involuntary" and "inadmissible" plainly cannot be synonymous. What is more, the Government's argument ignores the fact that under the *McNabb-Mallory* rule, which we presume Congress was aware of, "inadmissible" and "involuntary" mean different things. * * * *McNabb-Mallory* makes even voluntary confessions inadmissible if given after an unreasonable delay in presentment. So we cannot accept the Government's attempt to confuse the critically distinct terms "involuntary" and "inadmissible" by rewriting (c) into a bright-line rule doing nothing more than applying (a).

* * *

B

[Justice Souter reviews the legislative history and concludes that it supports the premise the § 3501(a) was directed solely at *Miranda* and that subdivision (c) was intended to limit, but not abrogate, *McNabb-Mallory*.]

C

It also counts heavily against the position of the United States that it would leave the Rule 5 presentment requirement without any teeth, for as the Government again is forced to admit, if there is no *McNabb-Mallory* there is no apparent remedy for delay in presentment. One might not care if the prompt presentment requirement were just some administrative nicety, but in fact the rule has always mattered in very practical ways and still does. As we said, it stretches back to the common law, when it was "one of the most important" protections "against unlawful arrest." *McLaughlin*, 500 U.S., at 60–61 (SCALIA, J., dissenting). Today presentment is the point at which the judge is required to take several key steps to foreclose Government over-reaching: informing the defendant of the charges against him, his right to remain silent, his right to counsel, the availability of bail, and any right to a preliminary hearing; giving the defendant a chance to con-

sult with counsel; and deciding between detention or release.

In a world without *McNabb-Mallory*, federal agents would be free to question suspects for extended periods before bringing them out in the open, and we have always known what custodial secrecy leads to. No one with any smattering of the history of 20th-century dictatorships needs a lecture on the subject, and we understand the need even within our own system to take care against going too far. "[C]ustodial police interrogation, by its very nature, isolates and pressures the individual," *Dickerson*, 530 U.S., at 435, and there is mounting empirical evidence that these pressures can induce a frighteningly high percentage of people to confess to crimes they never committed, see, e.g., Drizin & Leo, The Problem of False Confessions in the Post–DNA World, 82 N.C.L.Rev. 891, 906–907 (2004).

Justice Frankfurter's point in *McNabb* is as fresh as ever: "The history of liberty has largely been the history of observance of procedural safeguards." *McNabb-Mallory* is one of them, and neither the text nor the history of § 3501 makes out a case that Congress meant to do away with it.

III

* * *

IV

We hold that § 3501 modified *McNabb-Mallory* without supplanting it. Under the rule as revised by § 3501(c), a district court with a suppression claim must find whether the defendant confessed within six hours of arrest (unless a longer delay was "reasonable considering the means of transportation and the distance to be traveled to the nearest available [magistrate]"). If the confession came within that period, it is admissible, subject to the other Rules of Evidence, so long as it was "made voluntarily and ... the weight to be given [it] is left to the jury." If the confession occurred before presentment and beyond six hours, however, the court must decide whether delaying that long was unreasonable or unnecessary under the *McNabb-Mallory* cases, and if it was, the confession is to be suppressed.

In this case, the Third Circuit did not apply this rule and in consequence never conclusively determined whether Corley's oral confession "should be treated as having been made within six hours of arrest," as the District Court held. Nor did the Circuit consider the justifiability of any delay beyond six hours if the oral confession should be treated as given outside the six-hour window; and it did not make this enquiry with respect to Corley's written confession. We therefore vacate the judgment of the Court of Appeals and remand the case for consideration of those issues in the first instance, consistent with this opinion.

It is so ordered.

———

JUSTICE ALITO, with whom THE CHIEF JUSTICE, JUSTICE SCALIA, and JUSTICE THOMAS join, dissenting.

Section 3501(a) of Title 18, United States Code, directly and unequivocally answers the question presented in this case. After petitioner was arrested by federal agents, he twice waived his *Miranda* rights and voluntarily confessed, first orally and later in writing, that he had participated in an armed bank robbery. He was then taken before a Magistrate Judge for an initial appearance. The question that we must decide is whether this voluntary confession may be suppressed on the ground that there was unnecessary delay in bringing petitioner before the Magistrate Judge. Unless the unambiguous language of § 3501(a) is ignored, petitioner's confession may not be suppressed.

I

Section 3501(a) states: "In any criminal prosecution brought by the United States ... , a confession ... shall be admissible in evidence if it is voluntarily given."

Applying settled principles of statutory construction, we must first determine whether the statutory text is plain and unambiguous, and if it is, we must apply the statute according to its terms. Here, there is nothing ambiguous about the language of § 3501(a), and the Court does not claim otherwise. Although we normally presume that Congress means in a statute what it says there, the Court today concludes that § 3501(a) does not mean what it says and that a voluntary confession may be suppressed under the *McNabb-Mallory* rule. This supervisory rule, which requires the suppression of a confession where there was unnecessary delay in bringing a federal criminal defendant before a judicial officer after arrest, was announced long before 18 U.S.C. § 3501(a) was adopted. According to the Court, this rule survived the enactment of § 3501(a) because Congress adopted that provision for the sole purpose of abrogating *Miranda* and apparently never realized that the provision's broad language would also do away with the *McNabb-Mallory* rule. I disagree with the Court's analysis and therefore respectfully dissent.

II

A

* * *

B

* * *

C

The Court contends that a literal interpretation of § 3501(a) would leave the prompt presentment requirement set out in Federal Rule of Criminal Procedure 5(a)(1) "without any teeth, for . . . if there is no *McNabb-Mallory* there is no apparent remedy for delay in presentment." There is nothing strange, however, about a prompt presentment requirement that is not enforced by a rule excluding voluntary confessions made during a period of excessive prepresentment delay. As the Court notes, "[t]he common law obliged an arresting officer to bring his prisoner before a magistrate as soon as he reasonably could," but the *McNabb-Mallory* supervisory rule was not adopted until the middle of the 20th century. To this day, while the States are required by the Fourth Amendment to bring an arrestee promptly before a judicial officer, see, e.g., County of Riverside v. McLaughlin, 500 U.S. 44, 56 (1991), we have never held that this constitutional requirement is backed by an automatic exclusionary sanction. And although the

prompt presentment requirement serves interests in addition to the prevention of coerced confessions, the *McNabb-Mallory* rule provides no sanction for excessive prepresentment delay in those instances in which no confession is sought or obtained.

Moreover, the need for the *McNabb-Mallory* exclusionary rule is no longer clear. That rule, which was adopted long before *Miranda*, originally served a purpose that is now addressed by the giving of *Miranda* warnings upon arrest. As *Miranda* recognized, *McNabb* and *Mallory* were "responsive to the same considerations of Fifth Amendment policy" that the *Miranda* rule was devised to address.

In the pre-*Miranda* era, the requirement of prompt presentment ensured that persons taken into custody would, within a relatively short period, receive advice about their rights. Now, however, *Miranda* ensures that arrestees receive such advice at an even earlier point, within moments of being taken into custody. Of course, arrestees, after receiving *Miranda* warnings, may waive their rights and submit to questioning by law enforcement officers, and arrestees may likewise waive the prompt presentment requirement. It seems unlikely that many arrestees who are willing to waive the right to remain silent and the right to the assistance of counsel during questioning would balk at waiving the right to prompt presentment. More than a few courts of appeals have gone as far as to hold that a waiver of *Miranda* rights also constitutes a waiver under *McNabb-Mallory*. Whether or not those decisions are correct, it is certainly not clear that the *McNabb-Mallory* rule adds much protection beyond that provided by *Miranda*.

D

* * *

E

* * *

For all these reasons, I would affirm the decision of the Court of Appeals, and I therefore respectfully dissent.

IV. CONFESSIONS AND THE SIXTH AMENDMENT RIGHT TO COUNSEL

B. OBTAINING INFORMATION FROM FORMALLY CHARGED DEFENDANTS

Page 793. After the Headnote on *Gouveia*, add the following:

Right to Counsel Attaches at Arraignment Even if the Prosecutor Is Not Involved: Rothgery v. Gillespie County

In Rothgery v. Gillespie County, 128 S.Ct. 2578 (2008), Rothgery was arraigned at his first appearance before a magistrate. At that proceeding, the arresting officer submitted a sworn affidavit of probable cause that described the facts supporting the arrest and charged that Rothgery committed the offense of unlawful possession of a firearm by a felon. After reviewing the affidavit, the magistrate judge determined that probable cause existed for the arrest, informed Rothgery of the charge, and set his bail at $5,000. Under state procedure, the prosecutor was not involved in this arraignment procedure, and counsel was not provided to Rothgery. Eventually Rothgery was given a lawyer who got the charges dropped, and he brought a civil rights claim arguing that had he been given a lawyer at the initial proceeding, the charges would have been dropped at that point and he would have avoided incarceration. In the Supreme Court, the only question was whether the state arraignment procedure constituted a criminal prosecution that would trigger Rothgery's Sixth Amendment right to counsel; the Court was not asked to consider whether Rothgery's claim for damages had merit.

The Court, in an opinion by Justice Souter for eight Justices, held that the Sixth Amendment was triggered by the initial appearance before the magistrate, even though the prosecutor was not involved in the proceeding. Justice Souter relied on all of the Sixth Amendment right to counsel cases involving confessions, in which the Court had declared that the Sixth Amendment attached at the initial presentment to the magistrate. Justice Souter also reasoned that "what counts as a commitment to prosecute is an issue of federal law unaffected by allocations of power among state officials under a State's law." The majority concluded as follows:

Our holding is narrow. We do not decide whether the 6–month delay in appointment of counsel resulted in prejudice to Rothgery's Sixth Amendment rights, and have no occasion to consider what standards should apply in deciding this. We merely reaffirm what we have held before and what an overwhelming majority of American jurisdictions understand in practice: a criminal defendant's initial appearance before a judicial officer, where he learns the charge against him and his liberty is subject to restriction, marks the start of adversary judicial proceedings that trigger attachment of the Sixth Amendment right to counsel.

Chief Justice Roberts wrote a short concurring opinion, joined by Justice Scalia. Justice Alito wrote a concurring opinion joined by the Chief Justice and Justice Scalia, in which he emphasized the narrowness of the majority's holding. He declared that the initiation of a prosecution was only a triggering event, and that more is required before an accused has the right to counsel at a particular point:

I join the Court's opinion because I do not understand it to hold that a defendant is entitled to the assistance of appointed counsel as soon as his Sixth Amendment right attaches. As I interpret our precedents, the term "attachment" signifies nothing more than the beginning of the defendant's prosecution. It does not mark the beginning of a substantive entitlement to the assistance of counsel. * * * I interpret the Sixth Amendment to require the appointment of counsel only after the defendant's prosecution has begun, and then only as necessary to guarantee the defendant effective assistance at trial.

Justice Thomas dissented.

E. WAIVER OF SIXTH AMENDMENT PROTECTIONS

Page 804. Add at the bottom of the page.

MONTEJO v. LOUISIANA

Supreme Court of the United States, 2009.
129 S.Ct. 2079.

Justice Scalia delivered the opinion of the Court.

We consider in this case the scope and continued viability of the rule announced by this Court in Michigan v. Jackson, 475 U.S. 625 (1986), forbidding police to initiate interrogation of a criminal defendant once he has requested counsel at an arraignment or similar proceeding.

I

Petitioner Jesse Montejo was arrested on September 6, 2002, in connection with the robbery and murder of Lewis Ferrari, who had been found dead in his own home one day earlier. Suspicion quickly focused on Jerry Moore, a disgruntled former employee of Ferrari's dry cleaning business. Police sought to question Montejo, who was a known associate of Moore.

Montejo waived his rights under Miranda v. Arizona, and was interrogated at the sheriff's office by police detectives through the late afternoon and evening of September 6 and the early morning of September 7. During the interrogation, Montejo repeatedly changed his account of the crime, at first claiming that he had only driven Moore to the victim's home, and ultimately admitting that he had shot and killed Ferrari in the course of a botched burglary. These police interrogations were videotaped.

On September 10, Montejo was brought before a judge for what is known in Louisiana as a "72–hour hearing"—a preliminary hearing required under state law. Although the proceedings were not transcribed, the minute record indicates what transpired: "The defendant being charged with First Degree Murder, Court ordered N[o] Bond set in this matter. Further, Court ordered the Office of Indigent Defender be appointed to represent the defendant."

Later that same day, two police detectives visited Montejo back at the prison and requested that he accompany them on an excursion to locate the murder weapon (which Montejo had earlier indicated he had thrown into a lake). After some back-and-forth, the substance of which remains in dispute, Montejo was again read his *Miranda* rights and agreed to go along; during the excursion, he wrote an inculpatory letter of apology to the victim's widow. Only upon their return did Montejo finally meet his court-appointed attorney, who was quite upset that the detectives had interrogated his client in his absence.

At trial, the letter of apology was admitted over defense objection. The jury convicted Montejo of first-degree murder, and he was sentenced to death.

The Louisiana Supreme Court affirmed the conviction and sentence. As relevant here, the court rejected Montejo's argument that under the rule of *Jackson, supra,* the letter should have been suppressed. *Jackson* held that "if police initiate interrogation after a defendant's assertion, at an arraignment or similar proceeding, of his right to counsel, any waiver of the defendant's right to counsel for that police-initiated interrogation is invalid."

Citing a decision of the United States Court of Appeals for the Fifth Circuit, the Louisiana Supreme Court reasoned that the prophylactic protection of *Jackson* is not triggered unless and until the defendant has actually requested a lawyer or has otherwise asserted his Sixth Amendment right to counsel. Because Montejo simply stood mute at his 72–hour hearing while the judge ordered the appointment of counsel, he had made no such request or assertion. So the proper inquiry, the court ruled, was only whether he had knowingly, intelligently, and voluntarily waived his right to have counsel present during the interaction with the police. And because Montejo had been read his *Miranda* rights and agreed to waive them, the Court answered that question in the affirmative, and upheld the conviction.

We granted certiorari.

II

Montejo and his amici raise a number of pragmatic objections to the Louisiana Supreme Court's interpretation of *Jackson*. We agree that the approach taken below would lead either to an unworkable standard, or to arbitrary and anomalous distinctions between defendants in different States. Neither would be acceptable.

Under the rule adopted by the Louisiana Supreme Court, a criminal defendant must request counsel, or otherwise "assert" his Sixth Amendment right at the preliminary hearing, before the Jackson protections are triggered. If he does so, the police may not initiate further interrogation in the absence of counsel. But if the court on its own appoints counsel, with the defendant taking no affirmative action to invoke his right to counsel, then police are free to initiate further interrogations provided that they first obtain an otherwise valid waiver by the defendant of his right to have counsel present.

This rule would apply well enough in States that require the indigent defendant formally to request counsel before any appointment is made, which usually occurs after the court has informed him that he will receive counsel if he asks for it. That is how the system works in Michigan, for example, Mich. Ct. Rule 6.005(A) (2009), whose scheme produced the factual background for this Court's decision in Michigan v. Jackson. Jackson, like all other represented indigent defendants in the State, had requested counsel in accordance with the applicable state law.

But many States follow other practices. In some two dozen, the appointment of counsel is automatic upon a finding of indigency, e.g., Kan. Stat. Ann. § 22–4503(c) (2007); and in a number of others, appointment can be made either upon the defendant's request or sua sponte by the court, e.g., Del.Code Ann., Tit. 29, § 4602(a) (2003). Nothing in our *Jackson* opinion indicates whether we were then aware that not all States require that a defendant affirmatively request counsel before one is appointed; and of course we had no occasion there to decide how the rule we announced would apply to these other States.

The Louisiana Supreme Court's answer to that unresolved question is troublesome. The central distinction it draws—between defendants who "assert" their right to counsel and those who do not—is exceedingly hazy when applied to States that appoint counsel absent request from the defendant. How to categorize a defendant who merely asks, prior to appointment, whether he will be appointed counsel? Or who inquires, after the fact, whether he has been? What treatment for one who thanks the court after the appointment is made? And if the court asks a defendant whether he would object to appointment, will a quick shake of his head count as an assertion of his right?

To the extent that the Louisiana Supreme Court's rule also permits a defendant to trigger *Jackson* through the "acceptance" of counsel, that notion is even more mysterious: How does one affirmatively accept counsel appointed by court order? An indigent defendant has no right to choose his counsel, so it is hard to imagine what his "acceptance" would look like, beyond the passive silence that Montejo exhibited.

In practice, judicial application of the Louisiana rule in States that do not require a defendant to make a request for counsel could take either of two paths. Courts might ask on a case-by-case basis whether a defendant has somehow invoked his right to counsel, looking to his conduct at the preliminary hearing-his statements and gestures-and the totality of the circumstances. Or, courts might simply determine as a categorical matter that defendants in these States—over half of those in the Union—simply have no opportunity to assert their right to counsel at the hearing and are therefore out of luck.

Neither approach is desirable. The former would be particularly impractical in light of the fact that, as amici describe, preliminary hearings are often rushed, and are frequently not recorded or transcribed. The sheer volume of indigent defendants would render the monitoring of each particular defendant's reaction to the appointment of counsel almost impossible. And sometimes the defendant is not even present. E.g., La.Code Crim. Proc. Ann., Art. 230.1(A) (West Supp.2009) (allowing court to appoint counsel if defendant is "unable to appear"). Police who did not attend the hearing would have no way to know whether they could approach a particular defendant; and for a court to adjudicate that question ex post would be a fact-intensive and burdensome task, even if monitoring were possible and transcription available. Because "clarity of ...

command" and "certainty of ... application" are crucial in rules that govern law enforcement, Minnick v. Mississippi, 498 U.S. 146, 151 (1990), this would be an unfortunate way to proceed.

The second possible course fares no better, for it would achieve clarity and certainty only at the expense of introducing arbitrary distinctions: Defendants in States that automatically appoint counsel would have no opportunity to invoke their rights and trigger *Jackson*, while those in other States, effectively instructed by the court to request counsel, would be lucky winners. That sort of hollow formalism is out of place in a doctrine that purports to serve as a practical safeguard for defendants' rights.

III

But if the Louisiana Supreme Court's application of *Jackson* is unsound as a practical matter, then Montejo's solution is untenable as a theoretical and doctrinal matter. Under his approach, once a defendant is represented by counsel, police may not initiate any further interrogation. Such a rule would be entirely untethered from the original rationale of *Jackson*.

A

It is worth emphasizing first what is not in dispute or at stake here. Under our precedents, once the adversary judicial process has been initiated, the Sixth Amendment guarantees a defendant the right to have counsel present at all "critical" stages of the criminal proceedings. Interrogation by the State is such a stage.

Our precedents also place beyond doubt that the Sixth Amendment right to counsel may be waived by a defendant, so long as relinquishment of the right is voluntary, knowing, and intelligent. Patterson v. Illinois, 487 U.S. 285, 292, n. 4 (1988); Brewer v. Williams, 430 U.S. 387, 404 (1977). The defendant may waive the right whether or not he is already represented by counsel; the decision to waive need not itself be counseled. And when a defendant is read his *Miranda* rights (which include the right to have counsel present during interrogation) and agrees to waive those rights, that typically does the trick, even though the *Miranda* rights purportedly have their source in the Fifth Amendment:

> "As a general matter ... an accused who is admonished with the warnings prescribed by this Court in *Miranda* ... has been sufficiently apprised of the nature of his Sixth Amendment rights, and of the consequences of abandoning those rights, so that his waiver on this basis will be considered a knowing and intelligent one." *Patterson*, supra, at 296.

The only question raised by this case, and the only one addressed by the *Jackson* rule, is whether courts must presume that such a waiver is invalid under certain circumstances. We created such a presumption in *Jackson* by analogy to a similar prophylactic rule established to protect the Fifth Amendment based *Miranda* right to have counsel present at any custodial interrogation. Edwards v. Arizona, 451 U.S. 477 (1981), decided that once "an accused has invoked his right to have counsel present during custodial interrogation ... [he] is not subject to further interrogation by the authorities until counsel has been made available," unless he initiates the contact.

The *Edwards* rule is "designed to prevent police from badgering a defendant into waiving his previously asserted *Miranda* rights." It does this by presuming his postassertion statements to be involuntary, "even where the suspect executes a waiver and his statements would be considered voluntary under traditional standards." McNeil v. Wisconsin, 501 U.S. 171, 177 (1991). This prophylactic rule thus "protect[s] a suspect's voluntary choice not to speak outside his lawyer's presence." Texas v. Cobb, 532 U.S. 162, 175 (2001) (KENNEDY, J., concurring).

Jackson represented a wholesale importation of the *Edwards* rule into the Sixth Amendment. The *Jackson* Court decided that a request for counsel at an arraignment should be treated as an invocation of the Sixth Amendment right to counsel "at every critical stage of the prosecution," despite doubt that defendants "actually inten[d] their request for counsel to encompass representation during any further questioning," because doubts must be "resolved in favor of protecting the constitutional claim." Citing *Edwards*, the Court held that any subsequent waiver would thus be "insufficient to justify police-initiated interrogation." In other words, we presume such waivers involuntary "based on the supposition that suspects who assert their right to counsel are unlikely to waive that right voluntarily" in subsequent interactions with police.

The dissent presents us with a revisionist view of Jackson. The defendants' request for counsel, it contends, was important only because it proved that counsel had been appointed. Such a non sequitur (nowhere alluded to in the case) hardly needs rebuttal. Proceeding from this fanciful premise, the dissent claims that the decision actually established "a rule designed to safeguard a defendant's right to rely on the assistance of counsel," not one "designed to prevent police badgering." To safeguard the right to assistance of counsel from what? From a knowing and voluntary waiver by the defendant himself? Unless the dissent seeks to prevent a defendant altogether from waiving his Sixth Amendment rights, i.e., to "imprison a man in his privileges and call it the Constitution," Adams v. United States ex rel. McCann, 317 U.S. 269, 280 (1942)—a view with zero support in reason, history or case law—the answer must be: from police pressure, i.e., badgering. The antibadgering rationale is the only way to make sense of Jackson 's repeated citations of Edwards, and the only way to reconcile the opinion with our waiver jurisprudence.

B

With this understanding of what *Jackson* stands for and whence it came, it should be clear that Montejo's interpretation of that decision— that no represented defendant can ever be approached by the State and asked to consent to interrogation—is off the mark. When a court appoints counsel for an indigent defendant in the absence of any request on his part, there is no basis for a presumption that any subsequent waiver of the right to counsel will be involuntary. There is no "initial election" to exercise the right, that must be preserved through a prophylactic rule against later waivers. No reason exists to assume that a defendant like Montejo, who has done nothing at all to express his intentions with respect to his Sixth Amendment rights, would not be perfectly amenable to speaking with the police without having counsel present. And no reason exists to prohibit the police from inquiring. *Edwards* and *Jackson* are meant to prevent police from badgering defendants into changing their minds about their rights, but a defendant who never asked for counsel has not yet made up his mind in the first instance.

* * *

In practice, Montejo's rule would prevent police-initiated interrogation entirely once the Sixth Amendment right attaches, at least in those States that appoint counsel promptly without request from the defendant. As the dissent in Jackson pointed out, with no expressed disagreement from the majority, the opinion "most assuredly [did] not hold that the Edwards per se rule prohibiting all police-initiated interrogations applies from the moment the defendant's Sixth Amendment right to counsel attaches, with or without a request for counsel by the defendant." 475 U.S., at 640 (opinion of Rehnquist, J.). That would have constituted a "shockingly dramatic restructuring of the balance this Court has traditionally struck between the rights of the defendant and those of the larger society." Ibid.

The upshot is that even on *Jackson 's* own terms, it would be completely unjustified to presume that a defendant's consent to police-initiated interrogation was involuntary or coerced simply because he had previously been appointed a lawyer.

IV

So on the one hand, requiring an initial "invocation" of the right to counsel in order to trigger the *Jackson* presumption is consistent with the theory of that decision, but (as Montejo and his amici argue, see Part II, supra) would be unworkable in more than half the States of the Union. On the other hand, eliminating the invocation requirement would render the rule easy to apply but depart fundamentally from the *Jackson* rationale.

We do not think that *stare decisis* requires us to expand significantly the holding of a prior decision—fundamentally revising its theoretical basis in the process—in order to cure its practical deficiencies. To the contrary, the fact that a decision has proved "unworkable" is a traditional ground for overruling it. * * *

Beyond workability, the relevant factors in deciding whether to adhere to the principle of stare decisis include the antiquity of the precedent, the reliance interests at stake, and of course whether the decision was well reasoned. The first two cut in favor of abandoning *Jackson*: the opinion is only two decades old, and eliminating it would not upset expectations . Any criminal defendant learned enough to order his affairs based on the rule announced in *Jackson* would also be perfectly capable of interacting with the police on his own. Of course it is likely true that police and prosecutors have been trained to comply with *Jackson*, but that is hardly a basis for retaining it as a constitu-

tional requirement. If a State wishes to abstain from requesting interviews with represented defendants when counsel is not present, it obviously may continue to do so.

Which brings us to the strength of *Jackson's* reasoning. When this Court creates a prophylactic rule in order to protect a constitutional right, the relevant "reasoning" is the weighing of the rule's benefits against its costs. * * * We think that the marginal benefits of *Jackson* (viz., the number of confessions obtained coercively that are suppressed by its bright-line rule and would otherwise have been admitted) are dwarfed by its substantial costs (viz., hindering society's compelling interest in finding, convicting, and punishing those who violate the law).

What does the *Jackson* rule actually achieve by way of preventing unconstitutional conduct? Recall that the purpose of the rule is to preclude the State from badgering defendants into waiving their previously asserted rights. The effect of this badgering might be to coerce a waiver, which would render the subsequent interrogation a violation of the Sixth Amendment. Even though involuntary waivers are invalid even apart from *Jackson*, mistakes are of course possible when courts conduct case-by-case voluntariness review. A bright-line rule like that adopted in *Jackson* ensures that no fruits of interrogations made possible by badgering-induced involuntary waivers are ever erroneously admitted at trial.

But without *Jackson*, how many would be? The answer is few if any. The principal reason is that the Court has already taken substantial other, overlapping measures toward the same end. Under *Miranda's* prophylactic protection of the right against compelled self-incrimination, any suspect subject to custodial interrogation has the right to have a lawyer present if he so requests, and to be advised of that right .. Under *Edwards'* prophylactic protection of the *Miranda* right, once such a defendant "has invoked his right to have counsel present," interrogation must stop. And under *Minnick's* prophylactic protection of the *Edwards* right, no subsequent interrogation may take place until counsel is present, "whether or not the accused has consulted with his attorney."

These three layers of prophylaxis are sufficient. Under the *Miranda-Edwards-Minnick* line of cases (which is not in doubt), a defendant who does not want to speak to the police without counsel present need only say as much when he is first approached and given the *Miranda* warnings. At that point, not only must the immediate contact end, but "badgering" by later requests is prohibited. If that regime suffices to protect the integrity of "a suspect's voluntary choice not to speak outside his lawyer's presence" before his arraignment, *Cobb*, 532 U.S., at 175 (KENNEDY, J., concurring), it is hard to see why it would not also suffice to protect that same choice after arraignment, when Sixth Amendment rights have attached. And if so, then *Jackson* is simply superfluous.

It is true, as Montejo points out in his supplemental brief, that the doctrine established by *Miranda* and *Edwards* is designed to protect Fifth Amendment, not Sixth Amendment, rights. But that is irrelevant.

What matters is that these cases, like *Jackson*, protect the right to have counsel during custodial interrogation-which right happens to be guaranteed (once the adversary judicial process has begun) by *two* sources of law. Since the right under both sources is waived using the same procedure, *Patterson, supra*, at 296, doctrines ensuring voluntariness of the Fifth Amendment waiver simultaneously ensure the voluntariness of the Sixth Amendment waiver.

Montejo also correctly observes that the *Miranda-Edwards* regime is narrower than *Jackson* in one respect: The former applies only in the context of custodial interrogation. If the defendant is not in custody then those decisions do not apply; nor do they govern other, noninterrogative types of interactions between the defendant and the State (like pretrial lineups). However, those uncovered situations are the least likely to pose a risk of coerced waivers. When a defendant is not in custody, he is in control, and need only shut his door or walk away to avoid police badgering. And noninterrogative interactions with the State do not involve the "inherently compelling pressures" that one might reasonably fear could lead to involuntary waivers.

Jackson was policy driven, and if that policy is being adequately served through other means, there is no reason to retain its rule. *Miranda* and the cases that elaborate upon it already guarantee not simply noncoercion in the traditional sense, but what Justice Harlan referred to as "voluntariness with a vengeance," 384 U.S., at 505 (dissenting opinion). There is no need to take *Jackson's* further step of requiring voluntariness on stilts.

On the other side of the equation are the costs of adding the bright-line *Jackson* rule on top of Edwards and other extant protections. The principal cost of applying any exclusionary rule is, of course, letting guilty and possibly dangerous criminals go free. *Jackson* not only operates to invalidate a confession given by the free choice of suspects who have received proper advice of their *Miranda* rights but waived them nonetheless, but also deters law enforcement officers from even trying to obtain voluntary confessions. The "ready ability to obtain uncoerced confessions is not an evil but an unmitigated good." *McNeil,* 501 U.S., at 181. Without these confessions, crimes go unsolved and criminals unpunished. These are not negligible costs, and in our view the *Jackson* Court gave them too short shrift.

Notwithstanding this calculus, Montejo and his amici urge the retention of *Jackson.* Their principal objection to its elimination is that the *Edwards* regime which remains will not provide an administrable rule. But this Court has praised *Edwards* precisely because it provides "clear and unequivocal guidelines to the law enforcement profession," Arizona v. Roberson, 486 U.S. 675, 682 (1988). Our cases make clear which sorts of statements trigger its protections, see Davis v. United States, 512 U.S. 452, 459 (1994), and once triggered, the rule operates as a bright line. Montejo expresses concern that courts will have to determine whether statements made at preliminary hearings constitute *Edwards* invocations—

thus implicating all the practical problems of the Louisiana rule we discussed above. That concern is misguided. "We have in fact never held that a person can invoke his *Miranda* rights anticipatorily, in a context other than custodial interrogation." *McNeil, supra,* at 182, n. 3. What matters for *Miranda* and *Edwards* is what happens when the defendant is approached for interrogation, and (if he consents) what happens during the interrogation—not what happened at any preliminary hearing.

In sum, when the marginal benefits of the Jackson rule are weighed against its substantial costs to the truth-seeking process and the criminal justice system, we readily conclude that the rule does not "pay its way," United States v. Leon, 468 U.S. 897, 907–908, n. 6 (1984). Michigan v. Jackson should be and now is overruled.

V

Although our holding means that the Louisiana Supreme Court correctly rejected Montejo's claim under *Jackson*, we think that Montejo should be given an opportunity to contend that his letter of apology should still have been suppressed under the rule of *Edwards*. If Montejo made a clear assertion of the right to counsel when the officers approached him about accompanying them on the excursion for the murder weapon, then no interrogation should have taken place unless Montejo initiated it. Even if Montejo subsequently agreed to waive his rights, that waiver would have been invalid had it followed an unequivocal election of the right.

Montejo understandably did not pursue an *Edwards* objection, because *Jackson* served as the Sixth Amendment analogy to *Edwards* and offered broader protections. Our decision today, overruling *Jackson*, changes the legal landscape and does so in part based on the protections already provided by *Edwards*. Thus we think that a remand is appropriate so that Montejo can pursue this alternative avenue for relief. Montejo may also seek on remand to press any claim he might have that his Sixth Amendment waiver was not knowing and voluntary, e.g., his argument that the waiver was invalid because it was based on misrepresentations by police as to whether he had been appointed a lawyer. These matters have heightened importance in light of our opinion today.

We do not venture to resolve these issues ourselves, not only because we are a court of final review * * * but also because the relevant facts remain unclear. Montejo and the police gave inconsistent testimony about exactly what took place on the afternoon of September 10, 2002, and the Louisiana Supreme Court did not make an explicit credibility determination. Moreover, Montejo's testimony came not at the suppression hearing, but rather only at trial, and we are unsure whether under state law that testimony came too late to affect the propriety of the admission of the evidence. These matters are best left for resolution on remand.

We do reject, however, the dissent's revisionist legal analysis of the "knowing and voluntary" issue. In determining whether a Sixth Amendment waiver was knowing and voluntary, there is no reason categorically to distinguish an unrepresented defendant from a represented one. It is equally true for each that, as we held in *Patterson*, the *Miranda* warnings adequately inform him "of his right to have counsel present during the questioning," and make him "aware of the consequences of a decision by him to waive his Sixth Amendment rights." Somewhat surprisingly for an opinion that extols the virtues of stare decisis, the dissent complains that our "treatment of the waiver question rests entirely on the dubious decision in *Patterson*." The Court in *Patterson* did not consider the result dubious, nor does the Court today.

* * *

This case is an exemplar of Justice Jackson's oft quoted warning that this Court "is forever adding new stories to the temples of constitutional law, and the temples have a way of collapsing when one story too many is added." Douglas v. City of Jeannette, 319 U.S. 157, 181 (1943) (opinion concurring in result). We today remove Michigan v. Jackson 's fourth story of prophylaxis.

The judgment of the Louisiana Supreme Court is vacated, and the case is remanded for further proceedings not inconsistent with this opinion.

It is so ordered.

[The concurring opinion by Justice ALITO, joined by Justice KENNEDY, is omitted.]

JUSTICE STEVENS, **with whom** JUS-
TICE SOUTER **and** JUSTICE GINSBURG
join, and with whom JUSTICE BREY-
ER **joins, except for footnote 5,
dissenting.***

Today the Court properly concludes that the Louisiana Supreme
Court's parsimonious reading of
our decision in Michigan v. Jackson,
475 U.S. 625 (1986), is indefensible.
Yet the Court does not reverse.
Rather, on its own initiative and
without any evidence that the longstanding Sixth Amendment protections established in *Jackson* have
caused any harm to the workings of
the criminal justice system, the
Court rejects *Jackson* outright on
the ground that it is "untenable as a
theoretical and doctrinal matter."
That conclusion rests on a misinter-
pretation of *Jackson's* rationale and
a gross undervaluation of the rule
of stare decisis. The police interrogation in this case clearly violated
petitioner's Sixth Amendment right
to counsel.

I

* * *

II

* * *

The majority's analysis flagrantly
misrepresents *Jackson's* underlying
rationale and the constitutional interests the decision sought to protect. While it is true that the rule
adopted in *Jackson* was patterned
after the rule in *Edwards*, the *Jackson* opinion does not even mention
the anti-badgering considerations
that provide the basis for the
Court's decision today. Instead,
Jackson relied primarily on cases
discussing the broad protections
guaranteed by the Sixth Amendment right to counsel—not its Fifth

Amendment counterpart. *Jackson*
emphasized that the purpose of the
Sixth Amendment is to "protec[t]
the unaided layman at critical con-
frontations with his adversary "by
giving him "the right to rely on
counsel as a 'medium' between
him[self] and the State." * * *

Once *Jackson* is placed in its
proper Sixth Amendment context,
the majority's justifications for overruling the decision crumble. * * *

Paying lip service to the rule of
stare decisis, the majority acknowledges that the Court must consider
many factors before taking the dramatic step of overruling a past decision. Specifically, the majority focuses on four considerations: the
reasoning of the decision, the workability of the rule, the reliance interests at stake, and the antiquity of
the precedent. The Court exaggerates the considerations favoring reversal, however, and gives short
shrift to the valid considerations favoring retention of the *Jackson*
rule.

* * *

Despite the fact that the rule
established in Jackson remains
relevant, well grounded in constitutional precedent, and easily
administrable, the Court today
rejects it sua sponte. Such a decision can only diminish the
public's confidence in the reliability and fairness of our system
of justice.

III

Even if *Jackson* had never been
decided, it would be clear that Mon-

---

* Editors' Note: Footnote 5 is deleted
here. It involved a tussle among Justice
Alito and Justice Stevens as to whether

another opinion in the term, Arizona v.
Gant (discussed in Chapter 2, *supra*) was
properly decided.

tejo's Sixth Amendment rights were violated. Today's decision eliminates the rule that any waiver of Sixth Amendment rights given in a discussion initiated by police is presumed invalid once a defendant has invoked his right to counsel. Nevertheless, under the undisputed facts of this case, there is no sound basis for concluding that Montejo made a knowing and valid waiver of his Sixth Amendment right to counsel before acquiescing in police interrogation following his 72–hour hearing. Because police questioned Montejo without notice to, and outside the presence of, his lawyer, the interrogation violated Montejo's right to counsel even under pre-*Jackson* precedent.

* * *

The Court avoids confronting the serious Sixth Amendment concerns raised by the police interrogation in this case by assuming that Montejo validly waived his Sixth Amendment rights before submitting to interrogation. It does so by summarily concluding that "doctrines ensuring voluntariness of the Fifth Amendment waiver simultaneously ensure the voluntariness of the Sixth Amendment waiver"; thus, because Montejo was given *Miranda* warnings prior to interrogation, his waiver was presumptively valid. Ironically, while the Court faults *Jackson* for blurring the line between this Court's Fifth and Sixth Amendment jurisprudence, it commits the same error by assuming that the *Miranda* warnings given in this case, designed purely to safeguard the Fifth Amendment right against self-incrimination, were somehow adequate to protect Montejo's more robust Sixth Amendment right to counsel.

The majority's cursory treatment of the waiver question rests entirely on the dubious decision in *Patterson*, in which we addressed whether, by providing *Miranda* warnings, police had adequately advised an indicted but unrepresented defendant of his Sixth Amendment right to counsel. The majority held that "[a]s a general matter ... an accused who is admonished with the warnings prescribed ... in *Miranda*, ... has been sufficiently apprised of the nature of his Sixth Amendment rights, and of the consequences of abandoning those rights." The Court recognized, however, that "because the Sixth Amendment's protection of the attorney-client relationship ... extends beyond *Miranda 's* protection of the Fifth Amendment right to counsel, ... there will be cases where a waiver which would be valid under *Miranda* will not suffice for Sixth Amendment purposes." This is such a case.

As I observed in *Patterson*, the conclusion that *Miranda* warnings ordinarily provide a sufficient basis for a knowing waiver of the right to counsel rests on the questionable assumption that those warnings make clear to defendants the assistance a lawyer can render during post-indictment interrogation. See 487 U.S., at 307 (dissenting opinion). Because *Miranda* warnings do not hint at the ways in which a lawyer might assist her client during conversations with the police, I remain convinced that the warnings prescribed in *Miranda*, while sufficient to apprise a defendant of his Fifth Amendment right to remain silent, are inadequate to inform an unrepresented, indicted defendant of his Sixth Amendment right to have a lawyer present at all critical stages of a criminal prosecution. The inadequacy of those warnings is even more obvious in the case of a represented defendant. While it can be argued that informing an indicted but unrepresented defendant of his right to counsel at least alerts him to the fact that he is entitled to obtain something he does not already possess, providing that same warning to a defendant who has already secured counsel is more likely to confound than enlighten. By glibly assuming that that the Miranda warnings given in this case were sufficient to ensure Montejo's waiver was both knowing and voluntary, the Court conveniently avoids any comment on the actual advice Montejo received, which did not adequately inform him of his relevant Sixth Amendment rights or alert him to the possible consequences of waiving those rights.

* * *

IV

The Court's decision to overrule *Jackson* is unwarranted. Not only does it rests on a flawed doctrinal premise, but the dubious benefits it hopes to achieve are far outweighed by the damage it does to the rule of law and the integrity of the Sixth Amendment right to counsel. Moreover, even apart from the protections afforded by Jackson, the police interrogation in this case violated Jesse Montejo's Sixth Amendment right to counsel.

I respectfully dissent.

[The dissenting opinion of Justice BREYER is omitted.]

Note on the Consequences of the Court's Opinion in Montejo

Note that the result in *Montejo* not only invalidates *Jackson*. It also renders moot two Supreme Court cases decided after *Jackson*. McNeil v. Wisconsin set forth on page 805 of the Text, held that the *Jackson* rule was inapplicable if the interrogation was about a crime other than that with which the defendant was charged. And *Texas v. Cobb*, set forth on page 806 of the Text, employed a complicated analysis to determine which crimes are the same offense as the crime charged, interrogation on which would violate the *Jackson* rule. Neither of these cases are of any further practical effect—they both delineated a "different offense" exception to the *Jackson* rule, that had permitted interrogation of a charged suspect in the absence of initiation by the suspect, when the interrogation was on a new offense. But now that the *Jackson* rule itself is gone, the exception is no longer necessary—officers can now reinterrogate on the *same* offense on which the defendant is charged, so long as they obtain a knowing and voluntary waiver.

Chapter Eight

DISCOVERY

IV. THE PROSECUTOR'S CONSTITUTIONAL DUTY TO DISCLOSE

Page 1018. At the end of section 4, add the following new subpart D:

D. DOES THE *BRADY* DUTY EXTEND TO POST–TRIAL PROCEEDINGS?

DNA testing has been used in many cases to exonerate wrongfully convicted defendants. In District Attorney's Office for the Third Judicial District v. Osborne, 129 S.Ct. 2308 (2009), a convicted defendant argued that he had a constitutional right to DNA testing that he claimed would exonerate him. The state had in fact conducted a rudimentary form of DNA testing before the trial; that test tended to include Osborne as a possible perpetrator in a sex crime, but it was not definitive. Osborne's counsel decided not to ask for a more sophisticated test to be done, fearing that it would further incriminate Osborne. Osborne was convicted and several years later brought a civil rights action against the state, alleging that he had a due process right to an even more sophisticated DNA test than was available at the time of his trial.

In a 5–4 opinion, the Court held that convicted defendants have no freestanding due process right to DNA testing. Chief Justice Roberts, writing for the majority, declared as follows:

> DNA testing has an unparalleled ability both to exonerate the wrongly convicted and to identify the guilty. It has the potential to significantly improve both the criminal justice system and police investigative practices. The Federal Government and the States have recognized this, and have developed special approaches to ensure that this evidentiary tool can be effectively incorporated into established criminal procedure—usually but not always through legislation.

> Against this prompt and considered response, the respondent, William Osborne, proposes a different approach: the recognition of a

freestanding and far-reaching constitutional right of access to this new type of evidence. The nature of what he seeks is confirmed by his decision to file this lawsuit in federal court under 42 U. S. C. § 1983, not within the state criminal justice system. This approach would take the development of rules and procedures in this area out of the hands of legislatures and state courts shaping policy in a focused manner and turn it over to federal courts applying the broad parameters of the Due Process Clause. There is no reason to constitutionalize the issue in this way. Because the decision below would do just that, we reverse.

The lower court, in granting Osborne's demand for DNA testing, had relied on *Brady*. It reasoned that if the defendant had a constitutional right to exculpatory evidence before trial, he also had the right after conviction. Chief Justice Roberts rejected this reasoning in the following passage:

> The Court of Appeals went too far * * * in concluding that the Due Process Clause requires that certain familiar preconviction trial rights be extended to protect Osborne's postconviction liberty interest. After identifying Osborne's possible liberty interests, the court concluded that the State had an obligation to comply with the principles of Brady v. Maryland. In that case, we held that due process requires a prosecutor to disclose material exculpatory evidence to the defendant before trial. * * *

> A defendant proved guilty after a fair trial does not have the same liberty interests as a free man. At trial, the defendant is presumed innocent and may demand that the government prove its case beyond reasonable doubt. But once a defendant has been afforded a fair trial and convicted of the offense for which he was charged, the presumption of innocence disappears. * * *

> The State accordingly has more flexibility in deciding what procedures are needed in the context of postconviction relief. "[W]hen a State chooses to offer help to those seeking relief from convictions," due process does not "dictat[e] the exact form such assistance must assume." Pennsylvania v. Finley, 481 U.S. 551, 559 (1987). Osborne's right to due process is not parallel to a trial right, but rather must be analyzed in light of the fact that he has already been found guilty at a fair trial, and has only a limited interest in postconviction relief. *Brady* is the wrong framework.

> Instead, the question is whether consideration of Osborne's claim within the framework of the State's procedures for postconviction relief "offends some principle of justice so rooted in the traditions and conscience of our people as to be ranked as fundamental," or "transgresses any recognized principle of fundamental fairness in operation." Federal courts may upset a State's postconviction relief procedures only if they are fundamentally inadequate to vindicate the substantive rights provided.

Chief Justice Roberts reviewed the state post-conviction procedures and saw "nothing inadequate about the procedures Alaska has provided to vindicate its state right to postconviction relief in general, and nothing inadequate about how those procedures apply to those who seek access to DNA evidence." Accordingly, the Court denied Osborne federal relief.

Justice Alito filed a concurring opinion in which Justice Kennedy, joined, and in which Justice Thomas joined in part. He argued that it would be inappropriate to allow Osborne to forego testing at trial and then to request a different test many years later. In Justice Alito's view, this would "allow prisoners to play games with the criminal justice system" because "with nothing to lose, the defendant could demand DNA testing in the hope that some happy accident—for example, degradation or contamination of the evidence—would provide the basis for postconviction relief."

Justice Stevens filed a dissenting opinion, joined by Justices Ginsburg and Breyer and by Justice Souter in part. Justice Stevens noted that no prisoner had ever obtained DNA evidence for testing in Alaska and that he had "grave doubts about the adequacy of the procedural protections" in state law. He noted that DNA testing in this case would cost the state nothing because Osborne had offered to pay for it. Justice Souter also filed a dissenting opinion, concluding that state officials had "demonstrated a combination of inattentiveness and intransigence that add up to "procedural unfairness that violates the due process clause.".

Chapter Ten

TRIAL AND TRIAL–RELATED RIGHTS

I. THE RIGHT TO A SPEEDY TRIAL

C. ASSESSING SPEEDY TRIAL CLAIMS

Page 1102. Add at the end of the section.

Delay Caused By Appointed Counsel Is Not Attributable to the State: Vermont v. Brillon

The *Barker* test for assessing whether the right to speedy trial is violated focuses in part on "the reason for delay." A speedy trial violation cannot be found unless the delay can be attributed to the state. What happens if the delay is attributable to defense counsel who was *appointed* by the state? In Vermont v. Brillon, 129 S.Ct. 1283 (2009), the lower court found a speedy trial violation by attributing to the state the delays caused by the failure of Brillon's appointed counsel "to move his case forward." But the Supreme Court, in an opinion by Justice Ginsburg, held that "an assigned counsel's failure to move the case forward does not warrant attribution of delay to the state." While the Vermont Defender's office is funded by the State, Justice Ginsburg declared that "the individual counsel here acted only on behalf of Brillon, not the State." Justice Ginsburg noted the problems that would arise if delay by appointed counsel could be considered delay by the state:

A contrary conclusion could encourage appointed counsel to delay proceedings by seeking unreasonable continuances, hoping thereby to obtain a dismissal of the indictment on speedy-trial grounds. Trial courts might well respond by viewing continuance requests made by appointed counsel with skepticism, concerned that even an apparently genuine need for more time is in reality a delay tactic. Yet the same considerations would not attend a privately retained counsel's requests for time extensions. We see no justification for treating defendants' speedy-trial claims differently based on whether their counsel is privately retained or publicly assigned.

105

Justice Ginsburg noted that "the general rule attributing to the defendant delay caused by assigned counsel is not absolute." Specifically, delay resulting from a "systemic breakdown in the public defender system" could be charged to the State. But Justice Ginsburg found "nothing in the record suggests, that institutional problems caused any part of the delay in Brillon's case."

Justice Breyer, joined by Justice Stevens, wrote a short dissent, arguing that the writ of certiorari should have been dismissed as improvidently granted.

III. CONSTITUTIONALLY BASED PROOF REQUIREMENTS

C. THE SCOPE OF THE REASONABLE DOUBT REQUIREMENT: WHAT IS AN ELEMENT OF THE CRIME?

2. *Element of the Crime or a Sentencing Factor?*

Page 1148. Add at the bottom of the page:

State Sentencing Scheme Found Mandatory, Not Advisory: Cunningham v. California

What follows is another venture into the *Apprendi* line of cases. The Court strikes down the California sentencing system insofar as it requires a trial judge to impose a sentence in a higher sentencing range on the basis of facts found by the judge. Do you agree with Judge Alito that the California system is not meaningfully different from the federal system as the Court left it in *Booker*?

CUNNINGHAM v. CALIFORNIA

Supreme Court of the United States, 2007.
549 U.S. 270.

JUSTICE GINSBURG **delivered the opinion of the Court.**

California's determinate sentencing law (DSL) assigns to the trial judge, not to the jury, authority to find the facts that expose a defendant to an elevated "upper term" sentence. The facts so found are neither inherent in the jury's verdict nor embraced by the defendant's plea, and they need only be established by a preponderance of the evidence, not beyond a reasonable doubt. The question presented is whether the DSL, by placing sentence-elevating factfinding within the judge's province, violates a defendant's right to trial by jury safeguarded by the Sixth and Fourteenth Amendments. We hold that it does.

As this Court's decisions instruct, the Federal Constitution's jury-trial guarantee proscribes a sentencing scheme that allows a judge to impose a sentence above the statutory maximum based on a fact, other than a prior conviction, not found by a jury or admitted by the defendant. Apprendi v. New Jersey, 530 U.S. 466 (2000); Ring v. Arizona, 536 U.S. 584 (2002); Blakely v. Washington, 542 U.S. 296 (2004); United States v. Booker, 543 U.S. 220 (2005). "The relevant statutory maximum," this Court has clarified, "is not the maximum sentence a judge may impose after finding additional facts, but the maximum he may impose *without* any additional findings." *Blakely*, 542 U.S., at 303–304 (emphasis in original). In petitioner's case, the jury's verdict alone limited the permissible sentence to 12 years. Additional factfinding by the trial judge, however, yielded an upper term sentence of 16 years. The California Court of Appeal affirmed the harsher sentence. We reverse that disposition because the four-year elevation based on judicial factfinding denied petitioner his right to a jury trial.

I

A

Petitioner John Cunningham was tried and convicted of continuous sexual abuse of a child under the age of 14. Under the DSL, that offense is punishable by imprisonment for a lower term sentence of 6 years, a middle term sentence of 12 years, or an upper term sentence of 16 years. Cal. Penal Code Ann. § 288.5(a) (West 1999) (hereinafter Penal Code). As further explained below, the DSL obliged the trial judge to sentence Cunningham to the 12–year middle term unless the judge found one or more additional facts in aggravation. Based on a post-trial sentencing hearing, the trial judge found by a preponder-

ance of the evidence six aggravating circumstances, among them, the particular vulnerability of Cunningham's victim, and Cunningham's violent conduct, which indicated a serious danger to the community. In mitigation, the judge found one fact: Cunningham had no record of prior criminal conduct. Concluding that the aggravators outweighed the sole mitigator, the judge sentenced Cunningham to the upper term of 16 years.

A panel of the California Court of Appeal affirmed the conviction and sentence; one judge dissented in part, urging that this Court's precedent precluded the judge-determined four-year increase in Cunningham's sentence. The California Supreme Court denied review. In a reasoned decision published nine days earlier, that court considered the question here presented and held that the DSL survived Sixth Amendment inspection. People v. Black, 35 Cal. 4th 1238, 29 Cal. Rptr. 3d 740, 113 P. 3d 534 (2005).

B

Enacted in 1977, the DSL replaced an indeterminate sentencing regime in force in California for some 60 years. Under the prior regime, courts imposed open-ended prison terms (often one year to life), and the parole board—the Adult Authority—determined the amount of time a felon would ultimately spend in prison. In contrast, the DSL fixed the terms of imprisonment for most offenses, and eliminated the possibility of early release on parole. Through the DSL, California's lawmakers aimed to promote uniform and proportionate punishment.

For most offenses, including Cunningham's, the DSL regime is implemented in the following manner. The statute defining the offense prescribes three precise terms of imprisonment—a lower, middle, and upper term sentence. *E.g.*, Penal Code § 288.5(a) (a person convicted of continuous sexual abuse of a child "shall be punished by imprisonment in the state prison for a term of 6, 12, or 16 years"). Penal Code § 1170(b) controls the trial judge's choice; it provides that "the court shall order imposition of the middle term, unless there are circumstances in aggravation or mitigation of the crime." "Circumstances in aggravation or mitigation" are to be determined by the court after consideration of several items: the trial record; the probation officer's report; statements in aggravation or mitigation submitted by the parties, the victim, or the victim's family; "and any further evidence introduced at the sentencing hearing."

The DSL directed the State's Judicial Council to adopt Rules guiding the sentencing judge's decision whether to "impose the lower or upper prison term." Penal Code § 1170.3(a)(2). Restating § 1170(b), the Council's Rules provide that "the middle term shall be selected unless imposition of the upper or lower term is justified by circumstances in aggravation or mitigation." Rule 4.420(a). "Circumstances in aggravation," as crisply defined by the Judicial Council, means "*facts* which justify the imposition of the upper prison term." Rule 4.405(d) (emphasis added). Facts aggravating an offense, the Rules instruct, "shall be established by a preponderance of the evi-

dence," Rule 4.420(b), and must be "stated orally on the record." Rule 4.420(e).

The Rules provide a nonexhaustive list of aggravating circumstances, including "facts relating to the crime," Rule 4.421(a), "facts relating to the defendant," Rule 4.421(b), and "any other facts statutorily declared to be circumstances in aggravation," Rule 4.421(c). Beyond the enumerated circumstances, "the judge is free to consider any additional criteria reasonably related to the decision being made." "A fact that is an element of the crime," however, "shall not be used to impose the upper term." Rule 4.420(d). In sum, California's DSL, and the rules governing its application, direct the sentencing court to start with the middle term, and to move from that term only when the court itself finds and places on the record facts—whether related to the offense or the offender—beyond the elements of the charged offense.

Justice Alito maintains, however, that a circumstance in aggravation need not be a fact at all. In his view, a policy judgment, or even a judge's "subjective belief" regarding the appropriate sentence, qualifies as an aggravating circumstance. California's Rules, however, constantly refer to "facts." As just noted, the Rules define "circumstances in aggravation" as "*facts* which justify the imposition of the upper prison term." Rule 4.405(d) (emphasis added). And "circumstances in aggravation," the Rules unambiguously declare, "shall be established by a preponderance of the evidence," Rule 4.420(b), a clear factfinding directive to which there is no exception.

* * *

In line with the Rules, the California Supreme Court has repeatedly referred to circumstances in aggravation as facts. * * *

It is unsurprising, then, that State's counsel, at oral argument, acknowledged that he knew of no case in which a California trial judge had gone beyond the middle term based not on any fact the judge found, but solely on the basis of a policy judgment or subjective belief.

Notably, the Penal Code permits elevation of a sentence above the upper term based on specified statutory enhancements relating to the defendant's criminal history or circumstances of the crime. Unlike aggravating circumstances, statutory enhancements must be charged in the indictment, and the underlying facts must be proved to the jury beyond a reasonable doubt. Penal Code § 1170.1(e). A fact underlying an enhancement cannot do double duty; it cannot be used to impose an upper term sentence and, on top of that, an enhanced term. Penal Code § 1170(b). Where permitted by statute, however, a judge may use a fact qualifying as an enhancer to impose an upper term rather than an enhanced sentence. *Ibid.*; Rule 4.420(c).

II

This Court has repeatedly held that, under the Sixth Amendment, any fact that exposes a defendant to a greater potential sentence must be found by a jury, not a judge, and established beyond a reasonable doubt, not merely by a preponderance of the evidence. * * *

[Justice Ginsburg summarizes *Apprendi*.]

We have since reaffirmed the rule of *Apprendi*, applying it to facts subjecting a defendant to the death penalty, Ring v. Arizona, 536 U.S. 584 (2002), facts permitting a sentence in excess of the "standard range" under Washington's Sentencing Reform Act, Blakely v. Washington, 542 U.S. 296 (2004), and facts triggering a sentence range elevation under the then-mandatory Federal Sentencing Guidelines, United States v. Booker, 543 U.S. 220 (2005). *Blakely* and *Booker* bear most closely on the question presented in this case.

[Justice Ginsburg summarizes *Blakely* and *Booker*.]

We turn now to the instant case in light of both parts of the Court's *Booker* opinion, and our earlier decisions in point.

III

Under California's DSL, an upper term sentence may be imposed only when the trial judge finds an aggravating circumstance. An element of the charged offense, essential to a jury's determination of guilt, or admitted in a defendant's guilty plea, does not qualify as such a circumstance. Instead, aggravating circumstances depend on facts found discretely and solely by the judge. In accord with *Blakely*, therefore, the middle term prescribed in California's statutes, not the upper term, is the relevant statutory maximum. Because circumstances in aggravation are found by the judge, not the jury, and need only be established by a preponderance of the evidence, not beyond a reasonable doubt, the DSL violates *Apprendi*'s bright-line rule: Except for a prior conviction, "any fact that increases the penalty for a crime beyond the prescribed statutory maximum must be submitted to a jury, and proved beyond a reasonable doubt."

While "that should be the end of the matter," in People v. *Black*, the California Supreme Court held otherwise. In that court's view, the DSL survived examination under our precedent intact. The *Black* court acknowledged that California's system appears on surface inspection to be in tension with the rule of *Apprendi*. But in "operation and effect," the court said, the DSL "simply authorizes a sentencing court to engage in the type of factfinding that traditionally has been incident to the judge's selection of an appropriate sentence within a statutorily prescribed sentencing range." Therefore, the court concluded, "the upper term is the statutory maximum and a trial court's imposition of an upper term sentence does not violate a defendant's right to a jury trial under the principles set forth in *Apprendi*, *Blakely*, and *Booker*." * * *

The *Black* court's conclusion that the upper term, and not the middle term, qualifies as the relevant statutory maximum, rested on several considerations. First, the court reasoned that, given the ample discretion afforded trial judges to identify aggravating facts warranting an upper term sentence, the DSL

"does not represent a legislative effort to shift the proof of particular facts from elements of a crime (to be proved to a jury) to sentencing factors (to be decided by a judge).... Instead, it afforded

the sentencing judge the discretion to decide, with the guidance of rules and statutes, whether the facts of the case and the history of the defendant justify the higher sentence. Such a system does not diminish the traditional power of the jury."

We cautioned in *Blakely*, however, that broad discretion to decide what facts may support an enhanced sentence, or to determine whether an enhanced sentence is warranted in any particular case, does not shield a sentencing system from the force of our decisions. If the jury's verdict alone does not authorize the sentence, if, instead, the judge must find an additional fact to impose the longer term, the Sixth Amendment requirement is not satisfied.

The *Black* court also urged that the DSL is not cause for concern because it reduced the penalties for most crimes over the prior indeterminate sentencing regime. Furthermore, California's system is not unfair to defendants, for they "cannot reasonably expect a guarantee that the upper term will not be imposed" given judges' broad discretion to impose an upper term sentence or to keep their punishment at the middle term. The *Black* court additionally noted that the DSL requires statutory enhancements (as distinguished from aggravators)— *e.g.*, the use of a firearm or other dangerous weapon, infliction of great bodily injury—to be charged in the indictment and proved to a jury beyond a reasonable doubt.

The *Black* court's examination of the DSL, in short, satisfied it that California's sentencing system does not implicate significantly the concerns underlying the Sixth Amendment's jury-trial guarantee. Our decisions, however, leave no room for such an examination. Asking whether a defendant's basic jury-trial right is preserved, though some facts essential to punishment are reserved for determination by the judge, we have said, is the *very* inquiry *Apprendi*'s "bright-line rule" was designed to exclude.

Ultimately, the *Black* court relied on an equation of California's DSL system to the post-*Booker* federal system. "The level of discretion available to a California judge in selecting which of the three available terms to impose," the court said, "appears comparable to the level of discretion that the high court has chosen to permit federal judges in post-*Booker* sentencing." The same equation drives Justice Alito's dissent.

The attempted comparison is unavailing. * * * [T]his Court in *Booker* held the Federal Sentencing Guidelines incompatible with the Sixth Amendment because the Guidelines were "mandatory and imposed binding requirements on all sentencing judges." "Merely advisory provisions," recommending but not requiring "the selection of particular sentences in response to differing sets of facts," all Members of the Court agreed, "would not implicate the Sixth Amendment." To remedy the constitutional infirmity found in *Booker*, the Court's majority excised provisions that rendered the system mandatory, leaving the Guidelines in place as advisory only.

California's DSL does not resemble the advisory system the *Booker* Court had in view. Under California's system, judges are not free to exercise their "discretion to select a specific sentence within a defined range." California's Legislature has adopted sentencing triads, three fixed sentences with no ranges between them. Cunningham's sentencing judge had no discretion to select a sentence within a range of 6 to 16 years. His instruction was to select 12 years, nothing less and nothing more, unless he found facts allowing the imposition of a sentence of 6 or 16 years. Factfinding to elevate a sentence from 12 to 16 years, our decisions make plain, falls within the province of the jury employing a beyond-a-reasonable-doubt standard, not the bailiwick of a judge determining where the preponderance of the evidence lies.

Nevertheless, the *Black* court attempted to rescue the DSL's judicial factfinding authority by typing it simply a reasonableness constraint, equivalent to the constraint operative in the federal system post-*Booker*. ("Because an aggravating factor under California law may include any factor that the judge reasonably deems relevant, the [DSL's] requirement that an upper term sentence be imposed only if an aggravating factor exists is comparable to *Booker*'s requirement that a federal judge's sentencing decision not be unreasonable."). Reasonableness, however, is not, as the *Black* court would have it, the touchstone of Sixth Amendment analysis. The reasonableness requirement *Booker* anticipated for the federal system operates *within* the Sixth Amendment constraints delineated in our precedent, not as a substitute for those constraints. Because the DSL allocates to judges sole authority to find facts permitting the imposition of an upper term sentence, the system violates the Sixth Amendment. It is comforting, but beside the point, that California's system requires judge-determined DSL sentences to be reasonable. *Booker*'s remedy for the Federal Guidelines, in short, is not a recipe for rendering our Sixth Amendment case law toothless.

To summarize: Contrary to the *Black* court's holding, our decisions from *Apprendi* to *Booker* point to the middle term specified in California's statutes, not the upper term, as the relevant statutory maximum. Because the DSL authorizes the judge, not the jury, to find the facts permitting an upper term sentence, the system cannot withstand measurement against our Sixth Amendment precedent.

IV

As to the adjustment of California's sentencing system in light of our decision, "the ball ... lies in [California's] court." We note that several States have modified their systems in the wake of *Apprendi* and *Blakely* to retain determinate sentencing. They have done so by calling upon the jury—either at trial or in a separate sentencing proceeding—to find any fact necessary to the imposition of an elevated sentence. As earlier noted, California already employs juries in this manner to determine statutory sentencing enhancements. Other States have chosen to permit judges genuinely to exercise broad discretion within a statutory range, which everyone agrees encounters no Sixth Amendment shoal. California may follow the paths taken by its sister States or otherwise alter its system, so long as the State observes Sixth Amendment limitations declared in this Court's decisions.

* * *

For the reasons stated, the judgment of the California Court of Appeal is reversed in part, and the case is remanded for further proceedings not inconsistent with this opinion.

JUSTICE KENNEDY, with whom JUSTICE BREYER joins, dissenting.

The dissenting opinion by Justice Alito, which I join in full, well explains why the Court continues in a wrong and unfortunate direction in the cases following Apprendi v. New Jersey. * * * The discussion in his dissenting opinion is fully sufficient to show why, in my respectful view, the Court's analysis and holding are mistaken. It does seem appropriate to add this brief, further comment.

In my view the *Apprendi* line of cases remains incorrect. Yet there may be a principled rationale permitting those cases to control within the central sphere of their concern, while reducing the collateral, widespread harm to the criminal justice system and the corrections process now resulting from the Court's wooden, unyielding insistence on expanding the *Apprendi* doctrine far beyond its necessary boundaries. The Court could distinguish between sentencing enhancements based on the nature of the offense, where the *Apprendi* principle would apply, and sentencing enhancements based on the nature of the offender, where it would not. California attempted to make this initial distinction. Compare Cal. Rule of Court 4.421(a) (Criminal Cases) (listing aggravating "facts relating to the crime"), with Rule

4.421(b) (listing aggravating "facts relating to the defendant"). The Court should not foreclose its efforts.

California, as the Court notes, experimented earlier with an indeterminate sentencing system. The State reposed vast power and discretion in a nonjudicial agency to set a release date for convicted felons. That system, it seems, would have been untouched by *Apprendi*. When the State sought to reform its system, it might have chosen to give its judges the authority to sentence to a maximum but to depart downward for unexplained reasons. That too, by considerable irony, would be untouched by *Apprendi*. Instead, California sought to use a system based on guided discretion. *Apprendi*, the Court holds today, forecloses this option.

As dissenting opinions have suggested before, the Constitution ought not to be interpreted to strike down all aspects of sentencing systems that grant judicial discretion with some legislative direction and control. Judges and legislators must have the capacity to develop consistent standards, standards that individual juries empaneled for only a short time cannot elaborate in any permanent way. * * * Judges and sentencing officials have a broad view and long-term commitment to correctional systems. Juries do not. Judicial officers and corrections professionals, under the guidance and control of the legislature, should be encouraged to participate in an ongoing manner to improve the various sentencing schemes in our country.

This system of guided discretion would be permitted to a large extent if the Court confined the *Apprendi* rule to sentencing enhancements based on the nature of the offense. These would include, for example, the fact that a weapon was used; violence was employed; a stated amount of drugs or other contraband was involved; or the crime was motivated by the victim's race, gender, or other status protected by statute. Juries could consider these matters without serious disruption because these factors often are part of the statutory definition of an aggravated crime in any event and because the evidence to support these enhancements is likely to be a central part of the prosecution's case.

On the other hand, judicial determination is appropriate with regard to factors exhibited by the defendant. These would include, for example, prior convictions; cooperation or noncooperation with law enforcement; remorse or the lack of it; or other aspects of the defendant's history bearing upon his background and contribution to the community. This is so even if the relevant facts were to be found by the judge by a preponderance of the evidence. These are facts that should be taken into account at sentencing but have little if any significance for whether the defendant committed the crime. See Berman & Bibas, *Making Sentencing Sensible,* 4 Ohio St. J. Crim. L. 37, 55–57 (2006).

The line between offense and offender would not always be clear, but in most instances the nature of the offense is defined in a manner that ensures the problem of categories would not be difficult. *Apprendi* suffers from a similar line-drawing problem between facts that must be considered by the jury and other considerations that a judge can take into account. The main part of the *Apprendi* holding could be retained with far less systemic disruption. It is to be regretted that the Court's decision today appears to foreclose consideration of this approach or other reasonable efforts to develop systems of guided discretion within the general constraint that *Apprendi* imposes.

———

JUSTICE ALITO, with whom JUSTICE KENNEDY and JUSTICE BREYER join, dissenting.

The California sentencing law that the Court strikes down today is indistinguishable in any constitutionally significant respect from the advisory Guidelines scheme that the Court approved in United States v. Booker. Both sentencing schemes grant trial judges considerable discretion in sentencing; both subject the exercise of that discretion to appellate review for "reasonableness"; and both—the California law explicitly, and the federal scheme implicitly—require a sentencing judge to find some factor to justify a sentence above the minimum that could be imposed based solely on the jury's verdict. Because this Court has held unequivocally that the post-*Booker* federal sentencing system satisfies the requirements of the Sixth Amendment, the same should be true with regard to the California system. I therefore respectfully dissent.

I

In Apprendi v. New Jersey and the cases that have followed in its wake, the Court has held that under certain circumstances a criminal defendant possesses the Sixth Amendment right to have a jury find facts that result in an increased sentence. The Court, however, has never suggested that all factual findings that affect a defendant's sentence must be made by a jury. On the contrary, in *Apprendi* and later cases, the Court has consistently stated that when a trial court makes a fully discretionary sentencing decision (such as a sentencing decision under the pre-Sentencing Reform Act of 1984 federal sentencing system), the Sixth Amendment permits the court to base the sentence on its own factual findings.[1]

Applying this rule, the *Booker* Court unanimously agreed that judicial factfinding under a purely advisory guidelines system would likewise comport with the Sixth Amendment. * * *

* * *

———

1. The Court's recognition of this is hardly surprising since, as Judge McConnell has pointed out, "fully discretionary sentencing ... was the system [that was] in place when the Sixth Amendment was adopted" and that "prevailed in the federal courts from the Founding until enactment of the Sentencing Reform Act of 1984 ... without anyone ever suggesting a conflict with the Sixth Amendment." McConnell, The *Booker* Mess, 83 Denver U. L. Rev. 665, 679 (2006). Indeed, the original federal criminal statute enacted by the First Congress set forth indeterminate sentencing ranges for a variety of offenses, leaving the determination of the precise sentence to the judge's discretion. *See, e.g.,* Act of Apr. 30, 1790, ch. 9, § 2, 1 Stat. 112 (crime of misprision of treason punishable by imprisonment not exceeding seven years and fine not exceeding $1,000); § 6, *id.,* at 113 (crime of misprision of a felony punishable by imprisonment not exceeding three years and fine not exceeding $500); § 15, *id.,* at 115–116 (crime of falsifying federal records punishable by imprisonment not exceeding seven years, fine not exceeding $5,000, and whipping not exceeding 39 stripes).

In a similar vein, the remedial portion of the Court's opinion in *Booker*, written by Justice Breyer, held that the Sixth Amendment permits a system of advisory guidelines with reasonableness review.[3] Justice Breyer's opinion avoided a blanket invalidation of the Guidelines by excising the provision of the Sentencing Reform Act, 18 U.S.C. § 3553(b)(1), that required a sentencing judge to impose a sentence within the applicable Guidelines range. As Justice Breyer explained, "the existence of § 3553(b)(1) is a necessary condition of the constitutional violation. That is to say, without this provision . . . the statute falls outside the scope of *Apprendi*'s requirement."

Under the post-*Booker* federal sentencing system, "the district courts, while not bound to apply the Guidelines, must consult those Guidelines and take them into account when sentencing." In addition, sentencing courts must take account of the general sentencing goals set forth by Congress, including avoiding unwarranted sentencing disparities, providing restitution to victims, reflecting the seriousness of the offense, promoting respect for the law, providing just punishment, affording adequate deterrence, protecting the public, and effectively providing the defendant with needed educational or vocational training and medical care.

It is significant that *Booker*, while rendering the Guidelines advisory, did not reinstitute the pre-Guidelines federal sentencing system, under which "well-established doctrine barred review of the exercise of sentencing discretion" within the broad sentencing ranges imposed by the criminal statutes. Rather, *Booker* conditioned a district court's sentencing discretion on appellate review for "reasonableness" in light of the Guidelines and the § 3553(a) factors. * * *

Although the *Booker* Court did not spell out in detail how sentencing judges are to proceed under the new advisory Guidelines regime, it seems clear that this regime permits—and, indeed, requires—sentencing judges to make factual findings and to base their sentences on those findings. The federal criminal statutes generally set out wide sentencing ranges, and thus in each case a sentencing judge must use some criteria in selecting the sentence to be imposed. In doing this, federal judges have generally made and relied upon factual determinations about the nature of the offense and the offender—and it is impossible to imagine how federal judges could reasonably carry out their sentencing responsibilities without making such factual determinations.

Under the mandatory Federal Sentencing Guidelines regime, these factual determinations were relatively formal and precise. (For example, a trial judge under that regime might have found based on a post-trial proceeding that a drug

---

3. While the dissenters from the remedial portion of the Court's opinion disagreed with Justice Breyer's severability analysis, they did not suggest that the resulting "advisory Guidelines" structure was unconstitutional. Rather, they recognized—as Justice Stevens explained in his portion of the Court's opinion—that "if the Guidelines as currently written could be read as merely advisory provisions that recommended, rather than required, the selection of particular sentences in response to differing sets of facts, their use would not implicate the Sixth Amendment."

offense involved six kilograms of cocaine or that the loss caused by a mail fraud offense was $2.5 million.) By contrast, under the pre-Sentencing Reform Act federal system, the factual determinations were often relatively informal and imprecise. (A trial judge might have concluded from the presentence report that an offense involved "a large quantity of drugs" or that a mail fraud scheme caused "a great loss.") Under both systems, however, the judges made factual determinations about the nature of the offense and the offender and determined the sentence accordingly. And as the Courts of Appeals have unanimously concluded, the post-*Booker* federal sentencing regime also permits trial judges to make such factual findings and to rely on those findings in selecting the sentences that are appropriate in particular cases.[4]

* * * As noted, the post-*Booker* system permits a defendant to obtain appellate review of the reasonableness of a sentence, and a sentence that the sentencing court justifies solely on the basis of an erroneous finding of fact can hardly be regarded as reasonable. Thus, under the post-*Booker* system, there will be cases—and, in all likelihood, a good many cases—in which the question whether a defendant will be required to serve a greater or lesser sentence depends on whether a court of appeals sustains a finding of fact made by the sentencing judge.

A simple example illustrates this point. Suppose that a defendant is found guilty of 10 counts of mail fraud in that the defendant made 10 mailings in furtherance of a scheme to defraud. *See* 18 U.S.C. § 1341. Under the mail fraud statute, the district court would have discretion to sentence the defendant to any sentence ranging from probation up to 50 years of imprisonment (5 years on each count). Suppose that the sentencing judge imposes the maximum sentence allowed by statute—50 years of imprisonment—without identifying a single fact about the offense or the offender as a justification for this lengthy sentence. Surely that would be an unreasonable sentence that could not be sustained on appeal.

Suppose, alternatively, that the sentencing court finds that the mail fraud scheme caused a loss of $1 million and that the victims were elderly people of limited means, and suppose that the court, based on these findings, imposes a sentence of 10 years of imprisonment. If the defendant challenges the sentence on appeal on the ground that these findings are erroneous, the question whether the defendant will be required to serve 10 years or some lesser sentence may well de-

---

4. Every Court of Appeals to address the issue has held that a district court sentencing post-*Booker* may rely on facts found by the judge by a preponderance of the evidence. *See* United States v. Kilby, 443 F.3d 1135, 1141 (CA9 2006); United States v. Cooper, 437 F.3d 324, 330 (CA3 2006); United States v. Vaughn, 430 F.3d 518, 525–526 (CA2 2005); United States v. Morris, 429 F.3d 65, 72 (CA4 2005); United States v. Price, 418 F.3d 771, 788 (CA7 2005); United States v. Magallanez, 408 F.3d 672, 684–685 (CA10 2005); United States v. Pirani, 406 F.3d 543, 551, n. 4 (CA8 2005) (en banc); United States v. Yagar, 404 F.3d 967, 972 (CA6 2005); United States v. Mares, 402 F.3d 511, 519, and n. 6 (CA5 2005); United States v. Duncan, 400 F.3d 1297, 1304–1305 (CA11 2005); United States v. Antonakopoulos, 399 F.3d 68, 74 (CA1 2005).

pend on the validity of the district court's findings of fact.

Booker, then, approved a sentencing system that (1) requires a sentencing judge to "consult" and "take into account" legislatively defined sentencing factors and guidelines; (2) subjects a sentencing judge's exercise of sentencing discretion to appellate review for "reasonableness"; and (3) requires sentencing judges to make factual findings in order to support the exercise of this discretion.

II

The California sentencing law that the Court strikes down today is not meaningfully different from the federal scheme upheld in *Booker*.

As an initial matter, the California law gives a judge at least as much sentencing discretion as does the post-*Booker* federal scheme. California's system of sentencing triads and separate "enhancements"[5] was enacted to achieve sentences "in proportion to the seriousness of the offense as determined by the Legislature to be imposed by the court with specified discretion." Cal. Penal Code Ann. § 1170(a)(1). This "specified discretion" is quite broad. Under the statute, a sentencing court "shall order imposition of the middle term" of the base-term triad, "unless there are circumstances in aggravation or mitigation of the crime." § 1170(b). While the court may not rely on any fact that is an essential element of the crime

or of a proven enhancement, the "sentencing judge retains considerable discretion to identify aggravating factors." People v. Black, 35 Cal. 4th 1238, 1247, 29 Cal. Rptr. 3d 740, 113 P. 3d 534, 538 (2005).

In exercising its sentencing discretion, a California court can look to any of the 16 specific aggravating circumstances, see Cal. Rule of Court (Criminal Cases) 4.421, or 15 specific mitigating circumstances, *see* Rule 4.423, itemized in the California Rules of Court. A California trial court can also consider the "general objectives of sentencing," including protecting society, punishing the defendant, encouraging the defendant to lead a law-abiding life and deterring the defendant from committing future offenses, deterring others from criminal conduct by demonstrating its consequences, preventing the defendant from committing new crimes by means of incarceration, securing restitution for crime victims, and achieving uniformity in sentencing.[6] Rule 4.410(a). And if a California trial court finds that its sentencing authority is unduly restricted by these factors, which the California Supreme Court has recognized "are largely the articulation of considerations sentencing judges have always used in making these decisions," a California sentencing judge is also authorized to consider any "additional criteria reasonably related to the decision being made." Rule 4.408(a).

---

5. These enhancements, which add additional years onto the base-triad term selected by the court, must be pleaded and proved to a jury beyond a reasonable doubt. They are not at issue in this case.

6. These factors are similar to the federal sentencing policies set forth in 18 U.S.C.

§ 3553(a) (2000 ed. and Supp. IV), which directs a court to consider, among other things, the need to promote respect for the law, to provide just punishment for the offense, to afford adequate deterrence to criminal conduct and to protect the public.

In short, under California law, the "circumstances the sentencing judge may look to in aggravation or in mitigation of the crime include . . . practically everything which has a legitimate bearing on the matter in issue." * * * Indeed, as one California court has explained, sentencing discretion may even be guided by a "judge's subjective determination of . . . the appropriate aggregate sentence" based on his "experiences with prior cases and the record in the defendant's case." "A judge's subjective belief regarding the length of the sentence to be imposed is not improper as long as it is channeled by the guided discretion outlined in the myriad of statutory sentencing criteria."

The California scheme—like the federal "advisory Guidelines"—does require that this discretion be exercised *reasonably*. Indeed, the California Supreme Court, authoritatively construing the California statute, has explained that § 1170(b)'s "requirement that an aggravating factor exist is merely a requirement that the decision to impose the upper term be *reasonable*." * * * Even when a court imposes the "presumptive" middle term, its decision is reviewable for abuse of discretion—that is, its decision to sentence at the "standard" term must be reasonable. * * *

Moreover, the California system, like the post-*Booker* federal regime, recognizes that a sentencing judge must have the ability to look at *all* the relevant facts—even those outside the trial record and jury verdict—in exercising his or her discretion. "The judicial factfinding that occurs during that selection process is the same type of judicial factfind-

ing that traditionally has been a part of the sentencing process."

III

Despite these similarities between the California system and the "advisory Guidelines" scheme approved in *Booker*, the Court nevertheless holds that the California regime runs afoul of the Sixth Amendment. The Court reasons as follows: (1) California requires that some aggravating fact, apart from the elements of the offense found by the jury, must support an upper term sentence; (2) *Blakely* defined the "statutory maximum" to be "the maximum sentence a judge may impose *solely on the basis of the facts reflected in the jury verdict or admitted by the defendant*;" and therefore (3) the California regime violates "*Apprendi*'s bright-line rule" that "any fact that increases the penalty for a crime beyond the prescribed statutory maximum must be submitted to a jury, and proved beyond a reasonable doubt."

This argument is flawed. For one thing, it is not at all clear that a California court must find some case-specific, adjudicative "fact" (as opposed to identifying a relevant policy consideration) before imposing an upper term sentence. What a California sentencing court must find is a "circumstance in aggravation" which, California's Court Rules make clear, can include any "criteria reasonably related to the decision being made."

California courts are thus empowered to take into account the full panoply of factual and policy considerations that have traditionally been considered by judges operating under fully discretionary sentencing regimes—the constitutionality of which the Court has repeatedly reaffirmed. California law explicitly authorizes a sentencing court to take into account, for example, broad sentencing objectives like punishment, deterrence, restitution, and uniformity, *see* Rule 4.410, and even a judge's "subjective belief" as to the appropriateness of the sentence, as long as the final result is reasonable. Policy considerations like these have always been outside the province of the jury and do not implicate the Sixth Amendment concerns expressed in *Apprendi*.

In short, the requirement that a California court find some "circumstance in aggravation" before imposing an upper term sentence is not the same as a requirement that it find an aggravating *fact*. And if a California sentencing court need not find a fact beyond those "reflected in the jury verdict or admitted by the defendant," then *Apprendi*'s "bright-line rule" plainly does not apply.

But even if the California law did require that a sentencing court find some aggravating "fact" before imposing an upper term sentence, that would not make this case constitutionally distinguishable from *Booker*. As previously explained, the "advisory Guidelines," bounded by reasonableness review, effectively (albeit less explicitly) impose the same requirement on federal judges. *Booker*'s reasonableness review necessarily supposes that some sentences will be unreasonable in the absence of additional facts justifying them. * * * Thus, although the post-*Booker* Guidelines are labeled "advisory," reasonableness review imposes a very real constraint on a judge's ability to sentence across the full statutory range without finding some aggravating fact.

The Court downplays the significance of *Booker* reasonableness review on the ground that *Booker*-style "reasonableness ... operates *within* the Sixth Amendment constraints delineated in our precedent, not as a substitute for those constraints." But this begs the question, which concerns the scope of those "Sixth Amendment constraints." That question is answered by the Court's remedial holding in *Booker*, which necessarily stands for the proposition that it is consistent with the Sixth Amendment for the imposition of an enhanced sentence to be conditioned on a factual finding made by a sentencing judge and not by a jury.

The Court relies heavily on *Blakely*'s admonition that "the statutory maximum for *Apprendi* purposes is the maximum sentence a judge may impose *solely on the basis of the facts reflected in the jury verdict or admitted by the defendant.*" But the Court fails to recognize how this statement must be understood in the wake of *Booker*.

For each statutory offense, there must be a sentence that represents the least onerous sentence that can be regarded as reasonable in light of the bare statutory elements found by the jury. To return to our prior example of a mail fraud offense, there must be some sentence that represents the least onerous sentence that would be appropriate in a case in which the statutory elements of mail fraud are satisfied but in which the offense and the offender are as little deserving of punishment as can be imagined. * * * This sentence is "the maximum sentence" that could reasonably be imposed "solely on the basis of the facts reflected in the jury verdict or admitted by the defendant."

Booker's reasonableness review necessarily anticipates that the imposition of above this level may be conditioned upon findings of fact made by a judge and not by the jury. *Booker* held that a system of "advisory Guidelines" with reasonableness review is consistent with the Sixth Amendment, and the same

analysis should govern California's "requirement that the decision to impose the upper term be *reasonable*." That the California requirement is explicit, while the federal aggravating factor requirement is (at least for now) implicit, should not be constitutionally dispositive.

Unless the Court is prepared to overrule the remedial decision in *Booker*, the California sentencing scheme at issue in this case should be held to be consistent with the Sixth Amendment. I would therefore affirm the decision of the California Court of Appeal.

Apprendi and the Determination of Facts Necessary To Impose a Consecutive Sentence: Oregon v. Ice

OREGON v. ICE

Supreme Court of the United States, 2009.
129 S.Ct. 711.

JUSTICE GINSBURG **delivered the opinion of the Court.**

This case concerns the scope of the Sixth Amendment's jury-trial guarantee, as construed in Apprendi v. New Jersey, 530 U.S. 466 (2000), and Blakely v. Washington, 542 U.S. 296 (2004). Those decisions are rooted in the historic jury function—determining whether the prosecution has proved each element of an offense beyond a reasonable doubt. They hold that it is within the jury's province to determine any fact (other than the existence of a prior conviction) that increases the maximum punishment authorized for a particular offense. Thus far, the Court has not extended the *Apprendi* and *Blakely* line of decisions beyond the offense-specific context that supplied the historic grounding for the decisions. The question here presented

concerns a sentencing function in which the jury traditionally played no part: When a defendant has been tried and convicted of multiple offenses, each involving discrete sentencing prescriptions, does the Sixth Amendment mandate jury determination of any fact declared necessary to the imposition of consecutive, in lieu of concurrent, sentences?

Most States continue the common-law tradition: They entrust to judges' unfettered discretion the decision whether sentences for discrete offenses shall be served consecutively or concurrently. In some States, sentences for multiple offenses are presumed to run consecutively, but sentencing judges may order concurrent sentences upon finding cause therefor. Other States, including Oregon, constrain judges' discretion by requiring them to find certain facts before imposing consecutive, rather than concurrent, sentences. It is undisputed that States may proceed on the first two tracks without transgressing the Sixth Amendment. The sole issue in dispute, then, is whether the Sixth Amendment, as construed in *Apprendi* and *Blakely*, precludes the mode of proceeding chosen by Oregon and several of her sister States. We hold, in light of historical practice and the authority of States over administration of their criminal justice systems, that the Sixth Amendment does not exclude Oregon's choice.

I

A

State laws, as just observed, prescribe a variety of approaches to the decision whether a defendant's sentences for distinct offenses shall run concurrently or consecutively. Oregon might have followed the prevailing pattern by placing the decision within the trial court's discretion in all, or almost all, circumstances. Instead, Oregon and several other States have adopted a more restrained approach: they provide for judicial discretion, but constrain its exercise. In these States, to impose consecutive sentences, judges must make certain predicate fact findings.

The controlling statute in Oregon provides that sentences shall run concurrently unless the judge finds statutorily described facts. In most cases, finding such facts permits—but does not require—the judge to order consecutive sentences. Specifically, an Oregon judge may order consecutive sentences "[i]f a defendant is simultaneously sentenced for criminal offenses that do not arise from the same continuous and uninterrupted course of conduct." If the offenses do arise from the same course of conduct, the judge may still impose consecutive sentences if she finds either:

"(a) That the criminal offense . . . was an indication of defendant's willingness to commit more than one criminal offense; or

"(b) The criminal offense . . . caused or created a risk of causing greater or qualitatively different loss, injury or harm to the victim or . . . to a different victim . . . ."

B

On two occasions between December 1996 and July 1997, respondent Thomas Eugene Ice entered an apartment in the complex he managed and sexually assaulted an 11–year-old girl. An Oregon jury convicted Ice of six crimes. * * * At sentencing, the judge made findings * * * that permitted the imposition of consecutive sentences. [The judge found that the crimes constituted "separate incidents" and that Ice displayed a "willingness to commit more than one . . . offense" during each criminal episode, and his conduct "caused or created a risk of causing greater, qualitatively different loss, injury, or harm to the victim."] These findings gave the judge discretion to impose the sentence for each of those sexual assault offenses consecutive to the associated burglary sentence. The court elected to do so. * * * Ibid. In total, the court sentenced Ice to 340 months' imprisonment. [Had the judge ordered concurrent service of all sentences, Ice's time in prison would have been 90 months.]

Ice appealed his sentences. In relevant part, he argued that he had a Sixth Amendment right to have the jury, not the sentencing judge, find the facts that permitted the imposition of consecutive sentences. [The Oregon Supreme Court found an *Apprendi* violation because the judge found facts that increased the defendant's sentence.]

II

The Federal Constitution's jury-trial guarantee assigns the determination of certain facts to the jury's exclusive province. Under that guarantee, this Court held in *Apprendi*, "any fact that increases the penalty for a crime beyond the prescribed statutory maximum must be submitted to a jury, and proved beyond a reasonable doubt."

We have applied *Apprendi*'s rule to facts subjecting a defendant to the death penalty, Ring v. Arizona, 536 U.S. 584, 602 (2002), facts allowing a sentence exceeding the "standard" range in Washington's sentencing system, *Blakely*, and facts prompting an elevated sentence under then-mandatory Federal Sentencing Guidelines, United States v. Booker, 543 U.S. 220 (2005). Most recently, in Cunningham v. California, 549 U.S. 270 (2007), we applied *Apprendi*'s rule to facts permitting imposition of an "upper term" sentence under California's determinate sentencing law. All of these decisions involved sentencing for a discrete crime, not—as here—for multiple offenses different in character or committed at different times.

Our application of *Apprendi*'s rule must honor the "longstanding common-law practice" in which the rule is rooted. *Cunningham*, 549 U.S., at 281. The rule's animating principle is the preservation of the jury's historic role as a bulwark between the State and the accused at the trial for an alleged offense. Guided by that principle, our opinions make clear that the Sixth Amendment does not countenance legislative encroachment on the jury's traditional domain. We accordingly considered whether the finding of a particular fact was understood as within "the domain of the jury . . . by those who framed the Bill of Rights." Harris v. United States, 536 U.S. 545, 557 (2002) (plurality opinion). In undertaking this inquiry, we remain cognizant that administration of a discrete criminal justice system is among the basic sovereign prerogatives States retain. See, e.g., Patterson v. New York, 432 U.S. 197, 201 (1977).

These twin considerations—historical practice and respect for state sovereignty—counsel against extending *Apprendi*'s rule to the imposition of sentences for discrete crimes. The decision to impose sentences consecutively is not within the jury function that "extends down centuries into the common law." *Apprendi*, 530 U.S., at 477. Instead, specification of the regime for administering multiple sentences has long been considered the prerogative of state legislatures.

A

The historical record demonstrates that the jury played no role in the decision to impose sentences consecutively or concurrently. Rather, the choice rested exclusively with the judge. * * * The historical record further indicates that a judge's imposition of consecutive, rather than concurrent, sentences was the prevailing practice.

In light of this history, legislative reforms regarding the imposition of multiple sentences do not implicate the core concerns that prompted our decision in *Apprendi*. There is no encroachment here by the judge upon facts historically found by the jury, nor any threat to the jury's domain as a bulwark at trial between the State and the accused. Instead, the defendant—who historically may have faced consecutive sentences by default—has been granted by some modern legislatures statutory protections meant to temper the harshness of the historical practice.

It is no answer that, as Ice argues, "he was entitled to" concurrent sentences absent the fact findings Oregon law requires. In Ice's view, because "the Oregon Legislature deviated from tradition" and enacted a statute that hinges consecutive sentences on fact findings, *Apprendi*'s rule must be imported. As we have described, the scope of the constitutional jury right must be informed by the historical role of the jury at common law. It is therefore not the case that, as Ice suggests, the federal constitutional right attaches to every contemporary state-law "entitlement" to predicate findings.

For similar reasons, *Cunningham*, upon which Ice heavily relies, does not control his case. As stated earlier, we held in *Cunningham* that the facts permitting imposition of an elevated "upper term" sentence for a particular crime fell within the jury's province. The assignment of such a finding to the sentencing judge implicates *Apprendi*'s core concern: a legislative attempt to remove from the province of the jury the determination of facts that warrant punishment for a specific statutory offense. We had no occasion to consider the appropriate inquiry when no erosion of the jury's traditional role was at stake. *Cunningham* thus does not impede our conclusion that, as *Apprendi*'s core concern is inapplicable to the issue at hand, so too is the Sixth Amendment's restriction on judge-found facts.

B

States' interest in the development of their penal systems, and their historic dominion in this area, also counsel against the extension of *Apprendi* that Ice requests. Beyond question, the authority of States over the administration of their criminal justice systems lies at the core of their sovereign status. This Court should not diminish that role absent impelling reason to do so.

It bears emphasis that state legislative innovations like Oregon's seek to rein in the discretion judges possessed at common law to impose consecutive sentences at will. Limiting judicial discretion to impose consecutive sentences serves the "salutary objectives" of promoting sentences proportionate to "the gravity of the offense," *Blakely*, 542 U.S., at 308, and of reducing disparities in sentence length. All agree that a scheme making consecutive sentences the rule, and concurrent sentences the exception, encounters no Sixth Amendment shoal. To hem in States by holding that they may not equally choose to make concurrent sentences the rule, and consecutive sentences the exception, would make scant sense. Neither *Apprendi* nor our Sixth Amendment traditions compel straitjacketing the States in that manner.

Further, it is unclear how many other state initiatives would fall under Ice's proposed expansion of *Apprendi*. As 17 States have observed in an amici brief supporting Oregon, States currently permit judges to make a variety of sentencing determinations other than the length of incarceration. Trial judges often find facts about the nature of the offense or the character of the defendant in determining, for example, the length of supervised release following service of a prison sentence; required attendance at drug rehabilitation programs or terms of community service; and the imposition of statutorily prescribed fines and orders of restitution. Intruding *Apprendi*'s rule into these decisions on sentencing choices or accoutrements surely would cut the rule loose from its moorings.

Moreover, the expansion that Ice seeks would be difficult for States to administer. The predicate facts for consecutive sentences could substantially prejudice the defense at the guilt phase of a trial. As a result, bifurcated or trifurcated trials might often prove necessary. We will not so burden the Nation's trial courts absent any genuine affront to *Apprendi*'s instruction.

We recognize that not every state initiative will be in harmony with Sixth Amendment ideals. But as we have previously emphasized, "structural democratic constraints exist to discourage legislatures from" pernicious manipulation of the rules we articulate. *Apprendi*, 530 U.S., at 490, n. 16. In any event, if confronted with such a manipulation, we would be required to question whether the legislative measure was constitutional under this Court's prior decisions. The Oregon statute before us today raises no such concern.

III

Members of this Court have warned against "wooden, unyielding insistence on expanding the *Apprendi* doctrine far beyond its necessary boundaries." *Cunningham*, 549 U.S., at 295 (Kennedy, J., dissenting). The jury-trial right is best honored through a principled rationale that applies the rule of the *Apprendi* cases within the central sphere of their concern. Our disposition today—upholding an Oregon statute that assigns to judges a decision that has not traditionally belonged to the jury—is faithful to that aim.

———

For the reasons stated, the judgment of the Oregon Supreme Court is reversed, and the case is remanded for further proceedings not inconsistent with this opinion.

It is so ordered.

Justice Scalia, with whom The Chief Justice, Justice Souter, and Justice Thomas join, dissenting.

The rule of Apprendi v. New Jersey is clear: Any fact—other than that of a prior conviction—that increases the maximum punishment to which a defendant may be sentenced must be admitted by the defendant or proved beyond a reasonable doubt to a jury. Oregon's sentencing scheme allows judges rather than juries to find the facts necessary to commit defendants to longer prison sentences, and thus directly contradicts what we held eight years ago and have reaffirmed several times since. The Court's justification of Oregon's scheme is a virtual copy of the dissents in those cases.

The judge in this case could not have imposed a sentence of consecutive prison terms without making the factual finding that the defendant caused "separate harms" to the victim by the acts that produced two convictions. There can thus be no doubt that the judge's factual finding was essential to the punishment he imposed. That "should be the end of the matter." Blakely v. Washington, 542 U.S. 296, 313 (2004).

Instead, the Court attempts to distinguish Oregon's sentencing scheme by reasoning that the rule of *Apprendi* applies only to the length of a sentence for an individual crime and not to the total sentence for a defendant. I cannot understand why we would make such a strange exception to the treasured right of trial by jury. Neither the reasoning of the *Apprendi* line of cases, nor any distinctive history of the factfinding necessary to imposition of consecutive sentences, nor (of course) logic supports such an odd rule.

* * *

[There is] no room for a formalistic distinction between facts bearing on the number of years of imprisonment that a defendant will serve for one count (subject to the rule of *Apprendi*) and facts bearing on how many years will be served in total (now not subject to *Apprendi*). There is no doubt that consecutive sentences are a "greater punishment" than concurrent sentences. * * * The decision to impose consecutive sentences alters the single consequence most important to convicted noncapital defendants: their date of release from prison. For many defendants, the difference between consecutive and concurrent sentences is more important than a jury verdict of innocence on any single count: Two consecutive 10–year sentences are in most circumstances a more severe punishment than any number of concurrent 10–year sentences.

To support its distinction-without-a-difference, the Court puts forward the same (the very same) arguments regarding the history of sentencing that were rejected by *Apprendi*. Here, it is entirely irrelevant that common-law judges had discretion to impose either consecutive or concurrent sentences; just as there it was entirely irrelevant that common-law judges had discretion to impose greater or lesser sentences (within the prescribed statutory maximum) for individual convictions. There is no Sixth Amendment problem with a system that exposes defendants to a known range of sentences after a guilty verdict: "In a system that says the judge may punish burglary with 10 to 40 years, every burglar knows he is risking 40 years in jail." *Blakely, supra,* at 309. The same analysis applies to a system where both consecutive and concurrent sentences are authorized after only a jury verdict of guilt; the burglar-rapist knows he is risking consecutive sentences. Our concern here is precisely the same as our concern in *Apprendi*: What happens when a State breaks from the common-law practice of discretionary sentences and permits the imposition of an elevated sentence only upon the showing of extraordinary facts? In such a system, the defendant "is entitled to" the lighter sentence and by reason of the Sixth Amendment, the facts bearing upon that entitlement must be found by a jury. *Blakely*, 542 U.S., at 309.

The Court protests that in this case there is no "encroachment" on or "erosion" of the jury's role because traditionally it was for the judge to determine whether there would be concurrent terms. Alas, this argument too was made and rejected in *Apprendi*. The jury's role was not diminished, the *Apprendi* dissent contended, because it was traditionally up to judges, not juries, to determine what the sentence would be. 530 U.S., at 556, 559 (opinion of BREYER, J.). The Court's opinion acknowledged that in the 19th century it was the practice to leave sentencing up to the judges, within limits fixed by law. But, it said, that practice had no bearing upon whether the jury must find the fact where a law conditions the higher sentence upon the fact. The jury's role is diminished when the length of a sentence is made to depend upon a fact removed from its determination. The same is true here.

The Court then observes that the results of the Oregon system could readily be achieved, instead, by a system in which consecutive sen-

tences are the default rule but judges are permitted to impose concurrent sentences when they find certain facts. Undoubtedly the Sixth Amendment permits a system in which judges are authorized (or even required) to impose consecutive sentences unless the defendant proves additional facts to the Court's satisfaction. But the permissibility of that alternative means of achieving the same end obviously does not distinguish *Apprendi*, because the same argument (the very same argument) was raised and squarely rejected in that case. * * *

Ultimately, the Court abandons its effort to provide analytic support for its decision, and turns to what it thinks to be the "salutary objectives" of Oregon's scheme. Limiting judicial discretion, we are told, promotes sentences proportionate to the gravity of the offense, and reduces disparities in sentence length. The same argument (the very same argument) was made and rejected in *Booker* and *Blakely*. The protection of the Sixth Amendment does not turn on this Court's opinion of whether an alternative scheme is good policy, or whether the legislature had a compassionate heart in adopting it. The right to trial by jury and proof beyond a reasonable doubt is a given, and all legislative policymaking—good and bad, heartless and compassionate—must work within the confines of that reality.* * *

Finally, the Court summons up the parade of horribles assembled by the amicus brief of 17 States supporting Oregon. It notes that "[t]rial judges often find facts" in connection with "a variety of sentencing determinations other than the length of incarceration," and worries that even their ability to set the length of supervised release, impose community service, or order entry into a drug rehabilitation program, may be called into question. But if these courses reduce rather than augment the punishment that the jury verdict imposes, there is no problem. The last horrible the Court invokes is the prospect of bifurcated or even trifurcated trials in order to have the jury find the facts essential to consecutive sentencing without prejudicing the defendant's merits case. That is another déjà vu and déjà rejeté; we have watched it parade past before, in several of our *Apprendi*-related opinions, and have not saluted. See *Blakely*, supra, at 336–337 (BREYER, J., dissenting); *Apprendi*, supra, at 557 (same).

———

The Court's peroration says that "[t]he jury-trial right is best honored through a principled rationale that applies the rule of the *Apprendi* cases within the central sphere of their concern." Undoubtedly so. But we have hitherto considered "the central sphere of their concern" to be facts necessary to the increase of the defendant's sentence beyond what the jury verdict alone justifies. * * * If the doubling or tripling of a defendant's jail time through fact-dependent consecutive sentencing does not meet this description, nothing does. And as for a "principled rationale": The Court's reliance upon a distinction without a difference, and its repeated exhumation of arguments dead and buried by prior cases, seems to me the epitome of the opposite. Today's opinion muddies the waters, and gives cause to doubt whether the Court is willing to stand by *Apprendi*'s interpretation of the Sixth Amendment's jury-trial guarantee.

IV. TRIAL BY JURY

B. WHAT THE JURY DECIDES

Page 1165. Add the following after the paragraph on *Apprendi*:

In Cunningham v. California, 549 U.S. 270 (2007), the Court held that the California Determinative Sentencing Law violated *Apprendi* because it required a trial judge to impose a sentence in a higher sentencing category, upon the basis of certain aggravating facts found by the judge. Justice Ginsburg, writing for the six-person majority, declared as follows:

> Under California's DSL, an upper term sentence may be imposed only when the trial judge finds an aggravating circumstance. An element of the charged offense, essential to a jury's determination of guilt, or admitted in a defendant's guilty plea, does not qualify as such a circumstance. Instead, aggravating circumstances depend on facts found discretely and solely by the judge. * * * [T]he middle term prescribed in California's statutes [for the crime charged and proved to the jury], not the upper term, is the relevant statutory

maximum. Because circumstances in aggravation are found by the judge, not the jury, and need only be established by a preponderance of the evidence, not beyond a reasonable doubt, the DSL violates *Apprendi*'s bright-line rule: Except for a prior conviction, "any fact that increases the penalty for a crime beyond the prescribed statutory maximum must be submitted to a jury, and proved beyond a reasonable doubt."

The full opinion in *Cunningham,* including the dissents by Justice Kennedy (joined by Justice Breyer) and Justice Alito (joined by Justices Kennedy and Breyer) is set forth in this Supplement, supra, in the section on "Constitutionally Based Proof Requirements."

In Oregon v. Ice, 129 S.Ct. 711 (2009), the Court upheld a state law allowing the judge to impose consecutive, rather than concurrent, sentences after finding certain facts. The Court distinguished *Apprendi* as a case involving "sentencing for a discrete crime, not—as here—for multiple offenses different in character or committed at different times." The full opinion in *Ice* is also set forth in the section on constitutionally-based proof requirements, *supra.*

D. JURY SELECTION AND COMPOSITION

4. *Challenges for Cause*

a. *Jurors Who Cannot Be Challenged for Cause*

Page 1191. Add after the first full paragraph:

Trial Court Discretion to Strike Jurors to Maintain a Death–Qualified Jury: Uttecht v. Brown

In Uttecht v. Brown, 551 U.S. 1 (2007), a 5–4 majority of the Court held that a trial judge did not violate *Witherspoon* and its progeny by excusing a juror for cause. The majority emphasized the deference owed to a trial judge who is called upon to screen jurors to determine whether they will give fair consideration to the state's argument in favor of the death penalty. Justice Kennedy's majority opinion found that the Court's decisions established four relevant principles:

> First, a criminal defendant has the right to an impartial jury drawn from a venire that has not been tilted in favor of capital punishment by selective prosecutorial challenges for cause. * * * Second, the State has a strong interest in having jurors who are able to apply capital punishment within the framework state law prescribes. * * * Third, to balance these interests, a juror who is substantially impaired in his or her ability to impose the death penalty under the state-law framework can be excused for cause; but if the juror is not substantially impaired, removal for cause is impermissible. * * * Fourth, in determining whether the removal of a potential juror would vindicate the State's interest without violating the defen-

dant's right, the trial court makes a judgment based in part on the demeanor of the juror, a judgment owed deference by reviewing courts.

Justice Kennedy described the lengthy jury selection process in this case:

> Eleven days of the voir dire were devoted to determining whether the potential jurors were death-qualified. During that phase alone, the defense challenged 18 members of the venire for cause. Despite objections from the State, 11of those prospective jurors were excused. As for the State, it made 12 challenges for cause; defense counsel objected seven times; and only twice was the juror excused following an objection from the defense. Before deciding a contested challenge, the trial court gave each side a chance to explain its position and recall the potential juror for additional questioning. When issuing its decisions the court gave careful and measured explanations.

Justice Kennedy summarized the problems with the one juror that the defendant thought was erroneously struck for cause:

> Juror Z was examined on the seventh day of the voir dire and the fifth day of the death-qualification phase. The State argues that Juror Z was impaired not by his general outlook on the death penalty, but rather by his position regarding the specific circumstances in which the death penalty would be appropriate. The transcript of Juror Z's questioning reveals that, despite the preceding instructions and information, he had both serious misunderstandings about his responsibility as a juror and an attitude toward capital punishment that could have prevented him from returning a death sentence under the facts of this case.

In the end, Justice Kennedy found that there was ample reason for the trial judge to strike Juror Z:

> Juror Z's assurances that he would consider imposing the death penalty and would follow the law do not overcome the reasonable inference from his other statements that in fact he would be substantially impaired in this case because there was no possibility of release. His assurances did not require the trial court to deny the State's motion to excuse Juror Z. The defense itself had told the trial court that any juror would make similar guarantees and that they were worth little; instead, defense counsel explained, the court should listen to arguments concerning the substance of the juror's answers. The trial court in part relied, as diligent judges often must, upon both parties' counsel to explain why a challenged juror's problematic beliefs about the death penalty would not rise to the level of substantial impairment. Brown's counsel offered no defense of Juror Z. In light of the deference owed to the trial court the position Brown now maintains does not convince us the decision to excuse Juror Z was unreasonable.

The majority emphasized that defense counsel failed to object to the strike of Juror Z. Justice Kennedy stated that the failure to object was not dispositive of the appeal, because the applicable state law at trial provided that a failure to object is not a waiver. But despite the protective state law, Justice Kennedy found that defense counsel's failure to object had some relevance to the reasonableness of the trial judge's decision. Justice Kennedy explained as follows

It is true that in order to preserve a *Witherspoon* claim for federal habeas review there is no independent federal requirement that a defendant in state court object to the prosecution's challenge; state procedural rules govern. We nevertheless take into account voluntary acquiescence to, or confirmation of, a juror's removal. By failing to object, the defense did not just deny the conscientious trial judge an opportunity to explain his judgment or correct any error. It also deprived reviewing courts of further factual findings that would have helped to explain the trial court's decision.

Justice Stevens wrote a dissent, joined by Justices Souter, Ginsburg and Breyer. He contended that the majority mischaracterized Juror Z's stated attitude toward the death penalty:

When the State challenged Juror Z, it argued that he was "confused about the conditions under which [the death penalty] could be imposed and seemed to believe it only appropriate when there was a risk of release and recidivism." * * * A more accurate characterization of Juror Z's testimony is that although he harbored some general reservations about the death penalty, he stated that he could consider and would vote to impose the death penalty where appropriate. When asked for "an idea ... of the underlying reason why you think the death penalty is appropriate [or] what purpose it serves," Juror Z responded that "the type of situation" in which the death penalty would be appropriate was "if a person was incorrigible and would reviolate if released." * * * After it was explained to Juror Z that the only two sentencing alternatives available under Washington law would be life imprisonment without the possibility of parole and a death sentence, Juror Z repeatedly confirmed that even if he knew the defendant would never be released, he would still be able to consider and vote for the death penalty. * * * As for any general reservations Juror Z may have had about the imposition of the death penalty, it is clear from his testimony that he was in no way categorically opposed to it. When asked whether he was "a little more comfortable that it is being used some of the time," Juror Z responded in the affirmative.

Justice Stevens found the majority's analysis to be a departure from prior cases:

While such testimony might justify a prosecutor's peremptory challenge, until today not one of the many cases decided in the wake of *Witherspoon v. Illinois*, 391 U.S. 510 (1968), has suggested that such a view would support a challenge for cause. The distinction that our cases require trial judges to draw is not between jurors who are in favor of the death penalty and those who oppose it, but rather between two sub-classes within the latter class—those who will conscientiously apply the law and those whose conscientious scruples necessarily prevent them from doing so.

Justice Stevens concluded that the majority's reasoning was backwards:

> Today, the Court has fundamentally redefined—or maybe just misunderstood—the meaning of "substantially impaired," and, in doing so, has gotten it horribly backwards. It appears to be under the impression that trial courts should be encouraging the inclusion of jurors who will impose the death penalty rather than only ensuring the exclusion of those who say that, in all circumstances, they cannot. The Court emphasizes that "the State has a strong interest in having jurors who are able to apply capital punishment within the framework state law prescribes." But that does not and cannot mean that jurors must be willing to impose a death sentence in every situation in which a defendant is eligible for that sanction. That is exactly the outcome we aimed to protect against in developing the standard that, contrary to the Court's apparent temporary lapse, still governs today.

Justice Breyer, joined by Justice Souter, wrote a separate, short dissent. He contended that defense counsel's failure to object to the strike of Juror Z was entitled to no effect, because the applicable state procedural law provides that a failure to object is not a waiver. Thus it was unfair for the majority to draw a negative inference that the applicable rule at trial did not permit.

5. *The Use of Peremptory Challenges*

Page 1225. Add the following case after Miller v. Dretke:

Another Fact–Intensive Review of Peremptory Challenges: Snyder v. Louisiana

SNYDER v. LOUISIANA

Supreme Court of the United States, 2008.
128 S.Ct. 1203.

JUSTICE ALITO **delivered the opinion of the Court.**

Petitioner Allen Snyder was convicted of first-degree murder in a Louisiana court and was sentenced to death. He asks us to review a decision of the Louisiana Supreme Court rejecting his claim that the prosecution exercised some of its peremptory jury challenges based on race, in violation of Batson v. Kentucky, 476 U.S. 79 (1986). We hold that the trial court committed clear error in its ruling on a *Batson* objection, and we therefore reverse.

I

[Snyder was charged with the double murder of his wife and her friend. The government sought the death penalty.] *Voir dire* began on Tuesday, August 27, 1996, and proceeded as follows. During the first phase, the trial court screened the panel to identify jurors who did not meet Louisiana's requirements for jury service or claimed that service on the jury or sequestration for the duration of the trial would result in extreme hardship. More than 50 prospective jurors reported that they had work, family, or other commitments that would interfere with jury service. In each of those instances, the nature of the conflicting commitments was explored, and some of these jurors were dismissed.

In the next phase, the court randomly selected panels of 13 potential jurors for further questioning. The defense and prosecution addressed each panel and questioned the jurors both as a group and individually. At the conclusion of this questioning, the court ruled on challenges for cause. Then, the prosecution and the defense were given the opportunity to use peremptory challenges (each side had 12) to remove remaining jurors. The court continued this process of calling 13–person panels until the jury was filled. In accordance with Louisiana law, the parties were permitted to exercise "backstrikes." That is, they were allowed to use their peremptories up until the time when the final jury was sworn and thus were permitted to strike jurors whom they had initially accepted when the jurors' panels were called.

Eighty-five prospective jurors were questioned as members of a panel. Thirty-six of these survived challenges for cause; 5 of the 36 were black; and all 5 of the prospective black jurors were eliminated by the prosecution through the use of peremptory strikes. The jury found petitioner guilty of first-degree murder and determined that he should receive the death penalty. [The state courts rejected the defendant's *Batson* claims with respect to the prosecutor's peremptory strikes of two blacks on the panel.]

II

[Justice Alito reviewed the "three-step process" for determining whether a prospective juror is dismissed for discriminatory reasons, and noted that a trial judge's determination under *Batson* can only be reversed if it is clearly erroneous.]

III

Petitioner centers his *Batson* claim on the prosecution's strikes of two black jurors, Jeffrey Brooks and Elaine Scott. Because we find that the trial court committed clear error in overruling petitioner's *Batson* objection with respect to Mr. Brooks, we have no need to consider petitioner's claim regarding Ms. Scott. * * *

When defense counsel made a *Batson* objection concerning the strike of Mr. Brooks, a college senior who was attempting to fulfill his student-teaching obligation, the prosecution offered two race-neutral reasons for the strike. The prosecutor explained:

"I thought about it last night. Number 1, the main reason is that he looked very nervous to me throughout the questioning. Number 2, he's one of the fellows that came up at the beginning [of *voir dire*] and said he was going to miss class. He's a student teacher. My main concern is for that reason, that being that he might, to go home quickly, come back with guilty of a lesser verdict so there wouldn't be a penalty phase. Those are my two reasons.''

Defense counsel disputed both explanations, and the trial judge ruled as follows: "All right. I'm going to allow the challenge. I'm going to allow the challenge." We discuss the prosecution's two proffered grounds for striking Mr. Brooks in turn.

A

With respect to the first reason, the Louisiana Supreme Court was correct that "nervousness cannot be shown from a cold transcript, which is why ... the [trial] judge's evaluation must be given much deference." * * * [D]eference is especially appropriate where a trial judge has made a finding that an attorney credibly relied on demeanor in exercising a strike. Here, however, the record does not show that the trial judge actually made a determination concerning Mr. Brooks' demeanor. The trial judge was given two explanations for the strike. Rather than making a specific finding on the record concerning Mr. Brooks' demeanor, the trial judge simply allowed the challenge without explanation. It is possible that the judge did not have any impression one way or the other concerning Mr. Brooks' demeanor. Mr. Brooks was not challenged until the day after he was questioned, and by that time dozens of other jurors had been questioned. Thus, the trial

judge may not have recalled Mr. Brooks' demeanor. Or, the trial judge may have found it unnecessary to consider Mr. Brooks' demeanor, instead basing his ruling completely on the second proffered justification for the strike. For these reasons, we cannot presume that the trial judge credited the prosecutor's assertion that Mr. Brooks was nervous.

B

The second reason proffered for the strike of Mr. Brooks—his student-teaching obligation—fails even under the highly deferential standard of review that is applicable here. * * * The prosecutor claimed to be apprehensive that Mr. Brooks, in order to minimize the student-teaching hours missed during jury service, might have been motivated to find petitioner guilty, not of first-degree murder, but of a lesser included offense because this would obviate the need for a penalty phase proceeding. But this scenario was highly speculative. Even if Mr. Brooks had favored a quick resolution, that would not have necessarily led him to reject a finding of first-degree murder. If the majority of jurors had initially favored a finding of first-degree murder, Mr. Brooks' purported inclination might have led him to agree in order to speed the deliberations. Only if all or most of the other jurors had favored the lesser verdict would Mr. Brooks have been in a position to shorten the trial by favoring such a verdict.

Perhaps most telling, the brevity of petitioner's trial—something that the prosecutor anticipated on the record during *voir dire*—meant that serving on the jury would not have seriously interfered with Mr.

Brooks' ability to complete his required student teaching. As noted, petitioner's trial was completed by Friday, August 30. If Mr. Brooks, who reported to court and was peremptorily challenged on Wednesday, August 28, had been permitted to serve, he would have missed only two additional days of student teaching, Thursday, August 29, and Friday, August 30. Mr. Brooks' dean promised to "work with" Mr. Brooks to see that he was able to make up any student-teaching time that he missed due to jury service; the dean stated that he did not think that this would be a problem; and the record contains no suggestion that Mr. Brooks remained troubled after hearing the report of the dean's remarks. In addition, although the record does not include the academic calendar of Mr. Brooks' university, it is apparent that the trial occurred relatively early in the fall semester. With many weeks remaining in the term, Mr. Brooks would have needed to make up no more than an hour or two per week in order to compensate for the time that he would have lost due to jury service. When all of these considerations are taken into account, the prosecutor's second proffered justification for striking Mr. Brooks is suspicious.

The implausibility of this explanation is reinforced by the prosecutor's acceptance of white jurors who disclosed conflicting obligations that appear to have been at least as serious as Mr. Brooks'. We recognize that a retrospective comparison of jurors based on a cold appellate record may be very misleading when alleged similarities were not raised at trial. In that situation, an appellate court must be

mindful that an exploration of the alleged similarities at the time of trial might have shown that the jurors in question were not really comparable. In this case, however, the shared characteristic, *i.e.,* concern about serving on the jury due to conflicting obligations, was thoroughly explored by the trial court when the relevant jurors asked to be excused for cause.

A comparison between Mr. Brooks and Roland Laws, a white juror, is particularly striking. During the initial stage of *voir dire,* Mr. Laws approached the court and offered strong reasons why serving on the sequestered jury would cause him hardship. Mr. Laws stated that he was "a self-employed general contractor," with "two houses that are nearing completion, one [with the occupants] . . . moving in this weekend." He explained that, if he served on the jury, "the people won't [be able to] move in." Mr. Laws also had demanding family obligations:

> "[M]y wife just had a hysterectomy, so I'm running the kids back and forth to school, and we're not originally from here, so I have no family in the area, so between the two things, it's kind of bad timing for me."

Although these obligations seem substantially more pressing than Mr. Brooks', the prosecution questioned Mr. Laws and attempted to elicit assurances that he would be able to serve despite his work and family obligations. And the prosecution declined the opportunity to use a peremptory strike on Mr. Laws. If the prosecution had been sincerely concerned that Mr. Brooks would favor a lesser verdict than first-degree murder in order to shorten the trial, it is hard to see why the prosecution would not have had at least as much concern regarding Mr. Laws.

* * * The question presented at the third stage of the *Batson* inquiry is whether the defendant has shown purposeful discrimination. The prosecution's proffer of this pretextual explanation naturally gives rise to an inference of discriminatory intent. Purkett v. Elem, 514 U.S. 765, 768 (1995) *(per curiam)* ("At [the third] stage, implausible or fantastic justifications may (and probably will) be found to be pretexts for purposeful discrimination").

In other circumstances, we have held that, once it is shown that a discriminatory intent was a substantial or motivating factor in an action taken by a state actor, the burden shifts to the party defending the action to show that this factor was not determinative. See Hunter v. Underwood, 471 U.S. 222, 228 (1985). We have not previously applied this rule in a *Batson* case, and we need not decide here whether that standard governs in this context. For present purposes, it is enough to recognize that a peremptory strike shown to have been motivated in substantial part by discriminatory intent could not be sustained based on any lesser showing by the prosecution. And in light of the circumstances here—including absence of anything in the record showing that the trial judge credited the claim that Mr. Brooks was nervous, the prosecution's description of both of its proffered expla-

nations as "main concern[s]," and the adverse inference noted above—the record does not show that the prosecution would have pre-emptively challenged Mr. Brooks based on his nervousness alone. Nor is there any realistic possibility that this subtle question of causation could be profitably explored further on remand at this late date, more than a decade after petitioner's trial.

———

We therefore reverse the judgment of the Louisiana Supreme Court and remand the case for further proceedings not inconsistent with this opinion.

JUSTICE THOMAS, **with whom** JUSTICE SCALIA **joins, dissenting.**

Petitioner essentially asks this Court to second-guess the fact-based determinations of the Louisiana courts as to the reasons for a prosecutor's decision to strike two jurors. The evaluation of a prosecutor's motives for striking a juror is at bottom a credibility judgment, which lies "peculiarly within a trial judge's province." Hernandez v. New York, 500 U.S. 352, 365 (1991). * * * None of the evidence in the record as to jurors Jeffrey Brooks and Elaine Scott demonstrates that the trial court clearly erred in finding they were not stricken on the basis of race. Because the trial court's determination was a permissible view of the evidence, I would affirm the judgment of the Louisiana Supreme Court.

* * *

VII. THE RIGHT TO EFFECTIVE ASSISTANCE OF COUNSEL

A. INEFFECTIVENESS AND PREJUDICE

3. *Assessing Counsel's Effectiveness*

Page 1323. Add after Florida v. Nixon.

Ineffective Charge Against a Lawyer Who Refuses To Bring a Defense That Is Likely To Fail: Knowles v. Mirzayance

In Knowles v. Mirzayance, 129 S.Ct. 1411 (2009), the Court considered an ineffectiveness challenge to a defense lawyer's decision not to bring a claim at one phase of a trial, when that claim had already been rejected by the jury in an earlier phase. Justice Thomas, writing for the Court, recounted the facts:

> Mirzayance confessed that he stabbed his 19–year-old cousin nine times with a hunting knife and then shot her four times. At trial, he entered pleas of not guilty and not guilty by reason of insanity (NGI). Under California law, when both of these pleas are entered, the court must hold a bifurcated trial, with guilt determined during the first phase and the viability of the defendant's NGI plea during the second. During the guilt phase of Mirzayance's trial, he sought to avoid a conviction for first-degree murder by obtaining a verdict on the lesser included offense of second-degree murder. To that end, he presented medical testimony that he was insane at the time of the crime and was, therefore, incapable of the premeditation or deliberation necessary for a first-degree murder conviction. The jury nevertheless convicted Mirzayance of first-degree murder.

> The trial judge set the NGI phase to begin the day after the conviction was entered but, on the advice of counsel, Mirzayance abandoned his NGI plea before it commenced. He would have borne the burden of proving his insanity during the NGI phase to the same jury that had just convicted him of first-degree murder. Counsel had planned to meet that burden by presenting medical testimony similar to that presented in the guilt phase, including evidence that Mirzayance was insane and incapable of premeditating or deliberating. Because the jury rejected similar evidence at the guilt phase (where the State bore the burden of proof), counsel believed a defense verdict at the NGI phase (where the burden was on the defendant) was unlikely. He planned, though, to have Mirzayance's parents testify and thus provide an emotional account of Mirzayance's struggles with mental illness to supplement the medical evidence of insanity. But on the morning that the NGI phase was set to begin, Mirzayance's parents refused to testify. After consulting

with co-counsel, counsel advised Mirzayance that he should with-draw the NGI plea. Mirzayance accepted the advice.

After he was sentenced, Mirzayance challenged his conviction in state postconviction proceedings. Among other allegations, he claimed that counsel's recommendation to withdraw the NGI plea constituted ineffective assistance of counsel under Strickland. The California trial court denied the petition and the California Court of Appeal affirmed without offering any reason for its rejection of this particular ineffective assistance claim. Mirzayance then filed an application for federal habeas relief under 28 U.S.C. § 2254.

The Court unanimously rejected the contention that counsel was constitutionally ineffective for failing to bring the NGI claim. Justice Thomas reasoned as follows:

Mirzayance has not shown that counsel's representation fell below an objective standard of reasonableness. The proper measure of attorney performance remains simply reasonableness under pre-vailing professional norms. Judicial scrutiny of counsel's perform-ance must be highly deferential, and a court must indulge a strong presumption that counsel's conduct falls within the wide range of reasonable professional assistance. Strategic choices made after thorough investigation of law and facts relevant to plausible options are virtually unchallengeable.

Here, Mirzayance has not shown that his counsel violated these standards. Rather, his counsel merely recommended the withdrawal of what he reasonably believed was a claim doomed to fail. The jury had already rejected medical testimony about Mirzayance's mental state in the guilt phase, during which the State carried its burden of proving guilt beyond a reasonable doubt.* * *

In the NGI phase, the burden would have switched to Mirzay-ance to prove insanity by a preponderance of the evidence. Mirzay-ance's counsel reasonably believed that there was almost no chance that the same jury would have reached a different result when considering similar evidence, especially with Mirzayance bearing the burden of proof. Furthermore, counsel knew he would have had to present this defense without the benefit of the parents' testimony, which he believed to be his strongest evidence. Counsel reasonably concluded that this defense was almost certain to lose.

Mirzayance argued that even if the NGI defense was weak, counsel was nonetheless ineffective because it was the only defense available. Justice Thomas addressed this argument in the following passage:

But we are aware of no prevailing professional norms that prevent counsel from recommending that a plea be withdrawn when it is almost certain to lose. And in this case, counsel did not give up "the only defense available." Counsel put on a defense to first-degree murder during the guilt phase. Counsel also defended his client at the sentencing phase. The law does not require counsel to raise every available nonfrivolous defense. Counsel also is not required to have a tactical reason—above and beyond a reasonable appraisal of a claim's dismal prospects for success—for recommending that a weak claim be dropped altogether. Mirzayance has thus failed to demonstrate that his counsel's performance was deficient.

Finally, Justice Thomas found that even if ineffectiveness could be shown, Mirzayance had not been prejudiced by the decision not to pursue the NGI defense:

> To prevail on his ineffective-assistance claim, Mirzayance must show, therefore, that there is a "reasonable probability" that he would have prevailed on his insanity defense had he pursued it. This Mirzayance cannot do. It was highly improbable that a jury, which had just rejected testimony about Mirzayance's mental condition when the State bore the burden of proof, would have reached a different result when Mirzayance presented similar evidence at the NGI phase.

Page 1334. Add the following case at the end of the section:

Defendant's Unwillingness to Pursue a Strategy as a Waiver of the Right to Effective Assistance of Counsel: Schriro v. Landrigan.

In the following case the Court considers how the defendant's apparent refusal to permit a strategy affects his right to complain about counsel's ineffectiveness.

SCHRIRO v. LANDRIGAN

Supreme Court of the United States, 2007.
550 U.S. 465.

Justice Thomas delivered the opinion of the Court.

In cases where an applicant for federal habeas relief is not barred from obtaining an evidentiary hearing by 28 U.S.C. § 2254(e)(2), the decision to grant such a hearing rests in the discretion of the district court. Here, the District Court determined that respondent could not make out a colorable claim of ineffective assistance of counsel and therefore was not entitled to an evidentiary hearing. It did so after reviewing the state-court record and expanding the record to include additional evidence offered by the respondent. The Court of Appeals held that the District Court abused its discretion in refusing to grant the hearing. We hold that it did not.

I

Respondent Jeffrey Landrigan was convicted in Oklahoma of second-degree murder in 1982. In 1986, while in custody for that murder, Landrigan repeatedly stabbed another inmate and was subsequently convicted of assault and battery with a deadly weapon. Three years later, Landrigan escaped from prison and murdered Chester Dean Dyer in Arizona.

An Arizona jury found Landrigan guilty of theft, second-degree burglary, and felony murder for having caused the victim's death in the course of a burglary. At sentencing, Landrigan's counsel attempted to present the testimony of Landrigan's ex-wife and birth mother as mitigating evidence. But at Landrigan's request, both women refused to testify. When the trial judge asked why the witnesses refused, Landrigan's counsel responded that "it's at my client's wishes." Counsel explained that he had "advised [Landrigan] very strongly that I think it's very much against his interests to take that particular position." The court then questioned Landrigan:

> "THE COURT: Mr. Landrigan, have you instructed your lawyer that you do not wish for him to bring any mitigating circumstances to my attention?
>
> "THE DEFENDANT: Yeah.
>
> "THE COURT: Do you know what that means?
>
> "THE DEFENDANT: Yeah.
>
> "THE COURT: Mr. Landrigan, are there mitigating circumstances I should be aware of?
>
> "THE DEFENDANT: Not as far as I'm concerned."

Still not satisfied, the trial judge directly asked the witnesses to testify. Both refused. The judge then asked counsel to make a proffer of the witnesses' testimony. Counsel attempted to explain that the witnesses would testify that Landrigan's birth mother used drugs and alcohol (including while she was pregnant with Landrigan), that Landrigan abused drugs and alcohol, and that Landrigan had been a good father.

But Landrigan would have none of it. When counsel tried to explain that Landrigan had worked in a legitimate job to provide for his family, Landrigan interrupted and stated "if I wanted this to be heard, I'd have my wife say it." Landrigan then explained that he was not only working but also "doing robberies supporting my family." When counsel characterized Landrigan's first murder as having elements of self-defense, Landrigan interrupted and clarified: "He didn't grab me. I stabbed him." Responding to counsel's statement implying that the prison stabbing involved self-defense because the assaulted inmate knew Landrigan's first murder victim, Landrigan interrupted to clarify that the inmate was not acquainted with his first victim, but just "a guy I got in an argument with. I stabbed him 14 times. It was lucky he lived."

At the conclusion of the sentencing hearing, the judge asked Landrigan if he had anything to say. Landrigan made a brief statement that concluded, "I think if you want to give me the death penalty, just bring it right on. I'm ready for it."

The trial judge found two statutory aggravating circumstances: that Landrigan murdered Dyer in expectation of pecuniary gain and that Landrigan was previously convicted of two felonies involving the use or threat of violence on another person. In addition, the judge found two nonstatutory mitigating circumstances: that Landrigan's family loved him and an absence of premeditation. Finally, the trial judge stated that she considered Landrigan "a person who has no scruples and no regard for human life and human beings." Based on these findings, the court sentenced Landrigan to death. On direct appeal, the Arizona Supreme Court unanimously affirmed Landrigan's sentence and conviction. In addressing an ineffective-assistance-of-counsel claim not relevant here, the court noted that Landrigan had stated his "desire not to have mitigating evidence presented in his behalf."

On January 31, 1995, Landrigan filed a petition for state postconviction relief and alleged his counsel's "failure to explore additional grounds for arguing mitigation evidence." Specifically, Landrigan maintained that his counsel should have investigated the "biological component" of his violent behavior by interviewing his biological father and other relatives. In addition, Landrigan stated that his biological father could confirm that his biological mother used drugs and alcohol while pregnant with Landrigan.

The Arizona postconviction court, presided over by the same judge who tried and sentenced Landrigan, rejected Landrigan's claim. The court found that "[Landrigan] instructed his attorney not to present any evidence at the sentencing hearing, [so] it is difficult to comprehend how [Landrigan] can claim counsel should have presented other evidence at sentencing." Noting Landrigan's contention that he " 'would have cooperated' "had other mitigating evidence been presented, the court concluded that Landrigan's "statements at sentencing belie his new-found sense of cooperation." Describing Landrigan's claim as "frivolous," the court declined to hold an evidentiary hearing and dismissed Landrigan's

petition. The Arizona Supreme Court denied Landrigan's petition for review on June 19, 1996.

Landrigan then filed a federal habeas application under § 2254. The District Court determined, after "expanding the record to include ... evidence of [Landrigan's] troubled background, his history of drug and alcohol abuse, and his family's history of criminal behavior," that Landrigan could not demonstrate that he was prejudiced by any error his counsel may have made. Because Landrigan could not make out even a "colorable" ineffective-assistance-of-counsel claim, the District Court refused to grant him an evidentiary hearing.

On appeal, a unanimous panel of the Court of Appeals for the Ninth Circuit affirmed, but the full court granted rehearing en banc, and reversed. The en banc Court of Appeals held that Landrigan was entitled to an evidentiary hearing because he raised a "colorable claim" that his counsel's performance fell below the standard required by Strickland v. Washington, 466 U.S. 668 (1984). With respect to counsel's performance, the Ninth Circuit found that he "did little to prepare for the sentencing aspect of the case," and that investigation would have revealed a wealth of mitigating evidence, including the family's history of drug and alcohol abuse and propensity for violence.

Turning to prejudice, the court held the Arizona postconviction court's determination that Landrigan refused to permit his counsel to present any mitigating evidence was "an unreasonable determination of the facts." The Court of Appeals found that when Landrigan stated that he did not want his counsel to present any mitigating evidence, he was clearly referring only to the evidence his attorney was about to introduce—that of his ex-wife and birth mother. The court further held that, even if Landrigan intended to forgo the presentation of all mitigation evidence, such a "last-minute decision cannot excuse his counsel's failure to conduct an adequate investigation *prior* to the sentencing." In conclusion, the court found "a reasonable probability that, if Landrigan's allegations are true, the sentencing judge would have reached a different conclusion." The court therefore remanded the case for an evidentiary hearing.

We granted certiorari and now reverse.

II

Prior to the Antiterrorism and Effective Death Penalty Act of 1996 (AEDPA), the decision to grant an evidentiary hearing was generally left to the sound discretion of district courts. * * * AEDPA, however, changed the standards for granting federal habeas relief. Under AEDPA, Congress prohibited federal courts from granting habeas relief unless a state court's adjudication of a claim "resulted in a decision that was contrary to, or involved an unreasonable application of, clearly established Federal law, as determined by the Supreme Court of the United States," § 2254(d)(1), or the relevant state-court decision "was based on an unreasonable determination of the facts in light of the evidence presented in the State court proceeding" § 2254(d)(2). The question under AEDPA is not whether a

federal court believes the state court's determination was incorrect but whether that determination was unreasonable—a substantially higher threshold. *See* Williams v. Taylor, 529 U.S. 362, 410 (2000)[discussed in Chapter 13 of the Text]. AEDPA also requires federal habeas courts to presume the correctness of state courts' factual findings unless applicants rebut this presumption with "clear and convincing evidence." § 2254(e)(1).

In deciding whether to grant an evidentiary hearing, a federal court must consider whether such a hearing could enable an applicant to prove the petition's factual allegations, which, if true, would entitle the applicant to federal habeas relief. Because the deferential standards prescribed by § 2254 control whether to grant habeas relief, a federal court must take into account those standards in deciding whether an evidentiary hearing is appropriate. * * *

It follows that if the record refutes the applicant's factual allegations or otherwise precludes habeas relief, a district court is not required to hold an evidentiary hearing. * * *

* * *

III

For several reasons, the Court of Appeals believed that Landrigan might be entitled to federal habeas relief and that the District Court, therefore, abused its discretion by denying Landrigan an evidentiary hearing. To the contrary, the District Court was well within its discretion to determine that, even with the benefit of an evidentiary hearing, Landrigan could not develop a factual record that would entitle him to habeas relief.

A

The Court of Appeals first addressed the State's contention that Landrigan instructed his counsel not to offer any mitigating evidence. If Landrigan issued such an instruction, counsel's failure to investigate further could not have been prejudicial under *Strickland*. The Court of Appeals rejected the findings of the Arizona Supreme Court (on direct appeal) and the Arizona Superior Court (on habeas review) that Landrigan instructed his counsel not to introduce any mitigating evidence. According to the Ninth Circuit, those findings took Landrigan's colloquy with the sentencing court out of context in a manner that "amounts to an unreasonable determination of the facts."

Upon review of record material and the transcripts from the state courts, we disagree. As a threshold matter, the language of the colloquy plainly indicates that Landrigan informed his counsel not to present any mitigating evidence. When the Arizona trial judge asked Landrigan if he had instructed his lawyer not to present mitigating evidence, Landrigan responded affirmatively. Likewise, when asked if there was any relevant mitigating evidence, Landrigan answered, "Not as far as I'm concerned." These statements establish that the Arizona postconviction court's determination of the facts was reasonable. And it is worth noting, again, that the judge presiding on postconviction review was ideally situated to make this assessment because she is the same judge that sentenced Landrigan and discussed these issues with him.

Notwithstanding the plainness of these statements, the Court of Appeals concluded that they referred to only the specific testimony that counsel planned to offer—that of Landrigan's ex-wife and birth mother. The Court of Appeals further concluded that Landrigan, due to counsel's failure to investigate, could not have known about the mitigating evidence he now wants to explore. The record conclusively dispels that interpretation. First, Landrigan's birth mother would have offered testimony that overlaps with the evidence Landrigan now wants to present. For example, Landrigan wants to present evidence from his biological father that would "confirm [his biological mother's] alcohol and drug use during her pregnancy." But the record shows that counsel planned to call Landrigan's birth mother to testify about her "drug use during her pregnancy," and the possible effects of such drug use. Second, Landrigan interrupted repeatedly when counsel tried to proffer anything that could have been considered mitigating. He even refused to allow his attorney to proffer that he had worked a regular job at one point. This behavior confirms what is plain from the transcript of the colloquy: that Landrigan would have undermined the presentation of any mitigating evidence that his attorney might have uncovered.

On the record before us, the Arizona court's determination that Landrigan refused to allow the presentation of any mitigating evidence was a reasonable determination of the facts. * * *

Because the Arizona postconviction court reasonably determined that Landrigan "instructed his attorney not to bring any mitigation to the attention of the [sentencing] court," it was not an abuse of discretion for the District Court to conclude that Landrigan could not overcome § 2254(d)(2)'s bar to granting federal habeas relief. The District Court was entitled to conclude that regardless of what information counsel might have uncovered in his investigation, Landrigan would have interrupted and refused to allow his counsel to present any such evidence. Accordingly, the District Court could conclude that because of his established recalcitrance, Landrigan could not demonstrate prejudice under *Strickland* even if granted an evidentiary hearing.

B

The Court of Appeals offered two alternative reasons for holding that Landrigan's inability to make a showing of prejudice under *Strickland* did not bar any potential habeas relief and, thus, an evidentiary hearing.

1

The Court of Appeals held that, even if Landrigan did not want any mitigating evidence presented, the Arizona courts' determination that Landrigan's claims were "frivolous and meritless was an unreasonable application of United States Supreme Court precedent." This holding was founded on the belief, derived from Wiggins v. Smith, 539 U.S. 510 (2003), that "Landrigan's apparently last-minute decision cannot excuse his counsel's failure to conduct an adequate investigation *prior* to the sentencing."

Neither *Wiggins* nor *Strickland* addresses a situation in which a client interferes with counsel's efforts to present mitigating evidence to a sentencing court. * * * Indeed, we have never addressed a situation like this. In Rompilla v. Beard, 545 U.S. 374, 381 (2005), on which the Court of Appeals also relied, the defendant refused to assist in the development of a mitigation case, but did not inform the court that he did not want mitigating evidence presented. In short, at the time of the Arizona postconviction court's decision, it was not objectively unreasonable for that court to conclude that a defendant who refused to allow the presentation of any mitigating evidence could not establish *Strickland* prejudice based on his counsel's failure to investigate further possible mitigating evidence.

2

The Court of Appeals also stated that the record does not indicate that Landrigan's decision not to present mitigating evidence was "informed and knowing," and that "the trial court's dialogue with Landrigan tells us little about his understanding of the consequences of his decision." We have never imposed an "informed and knowing" requirement upon a defendant's decision not to introduce evidence. Even assuming, however, that an "informed and knowing" requirement exists in this case, Landrigan cannot benefit from it, for three reasons.

First, Landrigan never presented this claim to the Arizona courts. Rather, he argued that he would have complied had other evidence been offered. Thus, Landrigan failed to develop this claim properly before the Arizona courts, and § 2254(e)(2) therefore barred the District Court from granting an evidentiary hearing on that basis.

Second, in Landrigan's presence, his counsel told the sentencing court that he had carefully explained to Landrigan the importance of mitigating evidence, "especially concerning the fact that the State is seeking the death penalty." Counsel also told the court that he had explained to Landrigan that as counsel, he had a duty to disclose "any and all mitigating factors ... to the court for consideration regarding the sentencing." In light of Landrigan's demonstrated propensity for interjecting himself into the proceedings, it is doubtful that Landrigan would have sat idly by while his counsel lied about having previously discussed these issues with him. And as Landrigan's counsel conceded at oral argument before this Court, we have never required a specific colloquy to ensure that a defendant knowingly and intelligently refused to present mitigating evidence.

Third, the Court of Appeals overlooked Landrigan's final statement to the sentencing court: "I think if you want to give me the death penalty, just bring it right on. I'm ready for it." It is apparent from this statement that Landrigan clearly understood the consequences of telling the judge that, "as far as [he was] concerned," there were no mitigating circumstances of which she should be aware.

IV

Finally, the Court of Appeals erred in rejecting the District Court's finding that the poor quality of Landrigan's alleged mitigating evidence prevented him from making "a colorable claim" of prejudice. As summarized by the Court of Appeals, Landrigan wanted to introduce as mitigation evidence:

"[that] he was exposed to alcohol and drugs *in utero,* which may have resulted in cognitive and behavioral deficiencies consistent with fetal alcohol syndrome. He was abandoned by his birth mother and suffered abandonment and attachment issues, as well as other behavioral problems throughout his childhood. His adoptive mother was also an alcoholic, and Landrigan's own alcohol and substance abuse began at an early age. Based on his biological family's history of violence, Landrigan claims he may also have been genetically predisposed to violence."

As explained above, all but the last sentence refer to information that Landrigan's birth mother and ex-wife could have offered if Landrigan had allowed them to testify. Indeed, the state postconviction court had much of this evidence before it by way of counsel's proffer. The District Court could reasonably conclude that any additional evidence would have made no difference in the sentencing.

In sum, the District Court did not abuse its discretion in finding that Landrigan could not establish prejudice based on his counsel's failure to present the evidence he now wishes to offer. Landrigan's mitigation evidence was weak, and the postconviction court was well acquainted with Landrigan's exceedingly violent past and had seen first hand his belligerent behavior.

Again, it is difficult to improve upon the initial Court of Appeals panel's conclusion:

> "The prospect was chilling; before he was 30 years of age, Landrigan had murdered one man, repeatedly stabbed another one, escaped from prison, and within two months murdered still another man. As the Arizona Supreme Court so aptly put it when dealing with one of Landrigan's other claims, 'in his comments [to the sentencing judge], defendant not only failed to show remorse or offer mitigating evidence, but he flaunted his menacing behavior.' On this record, assuring the court that genetics made him the way he is could not have been very helpful. There was no prejudice."

V

The Court of Appeals erred in holding that the District Court abused its discretion in declining to grant Landrigan an evidentiary hearing. Even assuming the truth of all the facts Landrigan sought to prove at the evidentiary hearing, he still could not be granted federal habeas relief because the state courts' factual determination that Landrigan would not have allowed counsel to present any mitigating evidence at sentencing is not an unreasonable determination of the facts under § 2254(d)(2) and the mitigating evidence he seeks to introduce would not have changed the result. In such circumstances, a District Court has discretion to deny an evidentiary hearing. The judgment of the Court of Appeals for the Ninth Circuit is reversed, and the case is remanded for further proceedings consistent with this opinion.

It is so ordered.

JUSTICE STEVENS, with whom JUSTICE SOUTER, JUSTICE GINSBURG, and JUSTICE BREYER join, dissenting.

Significant mitigating evidence—evidence that may well have explained respondent's criminal conduct and unruly behavior at his capital sentencing hearing—was unknown at the time of sentencing. Only years later did respondent learn that he suffers from a serious psychological condition that sheds important light on his earlier actions. The reason why this and other mitigating evidence was unavailable is that respondent's counsel failed to conduct a constitutionally adequate investigation. In spite of this, the Court holds that respondent is not entitled to an evidentiary hearing to explore the prejudicial impact of his counsel's inadequate representation. It reasons that respondent "would have" waived his right to introduce any mitigating evidence that counsel might have uncovered, and that such evidence "would have" made no difference in the sentencing anyway. Without the benefit of an evidentiary hearing, this is pure guesswork.

The Court's decision rests on a parsimonious appraisal of a capital defendant's constitutional right to have the sentencing decision reflect meaningful consideration of all relevant mitigating evidence, a begrudging appreciation of the need for a knowing and intelligent waiver of constitutionally protected trial rights, and a cramped reading of the record. Unlike this Court, the en banc Court of Appeals properly accounted for these important constitutional and factual considerations. Its narrow holding that the

District Court abused its discretion in denying respondent an evidentiary hearing should be affirmed.

I

No one, not even the Court, seriously contends that counsel's investigation of possible mitigating evidence was constitutionally sufficient. * * * The list of evidence that counsel failed to investigate is long. For instance, counsel did not complete a psychological evaluation of respondent, which we now know would have uncovered a serious organic brain disorder. He failed to consult an expert to explore the effects of respondent's birth mother's drinking and drug use during pregnancy. And he never developed a history of respondent's troubled childhood with his adoptive family—a childhood marked by physical and emotional abuse, neglect by his adoptive parents, his own serious substance abuse problems (including an overdose in his eighth or ninth grade classroom), a stunted education, and recurrent placement in substance abuse rehabilitation facilities, a psychiatric ward, and police custody. Counsel's failure to develop this background evidence was so glaring that even the sentencing judge noted that she had "received very little information concerning the defendant's difficult family history." At the time of sentencing, counsel was only prepared to put on the testimony by respondent's ex-wife and birth mother. By any measure, and especially for a capital case, this meager investigation "fell below an objective standard of reasonableness."

Given this deficient performance, the only issue is whether counsel's inadequate investigation prejudiced the outcome of sentencing. The bulk of the Court's opinion argues that the District Court reasonably found that respondent waived his right to present any and all mitigating evidence. As I shall explain, this argument finds no support in the Constitution or the record of this case.

II

It is well established that a citizen's waiver of a constitutional right must be knowing, intelligent, and voluntary.

* * *

Given this unmistakable focus on trial rights, it makes little difference that we have not specifically "imposed an 'informed and knowing' requirement upon a defendant's decision not to introduce evidence." A capital defendant's right to present mitigating evidence is firmly established and can only be exercised at a sentencing *trial*. For a capital defendant, the right to have the sentencing authority give full consideration to mitigating evidence that might support a sentence other than death is of paramount importance * * * . Our longstanding precedent * * * requires that any waiver of the right to adduce such evidence be knowing, intelligent, and voluntary. As such, the state postconviction court's conclusion that respondent completely waived his right to present mitigating evidence involved an unreasonable application of clearly established federal law as determined by this Court. See 28 U.S.C. § 2254(d)(1).

Respondent's statements at the sentencing hearing do not qualify as an informed waiver under our precedents. To understand why, it is important to remember the context in which the waiver issue arose. In all of his postconviction proceedings, respondent has never brought a freestanding claim that he failed to knowingly or intelligently waive his right to present mitigating evidence. That is because respondent believes he never waived his right to present all available mitigating evidence. Respondent's only claim is that his counsel was ineffective for failing to investigate and present mitigating evidence.

In light of this posture, the Court's conclusion that respondent cannot make a knowing-and-intelligent-waiver argument because he failed to present it in the Arizona courts is nothing short of baffling. Respondent never intended for waiver to become an issue because he never thought it was an issue. Waiver only became a concern when he was forced to answer: (1) the State's argument that he could not establish prejudice under *Strickland* because he waived the right to present all mitigating evidence; and (2) the state postconviction court's conclusion that "since the defendant instructed his attorney not to bring any mitigation to the attention of the court, he cannot now claim counsel was ineffective because he did not 'explore additional grounds for arguing mitigation evidence.'" It is instructive that both the State and the postconviction court considered the waiver issue within the context of the prejudice prong of respondent's ineffective-assistance-of-counsel claim. Even now, respondent's only "claim" within the meaning of 28 U.S.C. § 2254(e)(2) is that his counsel was ineffective for not ade-

quately investigating and presenting mitigating evidence. An *argument*—particularly one made in the alternative and in response to another party—is fundamentally different from a *claim*.

Turning back to that claim, respondent's purported waiver can only be appreciated in light of his counsel's deficient performance. To take just one example, respondent's counsel asked a psychologist, Dr. Mickey McMahon, to conduct an initial interview with respondent. But Dr. McMahon has submitted an affidavit stating that his experience was "quite different from the working relationship [he] had with counsel on other death penalty cases in which the psychological study went through a series of steps." In this case, Dr. McMahon was "not authorized to conduct the next step in psychological testing that would have told [him] if . . . there were any cognitive or neuropsychological deficits not observed during just an interview." Even though Dr. McMahon told respondent's counsel that "much more work was needed to provide an appropriate psychological study for a death penalty case," *ibid.*, counsel refused to let him investigate any further.

A more thorough investigation would have revealed that respondent suffers from an organic brain disorder. Years after Dr. McMahon's aborted examination, another psychologist, Dr. Thomas C. Thompson, conducted a complete analysis of respondent. Based on extensive interviews with respondent and several of his family members, a review of his family history, and multiple clinical tests, Dr. Thompson diagnosed respondent with Antisocial Personality Disorder. Dr. Thompson filed an affidavit in the District Court describing his diagnosis:

> "[Respondent's] actions did not constitute a lifestyle choice in the sense of an individual operating with a large degree of freedom, as we have come to define free will. The inherited, prenatal, and early developmental factors severely impaired Mr. Landrigan's ability to function in a society that expects individuals to operate in an organized and adaptive manner, taking into account the actions and consequences of their behaviors and their impact on society and its individual members. Based on evaluation and investigation along with other relevant data, this type of responsible functioning is simply beyond Mr. Landrigan and, as far back as one can go, there is no indication that he ever had these capacities."

On the day of the sentencing hearing, the only mitigating evidence that respondent's counsel had investigated was the testimony of respondent's birth mother and ex-wife. None of this neuropsychological information was available to respondent at the time of his purported waiver. Yet the Court conspicuously avoids any mention of respondent's organic brain disorder. It instead provides an incomplete list of other mitigating evidence that respondent would have presented and incorrectly assumes that respondent's birth mother and ex-wife would have covered it all. Unless I missed the portion of the record indicating that respondent's ex-wife and birth mother were trained psychologists, neither could have offered expert testimony about respondent's organic brain disorder.

It is of course true that respondent was aware of many of the individual pieces of mitigating evidence that contributed to Dr. Thompson's subsequent diagnosis. He knew that his birth mother abandoned him at the age of six months; that his biological family had an extensive criminal history; that his adoptive mother had "affective disturbances and chronic alcoholism"; that she routinely drank vodka until she passed out; that she would frequently strike him, once even "hit[ting him] with a frying pan hard enough to leave a dent"; that his childhood was difficult and he exhibited abandonment and attachment problems at an early age; that he had a bad temper and often threw violent tantrums as a child; and that he began getting into trouble and using alcohol and drugs at an early age and, by adolescence, he had begun a series of placements in juvenile detention facilities, a psychiatric ward, and twice in drug abuse rehabilitation programs. Perhaps respondent also knew that his biological mother abused alcohol and amphetamines during her pregnancy, and that *in utero* exposure to drugs and alcohol has deleterious effects on the child.

But even if respondent knew all these things, we cannot assume that he could understand their consequences the way an expert psychologist could. Without years of advanced education and a battery of complicated testing, respondent could not know that these experiences resulted in a serious organic brain disorder or what effect such a disorder might have on his behavior. And precisely because his counsel failed to conduct a proper investigation, he did not know that this important evidence was available to him when he purportedly waived the right to present mitigating evidence. It is hard to see how respondent's claim of *Strickland* prejudice can be prejudiced by counsel's *Strickland* error.

Without ever acknowledging that respondent lacked this information, the Court clings to counsel's discussion with respondent about "the importance of mitigating evidence." * * * [C]ounsel's abstract explanation cannot satisfy the demands of [knowing and voluntary waiver]. Unless respondent knew of the most significant mitigation evidence available to him, he could not have made a knowing and intelligent waiver of his constitutional rights. * * *

III

Even if the putative waiver had been fully informed, the Arizona postconviction court's determination that respondent "instructed his attorney not to bring any mitigation to the attention of the [sentencing] court" is plainly contradicted by the record. The Court nevertheless defers to this finding, concluding that it was not an "unreasonable determination of the facts" under 28 U.S.C. § 2254(d)(2). * * * A careful examination of the "record material and the transcripts from the state courts," does not indicate that respondent intended to make a waiver that went beyond the testimony of his birth mother and ex-wife.

The Court reads the following exchange as definitive proof that respondent "informed his counsel not to present any mitigating evidence":

"THE COURT: Mr. Landrigan, have you instructed your lawyer that you do not wish for him to bring any mitigating circumstances to my attention?

"THE DEFENDANT: Yeah.

"THE COURT: Do you know what that means?

"THE DEFENDANT: Yeah.

"THE COURT: Mr. Landrigan, are there mitigating circumstances I should be aware of?

"THE DEFENDANT: Not as far as I'm concerned."

* * *

The brief exchange between respondent and the trial court must be considered in the context of the *entire* sentencing proceeding. The above-quoted dialogue came immediately after a lengthy colloquy between the trial court and respondent's counsel:

"MR. FARRELL: Your Honor, at this time ... I have two witnesses that I wished to testify before this Court, one I had brought in from out of state and is my client's ex-wife, Ms. Sandy Landrigan. The second witness is my client's natural mother, Virginia Gipson. I believe both of those people had some important evidence that I believed the Court should take into mitigation concerning my client. *However, Mr. Landrigan has made it clear to me ... that he does not wish anyone from his family to testify on his behalf today.*

"I have talked with Sandra Landrigan, his ex-wife. I have talked a number of times with her and confirmed what I thought was important evidence that she should present for the Court. And I have also talked with Ms. Gipson, and her evidence I think is very important and should have been brought to this Court's attention. Both of them, after talking with Jeff today, have agreed with their, in one case son and the other ex-husband, they will not testify in his behalf.

"THE COURT: Why not?

"MR. FARRELL: Basically it's at my client's wishes, Your Honor. I told him that in order to effectively represent him, especially concerning the fact that the State is seeking the death penalty, any and all mitigating factors, I was under a duty to disclose those factors to this Court for consideration regarding the sentencing. He is adamant he does not want any testimony from his family, specifically these two people that I have here, his mother, under subpoena, and as well as having flown in his ex-wife."

Respondent's answers to the trial judge's questions must be read in light of this discussion. When the judge immediately turned from counsel to respondent and asked about "any mitigating circumstances," the entire proceeding to that point had been about the possible testimony of his birth mother or ex-wife. Counsel had only informed the court that respondent did not want any testimony "from his family." Neither counsel nor respondent said anything about other mitigating evidence. A fair reading of the full sentencing transcript makes clear that respondent's answers referred only to the testimony of his ex-wife and birth mother.

What is more, respondent's answers were necessarily infected by his counsel's failure to investigate. Respondent does not dispute that he instructed his counsel not to present his family's testimony. But his limited waiver cannot change the fact that he was unaware that the words "any mitigating circumstances" could include his organic brain disorder, the medical consequences of his mother's drinking and drug use during pregnancy, and his abusive upbringing with his adoptive family. In respondent's mind, the words "any mitigating circumstances" just meant the incomplete evidence that counsel offered to present. As the en banc Court of Appeals explained, "had his lawyer conducted an investigation and uncovered other types of mitigating evidence, Landrigan might well have been able to direct the court to other mitigating circumstances." It is therefore error to read respondent's simple "Yeah" and "Not as far as I'm concerned" as waiving anything other than the little he knew was available to him.

Accordingly, the state postconviction court's finding that petitioner waived his right to present any mitigating evidence was an unreasonable determination of the facts under § 2254(d)(2). * * *

While I believe that neither the Constitution nor the record supports the Court's waiver holding, respondent is at least entitled to an evidentiary hearing on this question as well as his broader claim of ineffective assistance of counsel. Respondent insists that he never instructed his counsel not to investigate other mitigating evidence. Even the State concedes that there has been no finding on this issue.

He has long maintained that he would have permitted the presentation of mitigating evidence if only counsel was prepared to introduce evidence other than testimony from his birth mother and ex-wife. Respondent planned to call his counsel at an evidentiary hearing to testify about these very assertions. Because counsel is in the best position to clarify whether respondent gave any blanket instructions not to investigate or present mitigating evidence, the Court is wrong to decide this case before any evidence regarding respondent's instructions can be developed.

IV

* * *

V

In the end, the Court's decision can only be explained by its increasingly familiar effort to guard the floodgates of litigation. Immediately before turning to the facts of this case, it states that "if district courts were required to allow federal habeas applicants to develop even the most insubstantial factual allegations in evidentiary hearings, district courts would be forced to reopen factual disputes that were conclusively resolved in the state courts." However, habeas cases requiring evidentiary hearings have

been "few in number," and there is no clear evidence that this particular classification of habeas proceedings has burdened the dockets of the federal courts. Even prior to the passage of the Antiterriorism and Effective Death Act of 1996, district courts held evidentiary hearings in only 1.17% of all federal habeas cases. See Report to the Federal Courts Study Committee of the Subcommittee on the Role of the Federal Courts and their Relation to the States (Mar. 12, 1990) (Richard A. Posner, Chair), in 1 Federal Courts Study Committee, Working Papers and Subcommittee Reports 468–515 (July 1, 1990). This figure makes it abundantly clear that doing justice does not always cause the heavens to fall. * * *

It may well be true that respondent would have completely waived his right to present mitigating evidence if that evidence had been adequately investigated at the time of sentencing. It may also be true that respondent's mitigating evidence could not outweigh his violent past. What is certainly true, however, is that an evidentiary hearing would provide answers to these questions. I emphatically agree with the majority of judges on the en banc Court of Appeals that it was an abuse of discretion to refuse to conduct such a hearing in this capital case.

Accordingly, I respectfully dissent.

5. *Per Se Ineffectiveness and Prejudice*

Page 1343. Add the following note after the note on Sleeping Defense Counsel:

Counsel Present Only By Speakerphone:
Wright v. Van Patten

In *Wright v. Van Patten*, 128 S.Ct. 743 (2008), a habeas petitioner argued that he was *per se* prejudiced when his counsel participated at his plea hearing only through a speakerphone. He contended that this amounted to a virtual absence of counsel and therefore counsel was automatically ineffective under *Cronic*. The government argued that counsel's effectiveness should be evaluated under the *Strickland* standard—and under that standard all parties agree that the defendant could not prove ineffectiveness and prejudice. The state court had held that *Strickland* and not *Cronic* was applicable.

Because the Court was reviewing a habeas petition, the standard of review was whether the state court "unreasonably applied clearly established Federal law." 28 U.S.C. § 2254(d). [See Teague v. Lane, Chapter One.] The Court, in a per curiam decision, held that *Cronic* was not clearly applicable to the present circumstances. It analyzed the question as follows:

> Strickland v. Washington, 466 U.S. 668 (1984) ordinarily applies to claims of ineffective assistance of counsel at the plea hearing stage. * * * And it was in a different context that *Cronic* recognized a narrow exception to "*Strickland's* holding that a defendant who asserts ineffective assistance of counsel must demonstrate not only that his attorney's performance was deficient, but also that the deficiency prejudiced the defense. Florida v. Nixon," 543 U.S. 175, 190 (2004). *Cronic* held that a Sixth Amendment violation may be found without inquiring into counsel's actual performance or requiring the defendant to show the effect it had on the trial, when "circumstances [exist] that are so likely to prejudice the accused that the cost of litigating their effect in a particular case is unjustified," *Cronic, supra,* at 658. *Cronic,* not *Strickland,* applies "when . . . the likelihood that any lawyer, even a fully competent one, could provide effective assistance is so small that a presumption of prejudice is appropriate without inquiry into the actual conduct of the trial," and one circumstance warranting the presumption is the "complete denial of counsel," that is, when "counsel [is] either totally absent, or prevented from assisting the accused during a critical stage of the proceeding," id., at 659.
>
> No decision of this Court, however, squarely addresses the issue in this case, or clearly establishes that *Cronic* should replace *Strickland* in this novel factual context. Our precedents do not clearly hold that counsel's participation by speaker phone should be treated as a "complete denial of counsel," on par with total absence. Even if we agree with Van Patten that a lawyer physically present will tend to perform better than one on the phone, it does not necessarily follow that mere telephone contact amounted to total absence or "prevented [counsel] from assisting the accused," so as to entail application of *Cronic*. The question is not whether counsel in those circumstances will perform less well than he otherwise would, but whether the circumstances are likely to result in such poor performance that an inquiry into its effects would not be worth the time. Our cases provide no categorical answer to this question, and for that matter the several proceedings in this case hardly point toward one. * * *

Because our cases give no clear answer to the question presented, let alone one in Van Patten's favor, it cannot be said that the state court unreasonably applied clearly established Federal law. Under the explicit terms of § 2254(d)(1), therefore, relief is unauthorized.

Justice Stevens, the author of *Cronic*, reluctantly concurred in the judgment. He rued the fact that his opinion for the Court in *Cronic* did not make it clear that the *physical* presence of counsel at trial or a guilty plea hearing was critical. He elaborated as follows:

An unfortunate drafting error in the Court's opinion in United States v. Cronic makes it necessary to join the Court's judgment in this case.

In *Cronic,* this Court explained that some violations of the right to counsel arise in "circumstances that are so likely to prejudice the accused that the cost of litigating their effect in a particular case is unjustified." One such circumstance exists when the accused is "denied the presence of counsel at a critical stage of the prosecution." We noted that the "presence" of lawyers "is essential because they are the means through which the other rights of the person on trial are secured." Regrettably, *Cronic* did not "clearly establish" the full scope of the defendant's right to the presence of an attorney. See 28 U.S.C. § 2254(d)(1).

The Court of Appeals apparently read "the presence of counsel" in *Cronic* to mean "the presence of counsel *in open court.*" Initially, all three judges on the panel assumed that the constitutional right at stake was the right to have counsel by one's side at all critical stages of the proceeding. In my view, this interpretation is correct. The fact that in 1984, when *Cronic* was decided, neither the parties nor the Court contemplated representation by attorneys who were not present in the flesh explains the author's failure to add the words "in open court" after the word "present."

* * * In light of *Cronic's* references to the "complete denial of counsel" and "totally absent" counsel, and the opinion's failure to state more explicitly that the defendant is entitled to "the presence of counsel [in open court]," I acquiesce in this Court's conclusion that the state-court decision was not an unreasonable application of clearly established federal law. In doing so, however, I emphasize that today's opinion does not say that the state courts' interpretation of *Cronic* was correct, or that we would have accepted that reading if the case had come to us on direct review rather than by way of 28 U.S.C. § 2254.

VIII.   SELF–REPRESENTATION

A.   THE CONSTITUTIONAL RIGHT

Page 1393. Add at the end of the headnote on Competency to Waive the Right to Counsel and Proceed *Pro Se*:

INDIANA v. EDWARDS

Supreme Court of the United States, 2008.
128 S.Ct. 2379.

JUSTICE BREYER **delivered the opinion of the Court.**

This case focuses upon a criminal defendant whom a state court found mentally competent to stand trial if represented by counsel but not mentally competent to conduct that trial himself. We must decide whether in these circumstances the Constitution forbids a State from insisting that the defendant proceed to trial with counsel, the State thereby denying the defendant the right to represent himself. See Faretta v. California, 422 U.S. 806 (1975). We conclude that the Constitution does not forbid a State so to insist.

I

In July 1999 Ahmad Edwards, the respondent, tried to steal a pair of shoes from an Indiana department store. After he was discovered, he drew a gun, fired at a store security officer, and wounded a bystander. He was caught and then charged with attempted murder, battery with a deadly weapon, criminal recklessness, and theft. His mental condition subsequently became the subject of three competency proceedings and two self-representation requests, mostly before the same trial judge:

1.

First Competency Hearing: August 2000. Five months after Ed-wards' arrest, his court-appointed counsel asked for a psychiatric evaluation. After hearing psychiatrist and neuropsychologist witnesses (in February 2000 and again in August 2000), the court found Edwards incompetent to stand trial, App. 365a, and committed him to Logansport State Hospital for evaluation and treatment.

2.

Second Competency Hearing: March 2002. Seven months after his commitment, doctors found that Edwards' condition had improved to the point where he could stand trial. Several months later, however, but still before trial, Edwards' counsel asked for another psychiatric evaluation. In March 2002, the judge held a competency hearing, considered additional psychiatric evidence, and (in April) found that Edwards, while "suffer[ing] from mental illness," was "competent to assist his attorneys in his defense and stand trial for the charged crimes."

3.

Third Competency Hearing: April 2003. Seven months later but still before trial, Edwards' counsel sought yet another psychiatric evaluation of his client. And, in April

2003, the court held yet another competency hearing. Edwards' counsel presented further psychiatric and neuropsychological evidence showing that Edwards was suffering from serious thinking difficulties and delusions. * * * In November 2003, the court concluded that Edwards was not then competent to stand trial and ordered his recommitment to the state hospital.

4.

First Self–Representation Request and First Trial: June 2005. About eight months after his commitment, the hospital reported that Edwards' condition had again improved to the point that he had again become competent to stand trial. And almost one year after that Edwards' trial began. Just before trial, Edwards asked to represent himself. He also asked for a continuance, which, he said, he needed in order to proceed *pro se*. The court refused the continuance. Edwards then proceeded to trial represented by counsel. The jury convicted him of criminal recklessness and theft but failed to reach a verdict on the charges of attempted murder and battery.

5.

Second Self–Representation Request and Second Trial: December 2005. The State decided to retry Edwards on the attempted murder and battery charges. Just before the retrial, Edwards again asked the court to permit him to represent himself. Referring to the lengthy record of psychiatric reports, the trial court noted that Edwards still suffered from schizophrenia and concluded that "[w]ith these findings, he's competent to stand trial but I'm not going to find he's competent to defend himself." The court denied Edwards' self-representation request. Edwards was represented by appointed counsel at his retrial. The jury convicted Edwards on both of the remaining counts.

Edwards subsequently appealed to Indiana's intermediate appellate court. He argued that the trial court's refusal to permit him to represent himself at his retrial deprived him of his constitutional right of self-representation. The court agreed and ordered a new trial. The matter then went to the Indiana Supreme Court. That court found that "[t]he record in this case presents a substantial basis to agree with the trial court," but it nonetheless affirmed the intermediate appellate court on the belief that this Court's precedents, namely, *Faretta*, and Godinez v. Moran, 509 U.S. 389 (1993), required the State to allow Edwards to represent himself. At Indiana's request, we agreed to consider whether the Constitution required the trial court to allow Edwards to represent himself at trial.

II

Our examination of this Court's precedents convinces us that those precedents frame the question presented, but they do not answer it. The two cases that set forth the Constitution's "mental competence" standard, Dusky v. United States, 362 U.S. 402 (1960), and Drope v. Missouri, 420 U.S. 162 (1975), specify that the Constitution does not permit trial of an individual who lacks "mental competency." *Dusky* defines the competency standard as including both (1) "whether" the defendant has "a rational as well as factual understanding of the proceedings against him" and (2) whether the defendant "has sufficient present ability *to consult with his lawyer* with a reasonable degree of rational understanding." *Drope* repeats that standard, stating that it "has long been accepted that a person whose mental condition is such that he lacks the capacity to understand the nature and object of the proceedings against him, *to consult with counsel, and to assist in preparing his defense* may not be subjected to a trial." Neither case considered the mental competency issue presented here, namely, the relation of the mental competence standard to the right of self-representation.

The Court's foundational "self-representation" case, *Faretta*, held that the Sixth and Fourteenth Amendments include a "constitutional right to proceed *without* counsel when" a criminal defendant "voluntarily and intelligently elects to do so." * * *

Faretta does not answer the question before us both because it did not consider the problem of mental competency, and because *Faretta* itself and later cases have made clear that the right of self-representation is not absolute. The question here concerns a mental-illness-related limitation on the scope of the self-representation right.

The sole case in which this Court considered mental competence and self-representation together, *Godinez, supra,* presents a question closer to that at issue here. The case focused upon a borderline-competent criminal defendant who had asked a state trial court to permit him to represent himself and to change his pleas from not guilty to guilty. The state trial court had found that the defendant met *Dusky*'s mental competence standard, that he "knowingly and intelligently" waived his right to assistance of counsel, and that he "freely and voluntarily" chose to plead guilty. And the state trial court had consequently granted the defendant's self-representation and change-of-plea requests. A federal appeals court, however, had vacated the defendant's guilty pleas on the ground that the Constitution required the trial court to ask a further question, namely, whether the defendant was competent to waive his constitutional right to counsel. * * *

This Court, reversing the Court of Appeals, "reject[ed] the notion that competence to plead guilty or to waive the right to counsel must be measured by a standard that is higher than (or even different from) the *Dusky* standard." The decision to plead guilty, we said, "is no more complicated than the sum total of decisions that a [represented] defendant may be called upon to make during the course of a trial." Hence "there is no reason to believe that the decision to waive counsel requires an appreciably higher level of mental functioning than the decision to waive other constitutional rights." And even assuming that self-representation might pose special trial-related difficulties, "the competence that is required of a defendant seeking to waive his right to counsel is the competence to *waive the right,* not the competence to represent himself." * * *

We concede that *Godinez* bears certain similarities with the present case. Both involve mental competence and self-representation. Both involve a defendant who wants to represent himself. Both involve a mental condition that falls in a gray area between *Dusky*'s minimal constitutional requirement that measures a defendant's ability to stand trial and a somewhat higher standard that measures mental fitness for another legal purpose.

We nonetheless conclude that *Godinez* does not answer the question before us now. In part that is because the Court of Appeals higher standard at issue in *Godinez* differs in a critical way from the higher standard at issue here. In *Godinez,* the higher standard sought to measure the defendant's ability to proceed on his own to enter a guilty plea; here the higher standard seeks to measure the defendant's ability to conduct trial proceedings. To put the matter more specifically, the *Godinez* defendant sought only to change his pleas to guilty, he did not seek to conduct trial proceedings, and his ability to conduct a defense at trial was expressly not at issue. * * * In this case, the very matters that we did not consider in *Godinez* are directly before us.

For another thing, *Godinez* involved a State that sought to *permit* a gray-area defendant to represent himself. *Godinez*'s constitutional holding is that a State may do so. But that holding simply does not tell a State whether it may *deny* a gray-area defendant the right to represent himself—the matter at issue here. One might argue that *Godinez*'s grant (to a State) of permission to allow a gray-area defendant self-representation must implicitly include permission to deny self-representation. Yet one could more forcefully argue that *Godinez* simply did not consider whether the Constitution *requires* self-representation by gray-area defendants even in circumstances where the State seeks to disallow it (the question here). The upshot is that, in our view, the question before us is an open one.

III

We now turn to the question presented. We assume that a criminal defendant has sufficient mental competence to stand trial (*i.e.,* the defendant meets *Dusky*'s standard) and that the defendant insists on representing himself during that trial. We ask whether the Constitution permits a State to limit that defendant's self-representation right by insisting upon representation by counsel at trial—on the ground that the defendant lacks the mental capacity to conduct his trial defense unless represented.

Several considerations taken together lead us to conclude that the answer to this question is yes. First, the Court's precedent, while not answering the question, points slightly in the direction of our affirmative answer. *Godinez,* as we have just said, simply leaves the question open. But the Court's "mental competency" cases set forth a standard that focuses directly upon a defendant's "present ability to consult with his lawyer." These standards assume representation by counsel and emphasize the importance of counsel. They thus suggest (though do not hold) that an instance in which a defendant who would choose to forgo counsel at trial presents a very different set of circumstances, which in our view, calls for a different standard.

* * *

Second, the nature of the problem before us cautions against the use of a single mental competency standard for deciding both (1) whether a defendant who is represented by counsel can proceed to trial and (2) whether a defendant who goes to trial must be permitted to represent himself. Mental illness itself is not a unitary concept. It varies in degree. It can vary over time. It interferes with an individual's functioning at different times in different ways. * * * In certain instances an individual may well be able to satisfy *Dusky*'s mental competence standard, for he will be able to work with counsel at trial, yet at the same time he may be unable to carry out the basic tasks needed to present his own defense without the help of counsel.

The American Psychiatric Association (APA) tells us (without dispute) in its *amicus* brief filed in support of neither party that "[d]isorganized thinking, deficits in sustaining attention and concentration, impaired expressive abilities, anxiety, and other common symptoms of severe mental illnesses can impair the defendant's ability to play the significantly expanded role required for self-representation even if he can play the lesser role of represented defendant." * * *

Third, in our view, a right of self-representation at trial will not "affirm the dignity" of a defendant who lacks the mental capacity to conduct his defense without the assistance of counsel. To the contrary, given that defendant's uncertain mental state, the spectacle that could well result from his self-representation at trial is at least as likely to prove humiliating as ennobling. Moreover, insofar as a defendant's lack of capacity threatens an improper conviction or sentence, self-representation in that exceptional context undercuts the most basic of the Constitution's criminal law objectives, providing a fair trial. * * *

Further, proceedings must not only be fair, they must "appear fair to all who observe them." Wheat v. United States, 486 U.S. 153, 160 (1988). An *amicus* brief reports one psychiatrist's reaction to having observed a patient (a patient who had satisfied *Dusky*) try to conduct his own defense: "[H]ow in the world can our legal system allow an insane man to defend himself?" The application of *Dusky*'s basic mental competence standard can help in part to avoid this result. But given the different capacities needed to proceed to trial without counsel, there is little reason to believe that *Dusky* alone is sufficient. At the same time, the trial judge, particularly one such as the trial judge in this case, who presided over one of Edwards' competency hearings and his two trials, will often prove best able to make more fine-tuned mental capacity decisions, tailored to the individualized circumstances of a particular defendant.

We consequently conclude that the Constitution permits judges to take realistic account of the particular defendant's mental capacities by asking whether a defendant who seeks to conduct his own defense at trial is mentally competent to do so. That is to say, the Constitution permits States to insist upon representation by counsel for those competent enough to stand trial under *Dusky* but who still suffer from severe mental illness to the point where they are not competent to conduct trial proceedings by themselves.

IV

Indiana has also asked us to adopt, as a measure of a defendant's ability to conduct a trial, a more specific standard that would "deny a criminal defendant the right to represent himself at trial where the defendant cannot communicate coherently with the court or a jury." We are sufficiently uncertain, however, as to how that particular standard would work in practice to refrain from endorsing it as a federal constitutional standard here. We need not now, and we do not, adopt it.

Indiana has also asked us to overrule *Faretta*. We decline to do so. We recognize that judges have sometimes expressed concern that *Faretta,* contrary to its intent, has led to trials that are unfair. But recent empirical research suggests that such instances are not common. See, *e.g.*, Hashimoto, Defending the Right of Self–Representation: An Empirical Look at the Pro Se Felony Defendant, 85 N. C. L. Rev. 423, 427, 447, 428 (2007) (noting that of the small number of defendants who chose to proceed *pro se*—"roughly 0.3% to 0.5%" of the total, state felony defendants in particular "appear to have achieved higher felony acquittal rates than their represented counterparts in that they were less likely to have been convicted of felonies"). At the same time, instances in which the trial's fairness is in doubt may well be concentrated in the 20 percent or so of self-representation cases where the mental competence of the defendant is also at issue. If so, today's opinion, assuring trial judges the authority to deal appropriately with cases in the latter category, may well alleviate those fair trial concerns.

For these reasons, the judgment of the Supreme Court of Indiana is vacated, and the case is remanded for further proceedings not inconsistent with this opinion.

––––––––

APPENDIX

Excerpt from respondent's [pro se] filing entitled " 'Defendant's Version of the Instant Offense,' " which he had attached to his presentence investigation report:

" 'The appointed motion of permissive intervention filed therein the court superior on, 6–26–01 caused a stay of action and apon it's expiration or thereafter three years the plan to establish a youth program to and for the coordination of aspects of law enforcement to prevent and reduce crime amoung young people in Indiana became a diplomatic act as under the Safe Streets Act of 1967, "A omnibuc considerate agent: I membered clients within the public and others that at/production of the courts actions showcased causes. The costs of the stay (Trial Rule 60) has a derivative property that is: my knowledged events as not unexpended to contract the membered clients is the commission of finding a facilitie for this plan or project to become organization of administrative recommen-

dations conditioned by governors." ' "

JUSTICE SCALIA, with whom JUSTICE THOMAS joins, dissenting.

* * * In my view the Constitution does not permit a State to substitute its own perception of fairness for the defendant's right to make his own case before the jury—a specific right long understood as essential to a fair trial.

I

[Justice Scalia goes over the facts.]

II

A

* * *

When a defendant appreciates the risks of forgoing counsel and chooses to do so voluntarily, the Constitution protects his ability to present his own defense even when that harms his case. In fact waiving counsel "usually" does so. McKaskle v. Wiggins, 465 U.S. 168, 177, n. 8. * * * What the Constitution requires is not that a State's case be subject to the most rigorous adversarial testing possible—after all, it permits a defendant to eliminate *all* adversarial testing by pleading guilty. What the Constitution requires is that a defendant be given the right to challenge the State's case against him using the arguments *he* sees fit.

* * *

B

* * *

Until today, the right of self-representation has been accorded the same respect as other constitutional guarantees. The only circumstance in which we have permitted the State to deprive a defendant of this trial right is the one under which we have allowed the State to deny *other* such rights: when it is necessary to enable the trial to proceed in an orderly fashion. * * * This ground for terminating self-representation is unavailable here, however, because Edwards was not even allowed to begin to represent himself, and because he was respectful and compliant and did not provide a basis to conclude a trial could not have gone forward had he been allowed to press his own claims.

* * *

* * * I believe the Court's assessment of the purposes of the right of self-representation is inaccurate to boot. While there is little doubt that preserving individual " 'dignity' " (to which the Court refers), is paramount among those purposes, there is equally little doubt that the loss of "dignity" the right is designed to prevent is *not* the defendant's making a fool of himself by presenting an amateurish or even incoherent defense. Rather, the dignity at issue is the supreme human dignity of being master of one's fate rather than a ward of the State—the dignity of individual choice. * * * In sum, if the Court is to honor the particular conception of "dignity" that underlies the self-representation right, it should respect the autonomy of the individual by honoring his choices knowingly and voluntarily made.

A further purpose that the Court finds is advanced by denial of the right of self-representation is the purpose of assuring that trials "appear fair to all who observe them." To my knowledge we have never denied a defendant a right simply on the ground that it would make his trial appear less "fair" to outside observers, and I would not inaugurate that principle here. But were I to do so, I would not apply it to deny a defendant the right to represent himself when he knowingly and voluntarily waives counsel. When Edwards stood to say that "I have a defense that I would like to represent or present to the Judge," it seems to me the epitome of both actual and apparent unfairness for the judge to say, I have heard "your desire to proceed by yourself and I've denied your request, so your attorney will speak for you from now on."

III

It may be that the Court permits a State to deprive mentally ill defendants of a historic component of a fair trial because it is suspicious of the constitutional footing of the right of self-representation itself. The right is not explicitly set forth in the text of the Sixth Amendment, and some Members of this Court have expressed skepticism about *Faretta*'s holding.

While the Sixth Amendment makes no mention of the right to forgo counsel, it provides the defendant, and not his lawyer, the right to call witnesses in his defense and to confront witnesses against him, and counsel is permitted to assist in

"*his* defence" (emphasis added). Our trial system, however, allows the attorney representing a defendant "full authority to manage the conduct of the trial"—an authority without which "[t]he adversary process could not function effectively." Taylor v. Illinois, 484 U.S. 400, 418. We have held that "the client must accept the consequences of the lawyer's decision to forgo cross-examination, to decide not to put certain witnesses on the stand, or to decide not to disclose the identity of certain witnesses in advance of trial." *Taylor, supra,* at 418. Thus, in order for the defendant's right to call his own witnesses, to cross-examine witnesses, and to put on a defense to be anything more than "a tenuous and unacceptable legal fiction," a defendant must have consented to the representation of counsel. *Faretta, supra,* at 821. Otherwise, "the defense presented is not the defense guaranteed him by the Constitution, for in a very real sense, it is not *his* defense." Ibid.

The facts of this case illustrate this point with the utmost clarity. Edwards wished to take a self-defense case to the jury. His counsel preferred a defense that focused on lack of intent. Having been denied the right to conduct his own defense, Edwards was convicted without having had the opportunity to present to the jury the grounds he believed supported his innocence. I do not doubt that he likely would have been convicted anyway. But to hold that a defendant may be deprived of the right to make legal arguments for acquittal simply because a state-selected agent has made different arguments on his behalf is * * * to "imprison a man in his privileges and call it the Constitution." In singling out mentally ill defendants for this treatment, the Court's opinion does not even have the questionable virtue of being politically correct. At a time when all society is trying to mainstream the mentally impaired, the Court permits them to be deprived of a basic constitutional right—for their own good.

Today's holding is extraordinarily vague. The Court does not accept Indiana's position that self-representation can be denied "where the defendant cannot communicate coherently with the court or a jury." It does not even hold that Edwards was properly denied his right to represent himself. It holds only that lack of mental competence can under some circumstances form a ba-sis for denying the right to proceed. We will presumably give some meaning to this holding in the future, but the indeterminacy makes a bad holding worse. Once the right of self-representation for the mentally ill is a sometime thing, trial judges will have every incentive to make their lives easier—to avoid the painful necessity of deciphering occasional pleadings of the sort contained in the Appendix to today's opinion—by appointing knowledgeable and literate counsel.

Because I think a defendant who is competent to stand trial, and who is capable of knowing and voluntary waiver of assistance of counsel, has a constitutional right to conduct his own defense, I respectfully dissent.

———

IX.   NO RIGHT TO CRIMINAL TRIAL OR COUNSEL: THE STATUS OF ENEMY COMBATANTS AFTER SEPTEMBER 11, 2001

Page 1431. At the end of the section, add the following case:

Military Commissions Act Suspends the Writ of Habeas Corpus: Boumediene v. Bush

In the following case, the five-Justice majority invalidates certain procedures established by the Military Commissions Act on the ground that they operated as a suspension of the writ of habeas corpus, in violation of the Constitution.

BOUMEDIENE v. UNITED STATES

Supreme Court of the United States, 2008.
128 S.Ct. 2229.

JUSTICE KENNEDY **delivered the opinion of the Court.**

Petitioners are aliens designated as enemy combatants and detained at the United States Naval Station at Guantanamo Bay, Cuba. There are others detained there, also aliens, who are not parties to this suit.

Petitioners present a question not resolved by our earlier cases relating to the detention of aliens at Guantanamo: whether they have the constitutional privilege of habeas corpus, a privilege not to be withdrawn except in conformance with the Suspension Clause, Art. I, § 9, cl. 2. We hold these petitioners do have the habeas corpus privilege. Congress has enacted a statute, the Detainee Treatment Act of 2005 (DTA), that provides certain procedures for review of the detainees' status. We hold that those procedures are not an adequate and effective substitute for habeas corpus. Therefore § 7 of the Military Commissions Act of 2006 (MCA), 28 U.S.C. A. § 2241(e) (Supp. 2007), operates as an unconstitutional suspension of the writ. We do not address whether the President has authority to detain these petitioners nor do we hold that the writ must issue. These and other questions regarding the legality of the detention are to be resolved in the first instance by the District Court.

I

Under the Authorization for Use of Military Force (AUMF), § 2(a), the President is authorized "to use all necessary and appropriate force against those nations, organizations, or persons he determines planned, authorized, committed, or aided the terrorist attacks that occurred on September 11, 2001, or harbored such organizations or persons, in order to prevent any future acts of international terrorism against the United States by such nations, organizations or persons."

In Hamdi v. Rumsfeld, 542 U.S. 507 (2004), five Members of the Court recognized that detention of individuals who fought against the United States in Afghanistan "for the duration of the particular conflict in which they were captured, is so fundamental and accepted an incident to war as to be an exercise of the 'necessary and appropriate force' Congress has authorized the President to use." After *Hamdi*, the Deputy Secretary of Defense established Combatant Status Review Tribunals (CSRTs) to determine whether individuals detained at Guantanamo were "enemy combatants," as the Department defines that term. A later memorandum established procedures to implement the CSRTs. The Government maintains these procedures were designed to comply with the due process requirements identified by the plurality in *Hamdi*.

Interpreting the AUMF, the Department of Defense ordered the detention of these petitioners, and they were transferred to Guantanamo. Some of these individuals were apprehended on the battlefield in Afghanistan, others in places as far away from there as Bosnia and Gambia. All are foreign nationals, but none is a citizen of a nation now at war with the United States. Each denies he is a member of the al Qaeda terrorist network that carried out the September 11 attacks or of the Taliban regime that provided sanctuary for al Qaeda. Each petitioner appeared before a separate CSRT; was determined to be an enemy combatant; and has sought a writ of habeas corpus in the United States District Court for the District of Columbia.

The first actions commenced in February 2002. The District Court ordered the cases dismissed for lack of jurisdiction because the naval station is outside the sovereign territory of the United States. The Court of Appeals for the District of Columbia Circuit affirmed. We granted certiorari and reversed, holding that 28 U.S.C. § 2241 extended statutory habeas corpus jurisdiction to Guantanamo. See Rasul v. Bush, 542 U.S. 466, 473 (2004). The constitutional issue presented in the instant cases was not reached in *Rasul*.

After *Rasul*, petitioners' cases were consolidated and entertained in two separate proceedings. In the first set of cases, Judge Richard J. Leon granted the Government's motion to dismiss, holding that the detainees had no rights that could be vindicated in a habeas corpus action. In the second set of cases Judge Joyce Hens Green reached the opposite conclusion, holding the detainees had rights under the Due Process Clause of the Fifth Amendment.

While appeals were pending from the District Court decisions, Congress passed the DTA. Subsection (e) of § 1005 of the DTA amended 28 U.S.C. § 2241 to provide that "no court, justice, or judge shall have jurisdiction to hear or consider ... an application for a writ of habeas corpus filed by or on behalf of an alien detained by the Department of Defense at Guantanamo Bay, Cuba." Section 1005 further provides that the Court of Appeals for the District of Columbia Circuit shall have "exclusive" jurisdiction to review decisions of the CSRTs.

In Hamdan v. Rumsfeld, 548 U.S. 557, 576–577 (2006), the Court held this provision did not apply to cases (like petitioners') pending when the DTA was enacted. Congress responded by passing the MCA, 10 U.S.C. A. § 948a *et seq.* (Supp. 2007), which again amended § 2241.* * *

Petitioners' cases were consolidated on appeal, and the parties filed supplemental briefs in light of our decision in *Hamdan*. The Court of Appeals' ruling is the subject of our present review and today's decision.

The Court of Appeals concluded that MCA § 7 must be read to strip from it, and all federal courts, jurisdiction to consider petitioners' habeas corpus applications; that petitioners are not entitled to the privilege of the writ or the protections of the Suspension Clause; and, as a result, that it was unnecessary to consider whether Congress provided an adequate and effective substitute for habeas corpus in the DTA. We granted certiorari.

II

As a threshold matter, we must decide whether MCA § 7 denies the federal courts jurisdiction to hear habeas corpus actions pending at the time of its enactment. We hold the statute does deny that jurisdiction, so that, if the statute is valid, petitioners' cases must be dismissed.

As amended by the terms of the MCA, 28 U.S.C. A. § 2241(e) (Supp. 2007) now provides:

(1) No court, justice, or judge shall have jurisdiction to hear or consider an application for a writ of habeas corpus filed by or on behalf of an alien detained by the United States who has been determined by the United States to have been properly detained as an enemy combatant or is awaiting such determination.

(2) Except as provided in [§§ 1005(e)(2) and (e)(3) of the DTA] no court, justice, or judge

shall have jurisdiction to hear or consider any other action against the United States or its agents relating to any aspect of the detention, transfer, treatment, trial, or conditions of confinement of an alien who is or was detained by the United States and has been determined by the United States to have been properly detained as an enemy combatant or is awaiting such determination.

Section 7(b) of the MCA provides the effective date for the amendment of § 2241(e). It states:

The amendment made by [MCA § 7(a)] shall take effect on the date of the enactment of this Act, and shall apply to all cases, without exception, pending on or after the date of the enactment of this Act which relate to any aspect of the detention, transfer, treatment, trial, or conditions of detention of an alien detained by the United States since September 11, 2001.

There is little doubt that the effective date provision applies to habeas corpus actions. * * *

III

In deciding the constitutional questions now presented we must determine whether petitioners are barred from seeking the writ or invoking the protections of the Suspension Clause either because of their status, *i.e.*, petitioners' designation by the Executive Branch as enemy combatants, or their physical location, *i.e.*, their presence at Guantanamo Bay. The Government contends that noncitizens designated as enemy combatants and detained in territory located outside our Nation's borders have no constitutional rights and no privilege of habeas corpus. Petitioners contend they do have cognizable constitutional rights and that Congress, in seeking to eliminate recourse to habeas corpus as a means to assert those rights, acted in violation of the Suspension Clause. [Article I, Section 9, Clause 2 of the Constitution provides: "The Privilege of the Writ of Habeas Corpus shall not be suspended, unless when in Cases of Rebellion or Invasion the public Safety may require it."]

We begin with a brief account of the history and origins of the writ. Our account proceeds from two propositions. First, protection for the privilege of habeas corpus was one of the few safeguards of liberty specified in a Constitution that, at the outset, had no Bill of Rights. In the system conceived by the Framers the writ had a centrality that must inform proper interpretation of the Suspension Clause. Second, to the extent there were settled precedents or legal commentaries in 1789 regarding the extraterritorial scope of the writ or its application to enemy aliens, those authorities can be instructive for the present cases.

A

[Justice Kennedy discusses historical antecedents such as Magna Carta and the development of the Writ of Habeas Corpus in English constitutional history.]

This history was known to the Framers. It no doubt confirmed their view that pendular swings to and away from individual liberty were endemic to undivided, uncontrolled power. The Framers' inherent distrust of governmental power was the driving force behind the constitutional plan that allocated powers among three independent branches. This design serves not only to make Government accountable but also to secure individual liberty. * * *

That the Framers considered the writ a vital instrument for the protection of individual liberty is evident from the care taken to specify the limited grounds for its suspension: "The Privilege of the Writ of Habeas Corpus shall not be suspended, unless when in Cases of Rebellion or Invasion the public Safety may require it." Art. I, § 9, cl. 2. * * * Surviving accounts of the ratification debates provide additional evidence that the Framers deemed the writ to be an essential mechanism in the separation-of-powers scheme. In a critical exchange with Patrick Henry at the Virginia ratifying convention Edmund Randolph referred to the Suspension Clause as an "exception" to the "power given to Congress to regulate courts." See 3 Debates in the Several State Conventions on the Adoption of the Federal Constitution 460–464 (J. Elliot 2d ed. 1876) (hereinafter Elliot's Debates). * * * Alexander Hamilton likewise explained that by providing the detainee a judicial forum to challenge detention, the writ preserves limited government. [Justice Kennedy cites Hamilton's discussion of the writ in Federalist No. 84, and then moves to the suspension of the writ on various occasions in England.]

In our own system the Suspension Clause is designed to protect against these cyclical abuses. The Clause protects the rights of the detained by a means consistent with the essential design of the Constitution. It ensures that, except during periods of formal suspension, the Judiciary will have a time-tested device, the writ, to maintain the delicate balance of governance that is itself the surest safeguard of liberty. The Clause protects the rights of the detained by affirming the duty and authority of the Judiciary to call the jailer to account. The separation-of-powers doctrine, and the history that influenced its design, therefore must inform the reach and purpose of the Suspension Clause.

B

The broad historical narrative of the writ and its function is central to our analysis, but we seek guidance as well from founding-era authorities addressing the specific question before us: whether foreign nationals, apprehended and detained in distant countries during a time of serious threats to our Nation's security, may assert the privilege of the writ and seek its protection. * * *

To support their arguments, the parties in these cases have examined historical sources to construct a view of the common-law writ as it existed in 1789 * * *. The Government argues the common-law writ ran only to those territories over which the Crown was sovereign. Petitioners argue that jurisdiction followed the King's officers. Diligent search by all parties reveals no certain conclusions. * * *

[Justice Kennedy parses the case law as it existed as of 1789 in both England and America.]

Each side in the present matter argues that the very lack of a precedent on point supports its position. The Government points out there is no evidence that a court sitting in England granted habeas relief to an enemy alien detained abroad; petitioners respond there is no evidence that a court refused to do so for lack of jurisdiction.

Both arguments are premised, however, upon the assumption that the historical record is complete and that the common law, if properly understood, yields a definite answer to the questions before us. There are reasons to doubt both assumptions. Recent scholarship points to the inherent shortcomings in the historical record. [Justice Kennedy cites a treatise indicating that habeas decisions in the Eighteenth Century were unpublished.] And given the unique status of Guantanamo Bay and the particular dangers of terrorism in the modern age, the common-law courts simply may not have confronted cases with close parallels to this one. We decline, therefore, to infer too much, one way or the other, from the lack of historical evidence on point.

IV

Drawing from its position that at common law the writ ran only to territories over which the Crown was sovereign, the Government says the Suspension Clause affords petitioners no rights because the United States does not claim sovereignty over the place of detention.

Guantanamo Bay is not formally part of the United States. And under the terms of the lease between the United States and Cuba, Cuba retains "ultimate sovereignty" over the territory while the United States exercises "complete jurisdiction and control." See Lease of Lands for Coaling and Naval Stations, Feb. 23, 1903, U.S.-Cuba, Art. III, T. S. No. 418 (hereinafter 1903 Lease Agreement). Under the terms of the 1934 Treaty, however, Cuba effectively has no rights as a sovereign until the parties agree to modification of the 1903 Lease Agreement or the United States abandons the base. See Treaty Defining Relations with Cuba, May 29, 1934, U.S.-Cuba, Art. III, 48 Stat. 1683, T. S. No. 866.

The United States contends, nevertheless, that Guantanamo is not within its sovereign control. This was the Government's position well before the events of September 11, 2001. And in other contexts the Court has held that questions of sovereignty are for the political branches to decide. * * * Even if this were a treaty interpretation case that did not involve a political question, the President's construction of the lease agreement would be entitled to great respect.

We therefore do not question the Government's position that Cuba, not the United States, maintains sovereignty, in the legal and technical sense of the term, over Guantanamo Bay. But this does not end the analysis. Our cases do not hold it is improper for us to inquire into the objective degree of control the Nation asserts over foreign territory. * * * Indeed, it is not altogether uncommon for a territory to be under the *de jure* sovereignty of one nation, while under the plenary control, or practical sovereignty, of another. This condition can occur when the territory is seized during war, as Guantanamo was during the Spanish–American War. Accordingly, for purposes of our analysis, we accept the Government's position that Cuba, and not the United States, retains *de jure* sovereignty over Guantanamo Bay. As we did in *Rasul*, however, we take notice of the obvious and uncontested fact that the United States, by virtue of its complete jurisdiction and control over the base, maintains *de facto* sovereignty over this territory.

Were we to hold that the present cases turn on the political question doctrine, we would be required first to accept the Government's premise that *de jure* sovereignty is the touchstone of habeas corpus jurisdiction. This premise, however, is unfounded. For the reasons indicated above, the history of common-law habeas corpus provides scant support for this proposition; and, for the reasons indicated below, that position would be inconsistent with our precedents and contrary to fundamental separation-of-powers principles.

A

The Court has discussed the issue of the Constitution's extraterritorial application on many occasions. These decisions undermine the Government's argument that, at least as applied to noncitizens, the Constitution necessarily stops where *de jure* sovereignty ends.

The Framers foresaw that the United States would expand and acquire new territories. Article IV, § 3, cl. 1, grants Congress the power to admit new States. Clause 2 of the same section grants Congress the "Power to dispose of and make all needful Rules and Regulations respecting the Territory or other Property belonging to the United States." Save for a few notable (and notorious) exceptions, *e.g.*, Dred Scott v. Sandford, 19 How. 393 (1857), throughout most of our history there was little need to explore the outer boundaries of the Constitution's geographic reach. * * *

Fundamental questions regarding the Constitution's geographic scope first arose at the dawn of the 20th century when the Nation acquired noncontiguous Territories: Puerto Rico, Guam, and the Philippines— ceded to the United States by Spain at the conclusion of the Spanish–American War—and Hawaii—annexed by the United States in 1898. At this point Congress chose to discontinue its previous practice of extending constitutional rights to the territories by statute. In a series of opinions later known as the Insular Cases, the Court addressed whether the Constitution, by its own force, applies in any territory that is not a State. See De Lima v. Bidwell, 182 U.S. 1 (1901); Dooley v. United States, 182 U.S. 222 (1901); Armstrong v. United States, 182 U.S. 243 (1901); Downes v. Bidwell, 182 U.S. 244 (1901); Hawaii v. Mankichi, 190 U.S. 197 (1903); Dorr v. United States, 195 U.S. 138 (1904). The Court held that the Constitution has independent force in these territories, a force not contingent upon acts of legislative grace. Yet it took note of the difficulties inherent in that position. [Justice Kennedy engages in an extensive discussion of the case law on the applicability of the Constitution to territories outside the United States. He describes the doctrine of "territorial incorporation," under which the Constitution applies in full in incorporated Territories surely destined for statehood but only in part in unincorporated Territories.]

[N]oting the inherent practical difficulties of enforcing all constitutional provisions "always and everywhere," the Court devised in the Insular Cases a doctrine that allowed it to use its power sparingly and where it would be most needed. This century-old doctrine informs our analysis in the present matter.

* * *

Practical considerations weighed heavily as well in Johnson v. Eisentrager, 339 U.S. 763 (1950), where the Court addressed whether habeas corpus jurisdiction extended to enemy aliens who had been convicted of violating the laws of war. The prisoners were detained at Landsberg Prison in Germany during the Allied Powers' postwar occupation. The Court stressed the difficulties of ordering the Government to produce the prisoners in a habeas corpus proceeding. It "would require allocation of shipping space, guarding personnel, billeting and rations" and would damage the prestige of military commanders at a sensitive time. In considering these factors the Court sought to balance the constraints of military occupation with constitutional necessities.

True, the Court in *Eisentrager* denied access to the writ, and it noted the prisoners "at no relevant time were within any territory over which the United States is sovereign, and [that] the scenes of their offense, their capture, their trial and their punishment were all beyond the territorial jurisdiction of any court of the United States." The Government seizes upon this language as proof positive that the *Eisentrager* Court adopted a formalistic, sovereignty-based test for determining the reach of the Suspension Clause. We reject this reading for three reasons.

First, we do not accept the idea that the above-quoted passage from *Eisentrager* is the only authoritative language in the opinion and that all the rest is dicta. The Court's further determinations, based on practical considerations, were integral to Part II of its opinion and came before the decision announced its holding. See 339 U.S., at 781.

Second, because the United States lacked both *de jure* sovereignty and plenary control over Landsberg Prison, it is far from clear that the *Eisentrager* Court used the term sovereignty only in the narrow technical sense and not to connote the degree of control the military asserted over the facility. The Justices who decided *Eisentrager* would have understood sovereignty as a multifaceted concept. See Black's Law Dictionary 1568 (4th ed. 1951) (defining "sovereignty" as "[t]he supreme, absolute, and uncontrollable power by which any independent state is governed"; "the international independence of a state, combined with the right and power of regulating its internal affairs without foreign dictation"; and "[t]he power to do everything in a state without accountability"). In its principal brief in *Eisentrager*, the Government advocated a bright-line test for determining the scope of the writ, similar to the one it advocates in these cases. Yet the Court mentioned the concept of territorial sovereignty only twice in its opinion. That the Court devoted a significant portion of Part II to a discussion of practical barriers to the running of the writ suggests that the Court was not concerned exclusively with the formal legal status of Landsberg Prison but also with the objective degree of control the

United States asserted over it. Even if we assume the *Eisentrager* Court considered the United States' lack of formal legal sovereignty over Landsberg Prison as the decisive factor in that case, its holding is not inconsistent with a functional approach to questions of extraterritoriality. The formal legal status of a given territory affects, at least to some extent, the political branches' control over that territory. *De jure* sovereignty is a factor that bears upon which constitutional guarantees apply there.

Third, if the Government's reading of *Eisentrager* were correct, the opinion would have marked not only a change in, but a complete repudiation of, the Insular Cases' * * * functional approach to questions of extraterritoriality. We cannot accept the Government's view. Nothing in *Eisentrager* says that *de jure* sovereignty is or has ever been the only relevant consideration in determining the geographic reach of the Constitution or of habeas corpus. Were that the case, there would be considerable tension between *Eisentrager*, on the one hand, and the Insular Cases * * * on the other. Our cases need not be read to conflict in this manner. A constricted reading of *Eisentrager* overlooks what we see as a common thread * * * : the idea that questions of extraterritoriality turn on objective factors and practical concerns, not formalism.

B

The Government's formal sovereignty-based test raises troubling separation-of-powers concerns as well. The political history of Guantanamo illustrates the deficiencies of this approach. The United States

has maintained complete and uninterrupted control of the bay for over 100 years. At the close of the Spanish–American War, Spain ceded control over the entire island of Cuba to the United States and specifically "relinquishe[d] all claim[s] of sovereignty ... and title." See Treaty of Paris, Dec. 10, 1898, U.S.-Spain, Art. I, 30 Stat. 1755, T. S. No. 343. From the date the treaty with Spain was signed until the Cuban Republic was established on May 20, 1902, the United States governed the territory "in trust" for the benefit of the Cuban people. And although it recognized, by entering into the 1903 Lease Agreement, that Cuba retained "ultimate sovereignty" over Guantanamo, the United States continued to maintain the same plenary control it had enjoyed since 1898. Yet the Government's view is that the Constitution had no effect there, at least as to noncitizens, because the United States disclaimed sovereignty in the formal sense of the term. The necessary implication of the argument is that by surrendering formal sovereignty over any unincorporated territory to a third party, while at the same time entering into a lease that grants total control over the territory back to the United States, it would be possible for the political branches to govern without legal constraint.

Our basic charter cannot be contracted away like this. The Constitution grants Congress and the President the power to acquire, dispose of, and govern territory, not the power to decide when and where its terms apply. * * * Abstaining from questions involving formal sovereignty and territorial governance is one thing. To hold the political branches have the power to switch the Constitution on or off at will is quite another. The former position reflects this Court's recognition that certain matters requiring political judgments are best left to the political branches. The latter would permit a striking anomaly in our tripartite system of government, leading to a regime in which Congress and the President, not this Court, say "what the law is." Marbury v. Madison, 1 Cranch 137, 177 (1803).

These concerns have particular bearing upon the Suspension Clause question in the cases now before us, for the writ of habeas corpus is itself an indispensable mechanism for monitoring the separation of powers. The test for determining the scope of this provision must not be subject to manipulation by those whose power it is designed to restrain.

C

As we recognized in *Rasul*, 542 U.S., at 476; *id.*, at 487 (KENNEDY, J., concurring in judgment), the outlines of a framework for determining the reach of the Suspension Clause are suggested by the factors the Court relied upon in *Eisentrager*. In addition to the practical concerns discussed above, the *Eisentrager* Court found relevant that each petitioner:

> "(a) is an enemy alien; (b) has never been or resided in the United States; (c) was captured outside of our territory and there held in military custody as a prisoner of war; (d) was tried and convicted by a Military Commission sitting outside the United States; (e) for offenses against laws of war committed outside the United States; (f) and is at all

times imprisoned outside the United States." 339 U.S., at 777.

Based on this language from *Eisentrager*, and the reasoning in our other extraterritoriality opinions, we conclude that at least three factors are relevant in determining the reach of the Suspension Clause: (1) the citizenship and status of the detainee and the adequacy of the process through which that status determination was made; (2) the nature of the sites where apprehension and then detention took place; and (3) the practical obstacles inherent in resolving the prisoner's entitlement to the writ.

Applying this framework, we note at the onset that the status of these detainees is a matter of dispute. The petitioners, like those in *Eisentrager*, are not American citizens. But the petitioners in *Eisentrager* did not contest, it seems, the Court's assertion that they were "enemy alien[s]." In the instant cases, by contrast, the detainees deny they are enemy combatants. They have been afforded some process in CSRT proceedings to determine their status; but, unlike in *Eisentrager*, there has been no trial by military commission for violations of the laws of war. The difference is not trivial. The records from the *Eisentrager* trials suggest that, well before the petitioners brought their case to this Court, there had been a rigorous adversarial process to test the legality of their detention. The *Eisentrager* petitioners were charged by a bill of particulars that made detailed factual allegations against them. To rebut the accusations, they were entitled to representation by counsel, allowed to introduce evidence on their own behalf, and permitted to cross-examine the prosecution's witnesses.

In comparison the procedural protections afforded to the detainees in the CSRT hearings are far more limited, and, we conclude, fall well short of the procedures and adversarial mechanisms that would eliminate the need for habeas corpus review. Although the detainee is assigned a "Personal Representative" to assist him during CSRT proceedings, the Secretary of the Navy's memorandum makes clear that person is not the detainee's lawyer or even his "advocate." The Government's evidence is accorded a presumption of validity. The detainee is allowed to present "reasonably available" evidence, but his ability to rebut the Government's evidence against him is limited by the circumstances of his confinement and his lack of counsel at this stage. And although the detainee can seek review of his status determination in the Court of Appeals, that review process cannot cure all defects in the earlier proceedings. See Part V, *infra*.

As to the second factor relevant to this analysis, the detainees here are similarly situated to the *Eisentrager* petitioners in that the sites of their apprehension and detention are technically outside the sovereign territory of the United States. As noted earlier, this is a factor that weighs against finding they have rights under the Suspension Clause. But there are critical differences between Landsberg Prison, circa 1950, and the United States Naval Station at Guantanamo Bay in 2008. Unlike its present control over the naval station, the United States' control over the prison in Germany was neither absolute nor indefinite. Like all parts of occupied Germany, the prison was under the jurisdiction of the combined Allied Forces. The United States was therefore answerable to its Allies for all activities occurring there. The Allies had not planned a long-term occupation of Germany, nor did they intend to displace all German institutions even during the period of occupation. The Court's holding in *Eisentrager* was thus consistent with the Insular Cases, where it had held there was no need to extend full constitutional protections to territories the United States did not intend to govern indefinitely. Guantanamo Bay, on the other hand, is no transient possession. In every practical sense Guantanamo is not abroad; it is within the constant jurisdiction of the United States.

As to the third factor, we recognize, as the Court did in *Eisentrager*, that there are costs to holding the Suspension Clause applicable in a case of military detention abroad. Habeas corpus proceedings may require expenditure of funds by the Government and may divert the attention of military personnel from other pressing tasks. While we are sensitive to these concerns, we do not find them dispositive. Compliance with any judicial process requires some incremental expenditure of resources. Yet civilian courts and the Armed Forces have functioned along side each other at various points in our history. The Government presents no credible arguments that the military mission at Guantanamo would be compromised if habeas corpus courts had jurisdiction to hear the detainees' claims. And in light of the plenary control the United States asserts over the base, none are apparent to us.

The situation in *Eisentrager* was far different, given the historical context and nature of the military's mission in post-War Germany. When hostilities in the European Theater came to an end, the United States became responsible for an occupation zone encompassing over 57,000 square miles with a population of 18 million. In addition to supervising massive reconstruction and aid efforts the American forces stationed in Germany faced potential security threats from a defeated enemy. In retrospect the post-War occupation may seem uneventful. But at the time *Eisentrager* was decided, the Court was right to be concerned about judicial interference with the military's efforts to contain "enemy elements, guerilla fighters, and 'were-wolves.'" 339 U.S., at 784.

Similar threats are not apparent here; nor does the Government argue that they are. The United States Naval Station at Guantanamo Bay consists of 45 square miles of land and water. The base has been used, at various points, to house migrants and refugees temporarily. At present, however, other than the detainees themselves, the only long-term residents are American military personnel, their families, and a small number of workers. The detainees have been deemed enemies of the United States. At present, dangerous as they may be if released, they are contained in a secure prison facility located on an isolated and heavily fortified military base.

There is no indication, furthermore, that adjudicating a habeas corpus petition would cause friction with the host government. No Cuban court has jurisdiction over American military personnel at Guantanamo or the enemy combatants detained there. While obligated to abide by the terms of the lease, the United States is, for all practical purposes, answerable to no other sovereign for its acts on the base. Were that not the case, or if the detention facility were located in an active theater of war, arguments that issuing the writ would be impracticable or anomalous would have more weight. Under the facts presented here, however, there are few practical barriers to the running of the writ. To the extent barriers arise, habeas corpus procedures likely can be modified to address them. See Part VI–B, *infra*.

It is true that before today the Court has never held that noncitizens detained by our Government in territory over which another country maintains *de jure* sovereignty have any rights under our Constitution. But the cases before us lack any precise historical parallel. They involve individuals detained by executive order for the duration of a conflict that, if measured from September 11, 2001, to the present, is already among the longest wars in American history. The detainees, moreover, are held in a territory that, while technically not part of the United States, is under the complete and total control of our Government. Under these circumstances the lack of a precedent on point is no barrier to our holding.

We hold that Art. I, § 9, cl. 2, of the Constitution has full effect at Guantanamo Bay. If the privilege of habeas corpus is to be denied to the detainees now before us, Congress must act in accordance with the requirements of the Suspension Clause. This Court may not impose a *de facto* suspension by abstaining from these controversies. The MCA does not purport to be a formal suspension of the writ; and the Government, in its submissions to us, has not argued that it is. Petitioners, therefore, are entitled to the privilege of habeas corpus to challenge the legality of their detention.

V

In light of this holding the question becomes whether the statute stripping jurisdiction to issue the writ avoids the Suspension Clause mandate because Congress has provided adequate substitute procedures for habeas corpus. The Government submits there has been compliance with the Suspension Clause because the DTA review process in the Court of Appeals, see DTA § 1005(e), provides an adequate substitute. Congress has granted that court jurisdiction to consider

> "(i) whether the status determination of the [CSRT] . . . was consistent with the standards and procedures specified by the Secretary of Defense . . . and (ii) to the extent the Constitution and laws of the United States are applicable, whether the use of such standards and procedures to make the determination is consistent with the Constitution and laws of the United States." § 1005(e)(2)(C), 119 Stat. 2742.

The Court of Appeals, having decided that the writ does not run to the detainees in any event, found it unnecessary to consider whether an adequate substitute has been provided. In the ordinary course we would remand to the Court of Appeals to consider this question in the first instance. It is well settled, however, that the Court's practice of declining to address issues left unresolved in earlier proceedings is not an inflexible rule. Departure from the rule is appropriate in "exceptional" circumstances.

The gravity of the separation-of-powers issues raised by these cases and the fact that these detainees have been denied meaningful access to a judicial forum for a period of years render these cases exceptional. The parties before us have addressed the adequacy issue. While we would have found it informative to consider the reasoning of the Court of Appeals on this point, we must weigh that against the harms petitioners may endure from additional delay. And, given there are few precedents addressing what features an adequate substitute for habeas corpus must contain, in all likelihood a remand simply would delay ultimate resolution of the issue by this Court.

* * *

Under the circumstances we believe the costs of further delay substantially outweigh any benefits of remanding to the Court of Appeals to consider the issue it did not address in these cases.

A

Our case law does not contain extensive discussion of standards defining suspension of the writ or of circumstances under which suspension has occurred. This simply confirms the care Congress has taken throughout our Nation's history to preserve the writ and its function. Indeed, most of the major legislative enactments pertaining to habeas corpus have acted not to contract the writ's protection but to expand it or to hasten resolution of prisoners' claims.

There are exceptions, of course. Title I of the Antiterrorism and Effective Death Penalty Act of 1996 (AEDPA), § 106, 110 Stat. 1220, contains certain gatekeeping provisions that restrict a prisoner's ability to bring new and repetitive claims in "second or successive" habeas corpus actions. We upheld these provisions against a Suspension Clause challenge in Felker v. Turpin, 518 U.S. 651, 662–664 (1996). The provisions at issue in *Felker*, however, did not constitute a substantial departure from common-law habeas procedures. The provisions, for the most part, codified the longstanding abuse-of-the-writ doctrine. AEDPA applies, moreover, to federal, postconviction review after criminal proceedings in state court have taken place. As of this point, cases discussing the implementation of that statute give little helpful instruction (save perhaps by contrast) for the instant cases, where no trial has been held.

* * *

[T]he DTA's jurisdictional grant is quite limited. The Court of Appeals has jurisdiction not to inquire into the legality of the detention generally but only to assess whether the CSRT complied with the "standards and procedures specified by the Secretary of Defense" and whether those standards and procedures are lawful. If Congress had envisioned DTA review as coextensive with traditional habeas corpus, it would not have drafted the statute in this manner. * * * [M]oreover, there has been no effort to preserve habeas corpus review as an avenue of last resort. No saving clause exists in either the MCA or the DTA. And MCA § 7 eliminates habeas review for these petitioners.

The differences between the DTA and the habeas statute that would govern in MCA § 7's absence, 28 U.S.C. § 2241, are likewise telling. In § 2241 (2000 ed.) Congress confirmed the authority of "any justice" or "circuit judge" to issue the writ. Cf. *Felker*, 518 U.S., at 660–661 (interpreting Title I of AEDPA to not strip from this Court the power to entertain original habeas corpus petitions). That statute accommodates the necessity for factfinding that will arise in some cases by allowing the appellate judge or Justice to transfer the case to a district court of competent jurisdiction, whose institutional capacity for factfinding is superior to his or her own. See 28 U.S.C. § 2241(b). By granting the Court of Appeals "exclusive" jurisdiction over petitioners' cases, see DTA § 1005(e)(2)(A), Congress has foreclosed that option. This choice indicates Congress intended the Court of Appeals to have a more limited role in enemy combatant status determinations than a district court has in habeas corpus proceedings. * * * Otherwise there would have been no, or very little, purpose for enacting the DTA.

* * *

It is against this background that we must interpret the DTA and assess its adequacy as a substitute for habeas corpus. * * *

B

We do not endeavor to offer a comprehensive summary of the requisites for an adequate substitute for habeas corpus. We do consider it uncontroversial, however, that the privilege of habeas corpus entitles the prisoner to a meaningful opportunity to demonstrate that he is being held pursuant to the erroneous application or interpretation of relevant law. And the habeas court must have the power to order the conditional release of an individual unlawfully detained—though release need not be the exclusive remedy and is not the appropriate one in every case in which the writ is granted. These are the easily identified attributes of any constitutionally adequate habeas corpus proceeding. But, depending on the circumstances, more may be required.

Indeed, common-law habeas corpus was, above all, an adaptable remedy. Its precise application and scope changed depending upon the circumstances. See 3 Blackstone 131 (describing habeas as "the great and efficacious writ, in all manner of illegal confinement"); see also Schlup v. Delo, 513 U.S. 298, 319 (1995) (Habeas "is, at its core, an equitable remedy"); Jones v. Cunningham, 371 U.S. 236, 243 (1963) (Habeas is not "a static, narrow, formalistic remedy; its scope has grown to achieve its grand purpose"). It appears the common-law habeas court's role was most extensive in cases of pretrial and non-criminal detention, where there had been little or no previous judicial review of the cause for detention. * * * Justice McLean, on Circuit in 1855, expressed his view that a habeas court should consider a prior judgment conclusive "where there was clearly jurisdiction and a full and fair hearing; but that it might not be so considered when any of these requisites were wanting." Ex parte Robinson, 20 F. Cas. 969, 971 (No. 11,935) (CC Ohio 1855). To illustrate the circumstances in which the prior adjudication did not bind the habeas court, he gave the example of a case in which "[s]everal unimpeached witnesses" provided new evidence to exculpate the prisoner. *Ibid*.

* * *

Accordingly, where relief is sought from a sentence that resulted from the judgment of a court of record, * * * considerable deference is owed to the court that ordered confinement. Likewise in those cases the prisoner should exhaust adequate alternative remedies before filing for the writ in federal court. Both aspects of federal habeas corpus review are justified because it can be assumed that, in the usual course, a court of record provides defendants with a fair, adversary proceeding. In cases involving state convictions this framework also respects federalism; and in federal cases it has added justification because the prisoner already has had a chance to seek review of his conviction in a federal forum through a direct appeal. The present cases fall outside these categories, however; for here the detention is by executive order.

Where a person is detained by executive order, rather than, say, after being tried and convicted in a court, the need for collateral review is most pressing. A criminal conviction in the usual course occurs after a judicial hearing before a tribunal disinterested in the outcome and committed to procedures designed to ensure its own independence. These dynamics are not inherent in executive detention orders or executive review procedures. In this context the need for habeas corpus is more urgent. The intended duration of the detention and the reasons for it bear upon the precise scope of the inquiry. Habeas corpus proceedings need not resemble a criminal trial, even when the detention is by executive order. But the writ must be effective. The habeas court must have sufficient authority to conduct a meaningful review of both the cause for detention and the Executive's power to detain.

To determine the necessary scope of habeas corpus review, therefore, we must assess the CSRT process, the mechanism through which petitioners' designation as enemy combatants became final. Whether one characterizes the CSRT process as direct review of the Executive's battlefield determination that the detainee is an enemy combatant—as the parties have and as we do—or as the first step in the collateral review of a battlefield determination makes no difference in a proper analysis of whether the procedures Congress put in place are an adequate substitute for habeas corpus. What matters is the sum total of procedural protections afforded to the detainee at all stages, direct and collateral.

Petitioners identify what they see as myriad deficiencies in the CSRTs. The most relevant for our purposes are the constraints upon the detainee's ability to rebut the factual basis for the Government's assertion that he is an enemy combatant. * * * [A]t the CSRT stage the detainee has limited means to find or present evidence to challenge the Government's case against him. He does not have the assistance of counsel and may not be aware of the most critical allegations that the Government relied upon to order his detention. The detainee can confront witnesses that testify during the CSRT proceedings. But given that there are in effect no limits on the admission of hearsay evidence—the only requirement is that the tribunal deem the evidence "relevant and helpful"—the detainee's opportunity to question witnesses is likely to be more theoretical than real.

The Government defends the CSRT process, arguing that it was designed to conform to the procedures suggested by the plurality in *Hamdi*. Setting aside the fact that the relevant language in *Hamdi* did not garner a majority of the Court, it does not control the matter at hand. None of the parties in *Hamdi* argued there had been a suspension of the writ. Nor could they. The § 2241 habeas corpus process remained in place. Accordingly, the plurality concentrated on whether the Executive had the authority to detain and, if so, what rights the detainee had under the Due Process Clause. True, there are places in the *Hamdi* plurality opinion where it is difficult to tell where its extrapolation of § 2241 ends and its analysis of the petitioner's Due Process rights begins. But the Court had no occasion to define the necessary scope of habeas review, for Suspension Clause purposes, in the context of enemy combatant detentions. * * *

Even if we were to assume that the CSRTs satisfy due process standards, it would not end our inquiry. * * * Even when the procedures authorizing detention are structurally sound, the Suspension Clause remains applicable and the writ relevant. This is so * * * even where the prisoner is detained after a criminal trial conducted in full accordance with the protections of the Bill of Rights. * * *

Although we make no judgment as to whether the CSRTs, as currently constituted, satisfy due process standards, we agree with petitioners that, even when all the parties involved in this process act with diligence and in good faith, there is considerable risk of error in the tribunal's findings of fact. This is a risk inherent in any process that, in the words of the former Chief Judge of the Court of Appeals, is "closed and accusatorial." See *Bismullah III*, 514 F.3d at 1296 (Ginsburg, C. J., concurring in denial of rehearing en banc). And given that the consequence of error may be detention of persons for the duration of hostilities that may last a generation or more, this is a risk too significant to ignore.

For the writ of habeas corpus, or its substitute, to function as an effective and proper remedy in this context, the court that conducts the habeas proceeding must have the means to correct errors that occurred during the CSRT proceedings. This includes some authority to assess the sufficiency of the Government's evidence against the detainee. It also must have the authority to admit and consider relevant exculpatory evidence that was not introduced during the earlier proceeding. Federal habeas petitioners long have had the means to supplement the record on review, even in the postconviction habeas setting. Here that opportunity is constitutionally required.

* * *

The extent of the showing required of the Government in these cases is a matter to be determined. We need not explore it further at this stage. We do hold that when the judicial power to issue habeas corpus properly is invoked the judicial officer must have adequate authority to make a determination in light of the relevant law and facts and to formulate and issue appropriate orders for relief, including, if necessary, an order directing the prisoner's release.

C

We now consider whether the DTA allows the Court of Appeals to conduct a proceeding meeting these standards. We are obligated to construe the statute to avoid constitutional problems if it is fairly possible. There are limits to this principle, however. The canon of constitutional avoidance does not supplant traditional modes of statutory interpretation. We cannot ignore the text and purpose of a statute in order to save it.

* * *

Assuming the DTA can be construed to allow the Court of Appeals to review or correct the CSRT's factual determinations, as opposed to merely certifying that the tribunal applied the correct standard of proof, we see no way to construe the statute to allow what is also constitutionally required in this context: an opportunity for the detainee to present relevant exculpatory evidence that was not made part of the record in the earlier proceedings.

* * *

Under the DTA the Court of Appeals has the power to review CSRT determinations by assessing the legality of standards and procedures. This implies the power to inquire into what happened at the CSRT hearing and, perhaps, to remedy certain deficiencies in that proceeding. But should the Court of Appeals determine that the CSRT followed appropriate and lawful standards and procedures, it will have reached the limits of its jurisdiction. There is no language in the DTA that can be construed to allow the Court of Appeals to admit and consider newly discovered evidence that could not have been made part of the CSRT record because it was unavailable to either the Government or the detainee when the CSRT made its findings. This evidence, however, may be critical to the detainee's argument that he is not an enemy combatant and there is no cause to detain him.

This is not a remote hypothetical. One of the petitioners, Mohamed Nechla, requested at his CSRT hearing that the Government contact his employer. The petitioner claimed the employer would corroborate Nechla's contention he had no affiliation with al Qaeda. Although the CSRT determined this testimony would be relevant, it also found the witness was not reasonably available to testify at the time of the hearing. Petitioner's counsel, however, now represents the witness is available to be heard. If a detainee can present reasonably available evidence demonstrating there is no basis for his continued detention, he must have the opportunity to present this evidence to a habeas corpus court. * * * The role of an Article III court in the exercise of its habeas corpus function cannot be circumscribed in this manner.

By foreclosing consideration of evidence not presented or reasonably available to the detainee at the CSRT proceedings, the DTA disadvantages the detainee by limiting the scope of collateral review to a record that may not be accurate or complete. In other contexts, *e.g.*, in post-trial habeas cases where the prisoner already has had a full and fair opportunity to develop the factual predicate of his claims, similar limitations on the scope of habeas review may be appropriate. In this context, however, where the underlying detention proceedings lack the necessary adversarial character, the detainee cannot be held responsible for all deficiencies in the record.

The Government does not make the alternative argument that the DTA allows for the introduction of previously unavailable exculpatory evidence on appeal. It does point out, however, that if a detainee obtains such evidence, he can request that the Deputy Secretary of Defense convene a new CSRT. Whatever the merits of this procedure, it is an insufficient replacement for the factual review these detainees are entitled to receive through habeas corpus. The Deputy Secretary's determination whether to initiate new proceedings is wholly a discretionary one. And we see no way to construe the DTA to allow a detainee to challenge the Deputy Secretary's decision not to open a new CSRT * * *.

* * *

We do not imply DTA review would be a constitutionally sufficient replacement for habeas corpus but for these limitations on the detainee's ability to present exculpatory evidence. For even if it were possible, as a textual matter, to read into the statute each of the necessary procedures we have identified, we could not overlook the cumulative effect of our doing so. To hold that the detainees at Guantanamo may, under the DTA, challenge the President's legal authority to detain them, contest the CSRT's findings of fact, supplement the record on review with exculpatory evidence, and request an order of release would come close to reinstating the § 2241 habeas corpus process Congress sought to deny them. The language of the statute, read in light of Congress' reasons for enacting it, cannot bear this interpretation. Petitioners have met their burden of establishing that the DTA review process is, on its face, an inadequate substitute for habeas corpus.

Although we do not hold that an adequate substitute must duplicate § 2241 in all respects, it suffices that the Government has not established that the detainees' access to the statutory review provisions at issue is an adequate substitute for the writ of habeas corpus. MCA § 7 thus effects an unconstitutional suspension of the writ. In view of our holding we need not discuss the reach of the writ with respect to claims of unlawful conditions of treatment or confinement.

VI

A

* * *

The Government argues petitioners must seek review of their CSRT determinations in the Court of Appeals before they can proceed with their habeas corpus actions in the District Court. * * * [I]n other contexts and for prudential reasons this Court has required exhaustion of alternative remedies before a prisoner can seek federal habeas relief. Most of these cases were brought by prisoners in state custody, and thus involved federalism concerns that are not relevant here. But we have extended this rule to require defendants in courts-martial to exhaust their military appeals before proceeding with a federal habeas corpus action.

The real risks, the real threats, of terrorist attacks are constant and not likely soon to abate. The ways to disrupt our life and laws are so many and unforeseen that the Court should not attempt even some general catalogue of crises that might occur. Certain principles are apparent, however. Practical considerations and exigent circumstances inform the definition and reach of the law's writs, including habeas corpus. The cases and our tradition reflect this precept.

In cases involving foreign citizens detained abroad by the Executive, it likely would be both an impractical and unprecedented extension of judicial power to assume that habeas corpus would be available at the moment the prisoner is taken into custody. If and when habeas corpus jurisdiction applies, as it does in these cases, then proper deference can be accorded to reasonable procedures for screening and initial detention under lawful and proper conditions of confinement and treatment for a reasonable period of time. Domestic exigencies, furthermore, might also impose such onerous burdens on the Government that here, too, the Judicial Branch would be required to devise sensible rules for staying habeas corpus proceedings until the Government can comply with its requirements in a responsible way. Cf. *Ex parte Milligan*, 4 Wall., at 127 ("If, in foreign invasion or civil war, the courts are actually closed, and it is impossible to administer criminal justice according to law, *then*, on the theatre of active military operations, where war really prevails, there is a necessity to furnish a substitute for the civil authority, thus overthrown, to preserve the safety of the army and society; and as no power is left but the military, it is allowed to govern by martial rule until the laws can have their free course"). Here, as is true with detainees apprehended abroad, a relevant consideration in determining the courts' role is whether there are suitable alternative processes in place to protect against the arbitrary exercise of governmental power.

The cases before us, however, do not involve detainees who have been held for a short period of time while awaiting their CSRT determinations. Were that the case, or were it probable that the Court of Appeals could complete a prompt review of their applications, the case for requiring temporary abstention or exhaustion of alternative remedies would be much stronger. These qualifications no longer pertain here. In some of these cases six years have elapsed without the judicial oversight that habeas corpus or an adequate substitute demands. And there has been no showing that the Executive faces such onerous burdens that it cannot respond to habeas corpus actions. To require these detainees to complete DTA review before proceeding with their habeas corpus actions would be to require additional months, if not years, of delay. The first DTA review applications were filed over a year ago, but no decisions on the merits have been issued. While some delay in fashioning new procedures is unavoidable, the costs of delay can no longer be borne by those who are held in custody. The detainees in these cases are entitled to a prompt habeas corpus hearing.

Our decision today holds only that the petitioners before us are entitled to seek the writ; that the DTA review procedures are an inadequate substitute for habeas corpus; and that the petitioners in these cases need not exhaust the review procedures in the Court of Appeals before proceeding with their habeas actions in the District Court. The only law we identify as unconstitutional is MCA § 7, 28 U.S.C. A. § 2241(e) (Supp. 2007). Accordingly, both the DTA and the CSRT process remain intact. Our holding with regard to exhaustion should not be read to imply that a habeas court should intervene the moment an enemy combatant steps foot in a territory where the writ runs. The Executive is entitled to a reasonable period of time to determine a detainee's status before a court entertains that detainee's habeas corpus petition. The CSRT process is the mechanism Congress and the President set up to deal with these issues. Except in cases of undue delay, federal courts should refrain from entertaining an enemy combatant's habeas corpus petition at least until after the Department, acting via the CSRT, has had a chance to review his status.

B

Although we hold that the DTA is not an adequate and effective substitute for habeas corpus, it does not follow that a habeas corpus court may disregard the dangers the detention in these cases was intended to prevent. * * * [T]he Suspension Clause does not resist innovation in the field of habeas corpus. Certain accommodations can be made to reduce the burden habeas corpus proceedings will place on the military without impermissibly diluting the protections of the writ.

In the DTA Congress sought to consolidate review of petitioners' claims in the Court of Appeals. Channeling future cases to one district court would no doubt reduce administrative burdens on the Government. This is a legitimate objective that might be advanced even without an amendment to § 2241. If, in a future case, a detainee files a habeas petition in another judicial district in which a proper respondent can be served, the Government can move for change of venue to the court that will hear these petitioners' cases, the United States District Court for the District of Columbia. See 28 U.S.C. § 1404(a).

Another of Congress' reasons for vesting exclusive jurisdiction in the Court of Appeals, perhaps, was to avoid the widespread dissemination of classified information. * * * We make no attempt to anticipate all of the evidentiary and access-to-counsel issues that will arise during the course of the detainees' habeas corpus proceedings. We recognize, however, that the Government has a legitimate interest in protecting sources and methods of intelligence gathering; and we expect that the District Court will use its discretion to accommodate this interest to the greatest extent possible.

These and the other remaining questions are within the expertise and competence of the District Court to address in the first instance.

———

In considering both the procedural and substantive standards used to impose detention to prevent acts of terrorism, proper deference must be accorded to the political branches. Unlike the President and some designated Members of Congress, neither the Members of this Court nor most federal judges begin the day with briefings that may describe new and serious threats to our Nation and its people. The law must accord the Executive substantial authority to apprehend and detain those who pose a real danger to our security.

Officials charged with daily operational responsibility for our security may consider a judicial discourse on the history of the Habeas Corpus Act of 1679 and like matters to be far removed from the Nation's present, urgent concerns. Established legal doctrine, however, must be consulted for its teaching. Remote in time it may be; irrelevant to the present it is not. Security depends upon a sophisticated intelligence apparatus and the ability of our Armed Forces to act and to interdict. There are further considerations, however. Security subsists, too, in fidelity to freedom's first principles. Chief among these are freedom from arbitrary and unlawful restraint and the personal liberty that is secured by adherence to the separation of powers. It is from these principles that the judicial authority to consider petitions for habeas corpus relief derives.

Our opinion does not undermine the Executive's powers as Commander in Chief. On the contrary, the exercise of those powers is vindicated, not eroded, when confirmed by the Judicial Branch. Within the Constitution's separation-of-powers structure, few exercises of judicial power are as legitimate or as necessary as the responsibility to hear challenges to the authority of the Executive to imprison a person. Some of these petitioners have been in custody for six years with no definitive judicial determination as to the legality of their detention. Their access to the writ is a necessity to determine the lawfulness of their status, even if, in the end, they do not obtain the relief they seek.

Because our Nation's past military conflicts have been of limited duration, it has been possible to leave the outer boundaries of war powers undefined. If, as some fear, terrorism continues to pose dangerous threats to us for years to come, the Court might not have this luxury. This result is not inevitable, however. The political branches, consistent with their independent obligations to interpret and uphold the Constitution, can engage in a genuine debate about how best to preserve constitutional values while protecting the Nation from terrorism.

It bears repeating that our opinion does not address the content of the law that governs petitioners' detention. That is a matter yet to be determined. We hold that petitioners may invoke the fundamental procedural protections of habeas corpus. The laws and Constitution are designed to survive, and remain in force, in extraordinary times. Liberty and security can be reconciled; and in our system they are reconciled within the framework of the law. The Framers decided that habeas corpus, a right of first importance, must be a part of that framework, a part of that law.

The determination by the Court of Appeals that the Suspension Clause and its protections are inapplicable to petitioners was in error. The judgment of the Court of Appeals is reversed. The cases are remanded to the Court of Appeals with instructions that it remand the cases to the District Court for proceedings consistent with this opinion.

———

JUSTICE SOUTER, with whom JUSTICE GINSBURG and JUSTICE BREYER join, concurring.

A * * * fact insufficiently appreciated by the dissents is the length of the disputed imprisonments, some of the prisoners represented here today having been locked up for six years. Hence the hollow ring when the dissenters suggest that the Court is somehow precipitating the judiciary into reviewing claims that the military (subject to appeal to the Court of Appeals for the District of Columbia Circuit) could handle within some reasonable period of time. These suggestions of judicial haste are all the more out of place given the Court's realistic acknowledgment that in periods of exigency the tempo of any habeas review must reflect the immediate peril facing the country.

It is in fact the very lapse of four years from the time *Rasul* put everyone on notice that habeas process was available to Guantanamo prisoners, and the lapse of six years since some of these prisoners were captured and incarcerated, that stand at odds with the repeated suggestions of the dissenters that these cases should be seen as a judicial victory in a contest for power between the Court and the political branches. The several answers to the charge of triumphalism might start with a basic fact of Anglo–American constitutional history: that the power, first of the Crown and now of the Executive Branch of the United States, is necessarily limited by habeas corpus jurisdiction to enquire into the legality of executive detention. And one could explain that in this Court's exercise of responsibility to preserve habeas corpus something much more significant is involved than pulling and hauling between the judicial and political branches. Instead, though, it is enough to repeat that some of these petitioners have spent six years behind bars. After six years of sustained executive detentions in Guantanamo, subject to habeas jurisdiction but without any actual habeas scrutiny, today's decision is no judicial victory, but an act of perseverance in trying to make habeas re-

view, and the obligation of the courts to provide it, mean something of value both to prisoners and to the Nation.

———

Chief Justice Roberts, with whom Justice Scalia, Justice Thomas, and Justice Alito join, dissenting.

Today the Court strikes down as inadequate the most generous set of procedural protections ever afforded aliens detained by this country as enemy combatants. The political branches crafted these procedures amidst an ongoing military conflict, after much careful investigation and thorough debate. The Court rejects them today out of hand, without bothering to say what due process rights the detainees possess, without explaining how the statute fails to vindicate those rights, and before a single petitioner has even attempted to avail himself of the law's operation. And to what effect? The majority merely replaces a review system designed by the people's representatives with a set of shapeless procedures to be defined by federal courts at some future date. One cannot help but think, after surveying the modest practical results of the majority's ambitious opinion, that this decision is not really about the detainees at all, but about control of federal policy regarding enemy combatants.

The majority is adamant that the Guantanamo detainees are entitled to the protections of habeas corpus—its opinion begins by deciding that question. I regard the issue as a difficult one, primarily because of the unique and unusual jurisdictional status of Guantanamo Bay. I nonetheless agree with Justice Scalia's analysis of our precedents and the pertinent history of the writ, and accordingly join his dissent. The important point for me, however, is that the Court should have resolved these cases on other grounds. Habeas is most fundamentally a procedural right, a mechanism for contesting the legality of executive detention. The critical threshold question in these cases, prior to any inquiry about the writ's scope, is whether the system the political branches designed protects whatever rights the detainees may possess. If so, there is no need for any additional process, whether called "habeas" or something else.

Congress entrusted that threshold question in the first instance to the Court of Appeals for the District of Columbia Circuit, as the Constitution surely allows Congress to do .. But before the D. C. Circuit has addressed the issue, the Court cashiers the statute, and without answering this critical threshold question itself. The Court does eventually get around to asking whether review under the DTA is, as the Court frames it, an "adequate substitute" for habeas, but even then its opinion fails to determine what rights the detainees possess and whether the DTA system satisfies them. The majority instead compares the undefined DTA process to an equally undefined habeas right—one that is to be given shape only in the future by district courts on a case-by-case basis. This whole approach is misguided.

It is also fruitless. How the detainees' claims will be decided now that the DTA is gone is anybody's guess. But the habeas process the

Court mandates will most likely end up looking a lot like the DTA system it replaces, as the district court judges shaping it will have to reconcile review of the prisoners' detention with the undoubted need to protect the American people from the terrorist threat—precisely the challenge Congress undertook in drafting the DTA. All that today's opinion has done is shift responsibility for those sensitive foreign policy and national security decisions from the elected branches to the Federal Judiciary.

I believe the system the political branches constructed adequately protects any constitutional rights aliens captured abroad and detained as enemy combatants may enjoy. I therefore would dismiss these cases on that ground. With all respect for the contrary views of the majority, I must dissent.

I

* * *

It is grossly premature to pronounce on the detainees' right to habeas without first assessing whether the remedies the DTA system provides vindicate whatever rights petitioners may claim. The plurality in *Hamdi v. Rumsfeld*, 542 U.S. 507, 533 (2004), explained that the Constitution guaranteed an American *citizen* challenging his detention as an enemy combatant the right to "notice of the factual basis for his classification, and a fair opportunity to rebut the Government's factual assertions before a neutral decisionmaker." The plurality specifically stated that constitutionally adequate collateral process could be provided "by an appropriately authorized and properly constituted military tribunal," given the "uncommon potential to burden the Executive at a time of ongoing military conflict." This point is directly pertinent here, for surely the Due Process Clause does not afford *non*-citizens in such circumstances greater protection than citizens are due.

* * *

The Court acknowledges that "the ordinary course" would be not to decide the constitutionality of the DTA at this stage, but abandons that "ordinary course" in light of the "gravity" of the constitutional issues presented and the prospect of additional delay. It is, however, precisely when the issues presented are grave that adherence to the ordinary course is most important. A principle applied only when unimportant is not much of a principle at all, and charges of judicial activism are most effectively rebutted when courts can fairly argue they are following normal practices.

The Court is also concerned that requiring petitioners to pursue DTA review before proceeding with their habeas corpus actions could involve additional delay. The nature of the habeas remedy the Court instructs lower courts to craft on remand, however, is far more unsettled than the process Congress provided in the DTA. There is no reason to suppose that review according to procedures the Federal Judiciary will design, case by case, will proceed any faster than the DTA process petitioners disdained.

* * *

II

* * *

Because the central purpose of habeas corpus is to test the legality of executive detention, the writ requires most fundamentally an Article III court able to hear the prisoner's claims and, when necessary, order release. Beyond that, the process a given prisoner is entitled to receive depends on the circumstances and the rights of the prisoner. After much hemming and hawing, the majority appears to concede that the DTA provides an Article III court competent to order release. The only issue in dispute is the process the Guantanamo prisoners are entitled to use to test the legality of their detention. *Hamdi* concluded that American citizens detained as enemy combatants are entitled to only limited process, and that much of that process could be supplied by a military tribunal, with review to follow in an Article III court. That is precisely the system we have here. It is adequate to vindicate whatever due process rights petitioners may have.

A

* * *

B

* * *

Declaring that petitioners have a right to habeas in no way excuses the Court from explaining why the DTA does not protect whatever due process or statutory rights petitioners may have. Because if the DTA provides a means for vindicating petitioners' rights, it is necessarily an adequate substitute for habeas corpus.

For my part, I will assume that any due process rights petitioners may possess are no greater than those of American citizens detained as enemy combatants. It is worth noting * * * that the *Hamdi* controlling opinion said the Constitution guarantees citizen detainees only "basic" procedural rights, and that the process for securing those rights can "be tailored to alleviate [the] uncommon potential to burden the Executive at a time of ongoing military conflict." The majority, however, objects that "the procedural protections afforded to the detainees in the CSRT hearings are . . . limited." But the evidentiary and other limitations the Court complains of reflect the nature of the issue in contest, namely, the status of aliens captured by our Armed Forces abroad and alleged to be enemy combatants. Contrary to the repeated suggestions of the majority, DTA review need not parallel the habeas privileges enjoyed by noncombatant American citizens, as set out in 28 U.S.C. § 2241 (2000 ed. and Supp V). It need only provide process adequate for noncitizens detained as alleged combatants.

* * *

C

At the CSRT stage, every petitioner has the right to present evidence that he has been wrongfully detained. This includes the right to call witnesses who are reasonably available, question witnesses called by the tribunal, introduce documentary evidence, and testify before the tribunal.

* * *

Detainees not only have the opportunity to confront any witness who appears before the tribunal, they may call witnesses of their own. The Implementation Memo requires only that detainees' witnesses be "reasonably available," a requirement drawn from Army Regulation 190–8, ch. 1, § 1–6(*e*)(6), and entirely consistent with the Government's interest in avoiding a futile search for evidence that might burden warmaking responsibilities. The dangerous mission assigned to our forces abroad is to fight terrorists, not serve subpoenas. The Court is correct that some forms of hearsay evidence are admissible before the CSRT, but *Hamdi* expressly approved this use of hearsay by habeas courts.

As to classified information, while detainees are not permitted access to it themselves, the Implementation Memo provides each detainee with a "Personal Representative" who may review classified documents at the CSRT stage and summarize them for the detainee. The prisoner's counsel enjoys the same privilege on appeal before the D. C. Circuit. That is more access to classified material for alleged alien enemy combatants than ever before provided. I am not aware of a single instance—and certainly the majority cites none—in which detainees such as petitioners have been provided access to classified material in *any* form. * * *

What alternative does the Court propose? Allow free access to classified information and ignore the risk the prisoner may eventually convey what he learns to parties hostile to this country, with deadly consequences for those who helped apprehend the detainee? If the Court can design a better system for communicating to detainees the substance of any classified information relevant to their cases, without fatally compromising national security interests and sources, the majority should come forward with it. Instead, the majority fobs that vexing question off on district courts to answer down the road.

Prisoners of war are not permitted access to classified information, and neither are they permitted access to counsel, another supposed failing of the CSRT process. And yet the Guantanamo detainees are hardly denied all legal assistance. They are provided a "Personal Representative" who, as previously noted, may access classified information, help the detainee arrange for witnesses, assist the detainee's preparation of his case, and even aid the detainee in presenting his evidence to the tribunal. The provision for a personal representative on this order is one of several ways in which the CSRT procedures are *more* generous than those provided prisoners of war under Army Regulation 190–8.

Keep in mind that all this is just at the CSRT stage. Detainees receive additional process before the D. C. Circuit, including full access to appellate counsel and the right to challenge the factual and legal bases of their detentions. DTA § 1005(e)(2)(C) empowers the Court of Appeals to determine not only whether the CSRT observed the "procedures specified by the Secretary of Defense," but also "whether the use of such standards and procedures ... is consistent with the Constitution and laws of the United States." These provisions permit detainees to dispute the sufficiency of the evidence against them. They allow detainees to chal-

lenge a CSRT panel's interpretation of any relevant law, and even the constitutionality of the CSRT proceedings themselves. This includes, as the Solicitor General acknowledges, the ability to dispute the Government's right to detain alleged combatants in the first place, and to dispute the Government's definition of "enemy combatant." All this before an Article III court— plainly a neutral decisionmaker.

All told, the DTA provides the prisoners held at Guantanamo Bay adequate opportunity to contest the bases of their detentions, which is all habeas corpus need allow. The DTA provides more opportunity and more process, in fact, than that afforded prisoners of war or any other alleged enemy combatants in history.

D

Despite these guarantees, the Court finds the DTA system an inadequate habeas substitute, for one central reason: Detainees are unable to introduce at the appeal stage exculpatory evidence discovered after the conclusion of their CSRT proceedings. * * * If this is the most the Court can muster, the ice beneath its feet is thin indeed.

* * *

The Court's hand wringing over the DTA's treatment of later-discovered exculpatory evidence is the most it has to show after a roving search for constitutionally problematic scenarios. But "[t]he delicate power of pronouncing an Act of Congress unconstitutional," we have said, "is not to be exercised with reference to hypothetical cases thus imagined." The Court today invents a sort of reverse facial challenge and applies it with gusto: If there is *any* scenario in which the statute *might* be constitutionally infirm, the law must be struck down. The Court's new method of constitutional adjudication only underscores its failure to follow our usual procedures and require petitioners to demonstrate that *they* have been harmed by the statute they challenge. In the absence of such a concrete showing, the Court is unable to imagine a plausible hypothetical in which the DTA is unconstitutional.

E

* * *

III

For all its eloquence about the detainees' right to the writ, the Court makes no effort to elaborate how exactly the remedy it prescribes will differ from the procedural protections detainees enjoy under the DTA. The Court objects to the detainees' limited access to witnesses and classified material, but proposes no alternatives of its own. Indeed, it simply ignores the many difficult questions its holding presents. What, for example, will become of the CSRT process? The majority says federal courts should *generally* refrain from entertaining detainee challenges until after the petitioner's CSRT proceeding has finished. But to what deference, if any, is that CSRT determination entitled?

There are other problems. Take witness availability. What makes the majority think witnesses will become magically available when the review procedure is labeled "habeas"? Will the location of most of these witnesses change—will they suddenly become easily susceptible to service of process? Or will subpoenas issued by American habeas courts run to Basra? And if they did, how would they be enforced? Speaking of witnesses, will detainees be able to call active-duty military officers as witnesses? If not, why not?

The majority has no answers for these difficulties. What it does say leaves open the distinct possibility that its "habeas" remedy will, when all is said and done, end up looking a great deal like the DTA review it rejects. * * *

So who has won? Not the detainees. The Court's analysis leaves them with only the prospect of further litigation to determine the content of their new habeas right, followed by further litigation to resolve their particular cases, followed by further litigation before the D. C. Circuit—where they could have started had they invoked the DTA procedure. Not Congress, whose attempt to determine— through democratic means—how best to balance the security of the American people with the detainees' liberty interests, has been unceremoniously brushed aside. Not the Great Writ, whose majesty is hardly enhanced by its extension to a jurisdictionally quirky outpost, with no tangible benefit to anyone. Not the rule of law, unless by that is meant the rule of lawyers, who will now arguably have a greater role than military and intelligence officials in shaping policy for alien enemy combatants. And certainly not the American people, who today lose a bit more control over the conduct of this Nation's foreign policy to unelected, politically unaccountable judges.

I respectfully dissent.

———

JUSTICE SCALIA, with whom THE CHIEF JUSTICE, JUSTICE THOMAS, and JUSTICE ALITO join, dissenting.

Today, for the first time in our Nation's history, the Court confers a constitutional right to habeas corpus on alien enemies detained abroad by our military forces in the course of an ongoing war. The Chief Justice's dissent, which I join, shows that the procedures prescribed by Congress in the Detainee Treatment Act provide the essential protections that habeas corpus guarantees; there has thus been no suspension of the writ, and no basis exists for judicial intervention beyond what the Act allows. My problem with today's opinion is more fundamental still: The writ of habeas corpus does not, and never has, run in favor of aliens abroad; the Suspension Clause thus has no application, and the Court's intervention in this military matter is entirely *ultra vires.*

I shall devote most of what will be a lengthy opinion to the legal errors contained in the opinion of the Court. Contrary to my usual practice, however, I think it appropriate to begin with a description of the disastrous consequences of what the Court has done today.

I

America is at war with radical Islamists. The enemy began by killing Americans and American allies abroad: 241 at the Marine barracks in Lebanon, 19 at the Khobar Towers in Dhahran, 224 at our embassies in Dar es Salaam and Nairobi, and 17 on the USS Cole in Yemen. See National Commission on Terrorist Attacks upon the United States, The 9/11 Commission Report, pp. 60–61, 70, 190 (2004). On September 11, 2001, the enemy brought the battle to American soil, killing 2,749 at the Twin Towers in New York City, 184 at the Pentagon in Washington, D. C., and 40 in Pennsylvania. It has threatened further attacks against our homeland; one need only walk about buttressed and barricaded Washington, or board a plane anywhere in the country, to know that the threat is a serious one. Our Armed Forces are now in the field against the enemy, in Afghanistan and Iraq. Last week, 13 of our countrymen in arms were killed.

The game of bait-and-switch that today's opinion plays upon the Nation's Commander in Chief will make the war harder on us. It will almost certainly cause more Americans to be killed. That consequence would be tolerable if necessary to preserve a time-honored legal principle vital to our constitutional Republic. But it is this Court's blatant *abandonment* of such a principle that produces the decision today. The President relied on our settled precedent in Johnson v. Eisentrager, 339 U.S. 763 (1950), when he established the prison at Guantanamo Bay for enemy aliens. * * * Had the law been otherwise, the military surely would not have transported prisoners there, but would have kept them in Afghanistan, transferred them to another of our foreign military bases, or turned them over to allies for detention. Those other facilities might well have been worse for the detainees themselves.

In the long term, then, the Court's decision today accomplishes little, except perhaps to reduce the well-being of enemy combatants that the Court ostensibly seeks to protect. In the short term, however, the decision is devastating. At least 30 of those prisoners hitherto released from Guantanamo Bay have returned to the battlefield. See S. Rep. No. 110–90, pt. 7, p. 13 (2007) (Minority Views of Sens. Kyl, Sessions, Graham, Cornyn, and Coburn) (hereinafter Minority Report). Some have been captured or killed. But others have succeeded in carrying on their atrocities against innocent civilians. In one case, a detainee released from Guantanamo Bay masterminded the kidnapping of two Chinese dam workers, one of whom was later shot to death when used as a human shield against Pakistani commandoes. Another former detainee promptly resumed his post as a senior Taliban commander and murdered a United Nations engineer and three Afghan soldiers. Still another murdered an Afghan judge. See Minority Report 13. It was reported only last month that a released detainee carried out a suicide bombing against Iraqi soldiers in Mosul, Iraq. See White, Ex–Guantanamo Detainee Joined Iraq Suicide Attack, Washington Post, May 8, 2008, p. A18.

These, mind you, were detainees whom *the military* had concluded were not enemy combatants. Their return to the kill illustrates the in-

credible difficulty of assessing who is and who is not an enemy combatant in a foreign theater of operations where the environment does not lend itself to rigorous evidence collection. Astoundingly, the Court today raises the bar, requiring military officials to appear before civilian courts and defend their decisions under procedural and evidentiary rules that go beyond what Congress has specified. As THE CHIEF JUSTICE's dissent makes clear, we have no idea what those procedural and evidentiary rules are, but they will be determined by civil courts and (in the Court's contemplation at least) will be more detainee-friendly than those now applied, since otherwise there would no reason to hold the congressionally prescribed procedures unconstitutional. If they impose a higher standard of proof (from foreign battlefields) than current procedures require, the number of the enemy returned to combat will obviously increase.

But even when the military has evidence that it can bring forward, it is often foolhardy to release that evidence to the attorneys representing our enemies. And one escalation of procedures that the Court *is* clear about is affording the detainees increased access to witnesses (perhaps troops serving in Afghanistan?) and to classified information. During the 1995 prosecution of Omar Abdel Rahman, federal prosecutors gave the names of 200 unindicted co-conspirators to the "Blind Sheik's" defense lawyers; that information was in the hands of Osama Bin Laden within two weeks. See Minority Report 14–15. In another case, trial testimony revealed to the enemy that the United States had been monitoring their cellular network, whereupon they promptly stopped using it, enabling more of them to evade capture and continue their atrocities. See *id.*, at 15.

And today it is not just the military that the Court elbows aside. * * * It is * * * clear that Congress and the Executive—*both* political branches—have determined that limiting the role of civilian courts in adjudicating whether prisoners captured abroad are properly detained is important to success in the war that some 190,000 of our men and women are now fighting. As the Solicitor General argued, "the Military Commissions Act and the Detainee Treatment Act ... represent an effort by the political branches to strike an appropriate balance between the need to preserve liberty and the need to accommodate the weighty and sensitive governmental interests in ensuring that those who have in fact fought with the enemy during a war do not return to battle against the United States."

But it does not matter. The Court today decrees that no good reason to accept the judgment of the other two branches is "apparent." "The Government," it declares, "presents no credible arguments that the military mission at Guantanamo would be compromised if habeas corpus courts had jurisdiction to hear the detainees' claims." What competence does the Court have to second-guess the judgment of Congress and the President on such a point? None whatever. But the Court blunders in nonetheless. Henceforth, as today's opinion makes unnervingly clear, how to handle enemy prisoners in this war will ultimately lie with the branch that knows least about the national security concerns that the subject entails.

II

A

The Suspension Clause of the Constitution provides: "The Privilege of the Writ of Habeas Corpus shall not be suspended, unless when in Cases of Rebellion or Invasion the public Safety may require it." Art. I, § 9, cl. 2. As a court of law operating under a written Constitution, our role is to determine whether there is a conflict between that Clause and the Military Commissions Act. A conflict arises only if the Suspension Clause preserves the privilege of the writ for aliens held by the United States military as enemy combatants at the base in Guantanamo Bay, located within the sovereign territory of Cuba.

* * *

B

The Court purports to derive from our precedents a "functional" test for the extraterritorial reach of the writ, which shows that the Military Commissions Act unconstitutionally restricts the scope of habeas. That is remarkable because the most pertinent of those precedents, Johnson v. Eisentrager, 339 U.S. 763, conclusively establishes the opposite. There we were confronted with the claims of 21 Germans held at Landsberg Prison, an American military facility located in the American Zone of occupation in postwar Germany. They had been captured in China, and an American military commission sitting there had convicted them of war crimes—collaborating with the Japanese after Germany's surrender.

Like the petitioners here, the Germans claimed that their detentions violated the Constitution and international law, and sought a writ of habeas corpus. Writing for the Court, Justice Jackson held that American courts lacked habeas jurisdiction. * * *

Lest there be any doubt about the primacy of territorial sovereignty in determining the jurisdiction of a habeas court over an alien, Justice Jackson distinguished two cases in which aliens had been permitted to seek habeas relief, on the ground that the prisoners in those cases were in custody within the sovereign territory of the United States. * * * *Eisentrager* thus held—*held* beyond any doubt—that the Constitution does not ensure habeas for aliens held by the United States in areas over which our Government is not sovereign. * * * [Justice Scalia contests the majority's reading of *Eisenstrager* as establishing a "functional" test of sovereignty, and attacks the majority's reliance on the Insular Cases.]

There is simply no support for the Court's assertion that constitutional rights extend to aliens held outside U.S. sovereign territory, and *Eisentrager* could not be clearer that the privilege of habeas corpus does not extend to aliens abroad. By blatantly distorting *Eisentrager*, the Court avoids the difficulty of explaining why it should be overruled. The rule that aliens abroad are not constitutionally entitled to habeas corpus has not proved unworkable in practice; if anything, it is the Court's "functional" test that does not (and never will) provide clear guidance for the future. *Eisentrager* forms a coherent whole with the accepted proposition that aliens abroad have no substantive rights under our Constitution. Since it was announced, no relevant factual premises have changed. It has engendered considerable reliance on the part of our military. And, as the Court acknowledges, text and history do not clearly compel a contrary ruling. It is a sad day for the rule of law when such an important constitutional precedent is discarded without an *apologia*, much less an apology.

C

What drives today's decision is neither the meaning of the Suspension Clause, nor the principles of our precedents, but rather an inflated notion of judicial supremacy. The Court says that if the extraterritorial applicability of the Suspension Clause turned on formal notions of sovereignty, "it would be possible for the political branches to govern without legal constraint" in areas beyond the sovereign territory of the United States. That cannot be, the Court says, because it is the duty of this Court to say what the law is. It would be difficult to imagine a more question-begging analysis. * * * Our power "to say what the law is" is circumscribed by the limits of our statutorily and constitutionally conferred jurisdiction. And that is precisely the question in these cases: whether the Constitution confers habeas jurisdiction on federal courts to decide petitioners' claims. It is both irrational and arrogant to say that the answer must be yes, because otherwise we would not be supreme.

But so long as there are *some* places to which habeas does not run—so long as the Court's new "functional" test will not be satisfied *in every case*—then there will be circumstances in which "it would be possible for the political branches to govern without legal constraint." Or, to put it more impartially, areas in which the legal determinations of the *other* branches will be (shudder!) *supreme*. In other words, judicial supremacy is not really assured by the constitutional rule that the Court creates. The gap between rationale and rule leads me to conclude that the Court's ultimate, unexpressed goal is to preserve the power to review the confinement of enemy prisoners held by the Executive anywhere in the world. The "functional" test usefully evades the precedential landmine of *Eisentrager* but is so inherently subjective that it clears a wide path for the Court to traverse in the years to come.

III

Putting aside the conclusive precedent of *Eisentrager*, it is clear that the original understanding of the Suspension Clause was that habeas corpus was not available to aliens abroad, as Judge Randolph's thorough opinion for the court below detailed. See 476 F.3d 981, 988–990 (CADC 2007). * * *

It is entirely clear that, at English common law, the writ of habeas corpus did not extend beyond the sovereign territory of the Crown. [Justice Scalia engages in an extensive discussion of the history of the writ and the Suspension Clause.]

In sum, *all* available historical evidence points to the conclusion that the writ would not have been available at common law for aliens captured and held outside the sover-

eign territory of the Crown. Despite three opening briefs, three reply briefs, and support from a legion of *amici,* petitioners have failed to identify a single case in the history of Anglo–American law that supports their claim to jurisdiction. The Court finds it significant that there is no recorded case *denying* jurisdiction to such prisoners either. But a case standing for the remarkable proposition that the writ could issue to a foreign land would surely have been reported, whereas a case denying such a writ for lack of jurisdiction would likely not. At a minimum, the absence of a reported case either way leaves unrefuted the voluminous commentary stating that habeas was confined to the dominions of the Crown.

* * *

———

Today the Court warps our Constitution in a way that goes beyond the narrow issue of the reach of the Suspension Clause, invoking judicially brainstormed separation-of-powers principles to establish a manipulable "functional" test for the extraterritorial reach of habeas corpus (and, no doubt, for the extraterritorial reach of other constitutional protections as well). It blatantly misdescribes important precedents, most conspicuously Justice Jackson's opinion for the Court in *Johnson* v. *Eisentrager*. It breaks a chain of precedent as old as the common law that prohibits judicial inquiry into detentions of aliens abroad absent statutory authorization. And, most tragically, it sets our military commanders the impossible task of proving to a civilian court, under whatever standards this Court devises in the future, that evidence supports the confinement of each and every enemy prisoner.

The Nation will live to regret what the Court has done today. I dissent.

Chapter Eleven

SENTENCING

I. INTRODUCTION

D. CONSTITUTIONAL LIMITATIONS ON PUNISHMENT

1. *Sentencing Enhancements, the Right to Jury Trial, and the Right to Due Process*

Page 1437. Add after the section on *Booker*:

State Guidelines Found Distinguishable From the Federal Guidelines as Left by Booker: *Cunningham v. California*

In Cunningham v. California, 549 U.S. 270 (2007), the Court held that the California Determinative Sentencing Law violated *Apprendi* because it required a trial judge to impose a sentence in a higher sentencing category, upon the basis of certain aggravating facts found by the judge. Justice Ginsburg, writing for the six-person majority, declared as follows:

> Under California's DSL, an upper term sentence may be imposed only when the trial judge finds an aggravating circumstance. An element of the charged offense, essential to a jury's determination of guilt, or admitted in a defendant's guilty plea, does not qualify as such a circumstance. Instead, aggravating circumstances depend on facts found discretely and solely by the judge. In accord with *Blakely*, therefore, the middle term prescribed in California's statutes [for the crime charged and proved to the jury], not the upper term, is the relevant statutory maximum. Because circumstances in aggravation are found by the judge, not the jury, and need only be established by a preponderance of the evidence, not beyond a reasonable doubt, the DSL violates *Apprendi*'s bright-line rule: Except for a prior conviction, "any fact that increases the penalty for a crime beyond the prescribed statutory maximum must be submitted to a jury, and proved beyond a reasonable doubt."

California argued that the sentencing enhancements were left to the discretion of the trial judge and therefore were "advisory" in the same way as the Federal Sentencing Guidelines upheld in *Booker*. But Justice Ginsburg disagreed. The full opinion in *Cunningham,* including the dissents by Justice Kennedy (joined by Justice Breyer) and Justice Alito (joined by Justices Kennedy and Breyer) is set forth in this Supplement, supra, in the section on "Constitutionally Based Proof Requirements."

II. GUIDELINES SENTENCING

D. SUPREME COURT CONSTRUCTION OF THE FEDERAL SENTENCING GUIDELINES

2. *Application of Advisory Guidelines After Booker*

Page 1494. Add at the end of the section on Appellate Review of Advisory Guidelines:

Within-Guidelines Sentences Can Be Found Presumptively Reasonable: Rita v. United States

In the following case, the Court agrees with the position of courts described in the Text, that within-Guidelines sentences can be found presumptively reasonable by an appellate court.

RITA v. UNITED STATES

Supreme Court of the United States, 2007.
551 U.S. 338.

JUSTICE BREYER **delivered the opinion of the Court.**

The federal courts of appeals review federal sentences and set aside those they find "unreasonable." See, *e.g.*, United States v. Booker, 543 U.S. 220, 261–263 (2005). Several Circuits have held that, when doing so, they will presume that a sentence imposed within a properly calculated United States Sentencing Guidelines range is a reasonable sentence. The most important question before us is whether the law permits the courts of appeals to use this presumption. We hold that it does.

I

A

The basic crime in this case concerns two false statements which Victor Rita, the petitioner, made under oath to a federal grand jury. The jury was investigating a gun company called InterOrdnance. Prosecutors believed that buyers of an InterOrdnance kit, called a "PPSH 41 machinegun 'parts kit,' "could assemble a machinegun from the kit, that those kits consequently amounted to machineguns, and that InterOrdnance had not secured proper registrations for the importation of the guns.

Rita had bought a PPSH 41 machinegun parts kit. Rita, when contacted by the Bureau of Alcohol, Tobacco, and Firearms and Explosives (ATF), agreed to let a federal agent inspect the kit. But before meeting with the agent, Rita called InterOrdnance and then sent back the kit. He subsequently turned over to ATF a different kit that apparently did not amount to a machinegun.

The investigating prosecutor brought Rita before the grand jury, placed him under oath, and asked him about these matters. Rita denied that the Government agent had asked him for the PPSH kit, and also denied that he had spoken soon thereafter about the PPSH kit to someone at InterOrdnance. The Government claimed these statements were false, charged Rita with perjury, making false statements, and obstructing justice, and, after a jury trial, obtained convictions on all counts.

B

The parties subsequently proceeded to sentencing. Initially, a probation officer, with the help of the parties, and after investigating the background both of the offenses and of the offender, prepared a presentence report. See Fed. Rules Crim. Proc. 32(c)-(d). The completed report describes "offense characteristics," "offender characteristics," and other matters that might be relevant to the sentence, and then calculates a Guidelines sentence. The report also sets forth factors potentially relevant to a departure from the Guidelines or relevant to the imposition of an other-than-Guidelines sentence. It ultimately makes a sentencing recommendation based on the Guidelines.

In respect to "offense characteristics," for example, the report points out that the five counts of conviction all stem from a single incident. Hence, pursuant to the Guidelines, the report, in calculating a recommended sentence, groups the five counts of conviction together, treating them as if they amounted to the single most serious count among them (and ignoring all others). See USSG § 3D1.1. The single most serious offense in Rita's case is "perjury." The relevant Guideline, § 2J1.3(c)(1), instructs the sentencing court (and the probation officer) to calculate the Guidelines sentence for "perjury . . . in respect to a criminal offense" by applying the Guideline for an "accessory after the fact," as to that criminal offense. § 2X3.1. And that latter Guideline says that the judge, for calculation purposes, should take as a base offense level, a level that is "6 levels lower than the offense level for the *underlying offense*," (emphasis added) (the offense that the perjury may have helped someone commit). Here the "underlying offense" consisted of InterOrdnance's possible violation of the machinegun registration law. USSG § 2M5.2 (providing sentence for violation of 22 U.S.C. § 2778(b)(2), importation of defense articles without authorization). The base offense level for the gun registration crime is 26. See USSG § 2M5.2. Six levels less is 20. And 20, says the presentence report, is the base offense level applicable to Rita for purposes of Guidelines sentence calculation.

The presentence report next considers Rita's "Criminal History." Rita was convicted in May 1986, and sentenced to five years' probation for making false statements in connection with the purchase of fire-arms. Because this conviction took place more than 10 years before the present offense, it did not count against Rita. And because Rita had no other relevant convictions, the Guidelines considered him as having no "criminal history points." The report consequently places Rita in criminal history category I, the lowest category for purposes of calculating a Guidelines' sentence.

The report goes on to describe other "Offender Characteristics." The description includes Rita's personal and family data, Rita's physical condition (including a detailed description of ailments), Rita's mental and emotional health, the lack of any history of substance abuse, Rita's vocational and nonvocational education, and Rita's employment record. It states that he served in the Armed Forces for over 25 years, on active duty and in the Reserve. During that time he received 35 commendations, awards, or medals of different kinds. The report analyzes Rita's financial condition.

Ultimately, the report calculates the Guidelines sentencing range. The Guidelines specify for base level 20, criminal history category I, a sentence of 33–to–41 months' imprisonment. The report adds that there "appears to be no circumstance or combination of circumstances that warrant a departure from the prescribed sentencing guidelines."

C

At the sentencing hearing, both Rita and the Government presented their sentencing arguments. Each side addressed the report. Rita argued for a sentence outside (and lower than) the recommended Guidelines 33–to–41 month range.

The judge made clear that Rita's argument for a lower sentence could take either of two forms. First, Rita might argue *within the Guidelines' framework,* for a departure from the applicable Guidelines range on the ground that his circumstances present an "atypical case" that falls outside the "heartland" to which the United States Sentencing Commission intends each individual Guideline to apply. USSG § 5K2.0(a)(2). Second, Rita might argue that, independent of the Guidelines, application of the sentencing factors set forth in 18 U.S.C. § 3553(a) warrants a lower sentence. See *Booker,* 543 U.S., at 259–260.

Thus, the judge asked Rita's counsel, "Are you going to put on evidence to show that [Rita] should be getting a downward departure, or under 3553, your client would be entitled to a different sentence than he should get under sentencing guidelines?" And the judge later summarized:

> "You're asking for a departure from the guidelines or a sentence under 3553 that is lower than the guidelines, and here are the reasons:
>
> "One, he is a vulnerable defendant because he's been involved in [government criminal justice] work which has caused people to become convicted criminals who are in prison and there may be retribution against him.
>
> "Two, his military experience . . . ."

Counsel agreed, while adding that Rita's poor physical condition constituted a third reason. And counsel said that he rested his claim for a lower sentence on "just [those] three" special circumstances, "physical condition, vulnerability in prison and the military service." Rita presented evidence and argument related to these three factors. The Government, while not asking for a sentence higher than the report's recommended Guidelines range, said that Rita's perjury had interfered with the Government's potential "obstruction of justice" claim against InterOrdnance and that Rita, as a former Government criminal justice employee, should have known better than to commit perjury. The sentencing judge asked questions about each factor.

After hearing the arguments, the judge concluded that he was "unable to find that the [report's recommended] sentencing guideline range ... is an inappropriate guideline range for that, and under 3553 ... the public needs to be protected if it is true, and I must accept as true the jury verdict." The court concluded: "So the Court finds that it is appropriate to enter" a sentence at the bottom of the Guidelines range, namely a sentence of imprisonment "for a period of 33 months."

D

On appeal, Rita argued that his 33–month sentence was "unreasonable" because (1) it did not adequately take account of "the defendant's history and characteristics," and (2) it "is greater than necessary to comply with the purposes of sentencing set forth in 18 U.S.C. § 3553(a)(2)." The Fourth Circuit observed that it must set aside a sentence that is not "reasonable." The Circuit stated that "a sentence

imposed within the properly calculated Guidelines range ... is presumptively reasonable." It added that "while we believe that the appropriate circumstances for imposing a sentence outside the guideline range will depend on the facts of individual cases, we have no reason to doubt that most sentences will continue to fall within the applicable guideline range." The Fourth Circuit then rejected Rita's arguments and upheld the sentence.

E

Rita petitioned for a writ of certiorari. He pointed out that the Circuits are split as to the use of a presumption of reasonableness for within-Guidelines sentences. [Justice Breyer cites cases from the circuits.] We consequently granted Rita's petition. We agreed to decide whether a circuit court may afford a "presumption of reasonableness" to a "within-Guidelines" sentence. We also agreed to decide whether the District Court properly analyzed the relevant sentencing factors and whether, given the record, the District Court's ultimate choice of a 33–month sentence was "unreasonable."

II

The first question is whether a court of appeals may apply a presumption of reasonableness to a district court sentence that reflects a proper application of the Sentencing Guidelines. We conclude that it can.

A

For one thing, the presumption is not binding. It does not, like a trial-related evidentiary presumption, insist that one side, or the other, shoulder a particular burden of persuasion or proof lest they lose their case. Nor does the presumption reflect strong judicial deference of the kind that leads appeals courts to grant greater factfinding leeway to an expert agency than to a district judge. Rather, the presumption reflects the fact that, by the time an appeals court is considering a within-Guidelines sentence on review, *both* the sentencing judge and the Sentencing Commission will have reached the *same* conclusion as to the proper sentence in the particular case. That double determination significantly increases the likelihood that the sentence is a reasonable one.

Further, the presumption reflects the nature of the Guidelines-writing task that Congress set for the Commission and the manner in which the Commission carried out that task. In instructing both the sentencing judge and the Commission what to do, Congress referred to the basic sentencing objectives that the statute sets forth in 18 U.S.C. § 3553(a). That provision tells the sentencing judge to consider (1) offense and offender characteristics; (2) the need for a sentence to reflect the basic aims of sentencing, namely (a) "just punishment" (retribution), (b) deterrence, (c) incapacitation, (d) rehabilitation; (3) the sentences legally available; (4) the Sentencing Guidelines; (5) Sentencing Commission policy statements; (6) the need to avoid unwarranted disparities; and (7) the need for restitution. The provision also tells the sentencing judge to "impose a sentence sufficient, but not greater than necessary, to comply with" the basic aims of sentencing as set out above.

Congressional statutes then tell the Commission to write Guidelines that will carry out these same § 3553(a) objectives. Thus, 28 U.S.C. § 991(b) indicates that one of the Commission's basic objectives is to "assure the meeting of the purposes of sentencing as set forth in [§ 3553(a)(2)]." The provision adds that the Commission must seek to "provide certainty and fairness" in sentencing, to "avoid unwarranted sentencing disparities," to "maintain sufficient flexibility to permit individualized sentences when warranted by mitigating or aggravating factors not taken into account in the establishment of general sentencing practices," and to "reflect, to the extent practicable [sentencing-relevant] advancement in [the] knowledge of human behavior." Later provisions specifically instruct the Commission to write the Guidelines with reference to this statement of purposes, the statement that itself refers to § 3553(a). See 28 U.S.C. §§ 994(f), and 994(m).

The upshot is that the sentencing statutes envision both the sentencing judge and the Commission as carrying out the same basic § 3553(a) objectives, the one, at retail, the other at wholesale.

The Commission has made a serious, sometimes controversial, effort to carry out this mandate. The Commission, in describing its Guidelines-writing efforts, refers to these same statutory provisions. It says that it has tried to embody in the Guidelines the factors and considerations set forth in § 3553(a). The Commission's introductory statement recognizes that Congress "foresees guidelines that will further the basic purposes of criminal punishment, *i.e.*, deterring crime, incapacitating the offender, providing just punishment, and rehabilitating the offender." USSG § 1A.1, intro to comment., pt. A, P2 (The Statutory Mission). It adds that Congress "sought uniformity in sentencing by narrowing the wide disparity in sentences imposed by different federal courts for similar criminal conduct," as well as "proportionality in sentencing through a system that imposes appropriately different sentences for criminal conduct of different severity." *Ibid.* (The Basic Approach).

The Guidelines commentary explains how, despite considerable disagreement within the criminal justice community, the Commission has gone about writing Guidelines that it intends to embody these ends. It says, for example, that the goals of uniformity and proportionality often conflict. The commentary describes the difficulties involved in developing a practical sentencing system that sensibly reconciles the two ends. It adds that a "philosophical problem arose when the Commission attempted to reconcile the differing perceptions of the purposes of criminal punishment." Some would emphasize moral culpability and "just punishment"; others would emphasize the need for "crime control." Rather than choose among differing practical and philosophical objectives, the Commission took an "empirical approach," beginning with an empirical examination of 10,000 presentence reports setting forth what judges had done in the past and then modifying and adjusting past practice in the interests of greater rationality, avoiding inconsistency, complying with congressional instructions, and the like.

The Guidelines as written reflect the fact that the Sentencing Commission examined tens of thousands of sentences and worked with the help of many others in the law enforcement community over a long period of time in an effort to fulfill this statutory mandate. They also reflect the fact that different judges (and others) can differ as to how best to reconcile the disparate ends of punishment.

The Commission's work is ongoing. The statutes and the Guidelines themselves foresee continuous evolution helped by the sentencing courts and courts of appeals in that process. The sentencing courts, applying the Guidelines in individual cases may depart (either pursuant to the Guidelines or, since *Booker,* by imposing a non-Guidelines sentence). The judges will set forth their reasons. The Courts of Appeals will determine the reasonableness of the resulting sentence. The Commission will collect and examine the results. In doing so, it may obtain advice from prosecutors, defenders, law enforcement groups, civil liberties associations, experts in penology, and others. And it can revise the Guidelines accordingly.

The result is a set of Guidelines that seek to embody the § 3553(a) considerations, both in principle and in practice. Given the difficulties of doing so, the abstract and potentially conflicting nature of § 3553(a)'s general sentencing objectives, and the differences of philosophical view among those who work within the criminal justice community as to how best to apply general sentencing objectives, it is fair to assume that the Guidelines, insofar as practicable, reflect a rough approximation of sentences that might achieve § 3553(a)'s objectives.

An individual judge who imposes a sentence within the range recommended by the Guidelines thus makes a decision that is fully consistent with the Commission's judgment in general. Despite Justice Souter's fears to the contrary, (dissenting opinion), the courts of appeals' "reasonableness" presumption, rather than having independent legal effect, simply recognizes the real-world circumstance that when the judge's discretionary decision accords with the Commission's view of the appropriate application of § 3553(a) in the mine run of cases, it is probable that the sentence is reasonable. Indeed, even the Circuits that have declined to adopt a formal presumption also recognize that a Guidelines sentence will usually be reasonable, because it reflects both the Commission's and the sentencing court's judgment as to what is an appropriate sentence for a given offender.

We repeat that the presumption before us is an *appellate* court presumption. Given our explanation in *Booker* that appellate "reasonableness" review merely asks whether the trial court abused its discretion, the presumption applies only on appellate review. The sentencing judge, as a matter of process, will normally begin by considering the presentence report and its interpretation of the Guidelines. 18 U.S.C. § 3552(a); Fed. Rule Crim. Proc. 32. He may hear arguments by prosecution or defense that the Guidelines sentence should not apply, perhaps because (as the Guidelines themselves foresee) the case at hand falls outside the "heartland" to which the Commission intends individual Guidelines to apply, USSG § 5K2.O, perhaps because the Guidelines sentence itself fails properly to reflect § 3553(a) considerations, or perhaps because the case warrants a different sentence regardless. See Rule 32(f). Thus, the sentencing court subjects the defendant's sentence to the thorough adversarial testing contemplated by federal sentencing procedure. See Rules 32(f), (h), (i)(C) and (i)(D); see also Burns v. United States, 501 U.S. 129, 136 (1991) (recognizing importance of notice and meaningful opportunity to be heard at sentencing). In determining the merits of these arguments, the sentencing court does not enjoy the benefit of a legal presumption that the Guidelines sentence should apply. *Booker,* 543 U.S., at 259–260.

B

Rita and his supporting *amici* make two further arguments against use of the presumption. First, Rita points out that many individual Guidelines apply higher sentences in the presence of special facts, for example, brandishing a weapon. In many cases, the sentencing judge, not the jury, will determine the existence of those facts. A pro-Guidelines "presumption of reasonableness" will increase the likelihood that courts of appeals will affirm such sentences, thereby increasing the likelihood that sentencing judges will impose such sentences. For that reason, Rita says, the presumption raises Sixth Amendment "concerns."

In our view, however, the presumption, even if it increases the likelihood that the judge, not the jury, will find "sentencing facts," does not violate the Sixth Amendment. This Court's Sixth Amendment cases do not automatically forbid a sentencing court to take account of factual matters not determined by a jury and to increase the sentence in consequence. Nor do they prohibit the sentencing judge from taking account of the Sentencing Commission's factual findings or recommended sentences.

The Sixth Amendment question, the Court has said, is whether the law *forbids* a judge to increase a defendant's sentence *unless* the judge finds facts that the jury did not find (and the offender did not concede). * * *

A nonbinding appellate presumption that a Guidelines sentence is reasonable does not *require* the sentencing judge to impose that sentence. Still less does it *forbid* the sentencing judge from imposing a sentence higher than the Guidelines provide for the jury-determined facts standing alone. As far as the law is concerned, the judge could disregard the Guidelines and apply the same sentence (higher than the statutory minimum or the bottom of the unenhanced Guidelines range) in the absence of the special facts (say, gun brandishing) which, in the view of the Sentencing Commission, would warrant a higher sentence within the statutorily permissible range. Thus, our Sixth Amendment cases do not forbid appellate court use of the presumption.

Justice Scalia concedes that the Sixth Amendment concerns he foresees are not presented by this case.

(concurring in part and concurring in judgment). And his need to rely on *hypotheticals* to make his point is consistent with our view that the approach adopted here will not raise a multitude of constitutional problems. Similarly, Justice Scalia agrees that we have never held that "the Sixth Amendment prohibits judges from ever finding any facts" relevant to sentencing. In sentencing, as in other areas, district judges at time make mistakes that are substantive. At times, they will impose sentences that are unreasonable. Circuit courts exist to correct such mistakes when they occur. Our decision in *Booker* recognized as much. *Booker* held unconstitutional that portion of the Guidelines that made them mandatory. It also recognized that when district courts impose discretionary sentences, which are reviewed under normal appellate principles by courts of appeals, such a sentencing scheme will ordinarily raise no Sixth Amendment concern. See *Booker* at 233 (opinion for the Court by Stevens, J.) ("Indeed, everyone agrees that the constitutional issues presented by these cases would have been avoided entirely if Congress had omitted from the [federal sentencing statute] the provisions that make the Guidelines binding on district judges"). That being so, our opinion in *Booker* made clear that today's holding does not violate the Sixth Amendment.

Rita may be correct that the presumption will encourage sentencing judges to impose Guidelines sentences. But we do not see how that fact could change the constitutional calculus. Congress sought to diminish unwarranted sentencing disparity. It sought a Guidelines system that would bring about greater fairness in sentencing through increased uniformity. The fact that the presumption might help achieve these congressional goals does not provide cause for holding the presumption unlawful as long as the presumption remains constitutional. And, given our case law, we cannot conclude that the presumption itself violates the Sixth Amendment.

* * *

Second, Rita and his *amici* claim that use of a pro-Guidelines presumption on appeal conflicts with Congress' insistence that sentencing judges apply the factors set forth in 18 U.S.C. § 3553(a) (and that the resulting sentence be "sufficient, but not greater than necessary, to comply with the purposes" of sentencing set forth in that statute). We have explained above, however, why we believe that, where judge and Commission *both* determine that the Guidelines sentences is an appropriate sentence for the case at hand, that sentence likely reflects the § 3553(a) factors (including its "not greater than necessary" requirement). This circumstance alleviates any serious general conflict between § 3553(a) and the Guidelines, for the purposes of appellate review. And, for that reason, we find that nothing in § 3553(a) renders use of the presumption unlawful.

III

We next turn to the question whether the District Court properly analyzed the relevant sentencing factors. In particular, Rita argues that the court took inadequate account of § 3553(c), a provision that requires a sentencing judge, "at the time of sentencing," to "state in open court the reasons for its imposition of the particular sentence." In our view, given the straightforward, conceptually simple arguments before the judge, the judge's statement of reasons here, though brief, was legally sufficient.

The statute does call for the judge to "state" his "reasons." And that requirement reflects sound judicial practice. Judicial decisions are reasoned decisions. Confidence in a judge's use of reason underlies the public's trust in the judicial institution. A public statement of those reasons helps provide the public with the assurance that creates that trust.

That said, we cannot read the statute (or our precedent) as insisting upon a full opinion in every case. The appropriateness of brevity or length, conciseness or detail, when to write, what to say, depends upon circumstances. Sometimes a judicial opinion responds to every argument; sometimes it does not; sometimes a judge simply writes the word "granted," or "denied" on the face of a motion while relying upon context and the parties' prior arguments to make the reasons clear. The law leaves much, in this respect, to the judge's own professional judgment.

In the present context, a statement of reasons is important. The sentencing judge should set forth enough to satisfy the appellate court that he has considered the parties' arguments and has a reasoned basis for exercising his own legal decisionmaking authority. Nonetheless, when a judge decides simply to apply the Guidelines to a particular case, doing so will not necessarily require lengthy explanation. Circumstances may well make clear that the judge rests his decision upon the Commission's own reasoning that the Guidelines sentence is a proper sentence (in terms of § 3353(a) and other congressional mandates) in the typical case, and that the judge has found that the case before him is typical. Unless a party contests the Guidelines sentence generally under § 3553(a)—that is argues that the Guidelines reflect an unsound judgment, or, for example, that they do not generally treat certain defendant characteristics in the proper way—or argues for departure, the judge normally need say no more. (Although, often at sentencing a judge will speak at length to a defendant, and this practice may indeed serve a salutary purpose.)

Where the defendant or prosecutor presents nonfrivolous reasons for imposing a different sentence, however, the judge will normally go further and explain why he has rejected those arguments. Sometimes the circumstances will call for a brief explanation; sometimes they will call for a lengthier explanation. Where the judge imposes a sentence outside the Guidelines, the judge will explain why he has done so. To our knowledge, an ordinary explanation of judicial reasons as to why the judge has, or has not, applied the Guidelines triggers no Sixth Amendment "jury trial" requirement. Cf. *Booker*, 543 U.S., at 233 ("For when a trial judge exercises his discretion to select a specific sentence within a defined range, the defendant has no right to a jury determination of the facts that the judge deems relevant") and *id.*, at 242 (requirement of finding,

not articulation of it, creates Sixth Amendment problem).

By articulating reasons, even if brief, the sentencing judge not only assures reviewing courts (and the public) that the sentencing process is a reasoned process but also helps that process evolve. The sentencing judge has access to, and greater familiarity with, the individual case and the individual defendant before him than the Commission or the appeals court. That being so, his reasoned sentencing judgment, resting upon an effort to filter the Guidelines' general advice through § 3553(a)'s list of factors, can provide relevant information to both the court of appeals and ultimately the Sentencing Commission. The reasoned responses of these latter institutions to the sentencing judge's explanation should help the Guidelines constructively evolve over time, as both Congress and the Commission foresaw.

In the present case the sentencing judge's statement of reasons was brief but legally sufficient. Rita argued for a downward departure from the 33–to–41 month Guidelines sentence on the basis of three sets of special circumstances: health, fear of retaliation in prison, and military record. He added that, in any event, these same circumstances warrant leniency beyond that contemplated by the Guidelines.

The record makes clear that the sentencing judge listened to each argument. The judge considered the supporting evidence. The judge was fully aware of defendant's various physical ailments and imposed a sentence that takes them into account. The judge understood that

Rita had previously worked in the immigration service where he had been involved in detecting criminal offenses. And he considered Rita's lengthy military service, including over 25 years of service, both on active duty and in the Reserve, and Rita's receipt of 35 medals, awards, and nominations.

The judge then simply found these circumstances insufficient to warrant a sentence lower than the Guidelines range of 33 to 45 months. He said that this range was not "inappropriate." (This, of course, is not the legal standard for imposition of sentence, but taken in context it is plain that the judge so understood.) He immediately added that he found that the 33–month sentence at the bottom of the Guidelines range was "appropriate." He must have believed that there was not much more to say.

We acknowledge that the judge might have said more. He might have added explicitly that he had heard and considered the evidence and argument; that (as no one before him denied) he thought the Commission in the Guidelines had determined a sentence that was proper in the minerun of roughly similar perjury cases; and that he found that Rita's personal circumstances here were simply not different enough to warrant a different sentence. But context and the record make clear that this, or similar, reasoning, underlies the judge's conclusion. Where a matter is as conceptually simple as in the case at hand and the record makes clear that the sentencing judge considered the evidence and arguments, we do not believe the law requires the judge to write more extensively.

IV

We turn to the final question: Was the Court of Appeals, after applying its presumption, legally correct in holding that Rita's sentence (a sentence that applied, and did not depart from, the relevant sentencing Guideline) was not "unreasonable"? In our view, the Court of Appeals' conclusion was lawful.

As we previously said, the crimes at issue are perjury and obstruction of justice. In essence those offenses involved the making of knowingly false, material statements under oath before a grand jury, thereby impeding its criminal investigation. The Guidelines provide for a typical such offense a base offense level of 20, 6 levels below the level provided for a simple violation of the crime being investigated (here the unlawful importation of machine-guns). The offender, Rita, has no countable prior offenses and consequently falls within criminal history category I. The intersection of base offense level 20 and criminal history category I sets forth a sentencing range of imprisonment of 33 to 45 months.

Rita argued at sentencing that his circumstances are special. He based this argument upon his health, his fear of retaliation, and his prior military record. His sentence explicitly takes health into account by seeking assurance that the Bureau of Prisons will provide appropriate treatment. The record makes out no special fear of retaliation, asserting only that the threat is one that any former law enforcement official might suffer. Similarly, though Rita has a lengthy and distinguished military record, he did not claim at sentencing that military service should ordinarily lead to a sentence more lenient than the sentence the Guidelines impose. Like the District Court and the Court of Appeals, we simply cannot say that Rita's special circumstances are special enough that, in light of § 3553(a), they require a sentence lower than the sentence the Guidelines provide.

Finally, Rita and supporting *amici* here claim that the Guidelines sentence is not reasonable under § 3553(a) because it expressly declines to consider various personal characteristics of the defendant, such as physical condition, employment record, and military service, under the view that these factors are "not ordinarily relevant." USSG §§ 5H1.4, 5H1.5, 5H1.11. Rita did not make this argument below, and we shall not consider it.

* * *

For the foregoing reasons, the judgment of the Court of Appeals is *Affirmed*.

JUSTICE STEVENS, **with whom JUS-**TICE GINSBURG **joins as to all but Part II, concurring.**

It is no secret that the Court's remedial opinion in United States v. Booker, 543 U.S. 220 (2005), was not unanimous ... But *Booker* is now settled law and must be accepted as such. See B. Cardozo, The Nature of the Judicial Process 149 (1921) ("The labor of judges would be increased almost to the breaking point if every past decision could be reopened in every case, and one could not lay one's own course of bricks on the secure foundation of the courses laid by others who had gone before him"). Therefore, our task today is to apply *Booker*'s "reasonableness" standard

to a District Judge's decision to impose a sentence within the range recommended by United States Sentencing Guidelines that are now advisory, rather than binding.

I

* * *

Guided by [the] § 3553(a) factors, *Booker*'s abuse-of-discretion standard directs appellate courts to evaluate what motivated the District Judge's individualized sentencing decision. While reviewing courts may presume that a sentence within the advisory Guidelines is reasonable, appellate judges must still always defer to the sentencing judge's individualized sentencing determination. * * * The Commission has not developed any standards or recommendations that affect sentencing ranges for many individual characteristics. Matters such as age, education, mental or emotional condition, medical condition (including drug or alcohol addiction), employment history, lack of guidance as a youth, family ties, or military, civic, charitable, or public service are not ordinarily considered under the Guidelines. See United States Sentencing Commission, Guidelines Manual §§ 5H1.1–6, 11, and 12 (Nov. 2006). These are, however, matters that § 3553(a) authorizes the sentencing judge to consider. As such, they are factors that an appellate court must consider under *Booker*'s abuse-of-discretion standard.

My disagreement with Justice Scalia and Justice Souter rests on the above understanding of *Booker*'s standard of appellate review. I do not join Justice Scalia's opinion because I believe that the purely procedural review he advocates is inconsistent with our remedial opinion in *Booker*, which plainly contemplated that reasonableness review would contain a substantive component. After all, a district judge who gives harsh sentences to Yankees fans and lenient sentences to Red Sox fans would not be acting reasonably even if her procedural rulings were impeccable. Moreover, even if some future unusually harsh sentence might violate the Sixth Amendment because it exceeds some yet-to-be-defined judicial standard of reasonableness, Justice Scalia correctly acknowledges this case does not present such a problem. * * *

As to Justice Souter's opinion, I think he overestimates the "gravitational pull" towards the advisory Guidelines that will result from a presumption of reasonableness. *Booker*'s standard of review allows—indeed, requires—district judges to consider *all* of the factors listed in § 3553(a) and to apply them to the individual defendants before them. Appellate courts must then give deference to the sentencing decisions made by those judges, whether the resulting sentence is inside or outside the advisory Guidelines range, under traditional abuse-of-discretion principles. As the Court acknowledges, moreover, *presumptively* reasonable does not mean *always* reasonable; the presumption, of course, must be genuinely rebuttable. I am not blind to the fact that, as a practical matter, many federal judges continued to treat the Guidelines as virtually mandatory after our decision in *Booker*. One well-respected federal judge has even written that, "after

watching this Court—and the other Courts of Appeals, whether they have formally adopted such a presumption or not—affirm hundreds upon hundreds of within-Guidelines sentences, it seems to me that the rebuttability of the presumption is more theoretical than real." United States v. Pruitt, 487 F.3d 1298 (C.A.10 2007) (McConnell, J., concurring). Our decision today makes clear, however, that the rebuttability of the presumption is real. It should also be clear that appellate courts must review sentences individually and deferentially whether they are inside the Guidelines range (and thus potentially subject to a formal "presumption" of reasonableness) or outside that range. Given the clarity of our holding, I trust that those judges who had treated the Guidelines as virtually mandatory during the post-*Booker* interregnum will now recognize that the Guidelines are truly advisory.

Applying this standard, I would affirm the sentence imposed by the District Court. Although I would have imposed a lower sentence had I been the District Judge, I agree that he did not abuse his discretion in making the particular decision that he did. I also agree with the Court that his decision is entitled to added respect because it was consistent with the advice in the Guidelines.

II

That said, I do believe that there was a significant flaw in the sentencing procedure in this case. The petitioner is a veteran who received significant recognition for his service to his country. That aspect of his background is not taken into consideration in the sentencing guidelines and was not mentioned by the District Judge in his explanation of his choice of the sentence that defendant received. I regard this as a serious omission because I think the judge's statement to the defendant, made at the time of sentencing, is an especially important part of the criminal process. If the defendant is convinced that justice has been done in his case—that society has dealt with him fairly—the likelihood of his successful rehabilitation will surely be enhanced. Nevertheless, given the importance of paying appropriate respect to the exercise of a sentencing judge's discretion, I join the Court's opinion and judgment.

JUSTICE SCALIA, with whom JUSTICE THOMAS joins, concurring in part and concurring in the judgment.

In United States v. Booker, five Justices of this Court, I among them, held that our previous decision in Blakely v. Washington applied to sentences imposed under the Federal Sentencing Guidelines because those Guidelines were mandatory and binding on judges. * * * In response to this constitutional holding, a different majority of five Justices held that the appropriate remedy was to make the Guidelines nonmandatory in all cases and to review sentences on appeal only for reasonableness. I disagreed with the Court's remedial choice, believing instead that the proper remedy was to maintain the mandatory character of the Guidelines and simply to require, for that small category of cases in which a fact was legally essential to the sentence imposed, that the fact be proved to a jury beyond a reasonable doubt or admitted by the defendant.

I do not mean to reopen that debate. As a matter of statutory *stare decisis*, I accept *Booker*'s remedial holding that district courts are no longer bound by the Guidelines and that appellate courts should review the sentences imposed for reasonableness. As should be clear from our need to decide the case today, however, precisely what "reasonableness" review entails is not dictated by *Booker*. As I lamented then, "the worst feature of the scheme is that no one knows—and perhaps no one is meant to know—how advisory Guidelines and 'unreasonableness' review will function in practice."

* * *

* * * Nothing in the Court's opinion explains why, under the advisory Guidelines scheme, judge-found facts are *never* legally necessary to justify the sentence. By this I mean the Court has failed to establish that every sentence which will be imposed under the advisory Guidelines scheme could equally have been imposed had the judge relied upon no facts other than those found by the jury or admitted by the defendant. In fact, the Court implicitly, but quite plainly, acknowledges that this will not be the case, by treating as a permissible post-*Booker* claim petitioner's challenge of his within-Guidelines sentence as substantively excessive. Under the scheme promulgated today, some sentences reversed as excessive will be legally authorized in later cases only because additional judge-found facts are present; and, * * * some lengthy sentences will be affirmed (*i.e.*, held lawful) only because of the presence of aggravating facts, not found by the jury, that distinguish the case from the mine-run. The Court does not even attempt to explain how this is consistent with the Sixth Amendment.

No explanation is given because no explanation is possible. The Court has reintroduced the constitutional defect that *Booker* purported to eliminate. I cannot acquiesce in this course. If a sentencing system is permissible in which some sentences cannot lawfully be imposed by a judge unless the judge finds certain facts by a preponderance of the evidence, then we should have left in place the compulsory Guidelines that Congress enacted, instead of imposing this jerry-rigged scheme of our own. In order to avoid the possibility of a Sixth Amendment violation, which was the object of the *Booker* remedy, district courts must be able, without finding any facts not embraced in the jury verdict or guilty plea, to sentence to the maximum of the *statutory* range. Because, therefore, appellate courts cannot reverse within-range sentences for being too high; and because no one would contend that Congress intended that sentences be reviewed only for being too low; I would hold that reasonableness review cannot contain a substantive component at all. I believe, however, that appellate courts can nevertheless secure some amount of sentencing uniformity through the procedural reasonableness review made possible by the *Booker* remedial opinion.

I

A

* * * Two hypotheticals will suffice to reveal why the notion of excessive sentences within the statutory range, and the ability of appellate courts to reverse such sentences, inexorably produces, in violation of the Sixth Amendment, sentences whose legality is premised on a judge's finding some fact (or combination of facts) by a preponderance of the evidence.

First, consider two brothers with similar backgrounds and criminal histories who are convicted by a jury of respectively robbing two banks of an equal amount of money. Next assume that the district judge finds that one brother, fueled by racial animus, had targeted the first bank because it was owned and operated by minorities, whereas the other brother had selected the second bank simply because its location enabled a quick getaway. Further assume that the district judge imposes the statutory maximum upon both brothers, basing those sentences primarily upon his perception that bank robbery should be punished much more severely than the Guidelines base level advises, but explicitly noting that the racially biased decisionmaking of the first brother further justified his sentence. Now imagine that the appellate court reverses as excessive only the sentence of the nonracist brother. Given the dual holdings of the appellate court, the racist has a valid Sixth Amendment claim that his sentence was reasonable (and hence lawful) only because of the judicial finding of his motive in selecting his victim.

Second, consider the common case in which the district court imposes a sentence *within* an advisory Guidelines range that has been substantially enhanced by certain judge-found facts. For example, the base offense level for robbery under the Guidelines is 20, United States Sentencing Commission, Guidelines Manual § 2B3.1(a), which, if the defendant has a criminal history of I, corresponds to an advisory range of 33–41 months. If, however, a judge finds that a firearm was discharged, that a victim incurred serious bodily injury, and that more than $5 million was stolen, then the base level jumps by 18, §§ 2B3.1(b)(2), (3), (7), producing an advisory range of 235–293 months. When a judge finds all of those facts to be true and then imposes a within-Guidelines sentence of 293 months, those judge-found facts, or some combination of them, are not merely facts that the judge finds relevant in exercising his discretion; they are the legally essential predicate for his imposition of the 293–month sentence. His failure to find them would render the 293–month sentence unlawful. That is evident because, were the district judge explicitly to find *none* of those facts true and nevertheless to impose a 293–month sentence (simply because he thinks robbery merits seven times the sentence that the Guidelines provide) the sentence would surely be reversed as unreasonably excessive.

These hypotheticals are stylized ways of illustrating the basic problem with a system in which district courts lack full discretion to sentence within the statutory range. Under such a system, for every given crime there is some maximum sentence that will be upheld as reasonable based only on the facts found by the jury or admitted by the defendant. *Every* sentence higher than that is legally authorized only by some judge-found fact, in violation of the Sixth Amendment. Appellate courts' excessiveness review will explicitly or implicitly accept those judge-found facts as justifying sentences that would otherwise be unlawful. The only difference between this system and the pre-*Booker* mandatory Guidelines is that the maximum sentence based on the jury verdict or guilty plea was specified under the latter but must be established by appellate courts, in case-by-case fashion, under the former. This is, if anything, an additional constitutional disease, not a constitutional cure.

To be clear, I am not suggesting that the Sixth Amendment prohibits judges from ever finding any facts. We have repeatedly affirmed the proposition that judges can find facts that help guide their discretion *within* the sentencing range that is authorized by the facts found by the jury or admitted by the defendant. But there is a fundamental difference, one underpinning our entire *Apprendi* jurisprudence, between facts that *must* be found in order for a sentence to be lawful, and facts that individual judges *choose* to make relevant to the exercise of their discretion. The former, but not the latter, must be found by the jury beyond a reasonable doubt in order "to give intelligible content to the right of jury trial." *Blakely*, 542 U.S., at 305.

I am also not contending that there is a Sixth Amendment problem with the Court's affirmation of a presumption of reasonableness for within-Guidelines sentences. I agree with the Court that such a presumption never itself makes judge-found facts legally essential to the sentence imposed, since it has no direct relevance to whether the sentence would have been *unreasonable* in the *absence* of any judge-found facts. Nor is my claim that the Sixth Amendment was violated in this case, for petitioner cannot demonstrate that his relatively low sentence would have been unreasonable if the District Court had relied on nothing but jury-found or admitted facts.

Rather, my position is that there will inevitably be *some* constitutional violations under a system of substantive reasonableness review, because there will be some sentences that will be upheld as reasonable only because of the existence of judge-found facts. *Booker* itself reveals why that reality dooms the construct of reasonableness review established and applied by today's opinion. *Booker* made two things quite plain. First, reasonableness is the standard of review implicitly contained within the Sentencing Reform Act of 1984 (SRA). Second, Congress wanted a uniform system of sentencing review, rather than different schemes depending on whether there were Sixth Amendment problems in particular cases. Thus, if the contours of reasonableness review must be narrowed in *some* cases because of constitutional concerns, then they must be narrowed in *all* cases in light of Congress's desire for a uniform standard of review. * * *

Yet [the majority adopts] substantive reasonableness review without offering any rebuttal to my charge of patent constitutional flaw inher-

ent in such review. The one comfort to be found in the Court's opinion * * * is that it does not rule out as-applied Sixth Amendment challenges to sentences that would not have been upheld as reasonable on the facts encompassed by the jury verdict or guilty plea.

B

* * *

If it is true that some sentences under today's Court-prescribed system will still violate the Sixth Amendment, nonetheless allowing the system to go forward will produce chaos. Most cases do not resemble my stylized hypotheticals, and ordinarily defendants and judges will be unable to figure out, based on a comparison of the facts in their case with the facts of all of the previously decided appellate cases, whether the sentence imposed would have been upheld as reasonable based only on the facts supporting the jury verdict or guilty plea. That will not stop defendants from making the argument, however, and the Court certainly has not foreclosed them from trying. Judges will have in theory two options: create complicated charts and databases, based on appellate precedents, to ascertain what facts are legally essential to justify what sentences; or turn a deaf ear to these claims, though knowing full well that some of them are justified. I bet on the latter. Things were better under the mandatory Guidelines system, where every judge could readily identify when the Sixth Amendment was being violated, and could rule accordingly.

* * *

C

A final defense of substantive reasonableness review would be to invoke the intent of Congress or of the *Booker* remedial opinion. As for congressional intent: *Of course* Congress intended that judge-found facts be legally essential to the punishment imposed; that was the whole reason the mandatory Guidelines violated the Sixth Amendment. If we are now to indulge a newfound respect for unconstitutional congressional intent, we should reimpose the mandatory Guidelines system. The quasi-Guidelines system the Court creates today manages to contravene *both* congressional intent *and* the Sixth Amendment.

As for the "intent" of the *Booker* remedial opinion: That opinion purported to be divining congressional intent *in light of what the Sixth Amendment compelled*. Absent some explanation of why substantive reasonableness review does not cause judge-found facts to justify greater punishment than the jury's verdict or the defendant's guilty plea would sustain, I fail to understand how such review could possibly have been intended by all five Justices who composed the *Booker* remedial majority. * * *

II

Abandoning substantive reasonableness review does not require a return to the pre-SRA regime that the *Booker* remedial opinion sought to avoid. * * * I believe it is possible to give some effect to the *Booker* remedial opinion and the purposes that it sought to serve while still avoiding the constitutional defect identified in the *Booker* merits opinion. Specifically, I would limit reasonableness review to the sentencing *procedures* mandated by statute.

A

* * *

Booker's retention of * * * statutory procedural provisions furthered the congressional purpose of "ironing out sentencing differences," 543 U.S., at 263, and "avoiding excessive sentencing disparities," *id.*, at 264. It is important that appellate courts police their observance. *Booker* excised the provision of the SRA containing the standards for appellate review, see *id.*, at 260 (invalidating 18 U.S.C. § 3742(e)), but the remedial majority's creation of reasonableness review gave appellate courts the necessary means to reverse a district court that: appears not to have considered § 3553(a); considers impermissible factors; selects a sentence based on clearly erroneous facts; or does not comply with § 3553(c)'s requirement for a statement of reasons. n6 In addition to its direct effect on sentencing uniformity, this procedural review will indirectly produce, over time, reduction of sentencing disparities. By ensuring that district courts give reasons for their sentences, and more specific reasons when they decline to follow the advisory Guidelines range, see § 3553(c)(2), appellate courts will enable the Sentencing Commission to perform its function of revising the Guidelines to reflect the desirable sentencing practices of the district courts. And as that occurs, district courts will have less reason to depart from the Commission's recommendations, leading to more sentencing uniformity. * * *

The Court's decision today leaves unexplained why the mandatory Guidelines were unconstitutional, but the Court-created substantive-review system that contains the same potential for Sixth Amendment violation is not. It is irresponsible to leave this patent inconsistency hanging in the air, threatening in the future yet another major revision of Guidelines practices to which the district courts and courts of appeals will have to adjust. Procedural review would lay the matter to rest, comporting with both parts of the *Booker* opinion and achieving the maximum degree of sentencing uniformity on the basis of judge-found facts that the Constitution permits.

B

Applying procedural review in this case does not require much further discussion on my part. I join Part III of the Court's opinion.

———

JUSTICE SOUTER, **dissenting.**

Applying the Sixth Amendment to current sentencing law has gotten complicated, and someone coming cold to this case might wonder how we reached this point. A very general overview of the course of decisions over the past eight years may help to put today's holding in perspective.

[Justice Souter conducts a lengthy description of the *Apprendi* line of cases.]

If district judges treated the now-discretionary Guidelines simply as worthy of consideration but open to rejection in any given case, the *Booker* remedy would threaten a return to the old sentencing regime and would presumably produce the apparent disuniformity that convinced Congress to adopt Guidelines sentencing in the first place. But if sentencing judges attributed substantial gravitational pull to the now-discretionary Guidelines, if they treated the Guidelines result as persuasive or presumptively appropriate, the *Booker* remedy would in practical terms preserve the very feature of the Guidelines that threatened to trivialize the jury right. For a presumption of Guidelines reasonableness would tend to produce Guidelines sentences almost as regularly as mandatory Guidelines had done, with judges finding the facts needed for a sentence in an upper subrange. This would open the door to undermining *Apprendi* itself, and this is what has happened today.

Without a powerful reason to risk reversal on the sentence, a district judge faced with evidence supporting a high subrange Guidelines sentence will do the appropriate fact-finding in disparagement of the jury right and will sentence within the high subrange. This prediction is weakened not a whit by the Court's description of within-Guidelines reasonableness as an "appellate" presumption. What works on appeal determines what works at trial, and if the Sentencing Commission's views are as weighty as the Court says they are, a trial judge will find it far easier to make the appropriate findings and sentence within the appropriate Guideline, than to go through the unorthodox factfinding necessary to justify a sentence outside the Guidelines range, see 18 U.S.C. § 3553(c)(2). The upshot is that today's decision moves the threat to the practical value of the Sixth Amendment jury right closer to what it was when this Court flagged it in *Jones*, and it seems fair to ask just what has been accomplished in real terms by all the judicial labor imposed by *Apprendi* and its associated cases.

Taking the *Booker* remedy (of discretionary Guidelines) as a given, however, the way to avoid further risk to *Apprendi* and the jury right is to hold that a discretionary within-Guidelines sentence carries no presumption of reasonableness. Only if sentencing decisions are reviewed according to the same standard of reasonableness whether or not they fall within the Guidelines range will district courts be assured that the entire sentencing range set by statute is available to them. And only then will they stop replicating the unconstitutional system by imposing appeal-proof sentences within the Guidelines ranges determined by facts found by them alone.

I would therefore reject the presumption of reasonableness adopted in this case, not because it is pernicious in and of itself, but because I do not think we can recognize such a presumption and still retain the full effect of *Apprendi* in aid of the Sixth Amendment guarantee. But I would not stop at rejecting the presumption. Neither my preferred course nor the choice of today's majority can avoid being at odds to some degree with the intent of Congress; there is no question that Congress meant to impose mandatory Guidelines as the means of bringing greater uniformity to sentencing. So I point out that the congressional objective can still be attained, but that *Booker*'s remedial holding means that only Congress can restore the scheme to what it had in mind, and in a way that gives full measure to the right to a jury trial. If Congress has not had a change of heart about the value of a Guidelines system, it can reenact the Guidelines law to give it the same binding force it originally had, but with provision for jury, not judicial, determination of any fact necessary for a sentence within an upper Guidelines subrange. At this point, only Congress can make good on both its enacted policy of mandatory Guidelines sentencing and the guarantee of a robust right of jury trial.

I respectfully dissent.

Review of Outside–Guidelines Sentences for Reasonableness: Gall v. United States

In the following case the Court forbids an appellate court, in exercising *Booker* reasonableness review, from employing any rigid mathematical approach or any presumption of unreasonableness when reviewing a sentence outside the Guidelines.

GALL v. UNITED STATES

Supreme Court of the United States, 2007.
552 U.S. 38.

JUSTICE STEVENS **delivered the opinion of the Court.**

In two cases argued on the same day last Term we considered the standard that courts of appeals should apply when reviewing the reasonableness of sentences imposed by district judges. The first, Rita v. United States, [set forth immediately above] involved a sentence *within* the range recommended by the Federal Sentencing Guidelines; we held that when a district judge's discretionary decision in a particular case accords with the sentence the United States Sentencing Commission deems appropriate "in the mine run of cases," the court of appeals may presume that the sentence is reasonable.

The second case, Claiborne v. United States, involved a sentence *below* the range recommended by the Guidelines, and raised the converse question whether a court of appeals may apply a "proportionality test," and require that a sentence that constitutes a substantial variance from the Guidelines be justified by extraordinary circumstances. We did not have the opportunity to answer this question because the case was mooted by Claiborne's untimely death. We granted certiorari in the case before us today in order to reach that question, left unanswered last Term. We now hold that, while the extent of the difference between a particular sentence and the recommended Guidelines range is surely relevant, courts of appeals must review all sentences—whether inside, just outside, or significantly outside the Guidelines range—under a deferential abuse-of-discretion standard. We also hold that the sentence imposed by the experienced District Judge in this case was reasonable.

I

In February or March 2000, petitioner Brian Gall, a second-year college student at the University of Iowa, was invited by Luke Rinderknecht to join an ongoing enterprise distributing a controlled substance popularly known as "ecstasy." Gall—who was then a user of ecstasy, cocaine, and marijuana—accepted the invitation. During the ensuing seven months, Gall delivered ecstasy pills, which he received from Rinderknecht, to other conspirators, who then sold them to consumers. He netted over $30,000.

A month or two after joining the conspiracy, Gall stopped using ecstasy. A few months after that, in September 2000, he advised Rinderknecht and other co-conspirators that he was withdrawing from the conspiracy. He has not sold illegal drugs of any kind since. He has, in the words of the District Court, "self-rehabilitated." App. 75. He graduated from the University of Iowa in 2002, and moved first to Arizona, where he obtained a job in the construction industry, and later to Colorado, where he earned $18 per hour as a master carpenter. He has not used any illegal drugs since graduating from college.

After Gall moved to Arizona, he was approached by federal law enforcement agents who questioned him about his involvement in the ecstasy distribution conspiracy. Gall admitted his limited participation in the distribution of ecstasy, and the agents took no further action at that time. On April 28, 2004—approximately a year and a half after this initial interview, and three and a half years after Gall withdrew from the conspiracy—an indictment was returned in the Southern District of Iowa charging him and seven other defendants with participating in a conspiracy to distribute ecstasy, cocaine, and marijuana, that began in or about May 1996 and continued through October 30, 2002. The Government has never questioned the truthfulness of any of Gall's earlier statements or contended that he played any role in, or had any knowledge of, other aspects of the conspiracy described in the indictment. When he received notice of the indictment, Gall moved back to Iowa and surrendered to the authorities. While free on his own recognizance, Gall started his own business in the construction industry, primarily engaged in subcontracting for the installation of windows and doors. In his first year, his profits were over $2,000 per month.

Gall entered into a plea agreement with the Government, stipulating that he was "responsible for, but did not necessarily distribute himself, at least 2,500 grams of [ecstasy], or the equivalent of at least 87.5 kilograms of marijuana." In the agreement, the Government acknowledged that by "on or about September of 2000," Gall had communicated his intent to stop distributing ecstasy to Rinderknecht and other members of the conspiracy. The agreement further provided that recent changes in the Guidelines that enhanced the recommended punishment for distributing ecstasy were not applicable to Gall because he had withdrawn from the conspiracy prior to the effective date of those changes.

In her presentence report, the probation officer concluded that Gall had no significant criminal history; that he was not an organizer, leader, or manager; and that his offense did not involve the use of any weapons. The report stated that Gall had truthfully provided the Government with all of the evidence he had concerning the alleged offenses, but that his evidence was not useful because he provided no new information to the agents. The report also described Gall's substantial use of drugs prior to his offense and the absence of any such use in recent years. The report recommended a sentencing range of 30 to 37 months of imprisonment.

The record of the sentencing hearing held on May 27, 2005, includes a "small flood" of letters from Gall's parents and other relatives, his fiance, neighbors, and representatives of firms doing business with him, uniformly praising his character and work ethic. The transcript includes the testimony of several witnesses and the District Judge's colloquy with the Assistant United States Attorney (AUSA) and with Gall. The AUSA did not contest any of the evidence concerning Gall's law-abiding life during the preceding five years, but urged that "the Guidelines are appropriate and should be followed," and requested that the court impose a prison sentence within the Guidelines range.

He mentioned that two of Gall's co-conspirators had been sentenced to 30 and 35 months, respectively, but upon further questioning by the District Court, he acknowledged that neither of them had voluntarily withdrawn from the conspiracy.

The District Judge sentenced Gall to probation for a term of 36 months. In addition to making a lengthy statement on the record, the judge filed a detailed sentencing memorandum explaining his decision, and provided the following statement of reasons in his written judgment:

> "The Court determined that, considering all the factors under 18 U.S.C. 3553(a), the Defendant's explicit withdrawal from the conspiracy almost four years before the filing of the Indictment, the Defendant's post-offense conduct, especially obtaining a college degree and the start of his own successful business, the support of family and friends, lack of criminal history, and his age at the time of the offense conduct, all warrant the sentence imposed, which was sufficient, but not greater than necessary to serve the purposes of sentencing."

At the end of both the sentencing hearing and the sentencing memorandum, the District Judge reminded Gall that probation, rather than "an act of leniency," is a "substantial restriction of freedom." In the memorandum, he emphasized:

> "[Gall] will have to comply with strict reporting conditions along with a three-year regime of alcohol and drug testing. He will not be able to change or make decisions about significant cir-

cumstances in his life, such as where to live or work, which are prized liberty interests, without first seeking authorization from his Probation Officer or, perhaps, even the Court. Of course, the Defendant always faces the harsh consequences that await if he violates the conditions of his probationary term."

Finally, the District Judge explained why he had concluded that the sentence of probation reflected the seriousness of Gall's offense and that no term of imprisonment was necessary:

> "Any term of imprisonment in this case would be counter effective by depriving society of the contributions of the Defendant who, the Court has found, understands the consequences of his criminal conduct and is doing everything in his power to forge a new life. The Defendant's post-offense conduct indicates neither that he will return to criminal behavior nor that the Defendant is a danger to society. In fact, the Defendant's post-offense conduct was not motivated by a desire to please the Court or any other governmental agency, but was the pre-Indictment product of the Defendant's own desire to lead a better life."

II

The Court of Appeals reversed and remanded for resentencing. Relying on its earlier opinion in United States v. Claiborne, 439 F.3d 479 (CA8 2006), it held that a sentence outside of the Guidelines range must be supported by a justification that "is proportional to the extent of the difference between the advisory range and the sentence imposed." Characterizing the difference between a sentence of probation and the bottom of Gall's advisory Guidelines range of 30 months as "extraordinary" because it amounted to "a 100% downward variance," the Court of Appeals held that such a variance must be—and here was not—supported by extraordinary circumstances.

Rather than making an attempt to quantify the value of the justifications provided by the District Judge, the Court of Appeals identified what it regarded as five separate errors in the District Judge's reasoning: (1) He gave "too much weight to Gall's withdrawal from the conspiracy"; (2) given that Gall was 21 at the time of his offense, the District Judge erroneously gave "significant weight" to studies showing impetuous behavior by persons under the age of 18; (3) he did not "properly weigh" the seriousness of Gall's offense; (4) he failed to consider whether a sentence of probation would result in "unwarranted" disparities; and (5) he placed "too much emphasis on Gall's post-offense rehabilitation." As we shall explain, we are not persuaded that these factors, whether viewed separately or in the aggregate, are sufficient to support the conclusion that the District Judge abused his discretion. As a preface to our discussion of these particulars, however, we shall explain why the Court of Appeals' rule requiring "proportional" justifications for departures from the Guidelines range is not consistent with our remedial opinion in United States v. Booker.

III

In *Booker* we invalidated both the statutory provision, 18 U.S.C. § 3553(b)(1), which made the Sentencing Guidelines mandatory, and § 3742(e), which directed appellate courts to apply a *de novo* standard of review to departures from the Guidelines. As a result of our decision, the Guidelines are now advisory, and appellate review of sentencing decisions is limited to determining whether they are "reasonable." Our explanation of "reasonableness" review in the *Booker* opinion made it pellucidly clear that the familiar abuse-of-discretion standard of review now applies to appellate review of sentencing decisions.

It is also clear that a district judge must give serious consideration to the extent of any departure from the Guidelines and must explain his conclusion that an unusually lenient or an unusually harsh sentence is appropriate in a particular case with sufficient justifications. For even though the Guidelines are advisory rather than mandatory, they are, as we pointed out in *Rita*, the product of careful study based on extensive empirical evidence derived from the review of thousands of individual sentencing decisions.

In reviewing the reasonableness of a sentence outside the Guidelines range, appellate courts may therefore take the degree of variance into account and consider the extent of a deviation from the Guidelines. We reject, however, an appellate rule that requires "extraordinary" circumstances to justify a sentence outside the Guidelines range. We also reject the use of a rigid mathematical formula that uses the percentage of a departure as the standard for determining the strength of the justifications required for a specific sentence.

As an initial matter, the approaches we reject come too close to creating an impermissible presumption of unreasonableness for sentences outside the Guidelines range. Even the Government has acknowledged that such a presumption would not be consistent with *Booker.*

The mathematical approach also suffers from infirmities of application. On one side of the equation, deviations from the Guidelines range will always appear more extreme—in percentage terms—when the range itself is low, and a sentence of probation will always be a 100% departure regardless of whether the Guidelines range is 1 month or 100 years. Moreover, quantifying the variance as a certain percentage of the maximum, minimum, or median prison sentence recommended by the Guidelines gives no weight to the substantial restriction of freedom involved in a term of supervised release or probation.

* * *

On the other side of the equation, the mathematical approach assumes the existence of some ascertainable method of assigning percentages to various justifications. Does withdrawal from a conspiracy justify more or less than, say, a 30% reduction? Does it matter that the withdrawal occurred several years ago? Is it relevant that the withdrawal was motivated by a decision to discontinue the use of drugs and to lead a better life? What percentage, if any, should be assigned to evidence that a defendant poses no future threat to society, or to evidence that innocent third parties are dependent on

him? The formula is a classic example of attempting to measure an inventory of apples by counting oranges.

Most importantly, both the exceptional circumstances requirement and the rigid mathematical formulation reflect a practice—common among courts that have adopted "proportional review"—of applying a heightened standard of review to sentences outside the Guidelines range. This is inconsistent with the rule that the abuse-of-discretion standard of review applies to appellate review of all sentencing decisions—whether inside or outside the Guidelines range.

As we explained in *Rita*, a district court should begin all sentencing proceedings by correctly calculating the applicable Guidelines range. As a matter of administration and to secure nationwide consistency, the Guidelines should be the starting point and the initial benchmark. The Guidelines are not the only consideration, however. Accordingly, after giving both parties an opportunity to argue for whatever sentence they deem appropriate, the district judge should then consider all of the § 3553(a) factors to determine whether they support the sentence requested by a party. In so doing, he may not presume that the Guidelines range is reasonable. He must make an individualized assessment based on the facts presented. If he decides that an outside-Guidelines sentence is warranted, he must consider the extent of the deviation and ensure that the justification is sufficiently compelling to support the degree of the variance. We find it uncontroversial that a major departure should be supported by a more significant justification than a minor one. After settling on the appropriate sentence, he must adequately explain the chosen sentence to allow for meaningful appellate review and to promote the perception of fair sentencing.

Regardless of whether the sentence imposed is inside or outside the Guidelines range, the appellate court must review the sentence under an abuse-of-discretion standard. It must first ensure that the district court committed no significant procedural error, such as failing to calculate (or improperly calculating) the Guidelines range, treating the Guidelines as mandatory, failing to consider the § 3553(a) factors, selecting a sentence based on clearly erroneous facts, or failing to adequately explain the chosen sentence—including an explanation for any deviation from the Guidelines range. Assuming that the district court's sentencing decision is procedurally sound, the appellate court should then consider the substantive reasonableness of the sentence imposed under an abuse-of-discretion standard. When conducting this review, the court will, of course, take into account the totality of the circumstances, including the extent of any variance from the Guidelines range. If the sentence is within the Guidelines range, the appellate court may, but is not required to, apply a presumption of reasonableness. But if the sentence is outside the Guidelines range, the court may not apply a presumption of unreasonableness. It may consider the extent of the deviation, but must give due deference to the district court's decision that the § 3553(a) factors, on a whole, justify the extent of the variance. The fact that the appellate court might

reasonably have concluded that a different sentence was appropriate is insufficient to justify reversal of the district court.

Practical considerations also underlie this legal principle. The sentencing judge is in a superior position to find facts and judge their import under § 3553(a) in the individual case. The judge sees and hears the evidence, makes credibility determinations, has full knowledge of the facts and gains insights not conveyed by the record. "The sentencing judge has access to, and greater familiarity with, the individual case and the individual defendant before him than the Commission or the appeals court." *Rita*, 127 S. Ct. 2456, at 2469. Moreover, district courts have an institutional advantage over appellate courts in making these sorts of determinations, especially as they see so many more Guidelines sentences than appellate courts do.

"It has been uniform and constant in the federal judicial tradition for the sentencing judge to consider every convicted person as an individual and every case as a unique study in the human failings that sometimes mitigate, sometimes magnify, the crime and the punishment to ensue." Id. The uniqueness of the individual case, however, does not change the deferential abuse-of-discretion standard of review that applies to all sentencing decisions. As we shall now explain, the opinion of the Court of Appeals in this case does not reflect the requisite deference and does not support the conclusion that the District Court abused its discretion.

IV

As an initial matter, we note that the District Judge committed no significant procedural error. He correctly calculated the applicable Guidelines range, allowed both parties to present arguments as to what they believed the appropriate sentence should be, considered all of the § 3553(a) factors, and thoroughly documented his reasoning. The Court of Appeals found that the District Judge erred in failing to give proper weight to the seriousness of the offense, as required by § 3553(a)(2)(A), and failing to consider whether a sentence of probation would create unwarranted disparities, as required by § 3553(a)(6). We disagree.

Section 3553(a)(2)(A) requires judges to consider "the need for the sentence imposed . . . to reflect the seriousness of the offense, to promote respect for the law, and to provide just punishment for the offense." The Court of Appeals concluded that "the district court did not properly weigh the seriousness of Gall's offense" because it "ignored the serious health risks ecstasy poses." Contrary to the Court of Appeals' conclusion, the District Judge plainly did consider the seriousness of the offense. See, *e.g.,* App. 99 ("The Court, however, is bound to impose a sentence that reflects the seriousness of joining a conspiracy to distribute MDMA or ecstasy"). It is true that the District Judge did not make specific reference to the (unquestionably significant) health risks posed by ecstasy, but the prosecutor did not raise ecstasy's effects at the sentencing hearing. Had the prosecutor raised the issue, specific discussion of the point might have been in order, but it was not incumbent on the District Judge to raise every conceivably relevant issue on his own initiative.

The Government's legitimate concern that a lenient sentence for a serious offense threatens to promote disrespect for the law is at least to some extent offset by the fact that seven of the eight defendants in this case have been sentenced to significant prison terms. Moreover, the unique facts of Gall's situation provide support for the District Judge's conclusion that, in Gall's case, "a sentence of imprisonment may work to promote not respect, but derision, of the law if the law is viewed as merely a means to dispense harsh punishment without taking into account the real conduct and circumstances involved in sentencing." *Id.,* at 126.

Section 3553(a)(6) requires judges to consider "the need to avoid unwarranted sentence disparities among defendants with similar records who have been found guilty of similar conduct." The Court of Appeals stated that "the record does not show that the district court considered whether a sentence of probation would result in unwarranted disparities." As with the seriousness of the offense conduct, avoidance of unwarranted disparities was clearly considered by the Sentencing Commission when setting the Guidelines ranges. Since the District Judge correctly calculated and carefully reviewed the Guidelines range, he necessarily gave significant weight and consideration to the need to avoid unwarranted disparities. [Justice Stevens noted that the trial judge took into account the fact that Gall's coconspirators, who had all received harsher sentences, had never withdrawn from the conspiracy.]

From these facts, it is perfectly clear that the District Judge considered the need to avoid unwarranted disparities, but also considered the need to avoid unwarranted *similarities* among other co-conspirators who were not similarly situated. The District Judge regarded Gall's voluntary withdrawal as a reasonable basis for giving him a less severe sentence than the three codefendants discussed with the AUSA, who neither withdrew from the conspiracy nor rehabilitated themselves as Gall had done. We also note that neither the Court of Appeals nor the Government has called our attention to a comparable defendant who received a more severe sentence.

Since the District Court committed no procedural error, the only question for the Court of Appeals was whether the sentence was reasonable—*i.e.*, whether the District Judge abused his discretion in determining that the § 3553(a) factors supported a sentence of probation and justified a substantial deviation from the Guidelines range. As we shall now explain, the sentence was reasonable. The Court of Appeals' decision to the contrary was incorrect and failed to demonstrate the requisite deference to the District Judge's decision.

V

The Court of Appeals gave virtually no deference to the District Court's decision that the § 3553(a) factors justified a significant variance in this case. Although the Court of Appeals correctly stated that the appropriate standard of review was abuse of discretion, it engaged in an analysis that more closely resembled *de novo* review of the facts presented and determined that, in its view, the degree of variance was not warranted.

The Court of Appeals thought that the District Court "gave too much weight to Gall's withdrawal from the conspiracy because the court failed to acknowledge the significant benefit Gall received from being subject to the 1999 Guidelines." [Subsequently-implemented Guidelines provided a harsher sentence, but Gall withdrew from the conspiracy before their implementation so they were not applicable to him.] This criticism is flawed in that it ignores the critical relevance of Gall's voluntary withdrawal, a circumstance that distinguished his conduct not only from that of all his codefendants, but from the vast majority of defendants convicted of conspiracy in federal court. The District Court quite reasonably attached great weight to the fact that Gall voluntarily withdrew from the conspiracy after deciding, on his own initiative, to change his life. This lends strong support to the District Court's conclusion that Gall is not going to return to criminal behavior and is not a danger to society. See 18 U.S.C. §§ 3553(a)(2)(B), (C). Compared to a case where the offender's rehabilitation occurred after he was charged with a crime, the District Court here had greater justification for believing Gall's turnaround was genuine, as distinct from a transparent attempt to build a mitigation case.

The Court of Appeals thought the District Judge "gave significant weight to an improper factor" when he compared Gall's sale of ecstasy when he was a 21–year-old adult to the "impetuous and ill-considered" actions of persons under the age of 18. The appellate court correctly observed that the studies cited by the District Judge do not explain how Gall's "specific behavior in the instant case was impetuous or ill-considered."

In that portion of his sentencing memorandum, however, the judge was discussing the "character of the defendant," not the nature of his offense. He noted that Gall's criminal history included a ticket for underage drinking when he was 18 years old and possession of marijuana that was contemporaneous with his offense in this case. In summary, the District Judge observed that all of Gall's criminal history "including the present offense, occurred when he was twenty-one-years old or younger" and appeared "to stem from his addictions to drugs and alcohol." The District Judge appended a long footnote to his discussion of Gall's immaturity. The footnote includes an excerpt from our opinion in Roper v. Simmons, 543 U.S. 551, 569 (2005), which quotes a study stating that a lack of maturity and an undeveloped sense of responsibility are qualities that " 'often result in impetuous and ill-considered actions.' " The District Judge clearly stated the relevance of these studies in the opening and closing sentences of the footnote:

> "Immaturity at the time of the offense conduct is not an inconsequential consideration. Recent studies on the development of the human brain conclude that human brain development may not become complete until the age of twenty-five.... The recent [National Institute of Health] report confirms that there is no bold line demarcating at what age

a person reaches full maturity. While age does not excuse behavior, a sentencing court should account for age when inquiring into the conduct of a defendant."

Given the dramatic contrast between Gall's behavior before he joined the conspiracy and his conduct after withdrawing, it was not unreasonable for the District Judge to view Gall's immaturity at the time of the offense as a mitigating factor, and his later behavior as a sign that he had matured and would not engage in such impetuous and ill-considered conduct in the future. * * *

Finally, the Court of Appeals thought that, even if Gall's rehabilitation was dramatic and permanent, a sentence of probation for participation as a middleman in a conspiracy distributing 10,000 pills of ecstasy "lies outside the range of choice dictated by the facts of the case." If the Guidelines were still mandatory, and assuming the facts did not justify a Guidelines-based downward departure, this would provide a sufficient basis for setting aside Gall's sentence because the Guidelines state that probation alone is not an appropriate sentence for comparable offenses. But the Guidelines are not mandatory, and thus the "range of choice dictated by the facts of the case" is significantly broadened. Moreover, the Guidelines are only one of the factors to consider when imposing sentence, and § 3553(a)(3) directs the judge to consider sentences other than imprisonment.

* * *

The District Court quite reasonably attached great weight to Gall's self-motivated rehabilitation, which was undertaken not at the direction of, or under supervision by, any court, but on his own initiative. This also lends strong support to the conclusion that imprisonment was not necessary to deter Gall from engaging in future criminal conduct or to protect the public from his future criminal acts. See 18 U.S.C. §§ 3553(a)(2)(B), (C).

The Court of Appeals clearly disagreed with the District Judge's conclusion that consideration of the § 3553(a) factors justified a sentence of probation; it believed that the circumstances presented here were insufficient to sustain such a marked deviation from the Guidelines range. But it is not for the Court of Appeals to decide *de novo* whether the justification for a variance is sufficient or the sentence reasonable. On abuse-of-discretion review, the Court of Appeals should have given due deference to the District Court's reasoned and reasonable decision that the § 3553(a) factors, on the whole, justified the sentence. Accordingly, the judgment of the Court of Appeals is reversed.

JUSTICE SCALIA, **concurring.**

In Rita v. United States, I wrote separately to state my view that any appellate review of sentences for substantive reasonableness will necessarily result in a sentencing scheme constitutionally indistinguishable from the mandatory Guidelines struck down in United States v. Booker. Whether a sentencing scheme uses mandatory Guidelines, a "proportionality test" for Guidelines variances, or a deferential abuse-of-discretion standard, there will be some sentences up-

held only on the basis of additional judge-found facts.

Although I continue to believe that substantive-reasonableness review is inherently flawed, I give *stare decisis* effect to the statutory holding of *Rita*. The highly deferential standard adopted by the Court today will result in far fewer unconstitutional sentences than the proportionality standard employed by the Eighth Circuit. Moreover, as I noted in *Rita*, the Court has not foreclosed as-applied constitutional challenges to sentences. The door therefore remains open for a defendant to demonstrate that his sentence, whether inside or outside the advisory Guidelines range, would not have been upheld but for the existence of a fact found by the sentencing judge and not by the jury.

JUSTICE SOUTER, **concurring.**

* * * After *Booker*'s remedial holding, I continue to think that the best resolution of the tension between substantial consistency throughout the system and the right of jury trial would be a new Act of Congress: reestablishing a statutory system of mandatory sentencing guidelines (though not identical to the original in all points of detail), but providing for jury findings of all facts necessary to set the upper range of sentencing discretion.

JUSTICE THOMAS, **dissenting.**

* * * I would affirm the judgment of the Court of Appeals because the District Court committed statutory error when it departed below the applicable Guidelines range.

JUSTICE ALITO, **dissenting.**

The fundamental question in this case is whether, under the remedial decision in United States v. Booker, a district court must give the policy decisions that are embodied in the Sentencing Guidelines at least some significant weight in making a sentencing decision. I would answer that question in the affirmative and would therefore affirm the decision of the Court of Appeals.

I

* * * It is possible to read the [*Booker*] opinion to mean that district judges, after giving the Guidelines a polite nod, may then proceed essentially as if the Sentencing Reform Act had never been enacted. * * * While this is a possible understanding of the remedial opinion, a better reading is that sentencing judges must still give the Guidelines' policy decisions some significant weight and that the courts of appeals must still police compliance. In a key passage, the remedial opinion stated:

> "The district courts, while not bound to apply the Guidelines, must consult those Guidelines and take them into account when sentencing. * * * The courts of appeals review sentencing decisions for unreasonableness. These features of the remaining system, while not the system Congress enacted, nonetheless *continue to move sentencing in Congress' preferred direction, helping to avoid excessive sentencing disparities* while maintaining flexibility sufficient to individualize sentences where necessary." *Id.*, at 264–265 (emphasis added).

The implication of this passage is that district courts are still required to give some deference to the policy decisions embodied in the Guidelines and that appellate review must monitor compliance. * * * Moreover, in the passage quoted above and at other points in the remedial opinion, the Court expressed confidence that appellate review for reasonableness would help to avoid " 'excessive sentencing disparities' " and "would tend to iron out sentencing differences." Indeed, a major theme of the remedial opinion, as well as our decision last Term in Rita v. United States was that the post-*Booker* sentencing regime would still promote the Sentencing Reform Act's goal of reducing sentencing disparities.

It is unrealistic to think this goal can be achieved over the long term if sentencing judges need only give lip service to the Guidelines. The other sentencing factors set out in § 3553(a) are so broad that they impose few real restraints on sentencing judges. * * * [S]entencing disparities will gradually increase. Appellate decisions affirming sentences that diverge from the Guidelines (such as the Court's decision today) will be influential, and the sentencing habits developed during the pre-*Booker* era will fade.

Finally, in reading the *Booker* remedial opinion, we should not forget the decision's constitutional underpinnings. *Booker* and its antecedents are based on the Sixth Amendment right to trial by jury. The Court has held that (at least under a mandatory guidelines system) a defendant has the right to have a jury, not a judge, find facts that increase the defendant's authorized sentence. It is telling that the rules set out in the Court's opinion in the present case have nothing to do with juries or factfinding and, indeed, that not one of the facts that bears on petitioner's sentence is disputed. What is at issue, instead, is the allocation of the authority to decide issues of substantive sentencing policy, an issue on which the Sixth Amendment says absolutely nothing. The yawning gap between the Sixth Amendment and the Court's opinion should be enough to show that the *Blakely-Booker* line of cases has gone astray.

In *Blakely*, the Court drew a distinction—between judicial factfinding under a guidelines system and judicial factfinding under a discretionary sentencing system—that, in my judgment, cannot be defended as a matter of principle. It would be a coherent principle to hold that any fact that increases a defendant's sentence beyond the minimum required by the jury's verdict of guilt must be found by a jury. Such a holding, however, would clash with accepted sentencing practice at the time of the adoption of the Sixth Amendment. By that time, many States had enacted criminal statutes that gave trial judges the discretion to select a sentence from within a prescribed range, and the First Congress enacted federal criminal statutes that were cast in this mold.

Under a sentencing system of this type, trial judges inevitably make findings of fact (albeit informally) that increase sentences beyond the minimum required by the jury's verdict. For example, under a statute providing that the punishment for burglary is, say, imprisonment for up to *x* years, the sentencing court might increase the sentence that it would have otherwise imposed by some amount based on evidence introduced at trial that the defendant was armed or that, before committing the crime, the defendant had told a confederate that he would kill the occupants if they awakened during the burglary. The only difference between this sort of factfinding and the type that occurs under a guidelines system is that factfinding under a guidelines system is explicit and the effect of each critical finding is quantified. But in both instances, facts that cause a defendant to spend more time in prison are found by judges, not juries, and therefore no distinction can be drawn as a matter of Sixth Amendment principle.

The Court's acceptance of this distinction also produced strange collateral consequences. A sentencing system that gives trial judges the discretion to sentence within a specified range not only permits judicial factfinding that may increase a sentence, such a system also gives individual judges discretion to implement their own sentencing policies. This latter feature, whether wise or unwise, has nothing to do with the concerns of the Sixth Amendment, and a principal objective of the Sentencing Reform Act was to take this power out of the hands of individual district judges.

The *Booker* remedy, however, undid this congressional choice. In curing the Sentencing Reform Act's perceived defect regarding judicial factfinding, *Booker* restored to the district courts at least a measure of the policymaking authority that the Sentencing Reform Act had taken away. (How much of this authority was given back is, of course, the issue here.)

I recognize that the Court is committed to the *Blakely-Booker* line of cases, but we are not required to continue along a path that will take us further and further off course. Because the *Booker* remedial opinion may be read to require sentencing judges to give weight to the Guidelines, I would adopt that interpretation and thus minimize the gap between what the Sixth Amendment requires and what our cases have held.

II

A

* * * The District Court considered the sentence called for by the Guidelines, but I see no evidence that the District Court deferred to the Guidelines to any significant degree. Rather, the court determined what it thought was appropriate under the circumstances and sentenced petitioner accordingly.

If the question before us was whether a reasonable jurist could conclude that a sentence of probation was sufficient in this case to serve the purposes of punishment set out in 18 U.S.C. § 3553(a)(2), the District Court's decision could not be disturbed. But because I believe that sentencing judges must still give some significant weight to the Guidelines sentencing range, the Commission's policy statements, and the need to avoid unwarranted sentencing disparities, § 3553(a)(3), (4), and (5), I agree with the Eighth Circuit that the District Court did not properly exercise its discretion.

* * *

Here, the District Court "slighted" the factors set out in 18 U.S.C. §§ 3553(a)(3), (4), and (5)—namely, the Guidelines sentencing range, the Commission's policy statements, and the need to avoid unwarranted sentencing disparities. Although the Guidelines called for a prison term of at least 30 months, the District Court did not require any imprisonment—not one day. The opinion of the Court makes much of the restrictions and burdens of probation, but in the real world there is a huge difference between imprisonment and probation. If the District Court had given any appreciable weight to the Guidelines, the District Court could not have sentenced petitioner to probation without very strong countervailing considerations.

The court listed five considerations as justification for a sentence of probation: (1) petitioner's "voluntary and explicit withdrawal from the conspiracy," (2) his "exemplary behavior while on bond," (3) "the support manifested by family and friends," (4) "the lack of criminal history, especially a complete lack of any violent criminal history," (5) and his age at the time of the offense.

Two of the considerations that the District Court cited—"the support manifested by family and friends" and his age—amounted to a direct rejection of the Sentencing Commission's authority to decide the most basic issues of sentencing policy. In the Sentencing Reform Act, Congress required the Sentencing Commission to consider and decide whether certain specified factors—including "age," "education," "previous employment record," "physical condition," "family ties and responsibilities," and "community ties"—"have any relevance to the nature [and] extent ... of an appropriate sentence." 28 U.S.C. § 994(d). These factors come up with great frequency, and judges in the pre-Sentencing Reform Act era disagreed regarding their relevance. Indeed, some of these factors were viewed by some judges as reasons for increasing a sentence and by others as reasons for decreasing a sentence. For example, if a defendant had a job, a supportive family, and friends, those factors were sometimes viewed as justifying a harsher sentence on the ground that the defendant had squandered the opportunity to lead a law-abiding life. Alternatively, those same factors were sometimes viewed as justifications for a more lenient sentence on the ground that a defendant with a job and a network of support would be less likely to return to crime. If each judge is free to implement his or her personal views on such matters, sentencing disparities are inevitable.

In response to Congress' direction to establish uniform national sentencing policies regarding these common sentencing factors, the Sentencing Commission issued policy statements concluding that "age," "family ties," and "community ties" are relevant to sentencing only in unusual cases. The District Court in this case did not claim that there was anything particularly unusual about petitioner's family or community ties or his age, but the court cited these factors as justifications for a sentence of probation. Although the District Court was obligated to take into account the Commission's policy statements and the need to avoid sentencing disparities, the District Court rejected Commission policy statements that

are critical to the effort to reduce such disparities.

The District Court relied on petitioner's lack of criminal history, but criminal history (or the lack thereof) is a central factor in the calculation of the Guidelines range. Petitioner was given credit for his lack of criminal history in the calculation of his Guidelines sentence. Consequently, giving petitioner additional credit for this factor was nothing more than an expression of disagreement with the policy determination reflected in the Guidelines range.

The District Court mentioned petitioner's "exemplary behavior while on bond," but this surely cannot be regarded as a weighty factor.

Finally, the District Court was plainly impressed by petitioner's "voluntary and explicit withdrawal from the conspiracy." As the Government argues, the legitimate strength of this factor is diminished by petitioner's motivation in withdrawing. He did not leave the conspiracy for reasons of conscience, and he made no effort to stop the others in the ring. He withdrew because he had become afraid of apprehension. While the District Court was within its rights in regarding this factor and petitioner's "self-rehabilitation," as positive considerations, they are not enough, in light of the Guidelines' call for a 30- to 37-month prison term, to warrant a sentence of probation.

B

In reaching the opposite conclusion, the Court attacks straw men. The Court unjustifiably faults the Eighth Circuit for using what it characterizes as a "rigid mathematical formula." * * *

This criticism is quite unfair. It is apparent that the Seventh and Eighth Circuits did not mean to suggest that proportionality review could be reduced to a mathematical equation, and certainly the Eighth Circuit in this case did not assign numbers to the various justifications offered by the District Court. All that the Seventh and Eighth Circuits meant, I am convinced, is what this Court's opinion states, *i.e.*, that "the extent of the difference between a particular sentence and the recommended Guidelines range" is a relevant consideration in determining whether the District Court properly exercised its sentencing discretion.

This Court's opinion is also wrong in suggesting that the Eighth Circuit's approach was inconsistent with the abuse-of-discretion standard of appellate review. The Eighth Circuit stated unequivocally that it was conducting abuse-of-discretion review; abuse-of-discretion review is not toothless; and it is entirely proper for a reviewing court to find an abuse of discretion when important factors—in this case, the Guidelines, policy statements, and the need to avoid sentencing disparities—are slighted. The mere fact that the Eighth Circuit reversed is hardly proof that the Eighth Circuit did not apply the correct standard of review.

Because I believe that the Eighth Circuit correctly interpreted and applied the standards set out in the *Booker* remedial opinion, I must respectfully dissent.

District Court Rejection of the 100:1 Crack/Powder Ratio: Kimbrough v. United States

As discussed in the Text, the Sentencing Guidelines provide harsher sentences for offenses involving crack cocaine than those involving the same amount of powder cocaine. Before *Booker*, of course, that harsher treatment was binding on the sentencing court. The question in the following case is whether sentencing courts remain bound by the harsher sentencing policy after *Booker*.

KIMBROUGH v. UNITED STATES

Supreme Court of the United States, 2007.
552 U.S. 85.

JUSTICE GINSBURG **delivered the opinion of the Court.**

This Court's remedial opinion in United States v. Booker, 543 U.S. 220, 244 (2005), instructed district courts to read the United States Sentencing Guidelines as "effectively advisory." In accord with 18 U.S.C. § 3553(a), the Guidelines, formerly mandatory, now serve as one factor among several courts must consider in determining an appropriate sentence. *Booker* further instructed that "reasonableness" is the standard controlling appellate review of the sentences district courts impose.

Under the statute criminalizing the manufacture and distribution of crack cocaine, 21 U.S.C. § 841, and the relevant Guidelines prescription, § 2D1.1, a drug trafficker dealing in crack cocaine is subject to the same sentence as one dealing in 100 times more powder cocaine. The question here presented is whether, as the Court of Appeals held in this case, "a sentence ... outside the guidelines range is per se unreasonable when it is based on a disagreement with the sentencing disparity for crack and powder cocaine offenses." We hold that, under *Booker*, the cocaine Guidelines, like all other Guidelines, are advisory only, and that the Court of Appeals erred in holding the crack/powder disparity effectively mandatory. A district judge must include the Guidelines range in the array of factors warranting consideration. The judge may determine, however, that, in the particular case, a within-Guidelines sentence is "greater than necessary" to serve the objectives of sentencing. 18 U.S.C. § 3553(a). In making that determination, the judge may consider the disparity between the Guidelines' treatment of crack and powder cocaine offenses.

I

In September 2004, petitioner Derrick Kimbrough was indicted in the United States District Court for the Eastern District of Virginia and charged with four offenses: conspiracy to distribute crack and powder cocaine; possession with intent to distribute more than 50 grams of crack cocaine; possession with intent to distribute powder cocaine; and possession of a firearm in furtherance of a drug-trafficking offense. Kimbrough pleaded guilty to all four charges.

Under the relevant statutes, Kimbrough's plea subjected him to an aggregate sentence of 15 years to life in prison: 10 years to life for the three drug offenses, plus a consecutive term of 5 years to life for the firearm offense. In order to determine the appropriate sentence within this statutory range, the District Court first calculated Kimbrough's sentence under the advisory Sentencing Guidelines. Kimbrough's guilty plea acknowledged that he was accountable for 56 grams of crack cocaine and 92.1 grams of powder cocaine. This quantity of drugs yielded a base offense level of 32 for the three drug charges. See United States Sentencing Commission, Guidelines Manual § 2D1.1(c). Finding that Kimbrough, by asserting sole culpability for the crime, had testified falsely at his codefendant's trial, the District Court increased his offense level to 34. See § 3C1.1. In accord with the presentence report, the court determined that Kimbrough's criminal history category was II. An offense level of 34 and a criminal history category of II yielded a Guidelines range of 168 to 210 months for the three drug charges. The Guidelines sentence for the firearm offense was the statutory minimum, 60 months. See USSG § 2K2.4(b). Kimbrough's final advisory Guidelines range was thus 228 to 270 months, or 19 to 22.5 years.

A sentence in this range, in the District Court's judgment, would have been "greater than necessary" to accomplish the purposes of sentencing set forth in 18 U.S.C. § 3553(a). As required by § 3553(a), the court took into account the "nature and circumstances" of the offense and Kimbrough's "history and characteristics." The court also commented that the case exemplified the "disproportionate and unjust effect that crack cocaine guidelines have in sentencing." In this regard, the court contrasted Kimbrough's Guidelines range of 228 to 270 months with the range that would have applied had he been accountable for an equivalent amount of powder cocaine: 97 to 106 months, inclusive of the 5–year mandatory minimum for the firearm charge, see USSG § 2D1.1(c). Concluding that the statutory minimum sentence was "clearly long enough" to accomplish the objectives listed in § 3553(a), the court sentenced Kimbrough to 15 years, or 180 months, in prison plus 5 years of supervised release. [The Fourth Circuit reversed, under its precedent providing that a sentence outside the guidelines range is per se unreasonable when it is based on a disagreement with the sentencing disparity for crack and powder cocaine offenses.]

We granted certiorari to determine whether the crack/powder disparity adopted in the United States Sentencing Guidelines has been rendered "advisory" by our decision in *Booker*.

II

We begin with some background on the different treatment of crack and powder cocaine under the federal sentencing laws. Crack and powder cocaine are two forms of the same drug. Powder cocaine, or cocaine hydrochloride, is generally inhaled through the nose; it may also be mixed with water and injected. Crack cocaine, a type of cocaine base, is formed by dissolving powder cocaine and baking soda in boiling water. The resulting solid is divided into single-dose "rocks" that users smoke. The active ingredient in powder and crack cocaine is the same. The two forms of the drug also have the same physiological and psychotropic effects, but smoking crack cocaine allows the body to absorb the drug much faster than inhaling powder cocaine, and thus produces a shorter, more intense high.

Although chemically similar, crack and powder cocaine are handled very differently for sentencing purposes. The 100–to–1 ratio [under the Guidelines applicable at the time of Kimbrough's sentencing] yields sentences for crack offenses three to six times longer than those for powder offenses involving equal amounts of drugs. This disparity means that a major supplier of powder cocaine may receive a shorter sentence than a low-level dealer who buys powder from the supplier but then converts it to crack.

A

The crack/powder disparity originated in the Anti–Drug Abuse Act of 1986 (1986 Act), 100 Stat. 3207. The 1986 Act created a two-tiered scheme of five-and ten-year mandatory minimum sentences for drug manufacturing and distribution offenses. Congress sought "to link the ten-year mandatory minimum trafficking prison term to major drug dealers and to link the five-year minimum term to serious traffickers." The 1986 Act uses the weight of the drugs involved in the offense as the sole proxy to identify "major" and "serious" dealers. For example, any defendant responsible for 100 grams of heroin is subject to the five-year mandatory minimum, and any defendant responsible for 1,000 grams of heroin is subject to the ten-year mandatory minimum.

Cocaine was a relatively new drug when the 1986 Act was signed into law, but it was already a matter of great public concern * * * . Congress apparently believed that crack was significantly more dangerous than powder cocaine in that: (1) crack was highly addictive; (2) crack users and dealers were more likely to be violent than users and dealers of other drugs; (3) crack was more harmful to users than powder, particularly for children who had been exposed by their mothers' drug use during pregnancy; (4) crack use was especially prevalent among teenagers; and (5) crack's potency and low cost were making it increasingly popular.

Based on these assumptions, the 1986 Act adopted a "100–to–1 ratio" that treated every gram of crack cocaine as the equivalent of 100 grams of powder cocaine. The Act's five-year mandatory minimum applies to any defendant accountable for 5 grams of crack or 500 grams of powder, 21 U.S.C. § 841(b)(1) (B)(ii), (iii); its ten-year mandatory minimum applies to any defendant accountable for 50 grams of crack or 5,000 grams of powder, § 841(b)(1)(A)(ii), (iii).

While Congress was considering adoption of the 1986 Act, the Sentencing Commission was engaged in formulating the Sentencing Guidelines. In the main, the Commission developed Guidelines sentences using an empirical approach based on data about past sentencing practices, including 10,000 presentence investigation reports. The Commission modified and adjusted past practice in the interests of greater rationality, avoiding inconsistency, complying with congressional instructions, and the like.

The Commission did not use this empirical approach in developing the Guidelines sentences for drug-trafficking offenses. Instead, it employed the 1986 Act's weight-driven scheme. The Guidelines use a drug quantity table based on drug type and weight to set base offense levels for drug trafficking offenses. See USSG § 2D1.1(c). In setting offense levels for crack and powder cocaine, the Commission, in line with the 1986 Act, adopted the 100–to–1 ratio. The statute itself specifies only two quantities of each drug, but the Guidelines go further and set sentences for the full range of possible drug quantities using the same 100–to–1 quantity ratio. The Guidelines' drug quantity table sets base offense levels ranging from 12, for offenses involving less than 250 milligrams of crack (or 25 grams of powder), to 38, for offenses involving more than 1.5 kilograms of crack (or 150 kilograms of powder). USSG § 2D1.1(c).

B

Although the Commission immediately used the 100–to–1 ratio to define base offense levels for all crack and powder offenses, it later determined that the crack/powder sentencing disparity is generally unwarranted. Based on additional research and experience with the 100–to–1 ratio, the Commission concluded that the disparity "fails to meet the sentencing objectives set forth by Congress in both the Sentencing Reform Act and the

1986 Act." In a series of reports, the Commission identified three problems with the crack/powder disparity.

First, the Commission reported, the 100–to–1 ratio rested on assumptions about "the relative harmfulness of the two drugs and the relative prevalence of certain harmful conduct associated with their use and distribution that more recent research and data no longer support." See United States Sentencing Commission, Report to Congress: Cocaine and Federal Sentencing Policy 8 (May 2007), available at http://www.ussc.gov/r_congress/cocaine2007.pdf (hereinafter 2007 Report). For example, the Commission found that crack is associated with "significantly less trafficking-related violence ... than previously assumed." 2002 Report 100. It also observed that "the negative effects of prenatal crack cocaine exposure are identical to the negative effects of prenatal powder cocaine exposure." *Id.*, at 94. The Commission furthermore noted that "the epidemic of crack cocaine use by youth never materialized to the extent feared." *Id.*, at 96.

Second, the Commission concluded that the crack/powder disparity is inconsistent with the 1986 Act's goal of punishing major drug traffickers more severely than low-level dealers. Drug importers and major traffickers generally deal in powder cocaine, which is then converted into crack by street-level sellers. See 1995 Report 66–67. But the 100–to–1 ratio can lead to the "anomalous" result that "retail crack dealers get longer sentences than the wholesale drug distributors who supply them the powder cocaine from which their crack is produced." *Id.*, at 174.

Finally, the Commission stated that the crack/powder sentencing differential "fosters disrespect for and lack of confidence in the criminal justice system" because of a "widely-held perception" that it "promotes unwarranted disparity based on race." 2002 Report 103. Approximately 85 percent of defendants convicted of crack offenses in federal court are black; thus the severe sentences required by the 100–to–1 ratio are imposed "primarily upon black offenders." Ibid.

Despite these observations, the Commission's most recent reports do not urge identical treatment of crack and powder cocaine. In the Commission's view, "some differential in the quantity-based penalties" for the two drugs is warranted, *id.*, at 102, because crack is more addictive than powder, crack offenses are more likely to involve weapons or bodily injury, and crack distribution is associated with higher levels of crime, see *id.*, at 93–94, 101–102. But the 100–to–1 crack/powder ratio, the Commission concluded, significantly overstates the differences between the two forms of the drug. Accordingly, the Commission recommended that the ratio be "substantially" reduced.

C

The Commission has several times sought to achieve a reduction in the crack/powder ratio. In 1995, it proposed amendments to the Guidelines that would have replaced the 100–to–1 ratio with a 1–to–1 ratio. Complementing that change, the Commission would have installed special enhancements for trafficking offenses involving weapons or bodily injury. Congress

* * * rejected the amendments. See Pub. L. 104–38, § 1, 109 Stat. 334. Simultaneously, however, Congress directed the Commission to "propose revision of the drug quantity ratio of crack cocaine to powder cocaine under the relevant statutes and guidelines."

In response to this directive, the Commission issued reports in 1997 and 2002 recommending that Congress change the 100–to–1 ratio prescribed in the 1986 Act. The 1997 Report proposed a 5–to–1 ratio. See United States Sentencing Commission, Special Report to Congress: Cocaine and Federal Sentencing Policy 2 (Apr. 1997), http://www.ussc.gov/r_congress/newcrack.pdf. The 2002 Report recommended lowering the ratio "at least" to 20 to 1. 2002 Report viii. Neither proposal prompted congressional action.

The Commission's most recent report, issued in 2007, again urged Congress to amend the 1986 Act to reduce the 100–to–1 ratio. This time, however, the Commission did not simply await congressional action. Instead, the Commission adopted an ameliorating change in the Guidelines. The alteration, which became effective on November 1, 2007, reduces the base offense level associated with each quantity of crack by two levels. This modest amendment yields sentences for crack offenses between two and five times longer than sentences for equal amounts of powder. Describing the amendment as "only ... a partial remedy" for the problems generated by the crack/powder disparity, the Commission noted that "any comprehensive solution requires appropriate legislative action by Congress."

2007 Report 10. [Editor's Note: The Commission later determined that the amelioration in the Guidelines would be applied retroactively. But even under a retroactive application of the amendment, Kimbrough's Guidelines range would be 195 to 218 months—well above the 180–month sentence imposed by the District Court.]

III

With this history of the crack/powder sentencing ratio in mind, we next consider the status of the Guidelines tied to the ratio after our decision in *Booker*. In *Booker*, the Court held that the mandatory Sentencing Guidelines system violated the Sixth Amendment. The *Booker* remedial opinion determined that the appropriate cure was to sever and excise the provision of the statute that rendered the Guidelines mandatory, 18 U.S.C. § 3553(b)(1). This modification of the federal sentencing statute, we explained, "makes the Guidelines effectively advisory."

The statute, as modified by *Booker*, contains an overarching provision instructing district courts to "impose a sentence sufficient, but not greater than necessary" to accomplish the goals of sentencing, including "to reflect the seriousness of the offense," "to promote respect for the law," "to provide just punishment for the offense," "to afford adequate deterrence to criminal conduct," and "to protect the public from further crimes of the defendant." 18 U.S.C. § 3553(a). The statute further provides that, in determining the appropriate sentence, the court should consider a number of factors, including "the nature and circumstances of the offense," "the history and characteristics of the defendant," "the sentencing range established" by the Guidelines, "any pertinent policy statement" issued by the Sentencing Commission pursuant to its statutory authority, and "the need to avoid unwarranted sentence disparities among defendants with similar records who have been found guilty of similar conduct." In sum, while the statute still requires a court to give respectful consideration to the Guidelines, *Booker* "permits the court to tailor the sentence in light of other statutory concerns as well." 543 U.S., at 245–246.

The Government acknowledges that the Guidelines "are now advisory" and that, as a general matter, "courts may vary [from Guidelines ranges] based solely on policy considerations, including disagreements with the Guidelines." But the Government contends that the Guidelines adopting the 100–to–1 ratio are an exception to the "general freedom that sentencing courts have to apply the [§ 3553(a)] factors." That is so, according to the Government, because the ratio is a "specific policy determination that Congress has directed sentencing courts to observe." The Government offers three arguments in support of this position. We consider each in turn.

A

As its first and most heavily pressed argument, the Government urges that the 1986 Act itself prohibits the Sentencing Commission and sentencing courts from disagreeing with the 100–to–1 ratio. The Government acknowledges that the "Congress did not *expressly* direct the Sentencing Commission to incorporate the 100:1 ratio in the Guidelines." Nevertheless, it asserts that the Act "implicit[ly]" requires the Commission and sentencing courts to apply the 100–to–1 ratio. Any deviation, the Government urges, would be "logically incoherent" when combined with mandatory minimum sentences based on the 100–to–1 ratio.

This argument encounters a formidable obstacle: It lacks grounding in the text of the 1986 Act. The statute, by its terms, mandates only maximum and minimum sentences: A person convicted of possession with intent to distribute 5 grams or more of crack cocaine must be sentenced to a minimum of 5 years and the maximum term is 40 years. A person with 50 grams or more of crack cocaine must be sentenced to a minimum of 10 years and the maximum term is life. The statute says nothing about the appropriate sentences within these brackets, and we decline to read any implicit directive into that congressional silence. Drawing meaning from silence is particularly inappropriate here, for Congress has shown that it knows how to direct sentencing practices in express terms. For example, Congress has specifically required the Sentencing Commission to set Guidelines sentences for serious recidivist offenders "at or near" the statutory maximum. 28 U.S.C. § 994(h). See also § 994(i) ("The Commission shall assure that the guidelines specify a sentence to a substantial term of imprisonment" for specified categories of offenders.).

* * *

B

In addition to the 1986 Act, the Government relies on Congress' disapproval of the Guidelines amendment that the Sentencing Commission proposed in 1995. Congress "not only disapproved of the 1:1 ratio," the Government urges; it also made clear "that the 1986 Act required the Commission (and sentencing courts) to take drug quantities into account, and to do so in a manner that respects the 100:1 ratio."

* * * But nothing in Congress' 1995 reaction to the Commission-proposed 1–to–1 ratio suggested that crack sentences must exceed powder sentences by a ratio of 100 to 1. To the contrary, Congress' 1995 action required the Commission to recommend a "revision of the drug quantity ratio of crack cocaine to powder cocaine." § 2(a)(2), *id.*, at 335.

* * *

Moreover, as a result of the 2007 amendment, the Guidelines now advance a crack/powder ratio that varies (at different offense levels) between 25 to 1 and 80 to 1. Adopting the Government's analysis, the amended Guidelines would conflict with Congress' 1995 action, and with the 1986 Act, because the current Guidelines ratios deviate from the 100–to–1 statutory ratio. Congress, however, did not disapprove or modify the Commission-initiated 2007 amendment. Ordinarily, we resist reading congressional intent into congressional inaction. But in this case, Congress failed to act on a proposed amendment to the Guidelines in a high-profile area in which it had previously exercised its disapproval authority under 28 U.S.C. § 994(p). If nothing else, this tacit acceptance of the 2007 amendment undermines the Government's posi-tion, which is itself based on implications drawn from congressional silence.

C

Finally, the Government argues that if district courts are * * * permitted to vary from the Guidelines based on their disagreement with the crack/powder disparity, "defendants with identical real conduct will receive markedly different sentences, depending on nothing more than the particular judge drawn for sentencing." * * * [I]t is unquestioned that uniformity remains an important goal of sentencing. As we explained in *Booker*, however, advisory Guidelines combined with appellate review for reasonableness and ongoing revision of the Guidelines in response to sentencing practices will help to "avoid excessive sentencing disparities." 543 U.S., at 264. These measures will not eliminate variations between district courts, but our opinion in *Booker* recognized that some departures from uniformity were a necessary cost of the remedy we adopted. And as to crack cocaine sentences in particular, we note a congressional control on disparities: possible variations among district courts are constrained by the mandatory minimums Congress prescribed in the 1986 Act.

Moreover, to the extent that the Government correctly identifies risks of "unwarranted sentence disparities" within the meaning of 18 U.S.C. § 3553(a)(6), the proper solution is not to treat the crack/powder ratio as mandatory. Section 3553(a)(6) directs district courts to consider the need to avoid unwarranted disparities—along with other § 3553(a) factors—when imposing sentences. * * * To reach an appropriate sentence, these disparities must be weighed against the other § 3553(a) factors and any unwarranted disparity created by the crack/powder ratio itself.

IV

While rendering the Sentencing Guidelines advisory, we have nevertheless preserved a key role for the Sentencing Commission. * * * [D]istrict courts must treat the Guidelines as the "starting point and the initial benchmark," Gall v. United States, [*supra* in this Supplement] .. Congress established the Commission to formulate and constantly refine national sentencing standards. Carrying out its charge, the Commission fills an important institutional role: It has the capacity courts lack to base its determinations on empirical data and national experience, guided by a professional staff with appropriate expertise.

We have accordingly recognized that, in the ordinary case, the Commission's recommendation of a sentencing range will "reflect a rough approximation of sentences that might achieve § 3553(a)'s objectives." The sentencing judge, on the other hand, has greater familiarity with the individual case and the individual defendant before him than the Commission or the appeals court .. He is therefore in a superior position to find facts and judge their import under § 3553(a) in each particular case. In light of these discrete institutional strengths, a district court's decision to vary from the advisory Guidelines may attract greatest respect when the sentencing judge finds a particular case outside the "heartland" to which the Commission intends indi-

vidual Guidelines to apply. On the other hand, while the Guidelines are no longer binding, closer review may be in order when the sentencing judge varies from the Guidelines based solely on the judge's view that the Guidelines range fails properly to reflect § 3553(a) considerations even in a mine-run case.

The crack cocaine Guidelines, however, present no occasion for elaborative discussion of this matter because those Guidelines do not exemplify the Commission's exercise of its characteristic institutional role. In formulating Guidelines ranges for crack cocaine offenses, as we earlier noted, the Commission looked to the mandatory minimum sentences set in the 1986 Act, and did not take account of empirical data and national experience. Indeed, the Commission itself has reported that the crack/powder disparity produces disproportionately harsh sanctions, *i.e.*, sentences for crack cocaine offenses greater than necessary in light of the purposes of sentencing set forth in § 3553(a). Given all this, it would not be an abuse of discretion for a district court to conclude when sentencing a particular defendant that the crack/powder disparity yields a sentence greater than necessary to achieve § 3553(a)'s purposes, even in a mine-run case.

V

Taking account of the foregoing discussion in appraising the District Court's disposition in this case, we conclude that the 180–month sentence imposed on Kimbrough should survive appellate inspection. The District Court began by properly calculating and considering the advisory Guidelines range. It then addressed the relevant § 3553(a) factors. First, the court considered "the nature and circumstances" of the crime, see 18 U.S.C. § 3553(a)(1), which was an unremarkable drug-trafficking offense. ("This defendant and another defendant were caught sitting in a car with some crack cocaine and powder by two police officers—that's the sum and substance of it—[and they also had] a firearm."). Second, the court considered Kimbrough's "history and characteristics." § 3553(a)(1). The court noted that Kimbrough had no prior felony convictions, that he had served in combat during Operation Desert Storm and received an honorable discharge from the Marine Corps, and that he had a steady history of employment.

Furthermore, the court alluded to the Sentencing Commission's reports criticizing the 100–to–1 ratio, noting that the Commission "recognizes that crack cocaine has not caused the damage that the Justice Department alleges it has." Comparing the Guidelines range to the range that would have applied if Kimbrough had possessed an equal amount of powder, the court suggested that the 100–to–1 ratio itself created an unwarranted disparity within the meaning of § 3553(a). Finally, the court did not purport to establish a ratio of its own. Rather, it appropriately framed its final determination in line with § 3553(a)'s overarching instruction to "impose a sentence sufficient, but not greater than necessary" to accomplish the sentencing goals advanced in § 3553(a)(2). Concluding that "the crack cocaine guidelines [drove] the offense level to a point higher than is necessary to do justice in this case," the District Court thus rested its sentence on the appropriate considerations and committed no procedural error.

The ultimate question in Kimbrough's case is whether the sentence was reasonable—*i.e.*, whether the District Judge abused his discretion in determining that the § 3553(a) factors supported a sentence of [15 years] and justified a substantial deviation from the Guidelines range. The sentence the District Court imposed on Kimbrough was 4.5 years below the bottom of the Guidelines range. But in determining that 15 years was the appropriate prison term, the District Court properly homed in on the particular circumstances of Kimbrough's case and accorded weight to the Sentencing Commission's consistent and emphatic position that the crack/powder disparity is at odds with § 3553(a). Indeed, aside from its claim that the 100–to–1 ratio is mandatory, the Government did not attack the District Court's downward variance as unsupported by § 3553(a). Giving due respect to the District Court's reasoned appraisal, a reviewing court could not rationally conclude that the 4.5–year sentence reduction Kimbrough received qualified as an abuse of discretion.

For the reasons stated, the judgment of the United States Court of Appeals for the Fourth Circuit is reversed, and the case is remanded for further proceedings consistent with this opinion.

JUSTICE SCALIA, **concurring.**

The Court says that "closer review may be in order when the sentencing judge varies from the Guidelines based solely on the judge's view that the Guidelines range fails properly to reflect § 3553(a) considerations even in a mine-run case," but that this case "presents no occasion for elaborative discussion of this matter." I join the opinion only because I do not take this to be an unannounced abandonment of the following clear statements in our recent opinions:

[Justice Scalia takes quotes from *Booker* and later cases indicating that the sentencing court must consider the Guidelines in the first instance, but is not bound by them]

These statements mean that the district court is free to make its own reasonable application of the § 3553(a) factors, and to reject (after due consideration) the advice of the Guidelines. If there is any thumb on the scales; if the Guidelines *must* be followed even where the district court's application of the § 3553(a) factors is entirely reasonable; then the "advisory" Guidelines would, over a large expanse of their application, *entitle* the defendant to a lesser sentence *but for* the presence of certain additional facts found by judge rather than jury. This, as we said in *Booker,* would violate the Sixth Amendment.

Justice Thomas, dissenting.

I continue to disagree with the remedy fashioned in *United States v. Booker*, 543 U.S. 220, 258–265 (2005). The Court's post-*Booker* sentencing cases illustrate why the remedial majority in *Booker* was mistaken to craft a remedy far broader than necessary to correct constitutional error. The Court is now confronted with a host of questions about how to administer a sentencing scheme that has no basis in the statute. Because the Court's decisions in this area are necessarily grounded in policy considerations rather than law, I respectfully dissent.

* * *

* * * We are asked here to determine whether, under the new advisory Guidelines regime, district courts may impose sentences based in part on their disagreement with a categorical policy judgment reflected in the Guidelines. But the Court's answer to that question necessarily derives from something other than the statutory language or congressional intent because Congress, by making the Guidelines mandatory, quite clearly intended to bind district courts to the Sentencing Commission's categorical policy judgments. By rejecting this statutory approach, the *Booker* remedial majority has left the Court with no law to apply and forced it to assume the legislative role of devising a new sentencing scheme.

Although I joined JUSTICE SCALIA's dissent in *Rita* accepting the *Booker* remedial opinion as a matter of "statutory *stare decisis*," I am now convinced that there is no principled way to apply the *Booker* remedy—certainly not one based on the statute. Accordingly, I think it best to apply the statute as written, including 18 U.S.C. § 3553(b), which makes the Guidelines mandatory.

Applying the statute as written, it is clear that the District Court erred by departing below the mandatory Guidelines range. I would therefore affirm the judgment of the Court of Appeals vacating petitioner's sentence and remanding for resentencing.

JUSTICE ALITO, **dissenting.**

For the reasons explained in my dissent in Gall v. United States [immediately above in this Supplement] I would hold that, under the remedial decision in *United States v. Booker*, 543 U.S. 220, 258–265 (2005), a district judge is still required to give significant weight to the policy decisions embodied in the Guidelines. The *Booker* remedial decision, however, does not permit a court of appeals to treat the Guidelines' policy decisions as binding. I would not draw a distinction between the Guideline at issue here and other Guidelines. Accordingly, I would vacate the decision of the Court of Appeals and remand for reconsideration.

Appellate Court May Not Increase a Sentence in the Absence of a Government Appeal: Greenlaw v. United States

In Greenlaw v. United States, 128 S.Ct. 2559 (2008), the defendant appealed from his sentence, and the government filed no cross-appeal. The court of appeals rejected the defendant's challenge to his sentence and then proceeded *sua sponte* to determine whether the defendant's sentence was too low. Relying on the doctrine of plain error, the court of appeals entered an order increasing the defendant's sentence by 15 years. The Supreme Court, in an opinion by Justice Ginsburg for six Justices, held that the court of appeals could not use the plain error doctrine to increase a sentence from which the government had not appealed.

Justice Ginsburg relied on 18 U. S. C. § 3742(b), which provides that the government may not appeal a sentence "without the personal approval of the Attorney General, the Solicitor General, or a deputy solicitor general designated by the Solicitor General." She declared that "Congress, in § 3742(b), has accorded to the top representatives of the United States in litigation the prerogative to seek or forgo appellate correction of sentencing errors, however plain they may be. That measure should garner the Judiciary's full respect."

Justice Ginsburg found nothing in the plain error rule, Fed.R.Crim. P.52, to change the result mandated by 18 U. S. C. § 3742(b). She noted that the Court had ordered correction of plain errors not raised by defendants, "but we have done so only to benefit a defendant who had himself petitioned the Court for review on other grounds. In no case have we applied plain-error doctrine to the detriment of a petitioning party." Moreover, even if there might be circumstances in which it would be proper for an appellate court to initiate plain-error review, "sentencing errors that the Government refrained from pursuing would not fit the bill" because "Congress has provided a dispositive direction regarding sentencing errors that aggrieve the Government. In § 3742(b), as earlier explained, Congress designated leading Department of Justice officers as the decisionmakers responsible for determining when Government pursuit of a sentencing appeal is in order. Those high officers, Congress recognized, are best equipped to determine where the Government's interest lies. Rule 52(b) does not invite appellate court interference with their assessment."

Justice Alito, joined by Justices Breyer and Stevens, dissented. He argued that § 3742(b) "does not apportion authority over sentencing appeals between the Executive and Judicial Branches. By its terms, § 3742(b) simply apportions that authority *within* an executive department." According to Justice Alito, the rule that conditions increase of a sentence on an appeal from the government was one of "trial practice" that did not prevent an appellate court from increasing the sentences under the narrow circumstances permitted by the plain error rule.

E. SENTENCING DEVELOPMENTS IN THE STATES

Page 1497. Add the following at the end of the section:

In Cunningham v. California, 549 U.S. 270 (2007), the Court held that the California Determinative Sentencing Law violated *Apprendi* because it required a trial judge to impose a sentence in a higher sentencing category, upon the basis of certain aggravating facts found by the judge. Justice Ginsburg, writing for the six-person majority, declared as follows:

> Under California's DSL, an upper term sentence may be imposed only when the trial judge finds an aggravating circumstance. An element of the charged offense, essential to a jury's determination of guilt, or admitted in a defendant's guilty plea, does not qualify as such a circumstance. Instead, aggravating circumstances depend on facts found discretely and solely by the judge. In accord with *Blakely*, therefore, the middle term prescribed in California's statutes [for the crime charged and proved to the jury], not the upper term, is the relevant statutory maximum. Because circumstances in aggravation are found by the judge, not the jury, and need only be established by a preponderance of the evidence, not beyond a reasonable doubt, the DSL violates *Apprendi*'s bright-line rule: Except for a prior conviction, "any fact that increases the penalty for a crime beyond the prescribed statutory maximum must be submitted to a jury, and proved beyond a reasonable doubt."

California argued that the sentencing enhancements were left to the discretion of the trial judge and therefore were "advisory" in the same way as the Federal Sentencing Guidelines upheld in *Booker*. But Justice Ginsburg disagreed. The full opinion in *Cunningham,* including the dissents by Justice Kennedy (joined by Justice Breyer) and Justice Alito (joined by Justices Kennedy and Breyer) is set forth in this Supplement, supra, in the section on "Constitutionally Based Proof Requirements."

In Oregon v. Ice, 129 S.Ct. 711 (2009), the Court upheld a state law allowing the judge to impose consecutive, rather than concurrent, sentences after finding certain facts. The Court distinguished *Apprendi* as a case involving "sentencing for a discrete crime, not—as here—for multiple offenses different in character or committed at different times." The full opinion in *Ice* is also set forth in the section on constitutionally-based proof requirements, *supra*.

III. SENTENCING PROCEDURES

A. GENERAL PROCEDURES

Page 1500. Add the following headnote after the section on Pre–Sentence Reports and the Sentencing Guidelines:

Notice Requirement Does Not Apply to Court's Decision to Consider a Sentence Outside the Guidelines: Irizzary v. United States

Rule 32(h) of the Federal Rules of Criminal Procedure, promulgated in response to the Supreme Court's decision in Burns v. United States, 501 U.S. 129 (1991), states that "[b]efore the court may depart from the applicable sentencing range on a ground not identified for departure either in the presentence report or in a party's prehearing submission, the court must give the parties reasonable notice that it is contemplating such a departure." In Irizarry v. United States, 128 S.Ct. 2198 (2008), the Court held that this notice requirement does not apply to the sentencing court's consideration of whether to impose a sentence outside the Guidelines, which were made advisory in United States v. Booker, 543 U.S. 220 (2005). Justice Stevens, writing for the Court, found that the notice requirement was not appropriate as applied to the consideration of sentences outside the Guidelines. He explained as follows:

> At the time of our decision in *Burns*, the Guidelines were mandatory. * * * Confronted with the constitutional problems that might otherwise arise, we held that the provision of Rule 32 that allowed parties an opportunity to comment on the appropriate sentence * * * would be rendered meaningless unless the defendant were given notice of any contemplated departure. * * * Now faced with advisory Guidelines, neither the Government nor the defendant may place the same degree of reliance on the type of "expectancy" that gave rise to a special need for notice in *Burns*. Indeed, a sentence outside the Guidelines carries no presumption of unreasonableness. * * * The due process concerns that motivated the Court to require notice in a world of mandatory Guidelines no longer provide a basis for this Court to extend the rule set forth in *Burns* * * *.

Justice Stevens also noted the practical concerns of applying a notice requirement to the consideration of sentences outside the Guidelines:

> Adding a special notice requirement whenever a judge is contemplating a variance may create unnecessary delay; a judge who concludes during the sentencing hearing that a variance is appropriate may be forced to continue the hearing even where the content of the Rule 32(h) notice would not affect the parties' presentation of

argument and evidence. In the case before us today, even if we assume that the judge had contemplated a variance before the sentencing hearing began, the record does not indicate that a statement announcing that possibility would have changed the parties' presentations in any material way; nor do we think it would in most cases. The Government admits as much in arguing that the error here was harmless.

Sound practice dictates that judges in all cases should make sure that the information provided to the parties in advance of the hearing, and in the hearing itself, has given them an adequate opportunity to confront and debate the relevant issues. We recognize that there will be some cases in which the factual basis for a particular sentence will come as a surprise to a defendant or the Government. The more appropriate response to such a problem is not to extend the reach of Rule 32(h)'s notice requirement categorically, but rather for a district judge to consider granting a continuance when a party has a legitimate basis for claiming that the surprise was prejudicial. As Judge Boudin has noted,

> "In the normal case a competent lawyer ... will anticipate most of what might occur at the sentencing hearing—based on the trial, the pre-sentence report, the exchanges of the parties concerning the report, and the preparation of mitigation evidence. Garden variety considerations of culpability, criminal history, likelihood of re-offense, seriousness of the crime, nature of the conduct and so forth should not generally come as a surprise to trial lawyers who have prepared for sentencing."

Justice Thomas concurred. Justice Breyer, joined by Justices Kennedy, Souter and Ginsburg dissented. The dissenters argued that a notice requirement would provide an important procedural safeguard and would help to assure the effective advocacy made all the more important after the Court's decision in *Booker*.

Chapter Twelve

DOUBLE JEOPARDY

VII. COLLATERAL ESTOPPEL

Page 1557. Add after the section on "The Problem of General Verdicts":

Application of Ashe When There Is an Acquittal on Some Counts and a Deadlock on Others: Yeager v. United States

YEAGER v. UNITED STATES

Supreme Court of the United States, 2009.
129 S.Ct. 2360.

JUSTICE STEVENS **delivered the opinion of the Court.**

In Dunn v. United States, 284 U. S. 390, 393 (1932), the Court, speaking through Justice Holmes, held that a logical inconsistency between a guilty verdict and a verdict of acquittal does not impugn the validity of either verdict. The question presented in this case is whether an apparent inconsistency between a jury's verdict of acquittal on some counts and its failure to return a verdict on other counts affects the preclusive force of the acquittals under the Double Jeopardy Clause of the Fifth Amendment. We hold that it does not.

I

In 1997, Enron Corporation (Enron) acquired a telecommunications business that it expanded and ultimately renamed Enron Broadband Services (EBS). Petitioner F. Scott Yeager served as Senior Vice President of Strategic Development for EBS from October 1, 1998, until his employment was terminated a few months before Enron filed for bankruptcy on December 2, 2001. During his tenure, petitioner played an active role in EBS's attempt to develop a nationwide fiber-optic telecommunications system called the Enron Intelligent Network (EIN).

In the summer of 1999, Enron announced that EBS would become a "core" Enron business and a major part of its overall strategy. Thereafter, Enron issued press releases touting the advanced capabilities of EIN and claiming that the project was "lit,"or operational. On

January 20, 2000, at the company's annual equity analyst conference, petitioner and others allegedly made false and misleading statements about the value and performance of the EIN project. On January 21, 2000, the price of Enron stock rose from $54 to $67. The next day it reached $72. At that point petitioner sold more than 100,000 shares of Enron stock that he had received as part of his compensation. During the next several months petitioner sold an additional 600,000 shares. All told, petitioner's stock sales generated more than $54 million in proceeds and $19 million in personal profit. As for the EIN project, its value turned out to be illusory. The "intelligent" network showcased to the public in the press releases and at the analyst conference was riddled with technological problems and never fully developed.

On November 5, 2004, a grand jury returned a "Fifth Superseding Indictment" charging petitioner with 126 counts of five federal offenses: (1) conspiracy to commit securities and wire fraud; (2) securities fraud; (3) wire fraud; (4) insider trading; and (5) money laundering. The Government's theory of prosecution was that petitioner—acting in concert with other Enron executives—purposefully deceived the public about the EIN project in order to inflate the value of Enron's stock and, ultimately, to enrich himself.

Count 1 of the indictment described in some detail the alleged conspiracy to commit securities fraud and wire fraud and included as overt acts the substantive offenses charged in counts 2 through 6. Count 2, the securities fraud count, alleged that petitioner made false and misleading statements at the January 20, 2000, analyst conference or that he failed to state facts necessary to prevent statements made by others from being misleading. Counts 3 through 6 alleged that petitioner and others committed four acts of wire fraud when they issued four EBS-related press releases in 2000. Counts 27 through 46, the insider trading counts, alleged that petitioner made 20 separate sales of Enron stock "while in the possession of material non-public information regarding the technological capabilities, value, revenue and business performance of [EBS]." And counts 67 through 165, the money laundering counts, described 99 financial transactions involving petitioner's use of the proceeds of his sales of Enron stock, which the indictment characterized as "criminally derived property." To simplify our discussion, we shall refer to counts 1 through 6 as the "fraud counts" and the remaining counts as the "insider trading counts."

The trial lasted 13 weeks. After four days of deliberations, the jury notified the court that it had reached agreement on some counts but had deadlocked on others. The judge then gave the jury an *Allen* charge, see Allen v. United States, 164 U. S. 492, 501–502 (1896), urging the jurors to reexamine the grounds for their opinions and to continue deliberations "until the end of the day" to achieve a final verdict on all counts. When the jury failed to break the deadlock, the court told the jurors that it would "take their verdict" instead of prolonging deliberations. The jury acquitted petitioner on the fraud counts but failed to reach a verdict on the insider trading counts. The court entered judgment on the acquittals and declared a mistrial on the hung counts.

On November 9, 2005, the Government obtained a new indictment against petitioner. This "Eighth Superseding Indictment" recharged petitioner with some, but not all, of the insider trading counts on which the jury had previously hung. The new indictment refined the Government's case: Whereas the earlier indictment had named multiple defendants, the new indictment dealt exclusively with petitioner. And instead of alleging facts implicating a broader fraudulent scheme, the new indictment focused on petitioner's knowledge of the EIN project and his failure to disclose that information to the public before selling his Enron stock.

Petitioner moved to dismiss all counts in the new indictment on the ground that the acquittals on the fraud counts precluded the Government from retrying him on the insider trading counts. He argued that the jury's acquittals had necessarily decided that he did not possess material, nonpublic information about the performance of the EIN project and its value to Enron. In petitioner's view, because reprosecution for insider trading would require the Government to prove that critical fact, the issue-preclusion component of the Double Jeopardy Clause barred a second trial of that issue and mandated dismissal of all of the insider trading counts.

The District Court denied the motion. * * *

* * * Based on its independent review of the record, the Court of Appeals * * * concluded that "the jury must have found when it acquitted [petitioner] that [he] did not have any insider information that contradicted what was presented to the public." The court acknowledged that this factual determination would normally preclude the Government from retrying petitioner for insider trading or money laundering.

The court was nevertheless persuaded that a truly rational jury, having concluded that petitioner did not have any insider information, would have acquitted him on the insider trading counts. That the jury failed to acquit, and instead hung on those counts, was pivotal in the court's issue-preclusion analysis. Considering "the hung counts along with the acquittals," the court found it impossible "to decide with any certainty what the jury necessarily determined." Relying on Circuit precedent, United States v. Larkin, 605 F. 2d 1360 (1979), the court concluded that the conflict between the acquittals and the hung counts barred the application of issue preclusion in this case. 521 F. 3d, at 378–379.

Several courts have taken the contrary view and have held that a jury's failure to reach a verdict on some counts should play no role in determining the preclusive effect of an acquittal. We granted certiorari to resolve the conflict, and now reverse.

II

The Double Jeopardy Clause of the Fifth Amendment provides: "[N]or shall any person be subject for the same offence to be twice put in jeopardy of life or limb."

* * *

Our cases have recognized that the Clause embodies two vitally important interests. The first is the "deeply ingrained" principle that "the State with all its resources and power should not be allowed to make repeated attempts to convict an individual for an alleged offense, thereby subjecting him to embarrassment, expense and ordeal and compelling him to live in a continuing state of anxiety and insecurity, as well as enhancing the possibility that even though innocent he may be found guilty." The second interest is the preservation of "the finality of judgments."

The first interest is implicated whenever the State seeks a second trial after its first attempt to obtain a conviction results in a mistrial because the jury has failed to reach a verdict. In these circumstances, however, while the defendant has an interest in avoiding multiple trials, the Clause does not prevent the Government from seeking to reprosecute. Despite the argument's textual appeal, we have held that the second trial does not place the defendant in jeopardy "twice." Instead, a jury's inability to reach a decision is the kind of "manifest necessity" that permits the declaration of a mistrial and the continuation of the initial jeopardy that commenced when the jury was first impaneled. See Arizona v. Washington, 434 U. S. 497, 505–506 (1978). The "interest in giving the prosecution one complete opportunity to convict those who have violated its laws" justifies treating the jury's inability to reach a verdict as a none-

vent that does not bar retrial. Washington, 434 U. S., at 509.

While the case before us involves a mistrial on the insider trading counts, the question presented cannot be resolved by asking whether the Government should be given one complete opportunity to convict petitioner on those charges. Rather, the case turns on the second interest at the core of the Clause. We must determine whether the interest in preserving the finality of the jury's judgment on the fraud counts, including the jury's finding that petitioner did not possess insider information, bars a retrial on the insider trading counts. This requires us to look beyond the Clause's prohibition on being put in jeopardy "twice"; the jury's acquittals unquestionably terminated petitioner's jeopardy with respect to the issues finally decided in those counts. The proper question, under the Clause's text, is whether it is appropriate to treat the insider trading charges as the "same offence" as the fraud charges. Our opinion in Ashe v. Swenson, 397 U. S. 436 (1970), provides the basis for our answer.

In *Ashe*, we squarely held that the Double Jeopardy Clause precludes the Government from relitigating any issue that was necessarily decided by a jury's acquittal in a prior trial. [Justice Stevens sets forth the facts of *Ashe*.] We explained that "when an issue of ultimate fact has once been determined by a valid and final judgment" of acquittal, it "cannot again be litigated" in a second trial for a separate offense. To decipher what a jury has necessarily decided, we held that courts should "examine the record of a prior proceeding, taking into account the pleadings, evidence, charge, and other relevant matter, and conclude whether a rational jury could have grounded its verdict upon an issue other than that which the defendant seeks to foreclose from consideration." We explained that the inquiry "must be set in a practical frame and viewed with an eye to all the circumstances of the proceedings."

Unlike *Ashe*, the case before us today entails a trial that included multiple counts rather than a trial for a single offense. And, while *Ashe* involved an acquittal for that single offense, this case involves an acquittal on some counts and a mistrial declared on others. The reasoning in *Ashe* is nevertheless controlling because, for double jeopardy purposes, the jury's inability to reach a verdict on the insider trading counts was a nonevent and the acquittals on the fraud counts are entitled to the same effect as Ashe's acquittal.

[T]he Court of Appeals reasoned that the hung counts must be considered to determine what issues the jury decided in the first trial. Viewed in isolation, the court explained, the acquittals on the fraud charges would preclude retrial because they appeared to support petitioner's argument that the jury decided he lacked insider information. Viewed alongside the hung counts, however, the acquittals appeared less decisive. The problem, as the court saw it, was that, if "the jury found that [petitioner] did not have insider information, then the jury, acting rationally, would also have acquitted [him] of the insider trading counts." The fact that the jury hung was a logical wrinkle that made it impossible for the court "to decide with any certainty what the

jury necessarily determined." Because petitioner failed to show what the jury decided, the court refused to find the Government precluded from pursuing the hung counts in a new prosecution.

The Court of Appeals' issue-preclusion analysis was in error. A hung count is not a "relevant" part of the "record of [the] prior proceeding." See *Ashe,* 397 U. S., at 444. Because a jury speaks only through its verdict, its failure to reach a verdict cannot—by negative implication—yield a piece of information that helps put together the trial puzzle. A mistried count is therefore nothing like the other forms of record material that *Ashe* suggested should be part of the preclusion inquiry .. Unlike the pleadings, the jury charge, or the evidence introduced by the parties, there is no way to decipher what a hung count represents. Even in the usual sense of "relevance," a hung count hardly "make[s] the existence of any fact ... more probable or less probable." Fed. Rule Evid. 401. A host of reasons—sharp disagreement, confusion about the issues, exhaustion after a long trial, to name but a few—could work alone or in tandem to cause a jury to hang. To ascribe meaning to a hung count would presume an ability to identify which factor was at play in the jury room. But that is not reasoned analysis; it is guesswork. Such conjecture about possible reasons for a jury's failure to reach a decision should play no part in assessing the legal consequences of a unanimous verdict that the jurors did return.

A contrary conclusion would require speculation into what transpired in the jury room. Courts properly avoid such explorations into the jury's sovereign space, see Fed. Rule Evid. 606(b), and for good reason. The jury's deliberations are secret and not subject to outside examination. If there is to be an inquiry into what the jury decided, the evidence should be confined to the points in controversy on the former trial, to the testimony given by the parties, and to the questions submitted to the jury for their consideration.

Accordingly, we hold that the consideration of hung counts has no place in the issue-preclusion analysis. Indeed, if it were relevant, the fact that petitioner has already survived one trial should be a factor cutting in favor of, rather than against, applying a double jeopardy bar. To identify what a jury necessarily determined at trial, courts should scrutinize a jury's decisions, not its failures to decide. A jury's verdict of acquittal represents the community's collective judgment regarding all the evidence and arguments presented to it. * * * Thus, if the possession of insider information was a critical issue of ultimate fact in all of the charges against petitioner, a jury verdict that necessarily decided that issue in his favor protects him from prosecution for any charge for which that is an essential element.

III

The Government relies heavily on two of our cases, Richardson v. United States, 468 U. S. 317, and United States v. Powell, 469 U. S. 57, to argue that it is entitled to retry petitioner on the insider trading counts. Neither precedent can

bear the weight the Government places on it.

In *Richardson*, the defendant was indicted on three counts of narcotics violations. The jury acquitted him on one count but hung on the others. Richardson moved to bar retrial on the hung counts, insisting that reprosecution would place him twice in jeopardy for the same offense. Unlike petitioner in this case, Richardson did not argue that retrial was barred because the jury's verdict of acquittal meant that it necessarily decided an essential fact in his favor. He simply asserted that the hung counts, standing alone, shielded him from reprosecution. We disagreed and held that "the protection of the Double Jeopardy Clause by its terms applies only if there has been some event, such as an acquittal, which terminates the original jeopardy." The failure of the jury to reach a verdict, we explained, "is not an event which terminates jeopardy." From this the Government extrapolates the altogether different principle that retrial is always permitted whenever a jury convicts on some counts and hangs on others. But *Richardson* was not so broad. Rather, our conclusion was a rejection of the argument—similar to the one the Government urges today— that a mistrial is an event of significance. In so holding, we did not open the door to using a mistried count to ignore the preclusive effect of a jury's acquittal.

The Government next contends that an acquittal can never preclude retrial on a mistried count because it would impute irrationality to the jury in violation of the rule articulated in *Powell,* 469 U. S. 57. In *Powell,* the defendant was charged with various drug offenses. The jury acquitted Powell of the substantive drug charges but convicted her of using a telephone in "committing and in causing and facilitating" those same offenses. Powell attacked the verdicts on appeal as irrationally inconsistent and urged the reversal of her convictions. She insisted that "collateral estoppel should apply to verdicts rendered by a single jury, to preclude acceptance of a guilty verdict on a telephone facilitation count where the jury acquits the defendant of the predicate felony." We rejected this argument, reasoning that issue preclusion is "predicated on the assumption that the jury acted rationally."

Arguing that a jury that acquits on some counts while inexplicably hanging on others is not rational, the Government contends that issue preclusion is as inappropriate in this case as it was in *Powell*. There are two serious flaws in this line of reasoning. First, it takes Powell's treatment of inconsistent verdicts and imports it into an entirely different context involving both verdicts and seemingly inconsistent hung counts. But the situations are quite dissimilar. In *Powell*, respect for the jury's verdicts counseled giving each verdict full effect, however inconsistent. As we explained, the jury's verdict "brings to the criminal process, in addition to the collective judgment of the community, an element of needed finality." By comparison, hung counts have never been accorded respect as a matter of law or history, and are not similar to jury verdicts in any relevant sense. By equating them, the Government's argument fails. Second, the Government's reliance on *Powell* assumes that a mistried count

can, in context, be evidence of irrationality. But, as we explained above, the fact that a jury hangs is evidence of nothing—other than, of course, that it has failed to decide anything. By relying on hung counts to question the basis of the jury's verdicts, the Government violates the very assumption of rationality it invokes for support.

At bottom, the Government misreads our cases that have rejected attempts to question the validity of a jury's verdict. In *Powell* and, before that, in *Dunn*, we were faced with jury verdicts that, on their face, were logically inconsistent and yet we refused to impugn the legitimacy of either verdict. In this case, there is merely a suggestion that the jury may have acted irrationally. And instead of resting that suggestion on a verdict, the Government relies on a hung count, the thinnest reed of all. If the Court in *Powell* and *Dunn* declined to use a clearly inconsistent verdict to second-guess the soundness of another verdict, then, a fortiori, a potentially inconsistent hung count could not command a different result.

IV

* * *

V

The judgment is reversed, and the case is remanded to the Court of Appeals for further proceedings consistent with this opinion.

The opinion by JUSTICE KENNEDY, concurring in part and concurring in the judgment, is omitted.

JUSTICE SCALIA, with whom JUSTICE THOMAS and JUSTICE ALITO join, dissenting.

* * *

I

* * * This case would be easy indeed if our cases had adhered to the Clause's original meaning. The English common-law pleas of auterfoits acquit and auterfoits convict, on which the Clause was based, barred only repeated "prosecution for the same identical act and crime." As described by Sir Matthew Hale, "a man acquitted for stealing [a] horse" could be later "arraigned and convict[ed] for stealing the saddle, tho both were done at the same time." Under the common-law pleas, the jury's acquittal of Yeager on the fraud counts would have posed no bar to further prosecution for the distinct crimes of insider trading and money laundering.

But that is water over the dam. In *Ashe* the Court departed from the original meaning of the Double Jeopardy Clause, holding that it precludes successive prosecutions on distinct crimes when facts essential to conviction of the second crime have necessarily been resolved in the defendant's favor by a verdict of acquittal of the first crime. Even if I am to adhere to *Ashe* on stare decisis grounds, today's holding is an illogical extension of that case. *Ashe* held only that the Clause sometimes bars successive prosecution of facts found during "a prior proceeding." But today the Court bars retrial on hung counts after what was not, under this Court's theory of "continuing jeopardy," Justices of Boston Municipal Court v. Lydon, 466 U. S. 294, 308 (1984), a prior proceeding but simply an earlier stage of the same proceeding.

As an historical matter, the common-law pleas could be invoked only once there had been a conviction or an acquittal—after a complete trial. This Court has extended the protections of the Double Jeopardy Clause by holding that jeopardy attaches earlier: at the time a jury is empanelled and sworn. Although one might think that this early attachment would mean that any second trial with a new jury would constitute a second jeopardy, the Court amended its innovation by holding that discharge of a deadlocked jury does not "terminat[e] the original jeopardy," Richardson v. United States, 468 U. S. 317, 325 (1984). Under this continuing-jeopardy principle, retrial after a jury has failed to reach a verdict is not a new trial but part of the same proceeding.

Today's holding is inconsistent with this principle. It interprets the Double Jeopardy Clause, for the first time, to have effect internally within a single prosecution, even though the criminal proceedings against the accused have not run their full course. As a conceptual matter, it makes no sense to say that events occurring within a single prosecution can cause an accused to be "twice put in jeopardy." And our cases, until today, have acknowledged that. Ever since Dunn v. United States, 284 U. S. 390, 393 (1932), we have refused to set aside convictions that were inconsistent with acquittals in the same trial; and we made clear in United States v. Powell, 469 U. S. 57, 64–65 (1984), that *Ashe* does not mandate a different result. There is no reason to treat perceived inconsistencies between hung counts and acquittals any differently.

* * *

Jeopardy is commenced and terminated charge by charge, not issue by issue. And if the prosecution's failure to present sufficient evidence at a first trial cannot prevent retrial on a hung count because the retrial is considered part of the same proceeding, then there is no basis for invoking *Ashe* to prevent retrial in the present case. If a conviction can stand with a contradictory acquittal when both are pronounced at the same trial, there is no reason why an acquittal should prevent the State from pressing for a contradictory conviction in the continuation of the prosecution on the hung counts.

II

The Court's extension of *Ashe* to these circumstances cannot even be justified based on the rationales underlying that holding. Invoking issue preclusion to bar seriatim prosecutions has the salutary effect of preventing the Government from circumventing acquittals by forcing defendants "to 'run the gantlet' a second time" on effectively the same charges .. In cases where the prosecution merely seeks to get "one full and fair opportunity to convict" on all charges brought in an initial indictment, there is no risk of such gamesmanship. * * *

Moreover, barring retrial when a jury acquits on some counts and hangs on others bears only a tenuous relationship to preserving the finality of "an issue of ultimate fact [actually] determined by a valid and final judgment." *Ashe*, supra, at 443. There is no clear, unanimous jury finding here. In the unusual situation in which a factual finding upon which an acquittal must have been based would also logically require an acquittal on the hung count, all that can be said for certain is that the conflicting dispositions are irrational—the result of mistake, compromise, or lenity. It is at least as likely that the irrationality consisted of failing to make the factual finding necessary to support the acquittal as it is that the irrationality consisted of failing to adhere to that factual finding with respect to the hung count. While I agree that courts should avoid speculation as to why a jury reached a particular result, the Court's opinion steps in the wrong direction by pretending that the acquittals here mean something that they in all probability do not. * * *

* * *

Until today, this Court has consistently held that retrial after a jury has been unable to reach a verdict is part of the original prosecution and that there can be no second jeopardy where there has been no second prosecution. Because I believe holding that line against this extension of *Ashe* is more consistent with the Court's cases and with the original meaning of the Double Jeopardy Clause, I would affirm the judgment.

[The dissenting opinion by JUSTICE ALITO, joined by JUSTICE SCALIA and JUSTICE THOMAS, is omitted.]

Chapter Thirteen

POST-CONVICTION CHALLENGES

II. GROUNDS FOR DIRECT ATTACKS ON A CONVICTION

C. NEWLY DISCOVERED EVIDENCE CLAIMS

Page 1602. Add to the section on "New Forensic Techniques"

In District Attorney's Office for the Third Judicial District v. Osborne, 129 S.Ct. 2308 (2009), a convicted defendant argued that he had a constitutional right to DNA testing that he claimed would exonerate him. The state had in fact conducted a rudimentary form of DNA testing before the trial; that test tended to include Osborne as a possible perpetrator in a sex crime, but it was not definitive. Osborne's counsel decided not to ask for a more sophisticated test to be done, fearing that it would further incriminate Osborne. Osborne was convicted and several years later brought a civil rights action against the state, alleging that he had a due process right to an even more sophisticated DNA test than was available at the time of his trial.

In a 5–4 opinion, the Court held that convicted defendants have no freestanding due process right to DNA testing. Chief Justice Roberts, writing for the majority, declared as follows:

> DNA testing has an unparalleled ability both to exonerate the wrongly convicted and to identify the guilty. It has the potential to significantly improve both the criminal justice system and police investigative practices. The Federal Government and the States have recognized this, and have developed special approaches to ensure that this evidentiary tool can be effectively incorporated into established criminal procedure—usually but not always through legislation.

> Against this prompt and considered response, the respondent, William Osborne, proposes a different approach: the recognition of a freestanding and far-reaching constitutional right of access to this new type of evidence. The nature of what he seeks is confirmed by his decision to file this lawsuit in federal court under 42 U. S. C.

§ 1983, not within the state criminal justice system. This approach would take the development of rules and procedures in this area out of the hands of legislatures and state courts shaping policy in a focused manner and turn it over to federal courts applying the broad parameters of the Due Process Clause. There is no reason to constitutionalize the issue in this way. Because the decision below would do just that, we reverse.

The lower court, in granting Osborne's demand for DNA testing, had relied on *Brady*. It reasoned that if the defendant had a constitutional right to exculpatory evidence before trial, he also had the right after conviction. Chief Justice Roberts rejected this reasoning in the following passage:

> The Court of Appeals went too far * * * in concluding that the Due Process Clause requires that certain familiar preconviction trial rights be extended to protect Osborne's postconviction liberty interest. After identifying Osborne's possible liberty interests, the court concluded that the State had an obligation to comply with the principles of Brady v. Maryland. In that case, we held that due process requires a prosecutor to disclose material exculpatory evidence to the defendant before trial. * * *

> A defendant proved guilty after a fair trial does not have the same liberty interests as a free man. At trial, the defendant is presumed innocent and may demand that the government prove its case beyond reasonable doubt. But once a defendant has been afforded a fair trial and convicted of the offense for which he was charged, the presumption of innocence disappears. * * *

> The State accordingly has more flexibility in deciding what procedures are needed in the context of postconviction relief. "[W]hen a State chooses to offer help to those seeking relief from convictions," due process does not "dictat[e] the exact form such assistance must assume." Pennsylvania v. Finley, 481 U.S. 551, 559 (1987). Osborne's right to due process is not parallel to a trial right, but rather must be analyzed in light of the fact that he has already been found guilty at a fair trial, and has only a limited interest in postconviction relief. Brady is the wrong framework.

> Instead, the question is whether consideration of Osborne's claim within the framework of the State's procedures for postconviction relief "offends some principle of justice so rooted in the traditions and conscience of our people as to be ranked as fundamental," or "transgresses any recognized principle of fundamental fairness in operation." Federal courts may upset a State's postconviction relief procedures only if they are fundamentally inadequate to vindicate the substantive rights provided.

> We see nothing inadequate about the procedures Alaska has provided to vindicate its state right to postconviction relief in general, and nothing inadequate about how those procedures apply to those who seek access to DNA evidence. Alaska provides a

substantive right to be released on a sufficiently compelling showing of new evidence that establishes innocence. It exempts such claims from otherwise applicable time limits. The State provides for discovery in postconviction proceedings, and has—through judicial decision—specified that this discovery procedure is available to those seeking access to DNA evidence. These procedures are not without limits. The evidence must indeed be newly available to qualify under Alaska's statute, must have been diligently pursued, and must also be sufficiently material. These procedures are similar to those provided for DNA evidence by federal law and the law of other States, see, e.g., 18 U. S. C. § 3600(a), and they are not inconsistent with the "traditions and conscience of our people" or with "any recognized principle of fundamental fairness."

* * *

To the degree there is some uncertainty in the details of Alaska's newly developing procedures for obtaining postconviction access to DNA, we can hardly fault the State for that. Osborne has brought this § 1983 action without ever using these procedures in filing a state or federal habeas claim relying on actual innocence. In other words, he has not tried to use the process provided to him by the State or attempted to vindicate the liberty interest that is now the centerpiece of his claim. * * * His attempt to sidestep state process through a new federal lawsuit puts Osborne in a very awkward position. If he simply seeks the DNA through the State's discovery procedures, he might well get it. If he does not, it may be for a perfectly adequate reason, just as the federal statute and all state statutes impose conditions and limits on access to DNA evidence. It is difficult to criticize the State's procedures when Osborne has not invoked them. This is not to say that Osborne must exhaust state-law remedies. But it is Osborne's burden to demonstrate the inadequacy of the state-law procedures available to him in state postconviction relief. These procedures are adequate on their face, and without trying them, Osborne can hardly complain that they do not work in practice.

The Chief Justice concluded as follows:

DNA evidence will undoubtedly lead to changes in the criminal justice system. It has done so already. The question is whether further change will primarily be made by legislative revision and judicial interpretation of the existing system, or whether the Federal Judiciary must leap ahead-revising (or even discarding) the system by creating a new constitutional right and taking over responsibility for refining it.

Federal courts should not presume that state criminal procedures will be inadequate to deal with technological change. The criminal justice system has historically accommodated new types of evidence, and is a time-tested means of carrying out society's interest in convicting the guilty while respecting individual rights. That system, like any human endeavor, cannot be perfect. DNA evidence shows that it has not been. But there is no basis for Osborne's approach of assuming that because DNA has shown that these procedures are not flawless, DNA evidence must be treated as categorically outside the process, rather than within it. That is precisely what his § 1983 suit seeks to do, and that is the contention we reject.

Justice Alito filed a concurring opinion in which Justice Kennedy, joined, and in which Justice Thomas joined in part. He argued that it would be inappropriate to allow Osborne to forego testing at trial and then to request a different test many years later. In Justice Alito's view, this would "allow prisoners to play games with the criminal justice system" because "with nothing to lose, the defendant could demand DNA testing in the hope that some happy accident—for example, degradation or contamination of the evidence—would provide the basis for postconviction relief."

Justice Stevens filed a dissenting opinion, joined by Justices Ginsburg and Breyer and by Justice Souter in part. Justice Stevens argued that the state had no legitimate interest in denying the test, because Osborne had agreed to pay for it; and the state's interest in finality could not outweigh a plausible claim of innocence. Justice Stevens concluded as follows:

> [A]n individual's interest in his physical liberty is one of constitutional significance. That interest would be vindicated by providing postconviction access to DNA evidence, as would the State's interest in ensuring that it punishes the true perpetrator of a crime. In this case, the State has suggested no countervailing interest that justifies its refusal to allow Osborne to test the evidence in its possession and has not provided any other nonarbitrary explanation for its conduct. Consequently, I am left to conclude that the State's failure to provide Osborne access to the evidence constitutes arbitrary action that offends basic principles of due process. On that basis, I would affirm the judgment of the Ninth Circuit.

Justice Souter also filed a dissenting opinion, concluding that state officials had "demonstrated a combination of inattentiveness and intransigence that add up to "procedural unfairness that violates the due process clause.".

D. THE EFFECT OF AN ERROR ON THE VERDICT

1. Harmless Error

Page 1611. Add after the entry on Gonzalez–Lopez.

Breach of Plea Agreement Is Not a Structural Error Justifying Automatic Relief: Puckett v. United States

In Puckett v. United States, 129 S.Ct. 1423 (2009), Puckett entered into a plea agreement under which the government agreed to support a reduction of Puckett's sentence for acceptance of responsibility. But at the sentencing proceeding the government opposed a sentence reduction on those grounds. Yet Puckett's counsel did not object to, or even mention, the government's breach of its plea agreement. On appeal Puckett raised the issue of breach, but the reviewing court found that he had forfeited his claim of error. It reviewed for plain error and found none—specifically finding that the error did not affect Puckett's substantial rights because the sentencing court indicated that it would not reduce his sentence in any case.

In the Supreme Court, Puckett argued that the plain error standard was inappropriate because a breach of a plea agreement amounts to a "structural error"—rendering it unnecessary to show prejudice and mandating automatic relief. But the Supreme Court, in an opinion by Justice Scalia, rejected this argument. Justice Scalia declared as follows:

> This Court has several times declined to resolve whether "structural" errors—those that affect "the framework within which the trial proceeds," Arizona v. Fulminante, 499 U.S. 279, 310 (1991)—automatically satisfy the third prong of the plain-error test. Once again we need not answer that question, because breach of a plea deal is not a "structural" error as we have used that term. We have never described it as such, and it shares no common features with errors we have held structural. A plea breach does not "necessarily render a criminal trial fundamentally unfair or an unreliable vehicle for determining guilt or innocence," Neder v. United States, 527 U.S. 1, 9 (1999); it does not "defy analysis by harmless-error standards" by affecting the entire adjudicatory framework; and the "difficulty of assessing the effect of the error," United States v. Gonzalez–Lopez, 548 U.S. 140, 149, n. 4 (2006), is no greater with respect to plea breaches at sentencing than with respect to other procedural errors at sentencing, which are routinely subject to harmlessness review.

Puckett argued that the Court established an automatic reversal rule for breach of a plea agreement in Santobello v. New York, 404 U.S. 257 (1971) [discussed in the Text at page 1076]. But Justice Scalia emphasized that *Santobello* was a case in which the defendant had properly preserved his claim of error.

Santobello's holding "rested not upon the premise that plea—breach errors are (like 'structural' errors) somehow not susceptible, or not amenable, to review for harmlessness, but rather upon a policy interest in establishing the trust between defendants and prosecutors that is necessary to sustain plea bargaining-an 'essential' and 'highly desirable' part of the criminal process. But the rule of contemporaneous objection is equally essential and desirable, and when the two collide we see no need to relieve the defendant of his usual burden of showing prejudice."

Justice Souter, joined by Justice Stevens, dissented.

Improper Denial of a Peremptory Challenge Is Not Automatically Reversible: Rivera v. Illinois

The defendant in Rivera v. Illinois, 129 S.Ct. 1446 (2009), exercised a peremptory challenge at trial. The trial judge denied the challenge and seated the juror (who ended up serving as foreperson). The trial judge concluded that the defendant struck the juror on impermissible grounds under *Batson*. Rivera was convicted and appealed on the ground that he had a proper reason for striking the juror. The appellate court agreed, but nonetheless affirmed the conviction, on the ground that the trial court's error in seating the juror was harmless: Rivera conceded that the jury (including the juror he sought to strike) was unbiased. Rivera argued, however, that automatic reversal was necessary because it was impossible to tell whether the outcome would have been different had the juror been struck.

The Court, in a unanimous opinion by Justice Ginsburg, held that an improper denial of a peremptory strike did not warrant an automatic reversal. Justice Ginsburg emphasized that the defendant has no constitutional right to a peremptory challenge, and concluded as follows:

> If a defendant is tried before a qualified jury composed of individuals not challengeable for cause, the loss of a peremptory challenge due to a state court's good-faith error is not a matter of federal constitutional concern. Rather, it is a matter for the State to address under its own laws.

2. Plain Error

Page 1616. Add the following at the end of the section:

Plain Error Standard Applies to Forfeited Objection on Breach of Plea Agreement: Puckett v. United States

In Puckett v. United States, 129 S.Ct. 1423 (2009), Puckett entered into a plea agreement under which the government agreed to support a reduction of Puckett's sentence for acceptance of responsibility. But at the sentencing proceeding the government opposed a sentence reduction on those grounds. Yet Puckett's counsel did not object to, or even mention, the government's breach of its plea agreement. On appeal Puckett raised the issue of breach, but the reviewing court found that he had forfeited his claim of error. It reviewed for plain error and found none—specifically finding that the error did not affect Puckett's substantial rights because the sentencing court indicated that it would not reduce his sentence in any case.

In the Supreme Court, Puckett argued that the plain error standard was inappropriate when the error was the breach of a plea agreement. But the Court, in an opinion by Justice Scalia, disagreed. Justice Scalia reviewed the plain error doctrine, and found it applicable to the instant case, in the following passage:

> If a litigant believes that an error has occurred (to his detriment) during a federal judicial proceeding, he must object in order to preserve the issue. If he fails to do so in a timely manner, his claim for relief from the error is forfeited. "No procedural principle is more familiar to this Court than that a ... right may be forfeited in criminal as well as civil cases by the failure to make timely assertion of the right before a tribunal having jurisdiction to determine it." Yakus v. United States, 321 U.S. 414, 444 (1944).

> If an error is not properly preserved, appellate-court authority to remedy the error (by reversing the judgment, for example, or ordering a new trial) is strictly circumscribed. There is good reason for this; "anyone familiar with the work of courts understands that errors are a constant in the trial process, that most do not much matter, and that a reflexive inclination by appellate courts to reverse because of unpreserved error would be fatal." United States v. Padilla, 415 F.3d 211, 224 (C.A.1 2005) (en banc) (Boudin, C. J., concurring).

> This limitation on appellate-court authority serves to induce the timely raising of claims and objections, which gives the district court the opportunity to consider and resolve them. That court is ordinarily in the best position to determine the relevant facts and adjudicate the dispute. In the case of an actual or invited procedural error, the district court can often correct or avoid the mistake so that it cannot possibly affect the ultimate outcome. And of course the contemporaneous-objection rule prevents a litigant from " 'sandbagging' " the court—remaining silent about his objection and belatedly raising the error only if the case does not conclude in his favor.

> In federal criminal cases, Rule 51(b) tells parties how to preserve claims of error: "by informing the court—when the court ruling or order is made or sought—of the action the party wishes the court to take, or the party's objection to the court's action and the grounds for that objection." Failure to abide by this contemporaneous-objection rule ordinarily precludes the raising on appeal of the unpreserved claim of trial error. Rule 52(b), however, recognizes a limited exception to that preclusion. The Rule provides, in full: "A

plain error that affects substantial rights may be considered even though it was not brought to the court's attention."

* * *

We have repeatedly cautioned that any unwarranted extension of the authority granted by Rule 52(b) would disturb the careful balance it strikes between judicial efficiency and the redress of injustice; and that the creation of an unjustified exception to the Rule would be even less appropriate. The real question in this case is not whether plain-error review applies when a defendant fails to preserve a claim that the Government defaulted on its plea-agreement obligations, but rather what conceivable reason exists for disregarding its evident application. Such a breach is undoubtedly a violation of the defendant's rights, see Santobello v. New York, 404 U.S. 257, 262 (1971) [discussed in Chapter 9 of the Text], but the defendant has the opportunity to seek vindication of those rights in district court; if he fails to do so, Rule 52(b) as clearly sets forth the consequences for that forfeiture as it does for all others.

Justice Souter, joined by Justice Stevens, dissented.

Appellate Court May Not Invoke Plain Error to Increase a Sentence in the Absence of a Government Appeal: *Greenlaw v. United States*

In Greenlaw v. United States, 128 S.Ct. 2559 (2008), the defendant appealed from his sentence, and the government filed no cross-appeal. The court of appeals rejected the defendant's challenge to his sentence and then proceeded *sua sponte* to determine whether the defendant's sentence was too low. Relying on the doctrine of plain error, the court of appeals entered an order increasing the defendant's sentence by 15 years. The Supreme Court, in an opinion by Justice Ginsburg for six Justices, held that the court of appeals could not use the plain error doctrine to increase a sentence from which the government had not appealed.

Justice Ginsburg relied on 18 U.S.C. § 3742(b), which provides that the government may not appeal a sentence "without the personal approval of the Attorney General, the Solicitor General, or a deputy solicitor general designated by the Solicitor General." She declared that "Congress, in § 3742(b), has accorded to the top representatives of the United States in litigation the prerogative to seek or forgo appellate correction of sentencing errors, however plain they may be. That measure should garner the Judiciary's full respect."

Justice Ginsburg found nothing in the plain error rule, Fed.R.Crim. P.52, to change the result mandated by 18 U.S.C. § 3742(b). She noted that the Court had ordered correction of plain errors not raised by defendants, "but we have done so only to benefit a defendant who had himself petitioned the Court for review on other grounds. In no case have we applied plain-error doctrine to the detriment of a petitioning party.'' Moreover, even if there might be circumstances in which it would be proper for an appellate court to initiate plain-error review, ''sentencing errors that the Government refrained from pursuing would not fit the bill'' because ''Congress has provided a dispositive direction regarding sentencing errors that aggrieve the Government. In § 3742(b), as earlier explained, Congress designated leading Department of Justice officers as the decisionmakers responsible for determining when Government pursuit of a sentencing appeal is in order. Those high officers, Congress recognized, are best equipped to determine where the Government's interest lies. Rule 52(b) does not invite appellate court interference with their assessment.''

Justice Alito, joined by Justices Breyer and Stevens, dissented. He argued that § 3742(b) ''does not apportion authority over sentencing appeals between the Executive and Judicial Branches. By its terms, § 3742(b) simply apportions that authority *within* an executive department.'' According to Justice Alito, the rule that conditions increase of a sentence on an appeal from the government was one of ''trial practice'' that did not prevent an appellate court from increasing the sentences under the narrow circumstances permitted by the plain error rule.

III. COLLATERAL ATTACK

A. REMEDIES GENERALLY

3. *Habeas Corpus*

Page 1621. At the end of the entry on ''Congressional Power to Restrict Habeas Corpus'' add the following:

In Boumediene v. Bush, 128 S.Ct. 2229 (2008), a five-Justice majority invalidated the provision of the Military Commissions Act that purported to deprive the federal courts of habeas jurisdiction over the proceedings against alleged enemy combatants detained at Guantanamo. The Court held that this provision of the Military Commissions Act operated as a suspension of the writ of habeas corpus. The Court rejected the government's argument that the alternative procedures provided by the Act were the functional equivalent of the habeas remedy. The Court's opinion in *Boumediene*, together with the vigorous dissents filed by Chief Justice Roberts and Justice Scalia, are set forth at the end of the materials on Chapter 10 of this supplement, under the section discussing treatment of enemy combatants.

D. LIMITATIONS ON OBTAINING HABEAS RELIEF

7. *Limitations on Obtaining a Hearing*

Page 1688. Add at the end of the section:

In Schriro v. Landrigan, 550 U.S. 465 (2007), the Court found that a district court had not abused its discretion in refusing to grant a habeas petitioner's request for an evidentiary hearing to develop the facts supporting defense counsel's alleged ineffectiveness at a capital sentencing proceeding. Justice Thomas, writing for five members of the court, first set forth the applicable law governing the granting of an evidentiary hearing on a habeas petition:

> Prior to the Antiterrorism and Effective Death Penalty Act of 1996 (AEDPA), the decision to grant an evidentiary hearing was generally left to the sound discretion of district courts. * * * AEDPA, however, changed the standards for granting federal habeas relief. Under AEDPA, Congress prohibited federal courts from granting habeas relief unless a state court's adjudication of a claim "resulted in a decision that was contrary to, or involved an unreasonable application of, clearly established Federal law, as determined by the Supreme Court of the United States," § 2254(d)(1), or the relevant state-court decision "was based on an unreasonable determination of the facts in light of the evidence presented in the State court proceeding" § 2254(d)(2). The question under AEDPA is not whether a federal court believes the state court's determination was incorrect but whether that determination was unreasonable—a substantially higher threshold. *See Williams v. Taylor*, 529 U.S. 362, 410 (2000). AEDPA also requires federal habeas courts to presume the correctness of state courts' factual findings unless applicants rebut this presumption with "clear and convincing evidence." § 2254(e)(1).

> In deciding whether to grant an evidentiary hearing, a federal court must consider whether such a hearing could enable an applicant to prove the petition's factual allegations, which, if true, would entitle the applicant to federal habeas relief. Because the deferential standards prescribed by § 2254 control whether to grant habeas relief, a federal court must take into account those standards in deciding whether an evidentiary hearing is appropriate. * * *

> It follows that if the record refutes the applicant's factual allegations or otherwise precludes habeas relief, a district court is not required to hold an evidentiary hearing. * * *

Justice Thomas found that the record in the instant case demonstrated that the defendant himself objected to pursuing any avenues of mitigating evidence. Therefore the district court did not abuse discretion in refusing to grant an evidentiary hearing on counsel's effectiveness.

Justice Stevens, joined by Justices Souter, Ginsburg and Breyer, dissented. He argued that the record was not as clear as the majority would have it, and that at any rate defense counsel's effectiveness was not dependent on the defendant's willingness to agree to admitting favorable evidence.

The full opinion in *Landrigan* is reproduced in Chapter 10 of this supplement, in the section on effective assistance of counsel.

8. *Harmless Error in Habeas Corpus Cases*

Page 1691. At the end of the text, add the following note on harmless error, followed by a new section on the possibility of habeas relief for an American citizen suspected of criminal activity in a foreign country:

Brecht Standard of Harmlessness Applies When State Court Made No Harmlessness Review: Fry v. Pliler

In Fry v. Pliler, 551 U.S. 112 (2007), the Court held that a federal habeas court must assess the prejudicial impact of constitutional error in a state-court criminal trial under the "substantial and injurious effect" standard set forth in Brecht v. Abrahamson, 507 U.S. 619 (1993), when the state appellate court failed to recognize the error and did not review it for harmlessness under the "harmless beyond a reasonable doubt" standard set forth in Chapman v. California, 386 U.S. 18 (1967). Justice Scalia wrote for a unanimous Court except for footnote 1 and Part II B of the opinion.

Fry was convicted of murder in a California state court after two mistrials due to hung juries. Fry claimed that the trial judge violated Chambers v. Mississippi, 410 U.S. 284 (1973), in excluding the testimony of a witness who heard another man discussing murders that bore similarity to the two murders charged to Fry. (The Court in *Chambers* held that exclusion of a reliable statement that was critical to the defendant's case violated the defendant's constitutional right to an effective defense.) The California Court of Appeal affirmed Fry's convictions. It did not explicitly address the *Chambers* argument, but stated, without specifying the harmless error standard it was applying, that "no possible prejudice" could have resulted in light of the cumulative nature of the excluded witness's testimony. The California Supreme Court denied review. A federal Magistrate Judge found that the State Court of Appeals' failure to recognize *Chambers* error was an unreasonable application of clearly established United States Supreme Court law and disagreed with the "no possible prejudice" conclusion. But, the Magistrate Judge concluded that there was an insufficient showing that the improper exclusion had a "substantial and injurious effect" on the jury's verdict. The District Court denied relief, and the Ninth Circuit affirmed.

In footnote 1 of his opinion, Justice Scalia wrote the following: "As this case comes to the Court, we assume (without deciding) that the state appellate court's decision affirming the exclusion of Maples' testimony was an unreasonable application of Chambers v. Mississippi, 410 U.S. 284, 302 (1973). We also assume that the state appellate court did not determine the harmlessness of the error under the *Chapman* standard, notwithstanding its ambiguous conclusion that the exclusion of Maples' testimony resulted in 'no possible prejudice.' "

Justice Scalia reasoned that the Court's decision in *Brecht* to apply the more permissive Kotteakos v. United States, 328 U.S. 750 (1946), standard of review rather than the *Chapman* standard did not turn on whether the state court itself conducted *Chapman* review. Rather, *Brecht* represented a judgment that application of the high threshold of *Chapman* would undermine the state's interest in finality, infringe on state sovereignty over criminal matters, and undercut the historic limitation on the reach of habeas corpus. He noted that the *Brecht* Court clearly assumed that the *Kotteakos* standard would apply to virtually all state habeas petitioners, and suggested an exception only for the "unusual case" in which "a deliberate and especially egregious error of the trial type, or one that is combined with a pattern of prosecutorial misconduct . . . infect[s] the integrity of the proceeding."

In Part II B of the opinion, Justice Scalia concluded that Fry's argument that the trial court's error met even the *Brecht* standard of harmlessness was not fairly encompassed within the question presented on certiorari. Chief Justice Roberts and Justices Kennedy, Thomas and Alito agreed.

Justice Stevens, joined by Justices Souter and Ginsburg, and in part by Justice Breyer, argued that the Court should answer the question whether the exclusion of the witness at Fry's trial substantially and injuriously affected the jury's verdict, and that "[b]oth the history of this litigation and the nature of the constitutional error involved provide powerful support for the conclusion that if jurors had heard the testimony of Pamela Maples, they would at least have had a reasonable doubt concerning petitioner's guilt." Justice Stevens emphasized the following factors to indicate the importance of the excluded evidence to the outcome: there were two mistrials; the only eyewitness described the killer as 5'7" to 5'8" and weighing about 140 pounds while Fry was 6'2" and weighed 300 pounds; seven different witnesses linked the killing to another man; and the jury deliberated for a total of five weeks before returning a guilty verdict against Fry.

Justice Breyer's opinion, concurring in part and dissenting in part, agreed with the majority on the *Brecht* test for habeas cases and with Justice Stevens that the Court should reach the harmless error question on the merits. He would have remanded the case for the Court of Appeals to make a determination as to whether there was a *Chambers* violation.

9. *Limitations on Habeas Relief When It Impacts Interests of a Foreign Sovereign*

In the following case, the Court considers whether habeas relief is available to prevent an American citizen suspected of criminal activity in a foreign country from being transferred to the authorities of that country. The backdrop is the War in Iraq. Note the Court's distinction between habeas jurisdiction and habeas relief.

MUNAF v. GEREN

Supreme Court of the United States, 2008.
551 U.S. 47.

CHIEF JUSTICE ROBERTS **delivered the opinion of the Court.**

The Multinational Force–Iraq (MNF–I) is an international coalition force operating in Iraq composed of 26 different nations, including the United States. The force operates under the unified command of United States military officers, at the request of the Iraqi Government, and in accordance with United Nations (U. N.) Security Council Resolutions. Pursuant to the U. N. mandate, MNF–I forces detain individuals alleged to have committed hostile or warlike acts in Iraq, pending investigation and prosecution in Iraqi courts under Iraqi law.

These consolidated cases concern the availability of habeas corpus relief arising from the MNF–I's detention of American citizens who voluntarily traveled to Iraq and are alleged to have committed crimes there. We are confronted with two questions. *First*, do United States courts have jurisdiction over habeas corpus petitions filed on behalf of American citizens challenging their detention in Iraq by the MNF–I? *Second*, if such jurisdiction exists, may district courts exercise that jurisdiction to enjoin the MNF–I from transferring such individuals to Iraqi custody or allowing them to be tried before Iraqi courts?

We conclude that the habeas statute extends to American citizens held overseas by American forces operating subject to an American chain of command, even when those forces are acting as part of a multinational coalition. Under circumstances such as those presented here, however, habeas corpus provides petitioners with no relief.

I

Pursuant to its U. N. mandate, the MNF–I has " 'the authority to take all necessary measures to contribute to the maintenance of security and stability in Iraq.' " App. G to Pet. for Cert. in 07–394, p. 74a, P10 (quoting U. N. Security Council, U. N. Doc. S/Res/1546, P10 (June 2004)). To this end, the MNF–I engages in a variety of military and humanitarian activities. The multinational force, for example, conducts combat operations against insurgent factions, trains and equips Iraqi security forces, and aids in relief and reconstruction efforts.

MNF–I forces also detain individuals who pose a threat to the security of Iraq. The Government of Iraq retains ultimate responsibility for the arrest and imprisonment of individuals who violate its laws, but because many of Iraq's prison facilities have been destroyed, the MNF–I agreed to maintain physical custody of many such individuals during Iraqi criminal proceedings. MNF–I forces are currently holding approximately 24,000 detainees. An American military unit, Task Force 134, oversees detention operations and facilities in Iraq, including those located at Camp Cropper, the detention facility currently housing Shawqi Omar and Mohammad Munaf (hereinafter petitioners). The unit is under the command of United States military officers who report to General David Petraeus.

A

Petitioner Shawqi Omar, an American–Jordanian citizen, voluntarily traveled to Iraq in 2002. In October 2004, Omar was captured and detained in Iraq by U.S. military forces operating as part of the MNF–I during a raid of his Baghdad home. Omar is believed to have provided aid to Abu Musab al-Zarqawi—the late leader of al Qaeda in Iraq—by facilitating his group's connection with other terrorist groups, bringing foreign fighters into Iraq, and planning and executing kidnappings in Iraq. MNF–I searched his home in an effort to capture and detain insurgents who were associated with al-Zarqawi. The raid netted an Iraqi insurgent and four Jordanian fighters along with explosive devices and other weapons.

The captured insurgents gave sworn statements implicating Omar in insurgent cell activities. The four Jordanians testified that they had traveled to Iraq with Omar to commit militant acts against American and other Coalition Forces. Each of the insurgents stated that, while living in Omar's home, they had surveilled potential kidnap victims and conducted weapons training. The insurgents explained that Omar's fluency in English allowed him to lure foreigners to his home in order to kidnap and sell them for ransom.

Following Omar's arrest, a three-member MNF–I Tribunal composed of American military officers concluded that Omar posed a threat to the security of Iraq and designated him a "security internee." The tribunal also found that Omar had committed hostile and warlike acts, and that he was an enemy combatant in the war on terrorism. In accordance with Article 5 of the Geneva Convention, Omar was permitted to hear the basis for his detention, make a statement, and call immediately available witnesses.

In addition to the review of his detention by the MNF–I Tribunal, Omar received a hearing before the Combined Review and Release Board (CRRB)—a nine-member board composed of six representatives of the Iraqi Government and three MNF–I officers. The CRRB, like the MNF–I Tribunal, concluded that Omar's continued detention was necessary because he posed a threat to Iraqi security. At all times since his capture, Omar has remained in the custody of the United States military operating as part of the MNF–I.

Omar's wife and son filed a next-friend petition for a writ of habeas corpus on Omar's behalf in the District Court for the District of Columbia. After the Department of Justice informed Omar that the MNF–I had decided to refer him to the Central Criminal Court of Iraq (CCCI) for criminal proceedings, his attorney sought and obtained a preliminary injunction barring Omar's "remov[al] . . . from United States or MNF–I custody." * * * The United States appealed and the Court of Appeals for the District of Columbia Circuit affirmed. The Court of Appeals first upheld the District Court's exercise of habeas jurisdiction, finding that this Court's decision in Hirota v. MacArthur, 338 U.S. 197 (1948) did not preclude review. The Court of Appeals distinguished *Hirota* on the ground that

Omar, unlike the petitioner in that case, had yet to be convicted by a foreign tribunal. The Court of Appeals recognized, however, that the writ of habeas corpus could not be used to enjoin release. It therefore construed the injunction only to bar transfer to Iraqi custody and upheld the District Court's order insofar as it prohibited the United States from: (1) transferring Omar to Iraqi custody, (2) sharing details concerning any decision to release Omar with the Iraqi Government; and (3) presenting Omar to the Iraqi Courts for investigation and prosecution.

Judge Brown dissented. She joined the panel's jurisdictional ruling, but would have vacated the injunction because, in her view, the District Court had no authority to enjoin a transfer that would allow Iraqi officials to take custody of an individual captured in Iraq—something the Iraqi Government "undeniably h[ad] a right to do." * * *

B

Petitioner Munaf, a citizen of both Iraq and the United States, voluntarily traveled to Iraq with several Romanian journalists. He was to serve as the journalists' translator and guide. Shortly after arriving in Iraq, the group was kidnapped and held captive for two months. After the journalists were freed, MNF–I forces detained Munaf based on their belief that he had orchestrated the kidnappings.

A three-judge MNF–I Tribunal conducted a hearing to determine whether Munaf's detention was warranted. The MNF–I Tribunal reviewed the facts surrounding Munaf's capture, interviewed witnesses, and considered the available intelligence information. Munaf was present at the hearing and had an opportunity to hear the grounds for his detention, make a statement, and call immediately available witnesses. At the end of the hearing, the tribunal found that Munaf posed a serious threat to Iraqi security, designated him a "security internee," and referred his case to the CCCI for criminal investigation and prosecution.

During his CCCI trial, Munaf admitted on camera and in writing that he had facilitated the kidnapping of the Romanian journalists. He also appeared as a witness against his alleged co-conspirators. Later in the proceedings, Munaf recanted his confession, but the CCCI nonetheless found him guilty of kidnapping. On appeal, the Iraqi Court of Cassation vacated Munaf's conviction and remanded his case to the CCCI for further investigation. The Court of Cassation directed that Munaf was to "remain in custody pending the outcome" of further criminal proceedings. Ibid.

Meanwhile, Munaf's sister filed a next-friend petition for a writ of habeas corpus in the District Court for the District of Columbia. The District Court dismissed the petition for lack of jurisdiction, finding that this Court's decision in *Hirota* controlled: Munaf was "in the custody of coalition troops operating under the aegis of MNF–I, who derive their ultimate authority from the United Nations and the MNF–I member nations acting jointly." The Court of Appeals for the District of Columbia Circuit affirmed. The Court of Appeals, "[c]onstrained by precedent," agreed with the District Court that *Hirota* controlled and dismissed Munaf's petition for lack of jurisdiction. It distinguished the prior opinion in *Omar* on the ground that Munaf, like the habeas petitioner in *Hirota* but unlike Omar, had been convicted by a foreign tribunal. Judge Randolph concurred in the judgment. He concluded that the District Court had improperly dismissed for want of jurisdiction because "Munaf is an American citizen ... held by American forces overseas." Nevertheless, Judge Randolph would have held that Munaf's habeas petition failed on the merits. He relied on this Court's holding in Wilson v. Girard, 354 U.S. 524, 529 (1957), that a "sovereign nation has exclusive jurisdiction to punish offenses against its laws committed within its borders," and concluded that the fact that the United States was holding Munaf because of his conviction by a foreign tribunal was conclusive. * * *

II

The Solicitor General argues that the federal courts lack jurisdiction over the detainees' habeas petitions because the American forces holding Omar and Munaf operate as part of a multinational force. The habeas statute provides that a federal district court may entertain a habeas application by a person held "in custody under or by color of the authority of the United States," or "in custody in violation of the Constitution or laws or treaties of the United States." 28 U.S.C. §§ 2241(c)(1), (3). MNF–I forces, the argument goes, "are not operating solely under United States authority, but rather 'as the agent of' a multinational force." Omar and Munaf are thus held pursuant to international authority, not "the authori-

ty of the United States," § 2241(c)(1), and they are therefore not within the reach of the habeas statute.

The United States acknowledges that Omar and Munaf are American citizens held overseas in the immediate " 'physical custody' " of American soldiers who answer only to an American chain of command. The MNF–I itself operates subject to a unified American command. * * * In light of these admissions, it is unsurprising that the United States has never argued that it lacks the authority to release Munaf or Omar, or that it requires the consent of other countries to do so.

We think these concessions the end of the jurisdictional inquiry. The Government's argument—that the federal courts have no jurisdiction over American citizens held by American forces operating as multinational agents—is not easily reconciled with the text of § 2241(c)(1). That section applies to persons held "in custody under or by color of the authority of the United States." § 2241(c)(1). An individual is held "in custody" by the United States when the United States official charged with his detention has "the power to produce" him. The disjunctive "or" in § 2241(c)(1) makes clear that actual custody by the United States suffices for jurisdiction, even if that custody could be viewed as "under ... color of" another authority, such as the MNF–I.

The Government's primary contention is that the District Courts lack jurisdiction in these cases because of this Court's decision in *Hirota*. That slip of a case cannot bear the weight the Government would place on it. In *Hirota*, Japanese citizens sought permission to file habeas corpus applications directly in this Court. The petitioners were noncitizens detained in Japan. They had been convicted and sentenced by the International Military Tribunal for the Far East—an international tribunal established by General Douglas MacArthur acting, as the Court put it, in his capacity as "the agent of the Allied Powers." Although those familiar with the history of the period would appreciate the possibility of confusion over who General MacArthur took orders from, the Court concluded that the sentencing tribunal was "not a tribunal of the United States." * * *

The Court in *Hirota*, however, may have found it significant, in considering the nature of the tribunal established by General MacArthur, that the Solicitor General expressly contended that General MacArthur, as pertinent, was not subject to United States authority. * * *

Even if the Government is correct that the international authority at issue in *Hirota* is no different from the international authority at issue here, the present "circumstances" differ in another respect. These cases concern American citizens while *Hirota* did not, and the Court has indicated that habeas jurisdiction can depend on citizenship."Under the foregoing circumstances," we decline to extend our holding in *Hirota* to preclude American citizens held overseas by American soldiers subject to a United States chain of command from filing habeas petitions.

III

We now turn to the question whether United States district courts may exercise their habeas jurisdiction to enjoin our Armed Forces from transferring individuals detained within another sovereign's territory to that sovereign's government for criminal prosecution. The nature of that question requires us to proceed with the circumspection appropriate when this Court is adjudicating issues inevitably entangled in the conduct of our international relations. Here there is the further consideration that those issues arise in the context of ongoing military operations conducted by American Forces overseas. * * *

In *Omar*, the District Court granted and the D. C. Circuit upheld a preliminary injunction that, as interpreted by the Court of Appeals, prohibited the United States from (1) effectuating "Omar's transfer *in any form*, whether by an official handoff or otherwise," to Iraqi custody; (2) sharing details concerning any decision to release Omar with the Iraqi Government; and (3) "presenting Omar to the [Iraqi courts] for trial." This is not a narrow injunction. Even the habeas petitioners do not defend it in its entirety. They acknowledge the authority of the Iraqi courts to begin criminal proceedings against Omar and wisely concede that any injunction "clearly need not include a bar on 'information-sharing.' " As Judge Brown noted in her dissent, such a bar would impermissibly "enjoin the United States military from sharing information with an allied foreign sovereign in a war zone."

[The Court determined that a preliminary injunction should not have been entered given the close nature of the jurisdictional question, and the fact that the lower courts had not reviewed the merits of the habeas petition. It then proceeded to discuss the merits of that petition.]

Given that the present cases involve habeas petitions that implicate sensitive foreign policy issues in the context of ongoing military operations, reaching the merits is the wisest course. For the reasons we explain below, the relief sought by the habeas petitioners makes clear under our precedents that the power of the writ ought not to be exercised. Because the Government is entitled to judgment as a matter of law, it is appropriate for us to terminate the litigation now.

IV

The habeas petitioners argue that the writ should be granted in their cases because they have "a legally enforceable right" not to be transferred to Iraqi authority for criminal proceedings under both the Due Process Clause and the Foreign Affairs Reform and Restructuring Act of 1998 (FARR Act), div. G, 112 Stat. 2681–761, and because they are innocent civilians who have been unlawfully detained by the United States in violation of the Due Process Clause. With respect to the transfer claim, petitioners request an injunction prohibiting the United States from transferring them to Iraqi custody. With respect to the unlawful detention claim, petitioners seek "release"—but only to the extent that release would not result in "unlawful" transfer to Iraqi custody. Both of these requests would interfere with Iraq's sovereign right to "punish offenses against its laws committed within its borders." *Wilson*, 354 U.S., at 529. * * *

A

Habeas corpus is governed by equitable principles. We have therefore recognized that "prudential concerns," such as comity and the orderly administration of criminal justice, may "require a federal court to forgo the exercise of its habeas corpus power," Francis v. Henderson, 425 U.S. 536, 539 (1976).

The principle that a habeas court is "not bound in every case" to issue the writ, Ex parte Royall, 117 U.S. 241, 251 (1886), follows from the precatory language of the habeas statute, and from its common-law origins. The habeas statute provides only that a writ of habeas corpus "*may* be granted," § 2241(a), and directs federal courts to "dispose of [habeas petitions] as law and justice require," § 2243. * * *

At the outset, the nature of the relief sought by the habeas petitioners suggests that habeas is not appropriate in these cases. Habeas is at its core a remedy for unlawful executive detention. The typical remedy for such detention is, of course, release. But here the last thing petitioners want is simple release; that would expose them to apprehension by Iraqi authorities for criminal prosecution—precisely what petitioners went to federal court to avoid. At the end of the day, what petitioners are really after is a court order requiring the United States to shelter them from the sovereign government seeking to have them answer for alleged crimes committed within that sovereign's borders.

The habeas petitioners do not dispute that they voluntarily traveled to Iraq, that they remain detained within the sovereign territory of Iraq today, or that they are alleged to have committed serious crimes in Iraq. * * * Given these facts, our cases make clear that Iraq has a sovereign right to prosecute Omar and Munaf for crimes committed on its soil. * * *

This is true with respect to American citizens who travel abroad and commit crimes in another nation whether or not the pertinent criminal process comes with all the rights guaranteed by our Constitution. "When an American citizen commits a crime in a foreign country he cannot complain if required to submit to such modes of trial and to such punishment as the laws of that country may prescribe for its own people." Neely v. Henkel, 180 U.S. 109, 123 (1901).

The habeas petitioners nonetheless argue that the Due Process Clause includes a "[f]reedom from unlawful transfer" that is "protected *wherever* the government seizes a citizen." We disagree. Not only have we long recognized the principle that a nation state reigns sovereign within its own territory, we have twice applied that principle to reject claims that the Constitution precludes the Executive from transferring a prisoner to a foreign country for prosecution in an allegedly unconstitutional trial.

In *Wilson*, 354 U.S. 524, we reversed an injunction similar to the one at issue here. During a cavalry exercise at the Camp Weir range in Japan, Girard, a Specialist Third Class in the United States Army, caused the death of a Japanese woman. After Japan indicted Girard, but while he was still in United States custody, Girard filed a writ of habeas corpus in the United States District Court for the District of Columbia. The District Court granted a preliminary injunction against the United States, enjoining the proposed delivery of Girard to the Japanese Government. * * * We granted certiorari, and vacated the injunction. We noted that Japan had exclusive jurisdiction "to punish offenses against its laws committed within its borders," unless it had surrendered that jurisdiction. Consequently, even though Japan had ceded some of its jurisdiction to the United States pursuant to a bilateral Status of Forces Agreement, the United States could waive that jurisdiction—as it had done in Girard's case—and the habeas court was without authority to enjoin Girard's transfer to the Japanese authorities. Likewise, in *Neely v. Henkel, supra,* this Court held that habeas corpus was not available to defeat the criminal jurisdiction of a foreign sovereign, even when application of that sovereign's law would allegedly violate the Constitution. Neely—the habeas petitioner and an American citizen—was accused of violating Cuban law in Cuba. He was arrested and detained in the United States. The United States indicated its intent to extradite him, and Neely filed suit seeking to block his extradition on the grounds that Cuban law did not provide the panoply of rights guaranteed him by the Constitution of the United States. We summarily rejected this claim: "The answer to this suggestion is that those [constitutional] provisions have no relation to crimes committed without the jurisdiction of the United States against the laws of a foreign country." *Ibid.* Neely alleged no claim for which a "discharge on habeas corpus" could issue. Accordingly, the United States was free to transfer him to Cuban custody for prosecution.

In the present cases, the habeas petitioners concede that Iraq has the sovereign authority to prosecute them for alleged violations of its law, yet nonetheless request an injunction prohibiting the United States from transferring them to Iraqi custody. But as the foregoing cases make clear, habeas is not a means of compelling the United States to harbor fugitives from the criminal justice system of a sovereign with undoubted authority to prosecute them.

* * *

The habeas petitioners acknowledge that *some* interference with a foreign criminal system is too much. They concede that "it is axiomatic that an American court does not provide collateral review of proceedings in a foreign tribunal." We agree, but see no reason why habeas corpus should permit a prisoner detained within a foreign sovereign's territory to prevent a trial from going forward in the first place. It did not matter that the habeas petitioners in *Wilson* and *Neely* had not been convicted. Rather, the same principles of comity and respect for foreign sovereigns that preclude judicial scrutiny of foreign convictions necessarily render invalid attempts to shield citizens from foreign prosecution in order to preempt such nonreviewable adjudications.

* * *

There is of course even more at issue here: Neither *Neely* nor *Wilson* concerned individuals captured

and detained within an ally's territory during ongoing hostilities involving our troops. *Neely* involved a charge of embezzlement; *Wilson* the peacetime actions of a serviceman. Yet in those cases we held that the Constitution allows the Executive to transfer American citizens to foreign authorities for criminal prosecution. It would be passing strange to hold that the Executive lacks that same authority where, as here, the detainees were captured by our Armed Forces for engaging in serious hostile acts against an ally in what the Government refers to as "an active theater of combat."

Such a conclusion would implicate not only concerns about interfering with a sovereign's recognized prerogative to apply its criminal law to those alleged to have committed crimes within its borders, but also concerns about unwarranted judicial intrusion into the Executive's ability to conduct military operations abroad. * * * Those who commit crimes within a sovereign's territory may be transferred to that sovereign's government for prosecution; there is hardly an exception to that rule when the crime at issue is not embezzlement but unlawful insurgency directed against an ally during ongoing hostilities involving our troops.

B

* * *

Petitioners contend that these general principles are trumped in their cases because their transfer to Iraqi custody is likely to result in torture. * * * Such allegations are of course a matter of serious concern, but in the present context that concern is to be addressed by the political branches, not the judiciary. See M. Bassiouni, International Extradition: United States Law and Practice 921 (2007) ("*Habeas corpus* has been held not to be a valid means of inquiry into the treatment the relator is anticipated to receive in the requesting state").

* * *

The Executive Branch may, of course, decline to surrender a detainee for many reasons, including humanitarian ones. Petitioners here allege only the possibility of mistreatment in a prison facility; this is not a more extreme case in which the Executive has determined that a detainee is likely to be tortured but decides to transfer him anyway. Indeed, the Solicitor General states that it is the policy of the United States *not* to transfer an individual in circumstances where torture is likely to result. In these cases the United States explains that, although it remains concerned about torture among some sectors of the Iraqi Government, the State Department has determined that the Justice Ministry—the department that would have authority over Munaf and Omar—as well as its prison and detention facilities have "generally met internationally accepted standards for basic prisoner needs."
* * *

The Judiciary is not suited to second-guess such determinations—determinations that would require federal courts to pass judgment on foreign justice systems and undermine the Government's ability to speak with one voice in this area. In contrast, the political branches are well situated to consider sensitive foreign policy issues, such as whether there is a serious prospect of

torture at the hands of an ally, and what to do about it if there is. * * *

* * *

Munaf and Omar are alleged to have committed hostile and warlike acts within the sovereign territory of Iraq during ongoing hostilities there. Pending their criminal prosecution for those offenses, Munaf and Omar are being held in Iraq by American forces operating pursuant to a U. N. Mandate and at the request of the Iraqi Government. Petitioners concede that Iraq has a sovereign right to prosecute them for alleged violations of its law. Yet they went to federal court seeking an order that would allow them to defeat precisely that sovereign authority. Habeas corpus does not require the United States to shelter such fugitives from the criminal justice system of the sovereign with authority to prosecute them.

For all the reasons given above, petitioners state no claim in their habeas petitions for which relief can be granted, and those petitions should have been promptly dismissed. The judgments below and the injunction entered against the United States are vacated, and the cases are remanded for further proceedings consistent with this opinion.

It is so ordered.

———

JUSTICE SOUTER, **with whom JUS-TICE GINSBURG and JUSTICE BREYER join, concurring.**

The Court * * * reserves judgment on an "extreme case in which the Executive has determined that a detainee [in United States custody] is likely to be tortured but decides to transfer him anyway." I would add that nothing in today's opinion should be read as foreclosing relief for a citizen of the United States who resists transfer, say, from the American military to a foreign government for prosecution in a case of that sort, and I would extend the caveat to a case in which the probability of torture is well documented, even if the Executive fails to acknowledge it. Although the Court rightly points out that any likelihood of extreme mistreatment at the receiving government's hands is a proper matter for the political branches to consider, if the political branches did favor transfer it would be in order to ask whether substantive due process bars the Government from consigning its own people to torture. And although the Court points out that habeas is aimed at securing release, not protective detention, habeas would not be the only avenue open to an objecting prisoner; "where federally protected rights [are threatened], it has been the rule from the beginning that courts will be alert to adjust their remedies so as to grant the necessary relief," Bell v. Hood, 327 U.S. 678, 684 (1946).

THE FEDERAL RULES OF CRIMINAL PROCEDURE

(Including amendments that take effect on December 1, 2008)

TITLE I. APPLICABILITY

Rule 1. Scope; Definitions

(a) Scope.

(1) *In General.* These rules govern the procedure in all criminal proceedings in the United States district courts, the United States courts of appeals, and the Supreme Court of the United States.

(2) *State or Local Judicial Officer.* When a rule so states, it applies to a proceeding before a state or local judicial officer.

(3) *Territorial Courts.* These rules also govern the procedure in all criminal proceedings in the following courts:

(A) the district court of Guam;

(B) the district court for the Northern Mariana Islands, except as otherwise provided by law; and

(C) the district court of the Virgin Islands, except that the prosecution of offenses in that court must be by indictment or information as otherwise provided by law.

(4) *Removed Proceedings.* Although these rules govern all proceedings after removal from a state court, state law governs a dismissal by the prosecution.

(5) *Excluded Proceedings.* Proceedings not governed by these rules include:

(A) the extradition and rendition of a fugitive;

(B) a civil property forfeiture for violating a federal statute;

(C) the collection of a fine or penalty;

(D) a proceeding under a statute governing juvenile delinquency to the extent the procedure is inconsistent with the statute, unless Rule 20(d) provides otherwise;

(E) a dispute between seamen under 22 U.S.C. §§ 256–258; and

(F) a proceeding against a witness in a foreign country under 28 U.S.C. § 1784.

(b) Definitions. The following definitions apply to these rules:

(1) "Attorney for the government" means:

(A) the Attorney General or an authorized assistant;

(B) a United States attorney or an authorized assistant;

(C) when applicable to cases arising under Guam law, the Guam Attorney General or other person whom Guam law authorizes to act in the matter; and

(D) any other attorney authorized by law to conduct proceedings under these rules as a prosecutor.

(2) "Court" means a federal judge performing functions authorized by law.

(3) "Federal judge" means:

(A) a justice or judge of the United States as these terms are defined in 28 U.S.C. § 451;

(B) a magistrate judge; and

(C) a judge confirmed by the United States Senate and empowered by statute in any commonwealth, territory, or possession to perform a function to which a particular rule relates.

(4) "Judge" means a federal judge or a state or local judicial officer.

(5) "Magistrate judge" means a United States magistrate judge as defined in 28 U.S.C. §§ 631–639.

(6) "Oath" includes an affirmation.

(7) "Organization" is defined in 18 U.S.C. § 18.

(8) "Petty offense" is defined in 18 U.S.C. § 19.

(9) "State" includes the District of Columbia, and any commonwealth, territory, or possession of the United States.

(10) "State or local judicial officer" means:

(A) a state or local officer authorized to act under 18 U.S.C. § 3041; and

(B) a judicial officer empowered by statute in the District of Columbia or in any commonwealth, territory, or possession to perform a function to which a particular rule relates.

(11) "Victim" means a "crime victim" as defined in 18 U.S.C. § 3771(e).

(c) Authority of a Justice or Judge of the United States. When these rules authorize a magistrate judge to act, any other federal judge may also act.

Rule 2. Interpretation

These rules are to be interpreted to provide for the just determination of every criminal proceeding, to secure simplicity in procedure and fairness in administration, and to eliminate unjustifiable expense and delay.

TITLE II. PRELIMINARY PROCEEDINGS

Rule 3. The Complaint

The complaint is a written statement of the essential facts constituting the offense charged. It must be made under oath before a magistrate judge or, if none is reasonably available, before a state or local judicial officer.

Rule 4. Arrest Warrant or Summons on a Complaint

(a) Issuance. If the complaint or one or more affidavits filed with the complaint establish probable cause to believe that an offense has been committed and that the defendant committed it, the judge must issue an arrest warrant to an officer authorized to execute it. At the request of an attorney for the government, the judge must issue a summons, instead of a warrant, to a person authorized to serve it. A judge may issue more than one warrant or summons on the same complaint. If a defendant fails to appear in response to a summons, a judge may, and upon request of an attorney for the government must, issue a warrant.

(b) Form.

(1) *Warrant.* A warrant must:

(A) contain the defendant's name or, if it is unknown, a name or description by which the defendant can be identified with reasonable certainty;

(B) describe the offense charged in the complaint;

(C) command that the defendant be arrested and brought without unnecessary delay before a magistrate judge or, if none is reasonably available, before a state or local judicial officer; and

(D) be signed by a judge.

(2) *Summons.* A summons must be in the same form as a warrant except that it must require the defendant to appear before a magistrate judge at a stated time and place.

(c) Execution or Service, and Return.

(1) *By Whom.* Only a marshal or other authorized officer may execute a warrant. Any person authorized to serve a summons in a federal civil action may serve a summons.

(2) *Location.* A warrant may be executed, or a summons served, within the jurisdiction of the United States or anywhere else a federal statute authorizes an arrest.

(3) *Manner.*

(A) A warrant is executed by arresting the defendant. Upon arrest, an officer possessing the warrant must show it to the defendant. If the officer does not possess the warrant, the officer must inform the defendant of the warrant's existence and of the offense charged and, at the defendant's request, must show the warrant to the defendant as soon as possible.

(B) A summons is served on an individual defendant:

(i) by delivering a copy to the defendant personally; or

(ii) by leaving a copy at the defendant's residence or usual place of abode with a person of suitable age and discretion residing at that location and by mailing a copy to the defendant's last known address.

(C) A summons is served on an organization by delivering a copy to an officer, to a managing or general agent, or to another agent appointed or legally authorized to receive service of process. A copy must also be mailed to the organization's last known address within the district or to its principal place of business elsewhere in the United States.

(4) *Return*.

(A) After executing a warrant, the officer must return it to the judge before whom the defendant is brought in accordance with Rule 5. At the request of an attorney for the government, an unexecuted warrant must be brought back to and canceled by a magistrate judge or, if none is reasonably available, by a state or local judicial officer.

(B) The person to whom a summons was delivered for service must return it on or before the return day.

(C) At the request of an attorney for the government, a judge may deliver an unexecuted warrant, an unserved summons, or a copy of the warrant or summons to the marshal or other authorized person for execution or service.

Rule 5.   Initial Appearance

(a) In General.

(1) *Appearance Upon an Arrest*.

(A) A person making an arrest within the United States must take the defendant without unnecessary delay before a magistrate judge, or before a state or local judicial officer as Rule 5(c) provides, unless a statute provides otherwise.

(B) A person making an arrest outside the United States must take the defendant without unnecessary delay before a magistrate judge, unless a statute provides otherwise.

(2) *Exceptions*.

(A) An officer making an arrest under a warrant issued upon a complaint charging solely a violation of 18 U.S.C. § 1073 need not comply with this rule if:

(i) the person arrested is transferred without unnecessary delay to the custody of appropriate state or local authorities in the district of arrest; and

(ii) an attorney for the government moves promptly, in the district where the warrant was issued, to dismiss the complaint.

(B) If a defendant is arrested for violating probation or supervised release, Rule 32.1 applies.

(C) If a defendant is arrested for failing to appear in another district, Rule 40 applies.

(3) *Appearance Upon a Summons.* When a defendant appears in response to a summons under Rule 4, a magistrate judge must proceed under Rule 5(d) or (e), as applicable.

(b) Arrest Without a Warrant. If a defendant is arrested without a warrant, a complaint meeting Rule 4(a)'s requirement of probable cause must be promptly filed in the district where the offense was allegedly committed.

(c) Place of Initial Appearance; Transfer to Another District.

(1) *Arrest in the District Where the Offense Was Allegedly Committed.* If the defendant is arrested in the district where the offense was allegedly committed:

(A) the initial appearance must be in that district; and

(B) if a magistrate judge is not reasonably available, the initial appearance may be before a state or local judicial officer.

(2) *Arrest in a District Other Than Where the Offense Was Allegedly Committed.* If the defendant was arrested in a district other than where the offense was allegedly committed, the initial appearance must be:

(A) in the district of arrest; or

(B) in an adjacent district if:

(i) the appearance can occur more promptly there; or

(ii) the offense was allegedly committed there and the initial appearance will occur on the day of arrest.

(3) *Procedures in a District Other Than Where the Offense Was Allegedly Committed.* If the initial appearance occurs in a district other than where the offense was allegedly committed, the following procedures apply:

(A) the magistrate judge must inform the defendant about the provisions of Rule 20;

(B) if the defendant was arrested without a warrant, the district court where the offense was allegedly committed must first issue a warrant before the magistrate judge transfers the defendant to that district;

(C) the magistrate judge must conduct a preliminary hearing if required by Rule 5.1;

(D) the magistrate judge must transfer the defendant to the district where the offense was allegedly committed if:

(i) the government produces the warrant, a certified copy of the warrant, or a reliable electronic form of either; and

(ii) the judge finds that the defendant is the same person named in the indictment, information, or warrant; and

(E) when a defendant is transferred and discharged, the clerk must promptly transmit the papers and any bail to the clerk in the district where the offense was allegedly committed.

(d) Procedure in a Felony Case.

(1) *Advice.* If the defendant is charged with a felony, the judge must inform the defendant of the following:

(A) the complaint against the defendant, and any affidavit filed with it;

(B) the defendant's right to retain counsel or to request that counsel be appointed if the defendant cannot obtain counsel;

(C) the circumstances, if any, under which the defendant may secure pretrial release;

(D) any right to a preliminary hearing; and

(E) the defendant's right not to make a statement, and that any statement made may be used against the defendant.

(2) *Consulting with Counsel.* The judge must allow the defendant reasonable opportunity to consult with counsel.

(3) *Detention or Release.* The judge must detain or release the defendant as provided by statute or these rules.

(4) *Plea.* A defendant may be asked to plead only under Rule 10.

(e) Procedure in a Misdemeanor Case. If the defendant is charged with a misdemeanor only, the judge must inform the defendant in accordance with Rule 58(b)(2).

(f) Video Teleconferencing. Video teleconferencing may be used to conduct an appearance under this rule if the defendant consents.

Rule 5.1 Preliminary Hearing

(a) In General. If a defendant is charged with an offense other than a petty offense, a magistrate judge must conduct a preliminary hearing unless:

(1) the defendant waives the hearing;

(2) the defendant is indicted;

(3) the government files an information under Rule 7(b) charging the defendant with a felony;

(4) the government files an information charging the defendant with a misdemeanor; or

(5) the defendant is charged with a misdemeanor and consents to trial before a magistrate judge.

(b) Selecting a District. A defendant arrested in a district other than where the offense was allegedly committed may elect to have the preliminary hearing conducted in the district where the prosecution is pending.

(c) Scheduling. The magistrate judge must hold the preliminary hearing within a reasonable time, but no later than 14 days after the initial appearance if the defendant is in custody and no later than 21 days if not in custody.

(d) Extending the Time. With the defendant's consent and upon a showing of good cause—taking into account the public interest in the prompt disposition of criminal cases—a magistrate judge may extend the time limits in Rule 5.1(c) one or more times. If the defendant does not consent, the magistrate judge may extend the time limits only on a showing that extraordinary circumstances exist and justice requires the delay.

(e) Hearing and Finding. At the preliminary hearing, the defendant may cross-examine adverse witnesses and may introduce evidence but may not object to evidence on the ground that it was unlawfully acquired. If the magistrate judge finds probable cause to believe an offense has been committed and the defendant committed it, the magistrate judge must promptly require the defendant to appear for further proceedings.

(f) Discharging the Defendant. If the magistrate judge finds no probable cause to believe an offense has been committed or the defendant committed it, the magistrate judge must dismiss the complaint and discharge the defendant. A discharge does not preclude the government from later prosecuting the defendant for the same offense.

(g) Recording the Proceedings. The preliminary hearing must be recorded by a court reporter or by a suitable recording device. A recording of the proceeding may be made available to any party upon request. A copy of the recording and a transcript may be provided to any party upon request and upon any payment required by applicable Judicial Conference regulations.

(h) Producing a Statement.

(1) *In General.* Rule 26.2(a)-(d) and (f) applies at any hearing under this rule, unless the magistrate judge for good cause rules otherwise in a particular case.

(2) *Sanctions for Not Producing a Statement*. If a party disobeys a Rule 26.2 order to deliver a statement to the moving party, the magistrate judge must not consider the testimony of a witness whose statement is withheld.

TITLE III.   THE GRAND JURY, THE INDICTMENT, AND THE INFORMATION

Rule 6.   The Grand Jury

(a) Summoning a Grand Jury.

(1) *In General.* When the public interest so requires, the court must order that one or more grand juries be summoned. A grand jury must have 16 to 23 members, and the court must order that enough legally qualified persons be summoned to meet this requirement.

(2) *Alternate Jurors.* When a grand jury is selected, the court may also select alternate jurors. Alternate jurors must have the same qualifications and be selected in the same manner as any other juror. Alternate jurors replace jurors in the same sequence in which the alternates were selected. An alternate juror who replaces a juror is subject to the same challenges, takes the same oath, and has the same authority as the other jurors.

(b) Objection to the Grand Jury or to a Grand Juror.

(1) *Challenges.* Either the government or a defendant may challenge the grand jury on the ground that it was not lawfully drawn, summoned, or selected, and may challenge an individual juror on the ground that the juror is not legally qualified.

(2) *Motion to Dismiss an Indictment.* A party may move to dismiss the indictment based on an objection to the grand jury or on an individual juror's lack of legal qualification, unless the court has previously ruled on the same objection under Rule 6(b)(1). The motion to dismiss is governed by 28 U.S.C. § 1867(e). The court must not dismiss the indictment on the ground that a grand juror was not legally qualified if the record shows that at least 12 qualified jurors concurred in the indictment.

(c) Foreperson and Deputy Foreperson.
The court will appoint one juror as the foreperson and another as the deputy foreperson. In the foreperson's absence, the deputy foreperson will act as the foreperson. The foreperson may administer oaths and affirmations and will sign all indictments. The foreperson—or another juror designated by the foreperson—will record the number of jurors concurring in every indictment and will file the record with the clerk, but the record may not be made public unless the court so orders.

(d) Who May Be Present.

(1) *While the Grand Jury Is in Session.* The following persons may be present while the grand jury is in session: attorneys for the government, the witness being questioned, interpreters when needed, and a court reporter or an operator of a recording device.

(2) *During Deliberations and Voting.* No person other than the jurors, and any interpreter needed to assist a hearing-impaired or speech-impaired juror, may be present while the grand jury is deliberating or voting.

(e) Recording and Disclosing the Proceedings.

(1) *Recording the Proceedings.* Except while the grand jury is deliberating or voting, all proceedings must be recorded by a court reporter or by a suitable recording device. But the validity of a prosecution is not affected by the unintentional failure to make a recording. Unless the court orders otherwise, an attorney for the government will retain control of the recording, the reporter's notes, and any transcript prepared from those notes.

(2) *Secrecy.*

(A) No obligation of secrecy may be imposed on any person except in accordance with Rule 6(e)(2)(B).

(B) Unless these rules provide otherwise, the following persons must not disclose a matter occurring before the grand jury:

(i) a grand juror;

(ii) an interpreter;

(iii) a court reporter;

(iv) an operator of a recording device;

(v) a person who transcribes recorded testimony;

(vi) an attorney for the government; or

(vii) a person to whom disclosure is made under Rule 6(e)(3)(A)(ii)or (iii).

(3) *Exceptions.*

(A) Disclosure of a grand-jury matter—other than the grand jury's deliberations or any grand juror's vote—may be made to:

(i) an attorney for the government for use in performing that attorney's duty;

(ii) any government personnel—including those of a state, state subdivision, Indian tribe, or foreign government—that an attorney for the government considers necessary to assist in performing that attorney's duty to enforce federal criminal law; or

(iii) a person authorized by 18 U.S.C. § x3322.

(B) A person to whom information is disclosed under Rule 6(e)(3)(A)(ii) may use that information only to assist an attorney for the government in performing that attorney's duty to enforce federal criminal law. An attorney for the government must promptly provide the court that impaneled the grand jury with the names of all persons to whom a disclosure has been made, and must certify that the attorney has advised those persons of their obligation of secrecy under this rule.

(C) An attorney for the government may disclose any grand-jury matter to another federal grand jury.

(D) An attorney for the government may disclose any grand-jury matter involving foreign intelligence, counterintelligence (as defined in 50 U.S.C. § 401a), or foreign intelligence information (as defined in Rule 6(e)(3)(D)(iii)) to any federal law enforcement, intelligence, protective, immigration, national defense, or national security official to assist the official receiving the information in the performance of that official's duties. An attorney for the government may also disclose any grand-jury matter involving, within the United States or elsewhere, a threat of attack or other grave hostile acts of a foreign power or its agent, a threat of domestic or international sabotage or terrorism, or clandestine intelligence gathering activities by an intelligence service or network of a foreign power or by its agent, to any appropriate federal, state, state subdivision, Indian Tribal, or foreign government official, for the purpose of preventing or responding to such threat or activities.

(i) Any official who receives information under Rule 6(e)(3)(D) may use the information only as necessary in the conduct of that person's official duties subject to any limitations on the unauthorized disclosure of such information. Any state, state subdivision, Indian Tribal, or foreign government official who receives information under Rule 6(e)(3)(D) may use the information only in a manner consistent with any guidelines issued by the Attorney General and the Director of National Intelligence.

(ii) Within a reasonable time after disclosure is made under Rule 6(e)(3)(D), an attorney for the government must file, under seal, a notice with the court in the district where the grand jury convened stating that such information was disclosed and the departments, agencies, or entities to which the disclosure was made.

(iii) As used in Rule 6(e)(3)(D), the term "foreign intelligence information" means:

(a) information, whether or not it concerns a United States person, that relates to the ability of the United States to protect against—

actual or potential attack or other grave hostile acts of a foreign power or its agent;

sabotage or international terrorism by a foreign power or its agent; or

clandestine intelligence activities by an intelligence service or network of a foreign power or by its agent; or

(b) information, whether or not it concerns a United States person, with respect to a foreign power or foreign territory that relates to the national defense or the security of the United States; or the conduct of the foreign affairs of the United States.

(E) The court may authorize disclosure—at a time, in a manner, and subject to any other conditions that it directs—of a grand-jury matter:

(i) preliminarily to or in connection with a judicial proceeding;

(ii) at the request of a defendant who shows that a ground may exist to dismiss the indictment because of a matter that occurred before the grand jury;

(iii) at the request of the government, when sought by a foreign court or prosecutor for use in an official criminal investigation;

(iv) at the request of the government if it shows that the matter may disclose a violation of State, Indian tribal or foreign criminal law, as long as the disclosure is to an appropriate state, state-subdivision, Indian tribal, or foreign government official for the purpose of enforcing that law; or

(v) at the request of the government if it shows that the matter may disclose a violation of military criminal law under the Uniform Code of Military Justice, as long as the disclosure is to an appropriate military official for the purpose of enforcing that law.

(F) A petition to disclose a grand-jury matter under Rule 6(e)(3)(E)(i) must be filed in the district where the grand jury convened. Unless the hearing is ex parte—as it may be when the government is the petitioner—the petitioner must serve the petition on, and the court must afford a reasonable opportunity to appear and be heard to:

(i) an attorney for the government;

(ii) the parties to the judicial proceeding; and

(iii) any other person whom the court may designate.

(G) If the petition to disclose arises out of a judicial proceeding in another district, the petitioned court must transfer the petition to the other court unless the petitioned court can reasonably determine whether disclosure is proper. If the petitioned court decides to transfer, it must send to the transferee court the material sought to be disclosed, if feasible, and a written evaluation of the need for continued grand-jury secrecy. The transferee court must afford those persons identified in Rule 6(e)(3)(F) a reasonable opportunity to appear and be heard.

(4) *Sealed Indictment.* The magistrate judge to whom an indictment is returned may direct that the indictment be kept secret until the defendant is in custody or has been released pending trial. The clerk must then seal the indictment, and no person may disclose the indictment's existence except as necessary to issue or execute a warrant or summons.

(5) *Closed Hearing.* Subject to any right to an open hearing in a contempt proceeding, the court must close any hearing to the extent necessary to prevent disclosure of a matter occurring before a grand jury.

(6) *Sealed Records.* Records, orders, and subpoenas relating to grand-jury proceedings must be kept under seal to the extent and as long as necessary to prevent the unauthorized disclosure of a matter occurring before a grand jury.

(7) *Contempt.* A knowing violation of Rule 6, or of any guidelines jointly issued by the Attorney General and the Director of National Intelligence under Rule 6, may be punished as a contempt of court.

(f) Indictment and Return. A grand jury may indict only if at least 12 jurors concur. The grand jury—or its foreperson or deputy foreperson—must return the indictment to a magistrate judge in open court. If a complaint or information is pending against the defendant and 12 jurors do not concur in the indictment, the foreperson must promptly and in writing report the lack of concurrence to the magistrate judge.

(g) Discharging the Grand Jury. A grand jury must serve until the court discharges it, but it may serve more than 18 months only if the court, having determined that an extension is in the public interest, extends the grand jury's service. An extension may be granted for no more than 6 months, except as otherwise provided by statute.

(h) Excusing a Juror. At any time, for good cause, the court may excuse a juror either temporarily or permanently, and if permanently, the court may impanel an alternate juror in place of the excused juror.

(i) "Indian Tribe" Defined. "Indian tribe" means an Indian tribe recognized by the Secretary of the Interior on a list published in the Federal Register under 25 U.S.C. § 479a–1.

Rule 7. The Indictment and the Information

(a) When Used.

(1) *Felony.* An offense (other than criminal contempt) must be prosecuted by an indictment if it is punishable:

    (A) by death; or

    (B) by imprisonment for more than one year.

(2) *Misdemeanor.* An offense punishable by imprisonment for one year or less may be prosecuted in accordance with Rule 58(b)(1).

(b) Waiving Indictment. An offense punishable by imprisonment for more than one year may be prosecuted by information if the defendant—in open court and after being advised of the nature of the charge and of the defendant's rights—waives prosecution by indictment.

(c) Nature and Contents.

(1) *In General.* The indictment or information must be a plain, concise, and definite written statement of the essential facts constituting the offense charged and must be signed by an attorney for the government. It need not contain a formal introduction or conclusion. A count may incorporate by reference an allegation made in another count. A count may allege that the means by which the defendant committed the offense are unknown or that the defendant committed it by one or more specified means. For each count, the indictment or information must give the official or customary citation of the statute, rule, regulation, or other provision of law that the defendant is alleged to have violated. For purposes of an indictment referred to in section 3282 of title 18, United States Code, for which the identity of the defendant is unknown, it shall be sufficient for the indictment to describe the defendant as an individual whose name is unknown, but who has a particular DNA profile, as that term is defined in that section 3282.

(2) *Citation Error.* Unless the defendant was misled and thereby prejudiced, neither an error in a citation nor a citation's omission is a ground to dismiss the indictment or information or to reverse a conviction.

(d) Surplusage. Upon the defendant's motion, the court may strike surplusage from the indictment or information.

(e) Amending an Information. Unless an additional or different offense is charged or a substantial right of the defendant is prejudiced, the court may permit an information to be amended at any time before the verdict or finding.

(f) Bill of Particulars. The court may direct the government to file a bill of particulars. The defendant may move for a bill of particulars before or within 14 days after arraignment or at a later time if the court permits. The government may amend a bill of particulars subject to such conditions as justice requires.

Rule 8. Joinder of Offenses or Defendants

(a) Joinder of Offenses. The indictment or information may charge a defendant in separate counts with 2 or more offenses if the offenses charged—whether felonies or misdemeanors or both—are of the same or similar character, or are based on the same act or transaction, or are connected with or constitute parts of a common scheme or plan.

(b) Joinder of Defendants. The indictment or information may charge 2 or more defendants if they are alleged to have participated in the same act or transaction, or in the same series of acts or transactions, constituting an offense or offenses. The defendants may be charged in one or more counts together or separately. All defendants need not be charged in each count.

Rule 9. Arrest Warrant or Summons on an Indictment or Information

(a) Issuance. The court must issue a warrant—or at the government's request, a summons—for each defendant named in an indictment or named in an information if one or more affidavits accompanying the information establish probable cause to believe that an offense has been committed and that the defendant committed it. The court may issue more than one warrant or summons for the same defendant. If a defendant fails to appear in response to a summons, the court may, and upon request of an attorney for the government must, issue a warrant. The court must issue the arrest warrant to an officer authorized to execute it or the summons to a person authorized to serve it.

(b) Form.

(1) *Warrant.* The warrant must conform to Rule 4(b)(1) except that it must be signed by the clerk and must describe the offense charged in the indictment or information.

(2) *Summons.* The summons must be in the same form as a warrant except that it must require the defendant to appear before the court at a stated time and place.

(c) Execution or Service; Return; Initial Appearance.

(1) *Execution or Service.*

(A) The warrant must be executed or the summons served as provided in Rule 4(c)(1), (2), and (3).

(B) The officer executing the warrant must proceed in accordance with Rule 5(a)(1).

(2) *Return.* A warrant or summons must be returned in accordance with Rule 4(c)(4).

(3) *Initial Appearance.* When an arrested or summoned defendant first appears before the court, the judge must proceed under Rule 5.

TITLE IV. ARRAIGNMENT AND PREPARATION FOR TRIAL

Rule 10. Arraignment

(a) In General. An arraignment must be conducted in open court and must consist of:

(1) ensuring that the defendant has a copy of the indictment or information;

(2) reading the indictment or information to the defendant or stating to the defendant the substance of the charge; and then

(3) asking the defendant to plead to the indictment or information.

(b) Waiving Appearance. A defendant need not be present for the arraignment if:

(1) the defendant has been charged by indictment or misdemeanor information;

(2) the defendant, in a written waiver signed by both the defendant and defense counsel, has waived appearance and has affirmed that the defendant received a copy of the indictment or information and that the plea is not guilty; and

(3) the court accepts the waiver.

(c) Video Teleconferencing. Video teleconferencing may be used to arraign a defendant if the defendant consents.

Rule 11. Pleas

(a) Entering a Plea.

(1) *In General.* A defendant may plead not guilty, guilty, or (with the court's consent) nolo contendere.

(2) *Conditional Plea.* With the consent of the court and the government, a defendant may enter a conditional plea of guilty or nolo contendere, reserving in writing the right to have an appellate court review an adverse determination of a specified pretrial motion. A defendant who prevails on appeal may then withdraw the plea.

(3) *Nolo Contendere Plea.* Before accepting a plea of nolo contendere, the court must consider the parties' views and the public interest in the effective administration of justice.

(4) *Failure to Enter a Plea.* If a defendant refuses to enter a plea or if a defendant organization fails to appear, the court must enter a plea of not guilty.

(b) Considering and Accepting a Guilty or Nolo Contendere Plea.

(1) *Advising and Questioning the Defendant.* Before the court accepts a plea of guilty or nolo contendere, the defendant may be placed under oath, and the court must address the defendant personally in open court. During this address, the court must inform the defendant of, and determine that the defendant understands, the following:

(A) the government's right, in a prosecution for perjury or false statement, to use against the defendant any statement that the defendant gives under oath;

(B) the right to plead not guilty, or having already so pleaded, to persist in that plea;

(C) the right to a jury trial;

(D) the right to be represented by counsel—and if necessary have the court appoint counsel—at trial and at every other stage of the proceeding;

(E) the right at trial to confront and cross-examine adverse witnesses, to be protected from compelled self-incrimination, to testify and present evidence, and to compel the attendance of witnesses;

(F) the defendant's waiver of these trial rights if the court accepts a plea of guilty or nolo contendere;

(G) the nature of each charge to which the defendant is pleading;

(H) any maximum possible penalty, including imprisonment, fine, and term of supervised release;

(I) any mandatory minimum penalty;

(J) any applicable forfeiture;

(K) the court's authority to order restitution;

(L) the court's obligation to impose a special assessment;

(M) in determining a sentence, the court's obligation to calculate the applicable sentencing-guideline range and to consider that range, possible departures under the Sentencing Guidelines, and other sentencing factors under 18 U.S.C. § 3553(a); and

(N) the terms of any plea-agreement provision waiving the right to appeal or to collaterally attack the sentence.

(2) *Ensuring That a Plea Is Voluntary*. Before accepting a plea of guilty or nolo contendere, the court must address the defendant personally in open court and determine that the plea is voluntary and did not result from force, threats, or promises (other than promises in a plea agreement).

(3) *Determining the Factual Basis for a Plea*. Before entering judgment on a guilty plea, the court must determine that there is a factual basis for the plea.

(c) Plea Agreement Procedure.

(1) *In General*. An attorney for the government and the defendant's attorney, or the defendant when proceeding pro se, may discuss and reach a plea agreement. The court must not participate in these discussions. If the defendant pleads guilty or nolo contendere to either a charged offense or a lesser or related offense, the plea agreement may specify that an attorney for the government will:

(A) not bring, or will move to dismiss, other charges;

(B) recommend, or agree not to oppose the defendant's request, that a particular sentence or sentencing range is appropriate or that a particular provision of the Sentencing Guidelines, or policy statement, or sentencing factor does or does not apply (such a recommendation or request does not bind the court); or

(C) agree that a specific sentence or sentencing range is the appropriate disposition of the case, or that a particular provision of the Sentencing Guidelines, or policy statement, or sentencing factor does or does not apply (such a recommendation or request binds the court once the court accepts the plea agreement).

(2) *Disclosing a Plea Agreement.* The parties must disclose the plea agreement in open court when the plea is offered, unless the court for good cause allows the parties to disclose the plea agreement in camera.

(3) *Judicial Consideration of a Plea Agreement.*

(A) To the extent the plea agreement is of the type specified in Rule 11(c)(1)(A) or (C), the court may accept the agreement, reject it, or defer a decision until the court has reviewed the presentence report.

(B) To the extent the plea agreement is of the type specified in Rule 11(c)(1)(B), the court must advise the defendant that the defendant has no right to withdraw the plea if the court does not follow the recommendation or request.

(4) *Accepting a Plea Agreement.* If the court accepts the plea agreement, it must inform the defendant that to the extent the plea agreement is of the type specified in Rule 11(c)(1)(A) or (C), the agreed disposition will be included in the judgment.

(5) *Rejecting a Plea Agreement.* If the court rejects a plea agreement containing provisions of the type specified in Rule 11(c)(1)(A) or (C), the court must do the following on the record and in open court (or, for good cause, in camera):

(A) inform the parties that the court rejects the plea agreement;

(B) advise the defendant personally that the court is not required to follow the plea agreement and give the defendant an opportunity to withdraw the plea; and

(C) advise the defendant personally that if the plea is not withdrawn, the court may dispose of the case less favorably toward the defendant than the plea agreement contemplated.

(d) Withdrawing a Guilty or Nolo Contendere Plea. A defendant may withdraw a plea of guilty or nolo contendere:

(1) before the court accepts the plea, for any reason or no reason; or

(2) after the court accepts the plea, but before it imposes sentence if:

(A) the court rejects a plea agreement under Rule 11(c)(5); or

(B) the defendant can show a fair and just reason for requesting the withdrawal.

(e) Finality of a Guilty or Nolo Contendere Plea. After the court imposes sentence, the defendant may not withdraw a plea of guilty or nolo contendere, and the plea may be set aside only on direct appeal or collateral attack.

(f) Admissibility or Inadmissibility of a Plea, Plea Discussions, and Related Statements. The admissibility or inadmissibility of a plea, a plea discussion, and any related statement is governed by Federal Rule of Evidence 410.

(g) Recording the Proceedings. The proceedings during which the defendant enters a plea must be recorded by a court reporter or by a suitable recording device. If there is a guilty plea or a nolo contendere plea, the record must include the inquiries and advice to the defendant required under Rule 11(b) and (c).

(h) Harmless Error. A variance from the requirements of this rule is harmless error if it does not affect substantial rights.

Rule 12.   Pleadings and Pretrial Motions

(a) Pleadings. The pleadings in a criminal proceeding are the indictment, the information, and the pleas of not guilty, guilty, and nolo contendere.

(b) Pretrial Motions.

(1) *In General*. Rule 47 applies to a pretrial motion.

(2) *Motions That May Be Made Before Trial*. A party may raise by pretrial motion any defense, objection, or request that the court can determine without a trial of the general issue.

(3) *Motions That Must Be Made Before Trial*. The following must be raised before trial:

(A) a motion alleging a defect in instituting the prosecution;

(B) a motion alleging a defect in the indictment or information—but at any time while the case is pending, the court may hear a claim that the indictment or information fails to invoke the court's jurisdiction or to state an offense;

(C) a motion to suppress evidence;

(D) a Rule 14 motion to sever charges or defendants; and

(E) a Rule 16 motion for discovery.

(4) *Notice of the Government's Intent to Use Evidence*.

(A) *At the Government's Discretion*. At the arraignment or as soon afterward as practicable, the government may notify the defendant of its intent to use specified evidence at trial in order to afford the defendant an opportunity to object before trial under Rule 12(b)(3)(C).

(B) *At the Defendant's Request*. At the arraignment or as soon afterward as practicable, the defendant may, in order to have an opportunity to move to suppress evidence under Rule 12(b)(3)(C), request notice of the government's intent to use (in its evidence-in-chief at trial) any evidence that the defendant may be entitled to discover under Rule 16.

(c) Motion Deadline. The court may, at the arraignment or as soon afterward as practicable, set a deadline for the parties to make pretrial motions and may also schedule a motion hearing.

(d) Ruling on a Motion. The court must decide every pretrial motion before trial unless it finds good cause to defer a ruling. The court must not defer ruling on a pretrial motion if the deferral will adversely affect a party's right to appeal. When factual issues are involved in deciding a motion, the court must state its essential findings on the record.

(e) Waiver of a Defense, Objection, or Request. A party waives any Rule 12(b)(3) defense, objection, or request not raised by the deadline the court sets under Rule 12(c) or by any extension the court provides. For good cause, the court may grant relief from the waiver.

(f) Recording the Proceedings. All proceedings at a motion hearing, including any findings of fact and conclusions of law made orally by the court, must be recorded by a court reporter or a suitable recording device.

(g) Defendant's Continued Custody or Release Status. If the court grants a motion to dismiss based on a defect in instituting the prosecution, in the indictment, or in the information, it may order the defendant to be released or detained under 18 U.S.C. § 3142 for a specified time until a new indictment or information is filed. This rule does not affect any federal statutory period of limitations.

(h) Producing Statements at a Suppression Hearing. Rule 26.2 applies at a suppression hearing under Rule 12(b)(3)(C). At a suppression hearing, a law enforcement officer is considered a government witness.

Rule 12.1   Notice of an Alibi Defense

(a) Government's Request for Notice and Defendant's Response.

(1) *Government's Request.* An attorney for the government may request in writing that the defendant notify an attorney for the government of any intended alibi defense. The request must state the time, date, and place of the alleged offense.

(2) *Defendant's Response.* Within 14 days after the request, or at some other time the court sets, the defendant must serve written notice on an attorney for the government of any intended alibi defense. The defendant's notice must state:

(A) each specific place where the defendant claims to have been at the time of the alleged offense; and

(B) the name, address, and telephone number of each alibi witness on whom the defendant intends to rely.

(b) Disclosing Government Witnesses.

(1) *Disclosure.*

(A) *In General.* If the defendant serves a Rule 12.1(a)(2) notice, an attorney for the government must disclose in writing to the defendant or the defendant's attorney:

(i) the name of each witness—and the address and telephone number of each witness other than a victim—that the government intends to rely on to establish that the defendant was present at the scene of the alleged offense; and

(ii) each government rebuttal witness to the defendant's alibi defense.

(B) *Victim's Address and Telephone Number.* If the government intends to rely on a victim's testimony to establish that the defendant was present at the scene of the alleged offense and the defendant establishes a need for the victim's address and telephone number, the court may:

(i) order the government to provide the information in writing to the defendant or the defendant's attorney; or

(ii) fashion a reasonable procedure that allows preparation of the defense and also protects the victim's interests.

(2) *Time to Disclose.* Unless the court directs otherwise, an attorney for the government must give its Rule 12.1(b)(1) disclosure within 14 days after the defendant serves notice of an intended alibi defense under Rule 12.1(a)(2), but no later than 14 days before trial.

(c) Continuing Duty to Disclose.

(1) *In General.* Both an attorney for the government and the defendant must promptly disclose in writing to the other party the name of each additional witness—and the address and telephone number of each additional witness other than a victim—if:

(a) the disclosing party learns of the witness before or during trial; and

(b) the witness should have been disclosed under Rule 12.1(a) or (b) if the disclosing party had known of the witness earlier.

(2) *Address and Telephone Number of an Additional Victim Witness.* The address and telephone number of an additional victim witness must not be disclosed except as provided in Rule 12.1(b)(1)(B).

(d) Exceptions. For good cause, the court may grant an exception to any requirement of Rule 12.1(a)-(c).

(e) Failure to Comply. If a party fails to comply with this rule, the court may exclude the testimony of any undisclosed witness regarding the defendant's alibi. This rule does not limit the defendant's right to testify.

(f) Inadmissibility of Withdrawn Intention. Evidence of an intention to rely on an alibi defense, later withdrawn, or of a statement made in connection with that intention, is not, in any civil or criminal proceeding, admissible against the person who gave notice of the intention.

Rule 12.2   Notice of an Insanity Defense; Mental Examination

(a) Notice of an Insanity Defense. A defendant who intends to assert a defense of insanity at the time of the alleged offense must so notify an attorney for the government in writing within the time provided for filing a pretrial motion, or at any later time the court sets, and file a copy of the notice with the clerk. A defendant who fails to do so cannot rely on an insanity defense. The court may, for good cause, allow the defendant to file the notice late, grant additional trial-preparation time, or make other appropriate orders.

(b) Notice of Expert Evidence of a Mental Condition. If a defendant intends to introduce expert evidence relating to a mental disease or defect or any other mental condition of the defendant bearing on either (1) the issue of guilt or (2) the issue of punishment in a capital case, the defendant must—within the time provided for filing a pretrial motion or at any later time the court sets—notify an attorney for the government in writing of this intention and file a copy of the notice with the clerk. The court may, for good cause, allow the defendant to file the notice late, grant the parties additional trial-preparation time, or make other appropriate orders.

(c) Mental Examination.

(1) *Authority to Order an Examination; Procedures.*

(A) The court may order the defendant to submit to a competency examination under 18 U.S.C. § 4241.

(B) If the defendant provides notice under Rule 12.2(a), the court must, upon the government's motion, order the defendant to be examined under 18 U.S.C. § 4242. If the defendant provides notice under Rule 12.2(b) the court may, upon the government's motion, order the defendant to be examined under procedures ordered by the court.

(2) *Disclosing Results and Reports of Capital Sentencing Examination.* The results and reports of any examination conducted solely under Rule 12.2(c)(1) after notice under Rule 12.2(b)(2) must be sealed and must not be disclosed to any attorney for the government or the defendant unless the defendant is found guilty of one or more capital crimes and the defendant confirms an intent to offer during sentencing proceedings expert evidence on mental condition.

(3) *Disclosing Results and Reports of the Defendant's Expert Examination.* After disclosure under Rule 12.2(c)(2) of the results and reports of the government's examination, the defendant must disclose to the government the results and reports of any examination on mental condition conducted by the defendant's expert about which the defendant intends to introduce expert evidence.

(4) *Inadmissibility of a Defendant's Statements.* No statement made by a defendant in the course of any examination conducted under this rule (whether conducted with or without the defendant's consent), no testimony by the expert based on the statement, and no other fruits of the statement may be admitted into evidence against the defendant in any criminal proceeding except on an issue regarding mental condition on which the defendant:

(A) has introduced evidence of incompetency or evidence requiring notice under Rule 12.2(a) or (b)(1), or

(B) has introduced expert evidence in a capital sentencing proceeding requiring notice under Rule 12.2(b)(2).

(d) Failure to Comply.

(1) *Failure to Give Notice or to Submit to Examination.* The court may exclude any expert evidence from the defendant on the issue of the defendant's mental disease, mental defect, or any other mental condition bearing on the defendant's guilt or the issue of punishment in a capital case if the defendant fails to:

(A) give notice under Rule 12.2(b); or

(B) submit to an examination when ordered under Rule 12.2(c)

(2) *Failure to Disclose.* The court may exclude any expert evidence for which the defendant has failed to comply with the disclosure requirement of Rule 12.2(c)(3).

(e) Inadmissibility of Withdrawn Intention. Evidence of an intention as to which notice was given under Rule 12.2(a) or (b), later withdrawn, is not, in any civil or criminal proceeding, admissible against the person who gave notice of the intention.

Rule 12.3   Notice of a Public–Authority Defense

(a) Notice of the Defense and Disclosure of Witnesses.

(1) *Notice in General.* If a defendant intends to assert a defense of actual or believed exercise of public authority on behalf of a law enforcement agency or federal intelligence agency at the time of the alleged offense, the defendant must so notify an attorney for the government in writing and must file a copy of the notice with the clerk within the time provided for filing a pretrial motion, or at any later time the court sets. The notice filed with the clerk must be under seal if the notice identifies a federal intelligence agency as the source of public authority.

(2) *Contents of Notice.* The notice must contain the following information:

(A) the law enforcement agency or federal intelligence agency involved;

(B) the agency member on whose behalf the defendant claims to have acted; and

(C) the time during which the defendant claims to have acted with public authority.

(3) *Response to the Notice*. An attorney for the government must serve a written response on the defendant or the defendant's attorney within 14 days after receiving the defendant's notice, but no later than 21 days before trial. The response must admit or deny that the defendant exercised the public authority identified in the defendant's notice.

(4) *Disclosing Witnesses.*

(A) *Government's Request.* An attorney for the government may request in writing that the defendant disclose the name, address, and telephone number of each witness the defendant intends to rely on to establish a public-authority defense. An attorney for the government may serve the request when the government serves its response to the defendant's notice under Rule 12.3(a)(3), or later, but must serve the request no later than 21 days before trial.

(B) *Defendant's Response.* Within 14 days after receiving the government's request, the defendant must serve on an attorney for the government a written statement of the name, address, and telephone number of each witness.

(C) *Government's Reply.* Within 14 days after receiving the defendant's statement, an attorney for the government must serve on the defendant or the defendant's attorney a written statement of the name, address, and telephone number of each witness the government intends to rely on to oppose the defendant's public-authority defense.

(5) *Additional Time.* The court may, for good cause, allow a party additional time to comply with this rule.

(b) Continuing Duty to Disclose. Both an attorney for the government and the defendant must promptly disclose in writing to the other party the name, address, and telephone number of any additional witness if:

(1) the disclosing party learns of the witness before or during trial; and

(2) the witness should have been disclosed under Rule 12.3(a)(4) if the disclosing party had known of the witness earlier.

(c) Failure to Comply. If a party fails to comply with this rule, the court may exclude the testimony of any undisclosed witness regarding the public-authority defense. This rule does not limit the defendant's right to testify.

(d) Protective Procedures Unaffected. This rule does not limit the court's authority to issue appropriate protective orders or to order that any filings be under seal.

(e) Inadmissibility of Withdrawn Intention. Evidence of an intention as to which notice was given under Rule 12.3(a), later withdrawn, is not, in any civil or criminal proceeding, admissible against the person who gave notice of the intention.

Rule 12.4 Disclosure Statement

(a) Who Must File.

(1) *Nongovernmental Corporate Party.* Any nongovernmental corporate party to a proceeding in a district court must file a statement that identifies any parent corporation and any publicly held corporation that owns 10% or more of its stock or states that there is no such corporation.

(2) *Organizational Victim.* If an organization is a victim of the alleged criminal activity, the government must file a statement identifying the victim. If the organizational victim is a corporation, the statement must also disclose the information required by Rule 12.4(a)(1) to the extent it can be obtained through due diligence.

(b) Time for Filing; Supplemental Filing. A party must:

(1) file the Rule 12.4(a) statement upon the defendant's initial appearance; and

(2) promptly file a supplemental statement upon any change in the information that the statement requires.

Rule 13.   Joint Trial of Separate Cases

The court may order that separate cases be tried together as though brought in a single indictment or information if all offenses and all defendants could have been joined in a single indictment or information.

Rule 14.   Relief from Prejudicial Joinder

(a) Relief. If the joinder of offenses or defendants in an indictment, an information, or a consolidation for trial appears to prejudice a defendant or the government, the court may order separate trials of counts, sever the defendants' trials, or provide any other relief that justice requires.

(b) Defendant's Statements. Before ruling on a defendant's motion to sever, the court may order an attorney for the government to deliver to the court for in camera inspection any defendant's statement that the government intends to use as evidence.

Rule 15.   Depositions

(a) When Taken.

(1) *In General.* A party may move that a prospective witness be deposed in order to preserve testimony for trial. The court may grant the motion because of exceptional circumstances and in the interest of justice. If the court orders the deposition to be taken, it may also require the deponent to produce at the deposition any designated material that is not privileged, including any book, paper, document, record, recording, or data.

(2) *Detained Material Witness.* A witness who is detained under 18 U.S.C. § 3144 may request to be deposed by filing a written motion and giving notice to the parties. The court may then order that the deposition be taken and may discharge the witness after the witness has signed under oath the deposition transcript.

(b) Notice.

(1) *In General.* A party seeking to take a deposition must give every other party reasonable written notice of the deposition's date and location. The notice must state the name and address of each deponent. If requested by a party receiving the notice, the court may, for good cause, change the deposition's date or location.

(2) *To the Custodial Officer.* A party seeking to take the deposition must also notify the officer who has custody of the defendant of the scheduled date and location.

(c) Defendant's Presence.

(1) *Defendant in Custody.* The officer who has custody of the defendant must produce the defendant at the deposition and keep the defendant in the witness's presence during the examination, unless the defendant:

    (A) waives in writing the right to be present; or

    (B) persists in disruptive conduct justifying exclusion after being warned by the court that disruptive conduct will result in the defendant's exclusion.

(2) *Defendant Not in Custody.* A defendant who is not in custody has the right upon request to be present at the deposition, subject to any conditions imposed by the court. If the government tenders the defendant's expenses as provided in Rule 15(d) but the defendant still fails to appear, the defendant—absent good cause—waives both the right to appear and any objection to the taking and use of the deposition based on that right.

(d) Expenses. If the deposition was requested by the government, the court may—or if the defendant is unable to bear the deposition expenses, the court must—order the government to pay:

(1) any reasonable travel and subsistence expenses of the defendant and the defendant's attorney to attend the deposition; and

(2) the costs of the deposition transcript.

(e) Manner of Taking. Unless these rules or a court order provides otherwise, a deposition must be taken and filed in the same manner as a deposition in a civil action, except that:

(1) A defendant may not be deposed without that defendant's consent.

(2) The scope and manner of the deposition examination and cross-examination must be the same as would be allowed during trial.

(3) The government must provide to the defendant or the defendant's attorney, for use at the deposition, any statement of the deponent in the government's possession to which the defendant would be entitled at trial.

(f) Use as Evidence. A party may use all or part of a deposition as provided by the Federal Rules of Evidence.

(g) Objections. A party objecting to deposition testimony or evidence must state the grounds for the objection during the deposition.

(h) Depositions by Agreement Permitted. The parties may by agreement take and use a deposition with the court's consent.

Rule 16. Discovery and Inspection

(a) Government's Disclosure.

(1) *Information Subject to Disclosure.*

(A) *Defendant's Oral Statement.* Upon a defendant's request, the government must disclose to the defendant the substance of any relevant oral statement made by the defendant, before or after arrest, in response to interrogation by a person the defendant knew was a government agent if the government intends to use the statement at trial.

(B) *Defendant's Written or Recorded Statement.* Upon a defendant's request, the government must disclose to the defendant, and make available for inspection, copying, or photographing, all of the following:

(i) any relevant written or recorded statement by the defendant if: the statement is within the government's possession, custody, or control; and the attorney for the government knows—or through due diligence could know—that the statement exists;

(ii) the portion of any written record containing the substance of any relevant oral statement made before or after arrest if the defendant made the statement in response to interrogation by a person the defendant knew was a government agent; and

(iii) the defendant's recorded testimony before a grand jury relating to the charged offense.

(C) *Organizational Defendant.* Upon a defendant's request, if the defendant is an organization, the government must disclose to the defendant any statement described in Rule 16(a)(1)(A) and (B) if the government contends that the person making the statement:

(i) was legally able to bind the defendant regarding the subject of the statement because of that person's position as the defendant's director, officer, employee, or agent; or

(ii) was personally involved in the alleged conduct constituting the offense and was legally able to bind the defendant regarding that conduct because of that person's position as the defendant's director, officer, employee, or agent.

(D) *Defendant's Prior Record.* Upon a defendant's request, the government must furnish the defendant with a copy of the defendant's prior criminal record that is within the government's possession, custody, or control if the attorney for the government knows—or through due diligence could know—that the record exists.

(E) *Documents and Objects.* Upon a defendant's request, the government must permit the defendant to inspect and to copy or photograph books, papers, documents, data, photographs, tangible objects, buildings or places, or copies or portions of any of these items, if the item is within the government's possession, custody, or control and:

(i) the item is material to preparing the defense;

(ii) the government intends to use the item in its case-in-chief at trial; or

(iii) the item was obtained from or belongs to the defendant.

(F) *Reports of Examinations and Tests.* Upon a defendant's request, the government must permit a defendant to inspect and to copy or photograph the results or reports of any physical or mental examination and of any scientific test or experiment if:

(i) the item is within the government's possession, custody, or control;

(ii) the attorney for the government knows—or through due diligence could know—that the item exists; and

(iii) the item is material to preparing the defense or the government intends to use the item in its case-in-chief at trial.

(G) *Expert Witnesses.* At the defendant's request, the government must give the defendant a written summary of any testimony that the government intends to use under Rules 702, 703, or 705 of the Federal Rules of Evidence during its case-in-chief at trial. If the government requests discovery under subdivision (b)(1)(C)(ii) and the defendant complies, the government must, at the defendant's request, give to the defendant a written summary of testimony that the government intends to use under Rules 702, 703, or 705 of the Federal Rules of Evidence as evidence at trial on the issue of the defendant's mental condition. The summary provided under this subparagraph must describe the witness's opinions, the bases and reasons for those opinions, and the witness's qualifications.

(2) *Information Not Subject to Disclosure.* Except as Rule 16(a)(1) provides otherwise, this rule does not authorize the discovery or inspection of reports, memoranda, or other internal government documents made by an attorney for the government or other government agent in connection with investigating or prosecuting the case. Nor does this rule authorize the discovery or inspection of statements made by prospective government witnesses except as provided in 18 U.S.C. § 3500.

(3) *Grand Jury Transcripts.* This rule does not apply to the discovery or inspection of a grand jury's recorded proceedings, except as provided in Rules 6, 12(h), 16(a)(1), and 26.2.

(b) Defendant's Disclosure.

(1) *Information Subject to Disclosure.*

(A) *Documents and Objects.* If a defendant requests disclosure under Rule 16(a)(1)(E) and the government complies, then the defendant must permit the government, upon request, to inspect and to copy or photograph books, papers, documents, data, photographs, tangible objects, buildings or places, or copies or portions of any of these items if:

(i) the item is within the defendant's possession, custody, or control; and

(ii) the defendant intends to use the item in the defendant's case-in-chief at trial.

(B) *Reports of Examinations and Tests.* If a defendant requests disclosure under Rule 16(a)(1)(F) and the government complies, the defendant must permit the government, upon request, to inspect and to copy or photograph the results or reports of any physical or mental examination and of any scientific test or experiment if:

(i) the item is within the defendant's possession, custody, or control; and

(ii) the defendant intends to use the item in the defendant's case-in-chief at trial, or intends to call the witness who prepared the report and the report relates to the witness's testimony.

(C) *Expert Witnesses.* The defendant must, at the government's request, give to the government a written summary of any testimony that the defendant intends to use under Rules 702, 703, or 705 of the Federal Rules of Evidence as evidence at trial, if—

(i) the defendant requests disclosure under subdivision (a)(1)(G) and the government complies; or

(ii) the defendant has given notice under Rule 12.2(b) of an intent to present expert testimony on the defendant's mental condition.

This summary must describe the witness's opinions, the bases and reasons for those opinions, and the witness's qualifications.

(2) *Information Not Subject to Disclosure.* Except for scientific or medical reports, Rule 16(b)(1) does not authorize discovery or inspection of:

(A) reports, memoranda, or other documents made by the defendant, or the defendant's attorney or agent, during the case's investigation or defense; or

(B) a statement made to the defendant, or the defendant's attorney or agent, by:

(i) the defendant;

(ii) a government or defense witness; or

(iii) a prospective government or defense witness.

(c) Continuing Duty to Disclose. A party who discovers additional evidence or material before or during trial must promptly disclose its existence to the other party or the court if:

(1) the evidence or material is subject to discovery or inspection under this rule; and

(2) the other party previously requested, or the court ordered, its production.

(d) Regulating Discovery.

(1) *Protective and Modifying Orders.* At any time the court may, for good cause, deny, restrict, or defer discovery or inspection, or grant other appropriate relief. The court may permit a party to show good cause by a written statement that the court will inspect ex parte. If relief is granted, the court must preserve the entire text of the party's statement under seal.

(2) *Failure to Comply.* If a party fails to comply with this rule, the court may:

(A) order that party to permit the discovery or inspection; specify its time, place, and manner; and prescribe other just terms and conditions;

(B) grant a continuance;

(C) prohibit that party from introducing the undisclosed evidence; or

(D) enter any other order that is just under the circumstances.

Rule 17.   Subpoena

(a) Content. A subpoena must state the court's name and the title of the proceeding, include the seal of the court, and command the witness to attend and testify at the time and place the subpoena specifies. The clerk must issue a blank subpoena—signed and sealed—to the party requesting it, and that party must fill in the blanks before the subpoena is served.

(b) Defendant Unable to Pay. Upon a defendant's ex parte application, the court must order that a subpoena be issued for a named witness if the defendant shows an inability to pay the witness's fees and the necessity of the witness's presence for an adequate defense. If the court orders a subpoena to be issued, the process costs and witness fees will be paid in the same manner as those paid for witnesses the government subpoenas.

(c) Producing Documents and Objects.

(1) *In General.* A subpoena may order the witness to produce any books, papers, documents, data, or other objects the subpoena designates. The court may direct the witness to produce the designated items in court before trial or before they are to be offered in evidence. When the items arrive, the court may permit the parties and their attorneys to inspect all or part of them.

(2) *Quashing or Modifying the Subpoena.* On motion made promptly, the court may quash or modify the subpoena if compliance would be unreasonable or oppressive.

(3) *Subpoena for Personal or Confidential Information About a Victim.* After a complaint, indictment, or information is filed, a subpoena requiring the production of personal or confidential information about a victim may be served on a third party only by court order. Before entering the order and unless there are exceptional circumstances, the court must require giving notice to the victim so that the victim can move to quash or modify the subpoena or otherwise object.

(d) Service. A marshal, a deputy marshal, or any nonparty who is at least 18 years old may serve a subpoena. The server must deliver a copy of the subpoena to the witness and must tender to the witness one day's witness-attendance fee and the legal mileage allowance. The server need not tender the attendance fee or mileage allowance when the United States, a federal officer, or a federal agency has requested the subpoena.

(e) Place of Service.

(1) *In the United States.* A subpoena requiring a witness to attend a hearing or trial may be served at any place within the United States.

(2) *In a Foreign Country.* If the witness is in a foreign country, 28 U.S.C. § 1783 governs the subpoena's service.

(f) Issuing a Deposition Subpoena.

(1) *Issuance.* A court order to take a deposition authorizes the clerk in the district where the deposition is to be taken to issue a subpoena for any witness named or described in the order.

(2) *Place.* After considering the convenience of the witness and the parties, the court may order—and the subpoena may require—the witness to appear anywhere the court designates.

(g) Contempt. The court (other than a magistrate judge) may hold in contempt a witness who, without adequate excuse, disobeys a subpoena issued by a federal court in that district. A magistrate judge may hold in contempt a witness who, without adequate excuse, disobeys a subpoena issued by that magistrate judge as provided in 28 U.S.C. § 636(e).

(h) Information Not Subject to a Subpoena. No party may subpoena a statement of a witness or of a prospective witness under this rule. Rule 26.2 governs the production of the statement.

Rule 17.1   Pretrial Conference

On its own, or on a party's motion, the court may hold one or more pretrial conferences to promote a fair and expeditious trial. When a conference ends, the court must prepare and file a memorandum of any matters agreed to during the conference. The government may not use any statement made during the conference by the defendant or the defendant's attorney unless it is in writing and is signed by the defendant and the defendant's attorney.

TITLE V.   VENUE

Rule 18.   Place of Prosecution and Trial

Unless a statute or these rules permit otherwise, the government must prosecute an offense in a district where the offense was committed. The court must set the place of trial within the district with due regard for the convenience of the defendant, any victim, and the witnesses, and the prompt administration of justice.

Rule 19.   [Reserved]

Rule 20.   Transfer for Plea and Sentence

(a) Consent to Transfer. A prosecution may be transferred from the district where the indictment or information is pending, or from which a warrant on a complaint has been issued, to the district where the defendant is arrested, held, or present if:

(1) the defendant states in writing a wish to plead guilty or nolo contendere and to waive trial in the district where the indictment, information, or complaint is pending, consents in writing to the court's disposing of the case in the transferee district, and files the statement in the transferee district; and

(2) the United States attorneys in both districts approve the transfer in writing.

(b) Clerk's Duties. After receiving the defendant's statement and the required approvals, the clerk where the indictment, information, or complaint is pending must send the file, or a certified copy, to the clerk in the transferee district.

(c) Effect of a Not Guilty Plea. If the defendant pleads not guilty after the case has been transferred under Rule 20(a), the clerk must return the papers to the court where the prosecution began, and that court must restore the proceeding to its docket. The defendant's statement that the defendant wished to plead guilty or nolo contendere is not, in any civil or criminal proceeding, admissible against the defendant.

(d) Juveniles.

(1) *Consent to Transfer.* A juvenile, as defined in 18 U.S.C. § 5031, may be proceeded against as a juvenile delinquent in the district where the juvenile is arrested, held, or present if:

(A) the alleged offense that occurred in the other district is not punishable by death or life imprisonment;

(B) an attorney has advised the juvenile;

(C) the court has informed the juvenile of the juvenile's rights—including the right to be returned to the district where the offense allegedly occurred—and the consequences of waiving those rights;

(D) the juvenile, after receiving the court's information about rights, consents in writing to be proceeded against in the transferee district, and files the consent in the transferee district;

(E) the United States attorneys for both districts approve the transfer in writing; and

(F) the transferee court approves the transfer.

(2) *Clerk's Duties*. After receiving the juvenile's written consent and the required approvals, the clerk where the indictment, information, or complaint is pending or where the alleged offense occurred must send the file, or a certified copy, to the clerk in the transferee district.

Rule 21. Transfer for Trial

(a) For Prejudice. Upon the defendant's motion, the court must transfer the proceeding against that defendant to another district if the court is satisfied that so great a prejudice against the defendant exists in the transferring district that the defendant cannot obtain a fair and impartial trial there.

(b) For Convenience. Upon the defendant's motion, the court may transfer the proceeding, or one or more counts, against that defendant to another district for the convenience of the parties and witnesses and in the interest of justice.

(c) Proceedings on Transfer. When the court orders a transfer, the clerk must send to the transferee district the file, or a certified copy, and any bail taken. The prosecution will then continue in the transferee district.

(d) Time to File a Motion to Transfer. A motion to transfer may be made at or before arraignment or at any other time the court or these rules prescribe.

Rule 22. [Transferred]

TITLE VI. TRIAL

Rule 23. Jury or Nonjury Trial

(a) Jury Trial. If the defendant is entitled to a jury trial, the trial must be by jury unless:

(1) the defendant waives a jury trial in writing;

(2) the government consents; and

(3) the court approves.

(b) Jury Size.

(1) *In General.* A jury consists of 12 persons unless this rule provides otherwise.

(2) *Stipulation for a Smaller Jury.* At any time before the verdict, the parties may, with the court's approval, stipulate in writing that:

(A) the jury may consist of fewer than 12 persons; or

(B) a jury of fewer than 12 persons may return a verdict if the court finds it necessary to excuse a juror for good cause after the trial begins.

(3) *Court Order for a Jury of 11.* After the jury has retired to deliberate, the court may permit a jury of 11 persons to return a verdict, even without a stipulation by the parties, if the court finds good cause to excuse a juror.

(c) Nonjury Trial. In a case tried without a jury, the court must find the defendant guilty or not guilty. If a party requests before the finding of guilty or not guilty, the court must state its specific findings of fact in open court or in a written decision or opinion.

Rule 24. Trial Jurors

(a) Examination.

(1) *In General.* The court may examine prospective jurors or may permit the attorneys for the parties to do so.

(2) *Court Examination.* If the court examines the jurors, it must permit the attorneys for the parties to:

(A) ask further questions that the court considers proper; or

(B) submit further questions that the court may ask if it considers them proper.

(b) Peremptory Challenges. Each side is entitled to the number of peremptory challenges to prospective jurors specified below. The court may allow additional peremptory challenges to multiple defendants, and may allow the defendants to exercise those challenges separately or jointly.

(1) *Capital Case.* Each side has 20 peremptory challenges when the government seeks the death penalty.

(2) *Other Felony Case.* The government has 6 peremptory challenges and the defendant or defendants jointly have 10 peremptory challenges when the defendant is charged with a crime punishable by imprisonment of more than one year.

(3) *Misdemeanor Case.* Each side has 3 peremptory challenges when the defendant is charged with a crime punishable by fine, imprisonment of one year or less, or both.

(c) Alternate Jurors.

(1) *In General.* The court may impanel up to 6 alternate jurors to replace any jurors who are unable to perform or who are disqualified from performing their duties.

(2) *Procedure.*

(A) Alternate jurors must have the same qualifications and be selected and sworn in the same manner as any other juror.

(B) Alternate jurors replace jurors in the same sequence in which the alternates were selected. An alternate juror who replaces a juror has the same authority as the other jurors.

(3) *Retaining Alternate Jurors.* The court may retain alternate jurors after the jury retires to deliberate. The court must ensure that a retained alternate does not discuss the case with anyone until that alternate replaces a juror or is discharged. If an alternate replaces a juror after deliberations have begun, the court must instruct the jury to begin its deliberations anew.

(4) *Peremptory Challenges.* Each side is entitled to the number of additional peremptory challenges to prospective alternate jurors specified below. These additional challenges may be used only to remove alternate jurors.

(A) *One or Two Alternates.* One additional peremptory challenge is permitted when one or two alternates are impaneled.

(B) *Three or Four Alternates.* Two additional peremptory challenges are permitted when three or four alternates are impaneled.

(C) *Five or Six Alternates.* Three additional peremptory challenges are permitted when five or six alternates are impaneled.

Rule 25. Judge's Disability

(a) During Trial. Any judge regularly sitting in or assigned to the court may complete a jury trial if:

(1) the judge before whom the trial began cannot proceed because of death, sickness, or other disability; and

(2) the judge completing the trial certifies familiarity with the trial record.

(b) After a Verdict or Finding of Guilty.

(1) *In General.* After a verdict or finding of guilty, any judge regularly sitting in or assigned to a court may complete the court's duties if the judge who presided at trial cannot perform those duties because of absence, death, sickness, or other disability.

(2) *Granting a New Trial.* The successor judge may grant a new trial if satisfied that:

(A) a judge other than the one who presided at the trial cannot perform the post-trial duties; or

(B) a new trial is necessary for some other reason.

Rule 26. Taking Testimony

In every trial the testimony of witnesses must be taken in open court, unless otherwise provided by a statute or by rules adopted under 28 U.S.C. §§ 2072–2077.

Rule 26.1 Foreign Law Determination

A party intending to raise an issue of foreign law must provide the court and all parties with reasonable written notice. Issues of foreign law are questions of law, but in deciding such issues a court may consider any relevant material or source—including testimony—without regard to the Federal Rules of Evidence.

Rule 26.2 Producing a Witness's Statement

(a) Motion to Produce. After a witness other than the defendant has testified on direct examination, the court, on motion of a party who did not call the witness, must order an attorney for the government or the defendant and the defendant's attorney to produce, for the examination and use of the moving party, any statement of the witness that is in their possession and that relates to the subject matter of the witness's testimony.

(b) Producing the Entire Statement. If the entire statement relates to the subject matter of the witness's testimony, the court must order that the statement be delivered to the moving party.

(c) Producing a Redacted Statement. If the party who called the witness claims that the statement contains information that is privileged or does not relate to the subject matter of the witness's testimony, the court must inspect the statement in camera. After excising any privileged or unrelated portions, the court must order delivery of the redacted statement to the moving party. If the defendant objects to an excision, the court must preserve the entire statement with the excised portion indicated, under seal, as part of the record.

(d) Recess to Examine a Statement. The court may recess the proceedings to allow time for a party to examine the statement and prepare for its use.

(e) Sanction for Failure to Produce or Deliver a Statement. If the party who called the witness disobeys an order to produce or deliver a statement, the court must strike the witness's testimony from the record. If an attorney for the government disobeys the order, the court must declare a mistrial if justice so requires.

(f) "Statement" Defined. As used in this rule, a witness's "statement" means:

(1) a written statement that the witness makes and signs, or otherwise adopts or approves;

(2) a substantially verbatim, contemporaneously recorded recital of the witness's oral statement that is contained in any recording or any transcription of a recording; or

(3) the witness's statement to a grand jury, however taken or recorded, or a transcription of such a statement.

(g) Scope. This rule applies at trial, at a suppression hearing under Rule 12, and to the extent specified in the following rules:

(1) Rule 5.1(h) (preliminary hearing);

(2) Rule 32(i)(2) (sentencing);

(3) Rule 32.1(e) (hearing to revoke or modify probation or supervised release);

(4) Rule 46(j) (detention hearing); and

(5) Rule 8 of the Rules Governing Proceedings under 28 U.S.C. § 2255.

Rule 26.3 Mistrial

Before ordering a mistrial, the court must give each defendant and the government an opportunity to comment on the propriety of the order, to state whether that party consents or objects, and to suggest alternatives.

Rule 27. Proving an Official Record

A party may prove an official record, an entry in such a record, or the lack of a record or entry in the same manner as in a civil action.

Rule 28. Interpreters

The court may select, appoint, and set the reasonable compensation for an interpreter. The compensation must be paid from funds provided by law or by the government, as the court may direct.

Rule 29. Motion for a Judgment of Acquittal

(a) Before Submission to the Jury. After the government closes its evidence or after the close of all the evidence, the court on the defendant's motion must enter a judgment of acquittal of any offense for which the evidence is insufficient to sustain a conviction. The court may on its own consider whether the evidence is insufficient to sustain a conviction. If the court denies a motion for a judgment of acquittal at the close of the government's evidence, the defendant may offer evidence without having reserved the right to do so.

(b) Reserving Decision. The court may reserve decision on the motion, proceed with the trial (where the motion is made before the close of all the evidence), submit the case to the jury, and decide the motion either before the jury returns a verdict or after it returns a verdict of guilty or is discharged without having returned a verdict. If the court reserves decision, it must decide the motion on the basis of the evidence at the time the ruling was reserved.

(c) After Jury Verdict or Discharge.

(1) *Time for a Motion.* A defendant may move for a judgment of acquittal, or renew such a motion, within 14 days after a guilty verdict or after the court discharges the jury, whichever is later.

(2) *Ruling on the Motion.* If the jury has returned a guilty verdict, the court may set aside the verdict and enter an acquittal. If the jury has failed to return a verdict, the court may enter a judgment of acquittal.

(3) *No Prior Motion Required.* A defendant is not required to move for a judgment of acquittal before the court submits the case to the jury as a prerequisite for making such a motion after jury discharge.

(d) Conditional Ruling on a Motion for a New Trial.

(1) *Motion for a New Trial.* If the court enters a judgment of acquittal after a guilty verdict, the court must also conditionally determine whether any motion for a new trial should be granted if the judgment of acquittal is later vacated or reversed. The court must specify the reasons for that determination.

(2) *Finality.* The court's order conditionally granting a motion for a new trial does not affect the finality of the judgment of acquittal.

(3) *Appeal.*

(A) *Grant of a Motion for a New Trial.* If the court conditionally grants a motion for a new trial and an appellate court later reverses the judgment of acquittal, the trial court must proceed with the new trial unless the appellate court orders otherwise.

(B) *Denial of a Motion for a New Trial.* If the court conditionally denies a motion for a new trial, an appellee may assert that the denial was erroneous. If the appellate court later reverses the judgment of acquittal, the trial court must proceed as the appellate court directs.

Rule 29.1   Closing Argument

Closing arguments proceed in the following order:

(a) the government argues;

(b) the defense argues; and

(c) the government rebuts.

Rule 30.   Jury Instructions

(a) In General. Any party may request in writing that the court instruct the jury on the law as specified in the request. The request must be made at the close of the evidence or at any earlier time that the court reasonably sets. When the request is made, the requesting party must furnish a copy to every other party.

(b) Ruling on a Request. The court must inform the parties before closing arguments how it intends to rule on the requested instructions.

(c) Time for Giving Instructions. The court may instruct the jury before or after the arguments are completed, or at both times.

(d) Objections to Instructions. A party who objects to any portion of the instructions or to a failure to give a requested instruction must inform the court of the specific objection and the grounds for the objection before the jury retires to deliberate. An opportunity must be given to object out of the jury's hearing and, on request, out of the jury's presence. Failure to object in accordance with this rule precludes appellate review, except as permitted under Rule 52(b).

Rule 31. Jury Verdict

(a) Return. The jury must return its verdict to a judge in open court. The verdict must be unanimous.

(b) Partial Verdicts, Mistrial, and Retrial.

(1) *Multiple Defendants.* If there are multiple defendants, the jury may return a verdict at any time during its deliberations as to any defendant about whom it has agreed.

(2) *Multiple Counts.* If the jury cannot agree on all counts as to any defendant, the jury may return a verdict on those counts on which it has agreed.

(3) *Mistrial and Retrial.* If the jury cannot agree on a verdict on one or more counts, the court may declare a mistrial on those counts. The government may retry any defendant on any count on which the jury could not agree.

(c) Lesser Offense or Attempt. A defendant may be found guilty of any of the following:

(1) an offense necessarily included in the offense charged;

(2) an attempt to commit the offense charged; or

(3) an attempt to commit an offense necessarily included in the offense charged, if the attempt is an offense in its own right.

(d) Jury Poll. After a verdict is returned but before the jury is discharged, the court must on a party's request, or may on its own, poll the jurors individually. If the poll reveals a lack of unanimity, the court may direct the jury to deliberate further or may declare a mistrial and discharge the jury.

TITLE VII. POST–CONVICTION PROCEDURES

Rule 32. Sentencing and Judgment

(a) [Reserved.]

(b) Time of Sentencing.

(1) *In General.* The court must impose sentence without unnecessary delay.

(2) *Changing Time Limits.* The court may, for good cause, change any time limits prescribed in this rule.

(c) Presentence Investigation.

(1) *Required Investigation.*

(A) *In General.* The probation officer must conduct a presentence investigation and submit a report to the court before it imposes sentence unless:

(i) 18 U.S.C. § 3593(c) or another statute requires otherwise; or

(ii) the court finds that the information in the record enables it to meaningfully exercise its sentencing authority under 18 U.S.C. § 3553, and the court explains its finding on the record.

(B) *Restitution.* If the law permits restitution, the probation officer must conduct an investigation and submit a report that contains sufficient information for the court to order restitution.

(2) *Interviewing the Defendant.* The probation officer who interviews a defendant as part of a presentence investigation must, on request, give the defendant's attorney notice and a reasonable opportunity to attend the interview.

(d) Presentence Report.

(1) *Applying the Advisory Sentencing Guidelines.* The presentence report must:

(A) identify all applicable guidelines and policy statements of the Sentencing Commission;

(B) calculate the defendant's offense level and criminal history category;

(C) state the resulting sentencing range and kinds of sentences available;

(D) identify any factor relevant to:

(i) the appropriate kind of sentence, or

(ii) the appropriate sentence within the applicable sentencing range; and

(E) identify any basis for departing from the applicable sentencing range.

(2) *Additional Information.* The presentence report must also contain the following:

(A) the defendant's history and characteristics, including:

(i) any prior criminal record;

(ii) the defendant's financial condition; and

(iii) any circumstances affecting the defendant's behavior that may be helpful in imposing sentence or in correctional treatment;

(B) information that assesses any financial, social, psychological, and medical impact on any victim;

(C) when appropriate, the nature and extent of nonprison programs and resources available to the defendant;

(D) when the law provides for restitution, information sufficient for a restitution order;

(E) if the court orders a study under 18 U.S.C. § 3552(b), any resulting report and recommendation; and

(F) any other information that the court requires, including information relevant to the factors under 18 U.S.C. § 3553(a); and

(G) specify whether the government seeks forfeiture under Rule 32.2 and any other provision of law.

(3) *Exclusions.* The presentence report must exclude the following:

(A) any diagnoses that, if disclosed, might seriously disrupt a rehabilitation program;

(B) any sources of information obtained upon a promise of confidentiality; and

(C) any other information that, if disclosed, might result in physical or other harm to the defendant or others.

(e) Disclosing the Report and Recommendation.

(1) *Time to Disclose.* Unless the defendant has consented in writing, the probation officer must not submit a presentence report to the court or disclose its contents to anyone until the defendant has pleaded guilty or nolo contendere, or has been found guilty.

(2) *Minimum Required Notice.* The probation officer must give the presentence report to the defendant, the defendant's attorney, and an attorney for the government at least 35 days before sentencing unless the defendant waives this minimum period.

(3) *Sentence Recommendation.* By local rule or by order in a case, the court may direct the probation officer not to disclose to anyone other than the court the officer's recommendation on the sentence.

(f) Objecting to the Report.

(1) *Time to Object.* Within 14 days after receiving the presentence report, the parties must state in writing any objections, including objections to material information, sentencing guideline ranges, and policy statements contained in or omitted from the report.

(2) *Serving Objections.* An objecting party must provide a copy of its objections to the opposing party and to the probation officer.

(3) *Action on Objections.* After receiving objections, the probation officer may meet with the parties to discuss the objections. The probation officer may then investigate further and revise the presentence report as appropriate.

(g) Submitting the Report. At least 7 days before sentencing, the probation officer must submit to the court and to the parties the presentence report and an addendum containing any unresolved objections, the grounds for those objections, and the probation officer's comments on them.

(h) Notice of Possible Departure from Sentencing Guidelines. Before the court may depart from the applicable sentencing range on a ground not identified for departure either in the presentence report or in a party's prehearing submission, the court must give the parties reasonable notice that it is contemplating such a departure. The notice must specify any ground on which the court is contemplating a departure.

(i) Sentencing.

(1) *In General.* At sentencing, the court:

(A) must verify that the defendant and the defendant's attorney have read and discussed the presentence report and any addendum to the report;

(B) must give to the defendant and an attorney for the government a written summary of—or summarize in camera—any information excluded from the presentence report under Rule 32(d)(3) on which the court will rely in sentencing, and give them a reasonable opportunity to comment on that information;

(C) must allow the parties' attorneys to comment on the probation officer's determinations and other matters relating to an appropriate sentence; and

(D) may, for good cause, allow a party to make a new objection at any time before sentence is imposed.

(2) *Introducing Evidence; Producing a Statement.* The court may permit the parties to introduce evidence on the objections. If a witness testifies at sentencing, Rule 26.2(a)-(d) and (f) applies. If a party fails to comply with a Rule 26.2 order to produce a witness's statement, the court must not consider that witness's testimony.

(3) *Court Determinations.* At sentencing, the court:

(A) may accept any undisputed portion of the presentence report as a finding of fact;

(B) must—for any disputed portion of the presentence report or other controverted matter—rule on the dispute or determine that a ruling is unnecessary either because the matter will not affect sentencing, or because the court will not consider the matter in sentencing; and

(C) must append a copy of the court's determinations under this rule to any copy of the presentence report made available to the Bureau of Prisons.

(4) *Opportunity to Speak.*

(A) *By a Party.* Before imposing sentence, the court must:

(i) provide the defendant's attorney an opportunity to speak on the defendant's behalf;

(ii) address the defendant personally in order to permit the defendant to speak or present any information to mitigate the sentence; and

(iii) provide an attorney for the government an opportunity to speak equivalent to that of the defendant's attorney.

(B) *By a Victim.* Before imposing sentence, the court must address any victim of the crime who is present at sentencing and must permit the victim to be reasonably heard.

(C) *In Camera Proceedings.* Upon a party's motion and for good cause, the court may hear in camera any statement made under Rule 32(i)(4).

(j) Defendant's Right to Appeal.

(1) *Advice of a Right to Appeal.*

(A) *Appealing a Conviction.* If the defendant pleaded not guilty and was convicted, after sentencing the court must advise the defendant of the right to appeal the conviction.

(B) *Appealing a Sentence.* After sentencing—regardless of the defendant's plea—the court must advise the defendant of any right to appeal the sentence.

(C) *Appeal Costs.* The court must advise a defendant who is unable to pay appeal costs of the right to ask for permission to appeal in forma pauperis.

(2) *Clerk's Filing of Notice.* If the defendant so requests, the clerk must immediately prepare and file a notice of appeal on the defendant's behalf.

(k) Judgment.

(1) *In General*. In the judgment of conviction, the court must set forth the plea, the jury verdict or the court's findings, the adjudication, and the sentence. If the defendant is found not guilty or is otherwise entitled to be discharged, the court must so order. The judge must sign the judgment, and the clerk must enter it.

(2) *Criminal Forfeiture.* Forfeiture procedures are governed by Rule 32.2.

Rule 32.1 Revoking or Modifying Probation or Supervised Release

(a) Initial Appearance.

(1) *Person In Custody.* A person held in custody for violating probation or supervised release must be taken without unnecessary delay before a magistrate judge.

(A) If the person is held in custody in the district where an alleged violation occurred, the initial appearance must be in that district.

(B) If the person is held in custody in a district other than where an alleged violation occurred, the initial appearance must be in that district, or in an adjacent district if the appearance can occur more promptly there.

(2) *Upon a Summons.* When a person appears in response to a summons for violating probation or supervised release, a magistrate judge must proceed under this rule.

(3) *Advice.* The judge must inform the person of the following:

(A) the alleged violation of probation or supervised release;

(B) the person's right to retain counsel or to request that counsel be appointed if the person cannot obtain counsel; and

(C) the person's right, if held in custody, to a preliminary hearing under Rule 32.1(b)(1).

(4) *Appearance in the District With Jurisdiction.* If the person is arrested or appears in the district that has jurisdiction to conduct a revocation hearing—either originally or by transfer of jurisdiction—the court must proceed under Rule 32.1(b)–(e).

(5) *Appearance in a District Lacking Jurisdiction.* If the person is arrested or appears in a district that does not have jurisdiction to conduct a revocation hearing, the magistrate judge must:

(A) if the alleged violation occurred in the district of arrest, conduct a preliminary hearing under Rule 32.1(b) and either:

(i) transfer the person to the district that has jurisdiction, if the judge finds probable cause to believe that a violation occurred; or

(ii) dismiss the proceedings and so notify the court that has jurisdiction, if the judge finds no probable cause to believe that a violation occurred; or

(B) if the alleged violation did not occur in the district of arrest, transfer the person to the district that has jurisdiction if:

(i) the government produces certified copies of the judgment, warrant, and warrant application, or produces copies of those certified documents by reliable electronic means; and

(ii) the judge finds that the person is the same person named in the warrant.

(6) *Release or Detention.* The magistrate judge may release or detain the person under 18 U.S.C. § 3143(a) pending further proceedings. The burden of establishing that the person will not flee or pose a danger to any other person or to the community rests with the person.

(b) Revocation.

(1) *Preliminary Hearing.*

(A) *In General.* If a person is in custody for violating a condition of probation or supervised release, a magistrate judge must promptly conduct a hearing to determine whether there is probable cause to believe that a violation occurred. The person may waive the hearing.

(B) *Requirements.* The hearing must be recorded by a court reporter or by a suitable recording device. The judge must give the person:

> (i) notice of the hearing and its purpose, the alleged violation, and the person's right to retain counsel or to request that counsel be appointed if the person cannot obtain counsel;

> (ii) an opportunity to appear at the hearing and present evidence; and

> (iii) upon request, an opportunity to question any adverse witness, unless the judge determines that the interest of justice does not require the witness to appear.

(C) *Referral.* If the judge finds probable cause, the judge must conduct a revocation hearing. If the judge does not find probable cause, the judge must dismiss the proceeding.

(2) *Revocation Hearing.* Unless waived by the person, the court must hold the revocation hearing within a reasonable time in the district having jurisdiction. The person is entitled to:

(A) written notice of the alleged violation;

(B) disclosure of the evidence against the person;

(C) an opportunity to appear, present evidence, and question any adverse witness unless the court determines that the interest of justice does not require the witness to appear;

(D) notice of the person's right to retain counsel or to request that counsel be appointed if the person cannot obtain counsel; and

(E) an opportunity to make a statement and present any information in mitigation.

(c) Modification.

(1) *In General.* Before modifying the conditions of probation or supervised release, the court must hold a hearing, at which the person has the right to counsel and an opportunity to make a statement and present any information in mitigation.

(2) *Exceptions.* A hearing is not required if:

(A) the person waives the hearing; or

(B) the relief sought is favorable to the person and does not extend the term of probation or of supervised release; and

(C) an attorney for the government has received notice of the relief sought, has had a reasonable opportunity to object, and has not done so.

(d) Disposition of the Case. The court's disposition of the case is governed by 18 U.S.C. § 3563 and § 3565 (probation) and § 3583 (supervised release).

(e) Producing a Statement. Rule 26.2(a)–(d) and (f) applies at a hearing under this rule. If a party fails to comply with a Rule 26.2 order to produce a witness's statement, the court must not consider that witness's testimony.

Rule 32.2   Criminal Forfeiture

(a) Notice to the Defendant. A court must not enter a judgment of forfeiture in a criminal proceeding unless the indictment or information contains notice to the defendant that the government will seek the forfeiture of property as part of any sentence in accordance with the applicable statute. The notice should not be designated as a count of the indictment or information. The indictment or information need not identify the property subject to forfeiture or specify the amount of any forfeiture money judgment that the government seeks.

(b) Entering a Preliminary Order of Forfeiture.

(1) *Forfeiture Phase of the Trial.*

(A) Forfeiture Determinations. As soon as practical after a verdict or finding of guilty, or after a plea of guilty or nolo contendere is accepted, on any count in an indictment or information regarding which criminal forfeiture is sought, the court must determine what property is subject to forfeiture under the applicable statute. If the government seeks forfeiture of specific property, the court must determine whether the government has established the requisite nexus between the property and the offense. If the government seeks a personal money judgment, the court must determine the amount of money that the defendant will be ordered to pay.

(B) Evidence and Hearing. The court's determination may be based on evidence already in the record, including any written plea agreement, and on any additional evidence or information submitted by the parties and accepted by the court as relevant and reliable. If the forfeiture is contested, on either party's request the court must conduct a hearing after the verdict or finding of guilty.

(2) *Preliminary Order.*

(A) Contents of a Specific Order. If the court finds that property is subject to forfeiture, it must promptly enter a preliminary order of forfeiture setting forth the amount of any money judgment, directing the forfeiture of specific property, and directing the forfeiture of any substitute property if the government has met the statutory criteria. The court must enter the order without regard to any third party's interest in the property. Determining whether a third party has such an interest must be deferred until any third party files a claim in an ancillary proceeding under Rule 32.2(c).

(B) Timing. Unless doing so is impractical, the court must enter the preliminary order sufficiently in advance of sentencing to allow the parties to suggest revisions or modifications before the order becomes final as to the defendant under Rule 32.2(b)(4).

(C) General Order. If, before sentencing, the court cannot identify all the specific property subject to forfeiture or calculate the total amount of the money judgment, the court may enter a forfeiture order that:

    (i) lists any identified property;

    (ii) describes other property in general terms; and

    (iii) states that the order will be amended under Rule 32.2(e)(1) when additional specific property is identified or the amount of the money judgment has been calculated.

(3) *Seizing Property.* The entry of a preliminary order of forfeiture authorizes the Attorney General (or a designee) to seize the specific property subject to forfeiture; to conduct any discovery the court considers proper in identifying, locating, or disposing of the property; and to commence proceedings that comply with any statutes governing third-party rights. The court may include in the order of forfeiture conditions reasonably necessary to preserve the property's value pending any appeal.

(4) *Sentence and Judgment.*

(A) When Final. At sentencing—or at any time before sentencing if the defendant consents—the preliminary forfeiture order becomes final as to the defendant. If the order directs the defendant to forfeit specific property, it remains preliminary as to third parties until the ancillary proceeding is concluded under Rule 32.2(c).

(B) Notice and Inclusion in the Judgment. The court must include the forfeiture when orally announcing the sentence or must otherwise ensure that the defendant knows of the forfeiture at sentencing. The court must also include the forfeiture order, directly or by reference, in the judgment, but the court's failure to do so may be corrected at any time under Rule 36.

(C) Time to Appeal. The time for the defendant or the government to file an appeal from the forfeiture order, or from the court's failure to enter an order, begins to run when judgment is entered. If the court later amends or declines to amend a forfeiture order to include additional property under Rule 32.2(e), the defendant or the government may file an appeal regarding that property under Federal Rule of Appellate Procedure 4(b). The time for that appeal runs from the date when the order granting or denying the amendment becomes final.

(5) *Jury Determination.*

(A) Retaining the Jury. In any case tried before a jury, if the indictment or information states that the government is seeking forfeiture, the court must determine before the jury begins deliberating whether either party requests that the jury be retained to determine the forfeitability of specific property if it returns a guilty verdict.

(B) Special Verdict Form. If a party timely requests to have the jury determine forfeiture, the government must submit a proposed Special Verdict Form listing each property subject to forfeiture and asking the jury to determine whether the government has established the requisite nexus between the property and the offense committed by the defendant.

(6) *Notice of the Forfeiture Order.*

(A) Publishing and Sending Notice. If the court orders the forfeiture of specific property, the government must publish notice of the order and send notice to any person who reasonably appears to be a potential claimant with standing to contest the forfeiture in the ancillary proceeding.

(B) Content of the Notice. The notice must describe the forfeited property, state the times under the applicable statute when a petition contesting the forfeiture must be filed, and state the name and contact information for the government attorney to be served with the petition.

(C) Means of Publication; Exceptions to Publication Requirement. Publication must take place as described in Supplemental Rule G(4)(a)(iii) of the Federal Rules of Civil Procedure, and may be by any means described in Supplemental Rule G(4)(a)(iv). Publication is unnecessary if any exception in Supplemental Rule G(4)(a)(i) applies.

(D) Means of Sending the Notice. The notice may be sent in accordance with Supplemental Rules G(4)(b)(iii)-(v) of the Federal Rules of Civil Procedure.

(7) *Interlocutory Sale.* At any time before entry of a final forfeiture order, the court, in accordance with Supplemental Rule G(7) of the Federal Rules of Civil Procedure, may order the interlocutory sale of property alleged to be forfeitable.

(c) Ancillary Proceeding; Entering a Final Order of Forfeiture.

(1) *In General.* If, as prescribed by statute, a third party files a petition asserting an interest in the property to be forfeited, the court must conduct an ancillary proceeding, but no ancillary proceeding is required to the extent that the forfeiture consists of a money judgment.

(A) In the ancillary proceeding, the court may, on motion, dismiss the petition for lack of standing, for failure to state a claim, or for any other lawful reason. For purposes of the motion, the facts set forth in the petition are assumed to be true.

(B) After disposing of any motion filed under Rule 32.2(c)(1)(A) and before conducting a hearing on the petition, the court may permit the parties to conduct discovery in accordance with the Federal Rules of Civil Procedure if the court determines that discovery is necessary or desirable to resolve factual issues. When discovery ends, a party may move for summary judgment under Federal Rule of Civil Procedure 56.

(2) *Entering a Final Order.* When the ancillary proceeding ends, the court must enter a final order of forfeiture by amending the preliminary order as necessary to account for any third-party rights. If no third party files a timely petition, the preliminary order becomes the final order of forfeiture if the court finds that the defendant (or any combination of defendants convicted in the case) had an interest in the property that is forfeitable under the applicable statute. The defendant may not object to the entry of the final order on the ground that the property belongs, in whole or in part, to a codefendant or third party; nor may a third party object to the final order on the ground that the third party had an interest in the property.

(3) *Multiple Petitions.* If multiple third-party petitions are filed in the same case, an order dismissing or granting one petition is not appealable until rulings are made on all the petitions, unless the court determines that there is no just reason for delay.

(4) *Ancillary Proceeding Not Part of Sentencing.* An ancillary proceeding is not part of sentencing.

(d) Stay Pending Appeal. If a defendant appeals from a conviction or an order of forfeiture, the court may stay the order of forfeiture on terms appropriate to ensure that the property remains available pending appellate review. A stay does not delay the ancillary proceeding or the determination of a third party's rights or interests. If the court rules in favor of any third party while an appeal is pending, the court may amend the order of forfeiture but must not transfer any property interest to a third party until the decision on appeal becomes final, unless the defendant consents in writing or on the record.

(e) Subsequently Located Property; Substitute Property.

(1) *In General.* On the government's motion, the court may at any time enter an order of forfeiture or amend an existing order of forfeiture to include property that:

(A) is subject to forfeiture under an existing order of forfeiture but was located and identified after that order was entered; or

(B) is substitute property that qualifies for forfeiture under an applicable statute.

(2) *Procedure.* If the government shows that the property is subject to forfeiture under Rule 32.2(e)(1), the court must:

(A) enter an order forfeiting that property, or amend an existing preliminary or final order to include it; and

(B) if a third party files a petition claiming an interest in the property, conduct an ancillary proceeding under Rule 32.2(c).

(3) *Jury Trial Limited.* There is no right to a jury trial under Rule 32.2(e).

Rule 33.   New Trial

(a) Defendant's Motion. Upon the defendant's motion, the court may vacate any judgment and grant a new trial if the interest of justice so requires. If the case was tried without a jury, the court may take additional testimony and enter a new judgment.

(b) Time to File.

(1) *Newly Discovered Evidence.* Any motion for a new trial grounded on newly discovered evidence must be filed within 3 years after the verdict or finding of guilty. If an appeal is pending, the court may not grant a motion for a new trial until the appellate court remands the case.

(2) *Other Grounds.* Any motion for a new trial grounded on any reason other than newly discovered evidence must be filed within 14 days after the verdict or finding of guilty.

Rule 34.   Arresting Judgment

(a) In General. Upon the defendant's motion or on its own, the court must arrest judgment if:

(1) the indictment or information does not charge an offense; or

(2) the court does not have jurisdiction of the charged offense.

(b) Time to File. The defendant must move to arrest judgment within 14 days after the court accepts a verdict or finding of guilty, or after a plea of guilty or nolo contendere.

Rule 35.   Correcting or Reducing a Sentence

(a) Correcting Clear Error. Within 14 days after sentencing, the court may correct a sentence that resulted from arithmetical, technical, or other clear error.

(b) Reducing a Sentence for Substantial Assistance.

(1) *In General.* Upon the government's motion made within one year of sentencing, the court may reduce a sentence if the defendant, after sentencing, provided substantial assistance in investigating or prosecuting another person.

(2) *Later Motion.* Upon the government's motion made more than one year after sentencing, the court may reduce a sentence if the defendant's substantial assistance involved:

> (A) information not known to the defendant until one year or more after sentencing;

> (B) information provided by the defendant to the government within one year of sentencing, but which did not become useful to the government until more than one year after sentencing; or

> (C) information the usefulness of which could not reasonably have been anticipated by the defendant until more than one year after sentencing and which was promptly provided to the government after its usefulness was reasonably apparent to the defendant.

(3) *Evaluating Substantial Assistance.* In evaluating whether the defendant has provided substantial assistance, the court may consider the defendant's presentence assistance.

(4) *Below Statutory Minimum.* When acting under Rule 35(b), the court may reduce the sentence to a level below the minimum sentence established by statute.

(c) "Sentencing Defined". As used in this rule, "Sentencing" means the oral announcement of the sentence.

Rule 36.   Clerical Error

After giving any notice it considers appropriate, the court may at any time correct a clerical error in a judgment, order, or other part of the record, or correct an error in the record arising from oversight or omission.

Rule 37.   [Reserved]

Rule 38.   Staying a Sentence or a Disability

(a) Death Sentence. The court must stay a death sentence if the defendant appeals the conviction or sentence.

(b) Imprisonment.

(1) *Stay Granted.* If the defendant is released pending appeal, the court must stay a sentence of imprisonment.

(2) *Stay Denied; Place of Confinement.* If the defendant is not released pending appeal, the court may recommend to the Attorney General that the defendant be confined near the place of the trial or appeal for a period reasonably necessary to permit the defendant to assist in preparing the appeal.

(c) Fine. If the defendant appeals, the district court, or the court of appeals under Federal Rule of Appellate Procedure 8, may stay a sentence to pay a fine or a fine and costs. The court may stay the sentence on any terms considered appropriate and may require the defendant to:

(1) deposit all or part of the fine and costs into the district court's registry pending appeal;

(2) post a bond to pay the fine and costs; or

(3) submit to an examination concerning the defendant's assets and, if appropriate, order the defendant to refrain from dissipating assets.

(d) Probation. If the defendant appeals, the court may stay a sentence of probation. The court must set the terms of any stay.

(e) Restitution and Notice to Victims.

(1) *In General.* If the defendant appeals, the district court, or the court of appeals under Federal Rule of Appellate Procedure 8, may stay—on any terms considered appropriate—any sentence providing for restitution under 18 U.S.C. § 3556 or notice under 18 U.S.C. § 3555.

(2) *Ensuring Compliance.* The court may issue any order reasonably necessary to ensure compliance with a restitution order or a notice order after disposition of an appeal, including:

(A) a restraining order;

(B) an injunction;

(C) an order requiring the defendant to deposit all or part of any monetary restitution into the district court's registry; or

(D) an order requiring the defendant to post a bond.

(f) Forfeiture. A stay of a forfeiture order is governed by Rule 32.2(d).

(g) Disability. If the defendant's conviction or sentence creates a civil or employment disability under federal law, the district court, or the court of appeals under Federal Rule of Appellate Procedure 8, may stay the disability pending appeal on any terms considered appropriate. The court may issue any order reasonably necessary to protect the interest represented by the disability pending appeal, including a restraining order or an injunction.

Rule 39.   [Reserved]

TITLE VIII.   SUPPLEMENTARY AND SPECIAL PROCEEDINGS

Rule 40.   Arrest for Failing to Appear in Another District or for Violating Conditions of Release Set in Another District

(a) In General. A person must be taken without unnecessary delay before a magistrate judge in the district of arrest if the person has been arrested under a warrant issued in another district for:

(i) failing to appear as required by the terms of that person's release under 18 U.S.C. §§ 3141–3156 or by a subpoena; or

(ii) violating conditions of release set in another district.

(b) Proceedings. The judge must proceed under Rule 5(c)(3) as applicable.

(c) Release or Detention Order. The judge may modify any previous release or detention order issued in another district, but must state in writing the reasons for doing so.

Rule 41. Search and Seizure

(a) Scope and Definitions.

(1) *Scope.* This rule does not modify any statute regulating search or seizure, or the issuance and execution of a search warrant in special circumstances.

(2) *Definitions.* The following definitions apply under this rule:

(A) "Property" includes documents, books, papers, any other tangible objects, and information.

(B) "Daytime" means the hours between 6:00 a.m. and 10:00 p.m. according to local time.

(C) "Federal law enforcement officer" means a government agent (other than an attorney for the government) who is engaged in enforcing the criminal laws and is within any category of officers authorized by the Attorney General to request a search warrant.

(D) "Domestic terrorism" and "international terrorism" have the meanings set out in 18 U.S.C. § 2331.

(E) "Tracking device" has the meaning set out in 18 U.S.C. § 3117(b).

(b) Authority to Issue a Warrant. At the request of a federal law enforcement officer or an attorney for the government:

(1) a magistrate judge with authority in the district—or if none is reasonably available, a judge of a state court of record in the district—has authority to issue a warrant to search for and seize a person or property located within the district;

(2) a magistrate judge with authority in the district has authority to issue a warrant for a person or property outside the district if the person or property is located within the district when the warrant is issued but might move or be moved outside the district before the warrant is executed;

(3) a magistrate judge—in an investigation of domestic terrorism or international terrorism—with authority in any district in which activities related to the terrorism may have occurred, has authority to issue a warrant for a person or property within or outside that district; and

(4) a magistrate judge with authority in the district has authority to issue a warrant to install within the district a tracking device; the warrant may authorize use of the device to track the movement of a person or property located within the district, outside the district, or both; and

(5) a magistrate judge having authority in any district where activities related to the crime may have occurred, or in the District of Columbia, may issue a warrant for property that is located outside the jurisdiction of any state or district, but within any of the following:

(A) a United States territory, possession, or commonwealth;

(B) the premises—no matter who owns them—of a United States diplomatic or consular mission in a foreign state, including any appurtenant building, part of a building, or land used for the mission's purposes; or

(C) a residence and any appurtenant land owned or leased by the United States and used by United States personnel assigned to a United States diplomatic or consular mission in a foreign state.

(c) Persons or Property Subject to Search or Seizure. A warrant may be issued for any of the following:

(1) evidence of a crime;

(2) contraband, fruits of crime, or other items illegally possessed;

(3) property designed for use, intended for use, or used in committing a crime; or

(4) a person to be arrested or a person who is unlawfully restrained.

(d) Obtaining a Warrant.

(1) *In General.* After receiving an affidavit or other information, a magistrate judge—or if authorized by Rule 41(b), a judge of a state court of record—must issue the warrant if there is probable cause to search for and seize a person or property or to install and use a tracking device.

(2) *Requesting a Warrant in the Presence of a Judge.*

(A) *Warrant on an Affidavit.* When a federal law enforcement officer or an attorney for the government presents an affidavit in support of a warrant, the judge may require the affiant to appear personally and may examine under oath the affiant and any witness the affiant produces.

(B) *Warrant on Sworn Testimony.* The judge may wholly or partially dispense with a written affidavit and base a warrant on sworn testimony if doing so is reasonable under the circumstances.

(C) *Recording Testimony.* Testimony taken in support of a warrant must be recorded by a court reporter or by a suitable recording device, and the judge must file the transcript or recording with the clerk, along with any affidavit.

(3) *Requesting a Warrant by Telephonic or Other Means.*

(A) *In General.* A magistrate judge may issue a warrant based on information communicated by telephone or other reliable electronic means.

(B) *Recording Testimony*. Upon learning that an applicant is requesting a warrant under Rule 41(d)(3)(A), a magistrate judge must:

> (i) place under oath the applicant and any person on whose testimony the application is based; and

> (ii) make a verbatim record of the conversation with a suitable recording device, if available, or by a court reporter, or in writing.

(C) *Certifying Testimony*. The magistrate judge must have any recording or court reporter's notes transcribed, certify the transcription's accuracy, and file a copy of the record and the transcription with the clerk. Any written verbatim record must be signed by the magistrate judge and filed with the clerk.

(D) *Suppression Limited*. Absent a finding of bad faith, evidence obtained from a warrant issued under Rule 41(d)(3)(A) is not subject to suppression on the ground that issuing the warrant in that manner was unreasonable under the circumstances.

(e) Issuing the Warrant.

(1) *In General*. The magistrate judge or a judge of a state court of record must issue the warrant to an officer authorized to execute it.

(2) *Contents of the Warrant*.

(A) *Warrant to Search for and Seize a Person or Property*. Except for a tracking-device warrant, the warrant must identify the person or property to be searched, identify any person or property to be seized, and designate the magistrate judge to whom it must be returned. The warrant must command the officer to:

> (i) execute the warrant within a specified time no longer than 14 days;

> (ii) execute the warrant during the daytime, unless the judge for good cause expressly authorizes execution at another time; and

> (iii) return the warrant to the magistrate judge designated in the warrant.

(B) *Warrant Seeking Electronically Stored Information*. A warrant under Rule 41(e)(2)(A) may authorize the seizure of electronic storage media or the seizure or copying of electronically stored information. Unless otherwise specified, the warrant authorizes a later review of the media or information consistent with the warrant. The time for executing the warrant in Rule 41(e)(2)(A) and (f)(1)(A) refers to the seizure or on-site copying of the media or information, and not to any later off-site copying or review.

(C) *Warrant for a Tracking Device*. A tracking-device warrant must identify the person or property to be tracked, designate the magistrate judge to whom it must be returned, and specify a reasonable length of time that the device may be used. The time must not exceed 45 days from the date the warrant was issued. The court may, for good cause, grant one or more extensions for a reasonable period not to exceed 45 days each. The warrant must command the officer to:

(i) complete any installation authorized by the warrant within a specified time no longer than 10 calendar days;

(ii) perform any installation authorized by the warrant during the daytime, unless the judge for good cause expressly authorizes installation at another time; and

(iii) return the warrant to the judge designated in the warrant.

(3) *Warrant by Telephonic or Other Means*. If a magistrate judge decides to proceed under Rule 41(d)(3)(A), the following additional procedures apply:

(A) *Preparing a Proposed Duplicate Original Warrant*. The applicant must prepare a "proposed duplicate original warrant" and must read or otherwise transmit the contents of that document verbatim to the magistrate judge.

(B) *Preparing an Original Warrant*. If the applicant reads the contents of the proposed duplicate original warrant, the magistrate judge must enter the contents into an original warrant. If the applicant transmits those contents by reliable electronic means, that transmission may serve as the original warrant.

(C) *Modification*. The magistrate judge may modify the original warrant. The judge must transmit any modified warrant to the applicant by reliable electronic means under Rule 41(e)(3)(D) or direct the applicant to modify the proposed duplicate original warrant accordingly.

(D) *Signing the Warrant*. Upon determining to issue the warrant, the magistrate judge must immediately sign the original warrant, enter on its face the exact time and date it is issued, and transmit it by reliable electronic means to the applicant or direct the applicant to sign the judge's name on the duplicate original warrant.

(f) Executing and Returning the Warrant.

(1) Warrant to Search for and Seize a Person or Property.

(A) *Noting the Time*. The officer executing the warrant must enter on it the exact date and time it was executed.

(B) *Inventory*. An officer present during the execution of the warrant must prepare and verify an inventory of any property seized. The officer must do so in the presence of another officer and the person from whom, or from whose premises, the property was taken. If either one is not present, the officer must prepare and verify the inventory in the presence of at least one other credible person. In a case involving the seizure of electronic storage media or the seizure or copying of electronically stored information, the inventory may be limited to describing the physical storage media that were seized or copied. The officer may retain a copy of the electronically stored information that was seized or copied.

(C) *Receipt.* The officer executing the warrant must give a copy of the warrant and a receipt for the property taken to the person from whom, or from whose premises, the property was taken or leave a copy of the warrant and receipt at the place where the officer took the property.

(D) *Return.* The officer executing the warrant must promptly return it—together with a copy of the inventory—to the magistrate judge designated on the warrant. The judge must, on request, give a copy of the inventory to the person from whom, or from whose premises, the property was taken and to the applicant for the warrant.

(2) Warrant for a Tracking Device.

(A) *Noting the Time.* The officer executing a tracking-device warrant must enter on it the exact date and time the device was installed and the period during which it was used.

(B) *Return.* Within 10 calendar days after the use of the tracking device has ended, the officer executing the warrant must return it to the judge designated in the warrant.

(C) *Service.* Within 10 calendar days after the use of the tracking device has ended, the officer executing a tracking-device warrant must serve a copy of the warrant on the person who was tracked or whose property was tracked. Service may be accomplished by delivering a copy to the person who, or whose property, was tracked; or by leaving a copy at the person's residence or usual place of abode with an individual of suitable age and discretion who resides at that location and by mailing a copy to the person's last known address. Upon request of the government, the judge may delay notice as provided in Rule 41(f)(3).

(3) Delayed Notice. Upon the government's request, a magistrate judge—or if authorized by Rule 41(b), a judge of a state court of record—may delay any notice required by this rule if the delay is authorized by statute.

(g) Motion to Return Property. A person aggrieved by an unlawful search and seizure of property or by the deprivation of property may move for the property's return. The motion must be filed in the district where the property was seized. The court must receive evidence on any factual issue necessary to decide the motion. If it grants the motion, the court must return the property to the movant, but may impose reasonable conditions to protect access to the property and its use in later proceedings.

(h) Motion to Suppress. A defendant may move to suppress evidence in the court where the trial will occur, as Rule 12 provides.

(i) Forwarding Papers to the Clerk. The magistrate judge to whom the warrant is returned must attach to the warrant a copy of the return, of the inventory, and of all other related papers and must deliver them to the clerk in the district where the property was seized.

Rule 42. Criminal Contempt

(a) Disposition After Notice. Any person who commits criminal contempt may be punished for that contempt after prosecution on notice.

(1) *Notice.* The court must give the person notice in open court, in an order to show cause, or in an arrest order. The notice must:

(A) state the time and place of the trial;

(B) allow the defendant a reasonable time to prepare a defense; and

(C) state the essential facts constituting the charged criminal contempt and describe it as such.

(2) *Appointing a Prosecutor.* The court must request that the contempt be prosecuted by an attorney for the government, unless the interest of justice requires the appointment of another attorney. If the government declines the request, the court must appoint another attorney to prosecute the contempt.

(3) *Trial and Disposition.* A person being prosecuted for criminal contempt is entitled to a jury trial in any case in which federal law so provides and must be released or detained as Rule 46 provides. If the criminal contempt involves disrespect toward or criticism of a judge, that judge is disqualified from presiding at the contempt trial or hearing unless the defendant consents. Upon a finding or verdict of guilty, the court must impose the punishment.

(b) Summary Disposition. Notwithstanding any other provision of these rules, the court (other than a magistrate judge) may summarily punish a person who commits criminal contempt in its presence if the judge saw or heard the contemptuous conduct and so certifies; a magistrate judge may summarily punish a person as provided in 28 U.S.C. § 636(e). The contempt order must recite the facts, be signed by the judge, and be filed with the clerk.

TITLE IX. GENERAL PROVISIONS

Rule 43. Defendant's Presence

(a) When Required. Unless this rule, Rule 5, or Rule 10 provides otherwise, the defendant must be present at:

(1) the initial appearance, the initial arraignment, and the plea;

(2) every trial stage, including jury impanelment and the return of the verdict; and

(3) sentencing.

(b) When Not Required. A defendant need not be present under any of the following circumstances:

(1) *Organizational Defendant.* The defendant is an organization represented by counsel who is present.

(2) *Misdemeanor Offense.* The offense is punishable by fine or by imprisonment for not more than one year, or both, and with the defendant's written consent, the court permits arraignment, plea, trial, and sentencing to occur in the defendant's absence.

(3) *Conference or Hearing on a Legal Question.* The proceeding involves only a conference or hearing on a question of law.

(4) *Sentence Correction.* The proceeding involves the correction or reduction of sentence under Rule 35 or 18 U.S.C. § 3582(c).

(c) Waiving Continued Presence.

(1) *In General.* A defendant who was initially present at trial, or who had pleaded guilty or nolo contendere, waives the right to be present under the following circumstances:

(A) when the defendant is voluntarily absent after the trial has begun, regardless of whether the court informed the defendant of an obligation to remain during trial;

(B) in a noncapital case, when the defendant is voluntarily absent during sentencing; or

(C) when the court warns the defendant that it will remove the defendant from the courtroom for disruptive behavior, but the defendant persists in conduct that justifies removal from the courtroom.

(2) *Waiver's Effect.* If the defendant waives the right to be present, the trial may proceed to completion, including the verdict's return and sentencing, during the defendant's absence.

Rule 44.   Right to and Appointment of Counsel

(a) Right to Appointed Counsel. A defendant who is unable to obtain counsel is entitled to have counsel appointed to represent the defendant at every stage of the proceeding from initial appearance through appeal, unless the defendant waives this right.

(b) Appointment Procedure. Federal law and local court rules govern the procedure for implementing the right to counsel.

(c) Inquiry Into Joint Representation.

(1) *Joint Representation.* Joint representation occurs when:

(A) two or more defendants have been charged jointly under Rule 8(b) or have been joined for trial under Rule 13; and

(B) the defendants are represented by the same counsel, or counsel who are associated in law practice.

(2) *Court's Responsibilities in Cases of Joint Representation.* The court must promptly inquire about the propriety of joint representation and must personally advise each defendant of the right to the effective assistance of counsel, including separate representation. Unless there is good cause to believe that no conflict of interest is likely to arise, the court must take appropriate measures to protect each defendant's right to counsel.

Rule 45.   Computing and Extending Time

(a) Computing Time. The following rules apply in computing any time period specified in these rules, in any local rule or court order, or in any statute that does not specify a method of computing time.

(1) *Period Stated in Days or a Longer Unit*. When the period is stated in days or a longer unit of time:

(A) exclude the day of the event that triggers the period;

(B) count every day, including intermediate Saturdays, Sundays, and legal holidays; and

(C) include the last day of the period, but if the last day is a Saturday, Sunday, or legal holiday, the period continues to run until the end of the next day that is not a Saturday, Sunday, or legal holiday.

(2) *Period Stated in Hours.* When the period is stated in hours:

(A) begin counting immediately on the occurrence of the event that triggers the period;

(B) count every hour, including hours during intermediate Saturdays, Sundays, and legal holidays; and

(C) if the period would end on a Saturday, Sunday, or legal holiday, the period continues to run until the same time on the next day that is not a Saturday, Sunday, or legal holiday.

(3) *Inaccessibility of the Clerk's Office.* Unless the court orders otherwise, if the clerk's office is inaccessible:

(A) on the last day for filing under Rule 45(a)(1), then the time for filing is extended to the first accessible day that is not a Saturday, Sunday, or legal holiday; or

(B) during the last hour for filing under Rule 45(a)(2), then the time for filing is extended to the same time on the first accessible day that is not a Saturday, Sunday, or legal holiday.

(4) *"Last Day" Defined.* Unless a different time is set by a statute, local rule, or court order, the last day ends:

(A) for electronic filing, at midnight in the court's time zone; and

(B) for filing by other means, when the clerk's office is scheduled to close.

(5) *"Next Day" Defined.* The "next day" is determined by continuing to count forward when the period is measured after an event and backward when measured before an event.

(6) *"Legal Holiday" Defined.* "Legal holiday" means:

(A) the day set aside by statute for observing New Year's Day, Martin Luther King Jr.'s Birthday, Washington's Birthday, Memorial Day, Independence Day, Labor Day, Columbus Day, Veterans' Day, Thanksgiving Day, or Christmas Day;

(B) any day declared a holiday by the President or Congress; and

(C) for periods that are measured after an event, any other day declared a holiday by the state where the district court is located.

(b) Extending Time.

(1) *In General.* When an act must or may be done within a specified period, the court on its own may extend the time, or for good cause may do so on a party's motion made:

(A) before the originally prescribed or previously extended time expires; or

(B) after the time expires if the party failed to act because of excusable neglect.

(c) Additional Time After Certain Kinds of Service. Whenever a party must or may act within a specified period after service and service is made in the manner provided under Federal Rule of Civil Procedure 5(b)(2)(B), (C), or (D), 3 days are added after the period would otherwise expire under subdivision (a).

Rule 46. Release from Custody; Supervising Detention

(a) Before Trial. The provisions of 18 U.S.C. §§ 3142 and 3144 govern pretrial release.

(b) During Trial. A person released before trial continues on release during trial under the same terms and conditions. But the court may order different terms and conditions or terminate the release if necessary to ensure that the person will be present during trial or that the person's conduct will not obstruct the orderly and expeditious progress of the trial.

(c) Pending Sentencing or Appeal. The provisions of 18 U.S.C. § 3143 govern release pending sentencing or appeal. The burden of establishing that the defendant will not flee or pose a danger to any other person or to the community rests with the defendant.

(d) Pending Hearing on a Violation of Probation or Supervised Release. Rule 32.1(a)(6) governs release pending a hearing on a violation of probation or supervised release.

(e) Surety. The court must not approve a bond unless any surety appears to be qualified. Every surety, except a legally approved corporate surety, must demonstrate by affidavit that its assets are adequate. The court may require the affidavit to describe the following:

(1) the property that the surety proposes to use as security;

(2) any encumbrance on that property;

(3) the number and amount of any other undischarged bonds and bail undertakings the surety has issued; and

(4) any other liability of the surety.

(f) Bail Forfeiture.

(1) *Declaration.* The court must declare the bail forfeited if a condition of the bond is breached.

(2) *Setting Aside.* The court may set aside in whole or in part a bail forfeiture upon any condition the court may impose if:

(A) the surety later surrenders into custody the person released on the surety's appearance bond; or

(B) it appears that justice does not require bail forfeiture.

(3) *Enforcement.*

(A) *Default Judgment and Execution.* If it does not set aside a bail forfeiture, the court must, upon the government's motion, enter a default judgment.

(B) *Jurisdiction and Service.* By entering into a bond, each surety submits to the district court's jurisdiction and irrevocably appoints the district clerk as its agent to receive service of any filings affecting its liability.

(C) *Motion to Enforce.* The court may, upon the government's motion, enforce the surety's liability without an independent action. The government must serve any motion, and notice as the court prescribes, on the district clerk. If so served, the clerk must promptly mail a copy to the surety at its last known address.

(4) *Remission.* After entering a judgment under Rule 46(f)(3), the court may remit in whole or in part the judgment under the same conditions specified in Rule 46(f)(2).

(g) Exoneration. The court must exonerate the surety and release any bail when a bond condition has been satisfied or when the court has set aside or remitted the forfeiture. The court must exonerate a surety who deposits cash in the amount of the bond or timely surrenders the defendant into custody.

(h) Supervising Detention Pending Trial.

(1) *In General.* To eliminate unnecessary detention, the court must supervise the detention within the district of any defendants awaiting trial and of any persons held as material witnesses.

(2) *Reports.* An attorney for the government must report biweekly to the court, listing each material witness held in custody for more than 10 days pending indictment, arraignment, or trial. For each material witness listed in the report, an attorney for the government must state why the witness should not be released with or without a deposition being taken under Rule 15(a).

(i) Forfeiture of Property. The court may dispose of a charged offense by ordering the forfeiture of 18 U.S.C. § 3142(c)(1)(B)(xi) property under 18 U.S.C. § 3146(d), if a fine in the amount of the property's value would be an appropriate sentence for the charged offense.

(j) Producing a Statement.

(1) *In General.* Rule 26.2(a)-(d) and (f) applies at a detention hearing under 18 U.S.C. § 3142, unless the court for good cause rules otherwise.

(2) *Sanctions for Not Producing a Statement.* If a party disobeys a Rule 26.2 order to produce a witness's statement, the court must not consider that witness's testimony at the detention hearing.

Rule 47.   Motions and Supporting Affidavits

(a) In General. A party applying to the court for an order must do so by motion.

(b) Form and Content of a Motion. A motion—except when made during a trial or hearing—must be in writing, unless the court permits the party to make the motion by other means. A motion must state the grounds on which it is based and the relief or order sought. A motion may be supported by affidavit.

(c) Timing of a Motion. A party must serve a written motion—other than one that the court may hear ex parte—and any hearing notice at least 7 days before the hearing date, unless a rule or court order sets a different period. For good cause, the court may set a different period upon ex parte application.

(d) Affidavit Supporting a Motion. The moving party must serve any supporting affidavit with the motion. A responding party must serve any opposing affidavit at least one day before the hearing, unless the court permits later service.

Rule 48.   Dismissal

(a) By the Government. The government may, with leave of court, dismiss an indictment, information, or complaint. The government may not dismiss the prosecution during trial without the defendant's consent.

(b) By the Court. The court may dismiss an indictment, information, or complaint if unnecessary delay occurs in:

(1) presenting a charge to a grand jury;

(2) filing an information against a defendant; or

(3) bringing a defendant to trial.

Rule 49. Serving and Filing Papers

(a) When Required. A party must serve on every other party any written motion (other than one to be heard ex parte), written notice, designation of the record on appeal, or similar paper.

(b) How Made. Service must be made in the manner provided for a civil action. When these rules or a court order requires or permits service on a party represented by an attorney, service must be made on the attorney instead of the party, unless the court orders otherwise.

(c) Notice of a Court Order. When the court issues an order on any post-arraignment motion, the clerk must provide notice in a manner provided for in a civil action. Except as Federal Rule of Appellate Procedure 4(b) provides otherwise, the clerk's failure to give notice does not affect the time to appeal, or relieve—or authorize the court to relieve—a party's failure to appeal within the allowed time.

(d) Filing. A party must file with the court a copy of any paper the party is required to serve. A paper must be filed in a manner provided for in a civil action.

Rule 49.1 Privacy Protection for Filings Made with the Court

(a) Redacted Filings. Unless the court orders otherwise, in an electronic or paper filing with the court that contains an individual's social-security number, taxpayer-identification number, or birth date, the name of an individual known to be a minor, a financial-account number, or the home address of an individual, a party or nonparty making the filing may include only:

(1) the last four digits of the social-security number and taxpayer-identification number;

(2) the year of the individual's birth;

(3) the minor's initials;

(4) the last four digits of the financial-account number; and

(5) the city and state of the home address.

(b) Exemptions from the Redaction Requirement. The redaction requirement does not apply to the following:

(1) a financial-account number or real property address that identifies the property allegedly subject to forfeiture in a forfeiture proceeding;

(2) the record of an administrative or agency proceeding;

(3) the official record of a state-court proceeding;

(4) the record of a court or tribunal, if that record was not subject to the redaction requirement when originally filed;

(5) a filing covered by Rule 49.1(d);

(6) a pro se filing in an action brought under 28 U.S.C. §§ 2241, 2254, or 2255;

(7) a court filing that is related to a criminal matter or investigation and that is prepared before the filing of a criminal charge or is not filed as part of any docketed criminal case;

(8) an arrest or search warrant; and

(9) a charging document and an affidavit filed in support of any charging document.

(c) Immigration Cases. A filing in an action brought under 28 U.S.C. § 2241 that relates to the petitioner's immigration rights is governed by Federal Rule of Civil Procedure 5.2.

(d) Filings Made Under Seal. The court may order that a filing be made under seal without redaction. The court may later unseal the filing or order the person who made the filing to file a redacted version for the public record.

(e) Protective Orders. For good cause, the court may by order in a case:

(1) require redaction of additional information; or

(2) limit or prohibit a nonparty's remote electronic access to a document filed with the court.

(f) Option for Additional Unredacted Filing Under Seal. A person making a redacted filing may also file an unredacted copy under seal. The court must retain the unredacted copy as part of the record.

(g) Option for Filing a Reference List. A filing that contains redacted information may be filed together with a reference list that identifies each item of redacted information and specifies an appropriate identifier that uniquely corresponds to each item listed. The list must be filed under seal and may be amended as of right. Any reference in the case to a listed identifier will be construed to refer to the corresponding item of information.

(h) Waiver of Protection of Identifiers. A person waives the protection of Rule 49.1 (a) as to the person's own information by filing it without redaction and not under seal.

Rule 50. Prompt Disposition

Scheduling preference must be given to criminal proceedings as far as practicable.

Rule 51. Preserving Claimed Error

(a) Exceptions Unnecessary. Exceptions to rulings or orders of the court are unnecessary.

(b) Preserving a Claim of Error. A party may preserve a claim of error by informing the court—when the court ruling or order is made or sought—of the action the party wishes the court to take, or the party's objection to the court's action and the grounds for that objection. If a party does not have an opportunity to object to a ruling or order, the absence of an objection does not later prejudice that party. A ruling or order that admits or excludes evidence is governed by Federal Rule of Evidence 103.

Rule 52.   Harmless and Plain Error

(a) Harmless Error. Any error, defect, irregularity, or variance that does not affect substantial rights must be disregarded.

(b) Plain Error. A plain error that affects substantial rights may be considered even though it was not brought to the court's attention.

Rule 53.   Courtroom Photographing and Broadcasting Prohibited

Except as otherwise provided by a statute or these rules, the court must not permit the taking of photographs in the courtroom during judicial proceedings or the broadcasting of judicial proceedings from the courtroom.

Rule 54.   [Transferred]

[Editor's Note: All of Rule 54 was moved to Rule 1]

Rule 55.   Records

The clerk of the district court must keep records of criminal proceedings in the form prescribed by the Director of the Administrative Office of the United States Courts. The clerk must enter in the records every court order or judgment and the date of entry.

Rule 56.   When Court Is Open

(a) In General. A district court is considered always open for any filing, and for issuing and returning process, making a motion, or entering an order.

(b) Office Hours. The clerk's office—with the clerk or a deputy in attendance—must be open during business hours on all days except Saturdays, Sundays, and legal holidays.

(c) Special Hours. A court may provide by local rule or order that its clerk's office will be open for specified hours on Saturdays or legal holidays other than those set aside by statute for observing New Year's Day, Martin Luther King, Jr.'s Birthday, Washington's Birthday, Memorial Day, Independence Day, Labor Day, Columbus Day, Veterans' Day, Thanksgiving Day, and Christmas Day.

Rule 57.   District Court Rules

(a) In General.

(1) *Adopting Local Rules.* Each district court acting by a majority of its district judges may, after giving appropriate public notice and an opportunity to comment, make and amend rules governing its practice. A local rule must be consistent with—but not duplicative of—federal statutes and rules adopted under 28 U.S.C. § 2072 and must conform to

342 FEDERAL RULES OF CRIMINAL PROCEDURE

any uniform numbering system prescribed by the Judicial Conference of the United States.

(2) *Limiting Enforcement.* A local rule imposing a requirement of form must not be enforced in a manner that causes a party to lose rights because of an unintentional failure to comply with the requirement.

(b) Procedure When There Is No Controlling Law. A judge may regulate practice in any manner consistent with federal law, these rules, and the local rules of the district. No sanction or other disadvantage may be imposed for noncompliance with any requirement not in federal law, federal rules, or the local district rules unless the alleged violator was furnished with actual notice of the requirement before the noncompliance.

(c) Effective Date and Notice. A local rule adopted under this rule takes effect on the date specified by the district court and remains in effect unless amended by the district court or abrogated by the judicial council of the circuit in which the district is located. Copies of local rules and their amendments, when promulgated, must be furnished to the judicial council and the Administrative Office of the United States Courts and must be made available to the public.

Rule 58. Petty Offenses and Other Misdemeanors

(a) Scope.

(1) *In General.* These rules apply in petty offense and other misdemeanor cases and on appeal to a district judge in a case tried by a magistrate judge, unless this rule provides otherwise.

(2) *Petty Offense Case Without Imprisonment.* In a case involving a petty offense for which no sentence of imprisonment will be imposed, the court may follow any provision of these rules that is not inconsistent with this rule and that the court considers appropriate.

(3) *Definition.* As used in this rule, the term "petty offense for which no sentence of imprisonment will be imposed" means a petty offense for which the court determines that, in the event of conviction, no sentence of imprisonment will be imposed.

(b) Pretrial Procedure.

(1) *Charging Document.* The trial of a misdemeanor may proceed on an indictment, information, or complaint. The trial of a petty offense may also proceed on a citation or violation notice.

(2) *Initial Appearance.* At the defendant's initial appearance on a petty offense or other misdemeanor charge, the magistrate judge must inform the defendant of the following:

    (A) the charge, and the minimum and maximum penalties, including imprisonment, fines, any special assessment under 18 U.S.C. § 3013, and restitution under 18 U.S.C. § 3556;

    (B) the right to retain counsel;

(C) the right to request the appointment of counsel if the defendant is unable to retain counsel—unless the charge is a petty offense for which the appointment of counsel is not required;

(D) the defendant's right not to make a statement, and that any statement made may be used against the defendant;

(E) the right to trial, judgment, and sentencing before a district judge—unless:

(i) the charge is a petty offense; or

(ii) the defendant consents to trial, judgment, and sentencing before a magistrate judge;

(F) the right to a jury trial before either a magistrate judge or a district judge—unless the charge is a petty offense; and

(G) any right to a preliminary hearing under Rule 5.1, and the general circumstances, if any, under which the defendant may secure pretrial release.

(3) *Arraignment.*

(A) *Plea Before a Magistrate Judge.* A magistrate judge may take the defendant's plea in a petty offense case. In every other misdemeanor case, a magistrate judge may take the plea only if the defendant consents either in writing or on the record to be tried before a magistrate judge and specifically waives trial before a district judge. The defendant may plead not guilty, guilty, or (with the consent of the magistrate judge) nolo contendere.

(B) *Failure to Consent.* Except in a petty offense case, the magistrate judge must order a defendant who does not consent to trial before a magistrate judge to appear before a district judge for further proceedings.

(c) Additional Procedures in Certain Petty Offense Cases. The following procedures also apply in a case involving a petty offense for which no sentence of imprisonment will be imposed:

(1) *Guilty or Nolo Contendere Plea.* The court must not accept a guilty or nolo contendere plea unless satisfied that the defendant understands the nature of the charge and the maximum possible penalty.

(2) *Waiving Venue.*

(A) *Conditions of Waiving Venue.* If a defendant is arrested, held, or present in a district different from the one where the indictment, information, complaint, citation, or violation notice is pending, the defendant may state in writing a desire to plead guilty or nolo contendere; to waive venue and trial in the district where the proceeding is pending; and to consent to the court's disposing of the case in the district where the defendant was arrested, is held, or is present.

(B) *Effect of Waiving Venue.* Unless the defendant later pleads not guilty, the prosecution will proceed in the district where the defendant was arrested, is held, or is present. The district clerk must notify the clerk in the original district of the defendant's waiver of venue. The defendant's statement of a desire to plead guilty or nolo contendere is not admissible against the defendant.

(3) *Sentencing.* The court must give the defendant an opportunity to be heard in mitigation and then proceed immediately to sentencing. The court may, however, postpone sentencing to allow the probation service to investigate or to permit either party to submit additional information.

(4) *Notice of a Right to Appeal.* After imposing sentence in a case tried on a not-guilty plea, the court must advise the defendant of a right to appeal the conviction and of any right to appeal the sentence. If the defendant was convicted on a plea of guilty or nolo contendere, the court must advise the defendant of any right to appeal the sentence.

(d) Paying a Fixed Sum in Lieu of Appearance.

(1) *In General.* If the court has a local rule governing forfeiture of collateral, the court may accept a fixed-sum payment in lieu of the defendant's appearance and end the case, but the fixed sum may not exceed the maximum fine allowed by law.

(2) *Notice to Appear.* If the defendant fails to pay a fixed sum, request a hearing, or appear in response to a citation or violation notice, the district clerk or a magistrate judge may issue a notice for the defendant to appear before the court on a date certain. The notice may give the defendant an additional opportunity to pay a fixed sum in lieu of appearance. The district clerk must serve the notice on the defendant by mailing a copy to the defendant's last known address.

(3) *Summons or Warrant.* Upon an indictment, or upon a showing by one of the other charging documents specified in Rule 58(b)(1) of probable cause to believe that an offense has been committed and that the defendant has committed it, the court may issue an arrest warrant or, if no warrant is requested by an attorney for the government, a summons. The showing of probable cause must be made under oath or under penalty of perjury, but the affiant need not appear before the court. If the defendant fails to appear before the court in response to a summons, the court may summarily issue a warrant for the defendant's arrest.

(e) Recording the Proceedings. The court must record any proceedings under this rule by using a court reporter or a suitable recording device.

(f) New Trial. Rule 33 applies to a motion for a new trial.

(g) Appeal.

(1) *From a District Judge's Order or Judgment.* The Federal Rules of Appellate Procedure govern an appeal from a district judge's order or a judgment of conviction or sentence.

(2) *From a Magistrate Judge's Order or Judgment.*

(A) *Interlocutory Appeal.* Either party may appeal an order of a magistrate judge to a district judge within 14 days of its entry if a district judge's order could similarly be appealed. The party appealing must file a notice with the clerk specifying the order being appealed and must serve a copy on the adverse party.

(B) *Appeal from a Conviction or Sentence.* A defendant may appeal a magistrate judge's judgment of conviction or sentence to a district judge within 14 days of its entry. To appeal, the defendant must file a notice with the clerk specifying the judgment being appealed and must serve a copy on an attorney for the government.

(C) *Record.* The record consists of the original papers and exhibits in the case; any transcript, tape, or other recording of the proceedings; and a certified copy of the docket entries. For purposes of the appeal, a copy of the record of the proceedings must be made available to a defendant who establishes by affidavit an inability to pay or give security for the record. The Director of the Administrative Office of the United States Courts must pay for those copies.

(D) *Scope of Appeal.* The defendant is not entitled to a trial de novo by a district judge. The scope of the appeal is the same as in an appeal to the court of appeals from a judgment entered by a district judge.

(3) *Stay of Execution and Release Pending Appeal.* Rule 38 applies to a stay of a judgment of conviction or sentence. The court may release the defendant pending appeal under the law relating to release pending appeal from a district court to a court of appeals.

Rule 59.   Matters Before a Magistrate Judge

(a) Nondispositive Matters. A district judge may refer to a magistrate judge for determination any matter that does not dispose of a charge or defense. The magistrate judge must promptly conduct the required proceedings and, when appropriate, enter on the record an oral or written order stating the determination. A party may serve and file objections to the order within 14 days after being served with a copy of a written order or after the oral order is stated on the record, or at some other time the court sets. The district judge must consider timely objections and modify or set aside any part of the order that is contrary to law or clearly erroneous. Failure to object in accordance with this rule waives a party's right to review.

(b) Dispositive Matters.

(1) *Referral to Magistrate Judge.* A district judge may refer to a magistrate judge for recommendation a defendant's motion to dismiss or quash an indictment or information, a motion to suppress evidence, or any matter that may dispose of a charge or defense. The magistrate judge must promptly conduct the required proceedings. A record must be made of any evidentiary proceeding and of any other proceeding if the magistrate judge considers it necessary. The magistrate judge must enter on the record a recommendation for disposing of the matter, including any proposed findings of fact. The clerk must immediately serve copies on all parties.

(2) *Objections to Findings and Recommendations.* Within 14 days after being served with a copy of the recommended disposition, or at some other time the court sets, a party may serve and file specific written objections to the proposed findings and recommendations. Unless the district judge directs otherwise, the objecting party must promptly arrange for transcribing the record, or whatever portions of it the parties agree to or the magistrate judge considers sufficient. Failure to object in accordance with this rule waives a party's right to review.

(3) De Novo *Review of Recommendations.* The district judge must consider de novo any objection to the magistrate judge's recommendations. The district judge may accept, reject, or modify the recommendation, receive further evidence, or resubmit the matter to the magistrate judge with instructions.

Rule 60.   Victim's Rights

(a) In General.

(1) *Notice of a Proceeding.* The government must use its best efforts to give the victim reasonable, accurate, and timely notice of any public court proceeding involving the crime.

(2) *Attending the Proceeding.* The court must not exclude a victim from a public court proceeding involving the crime, unless the court determines by clear and convincing evidence that the victim's testimony would be materially altered if the victim heard other testimony at that proceeding. In determining whether to exclude a victim, the court must make every effort to permit the fullest attendance possible by the victim and must consider reasonable alternatives to exclusion. The reasons for any exclusion must be clearly stated on the record.

(3) *Right to Be Heard on Release, a Plea, or Sentencing.* The court must permit a victim to be reasonably heard at any public proceeding in the district court concerning release, plea, or sentencing involving the crime.

(b) Enforcement and Limitations.

(1) *Time for Deciding a Motion.* The court must promptly decide any motion asserting a victim's rights described in these rules.

(2) *Who May Assert the Rights.* A victim's rights described in these rules may be asserted by the victim, the victim's lawful representative, the attorney for the government, or any other person authorized by 18 U.S.C. § 3771(d) and (e).

(3) *Multiple Victims.* If the court finds that the number of victims makes it impracticable to accord all of them their rights as described in these rules, the court must fashion a reasonable procedure that gives effect to these rights without unduly complicating or prolonging the proceedings.

(4) ***Where Rights May Be Asserted.*** A victim's rights described in these rules must be asserted in the district where the defendant is being prosecuted for the crime.

(5) ***Limitations on Relief.*** A victim may move to reopen a plea or sentence only if:

> (A) the victim asked to be heard before or during the proceeding at issue, and the request was denied;

> (B) the victim petitions the court of appeals for a writ of mandamus within 10 days after the denial, and the writ is granted; and

> (C) in the case of a plea, the accused has not pleaded to the highest offense charged.

(6) ***No New Trial.*** A failure to afford a victim any right described in these rules is not grounds for a new trial.

Rule 61. Title

These rules may be known and cited as the Federal Rules of Criminal Procedure.

†